Title:	Helltown
Author:	Casey Sherman
Agent:	Peter Steinberg
	Fletcher & Co.
Publication date:	July 12, 2022
Category:	True Crime
Format:	Hardcover
ISBN:	978-1-7282-4595-9
Price:	$26.99 U.S.
Pages:	464 pages

D1014248

Please send all reviews or mentions of this book to the Sourcebooks marketing department:
marketing@sourcebooks.com

For sales inquiries, please contact: **sales@sourcebooks.com**

For librarian and educator resources, visit:
sourcebooks.com/library

ALSO BY CASEY SHERMAN

A Rose for Mary: The Hunt for the Real Boston Strangler
Search for the Strangler: My Hunt for Boston's Most Notorious Killer
Black Irish
Black Dragon
The Finest Hours: The True Story of the U.S. Coast Guard's
Most Daring Sea Rescue
Bad Blood: Freedom and Death in the White Mountains
Animal: The Bloody Rise and Fall of the Mob's Most Feared Assassin
Boston Strong: A City's Triumph over Tragedy
The Ice Bucket Challenge: Pete Frates and the Fight against ALS
Above and Beyond: John F. Kennedy
and America's Most Dangerous Cold War Spy Mission
12: Inside the Story of Tom Brady's Fight for Redemption
Hunting Whitey: The Inside Story of the Capture
and Killing of America's Most Wanted Crime Boss
The Last Days of John Lennon

HELL TOWN

THE UNTOLD STORY OF
A SERIAL KILLER ON CAPE COD

CASEY SHERMAN

sourcebooks

Published by Sourcebooks
P.O. Box 4410, Naperville, Illinois 60567–4410
(630) 961-3900
sourcebooks.com

[Library of Congress Cataloging-in-Publication Data]

Printed and bound in [Country of Origin—confirm when printer is selected].
XX 10 9 8 7 6 5 4 3 2 1

In Memory of the Dead—Christine Gallant, Sydney Monzon,
Susan Perry, Patricia Walsh, Mary Anne Wysocki, and so on.

PROLOGUE

The prisoner closed his dark eyes and inhaled, taking the warm air of midspring deep into his lungs. He blocked out all the noises around him and, for a brief moment, imagined himself back in Provincetown, sitting at the far edge of MacMillan Pier, staring out at the seemingly endless horizon of Cape Cod Bay where the Pilgrims had first set foot in the New World in 1620. He could almost hear the squawk of seagulls dive-bombing for squid and the echo of waves slapping against the old wooden pylons while his bare feet dangled carefree over the side. For the past four years, he had held on to the belief that he would return there one day.

Along with that belief had come a promise, a wager he had made with himself. He would try desperately to swallow any sudden urges to kill again.

Tony Costa opened his eyes and rubbed his spectacles with his denim shirtsleeve. Before him stood not the shifting sands and rolling dunes of Race Point. Instead, he gazed wearily at the twenty-foot-high walls of concrete that surrounded him and the prison guards with cocked, loaded rifles perched atop eight observation towers that offered them a clear view of the crowded yard below.

The bell sounded, and the prisoner soon fell into a long line with his fellow inmates. The new guys, those freshly convicted of serious offenses such as armed robbery, rape, and murder, stared at him and whispered among themselves. All were hardened criminals, but none were like him. They had not done what he had done.

Since the killing of self-professed Boston Strangler Albert DeSalvo, who was stabbed nineteen times in the prison infirmary six months earlier, the prisoner had become the most notorious resident at the Massachusetts state penitentiary at Walpole. Much had been written about all the gruesome crimes that had been attributed to him, but in his mind, no one had told the story the right way—from his point of view, from the killer's perspective.

Costa dawdled for a moment, allowing himself to get pushed to the back of the line. One by one, the inmates escaped the light of late afternoon and disappeared into the catacombs inside the prison that eventually led them back to their narrow, steel-encrusted cells. Costa craned his neck to allow the sun to touch his nose one last time before the natural light was replaced by the flickering fluorescent bulbs inside the jail that had plagued him with constant headaches since the moment he had arrived there four years earlier.

He returned to his cramped first floor cell with its double bunk, exposed metal toilet, and small writing desk and sat himself in front of an old borrowed typewriter, the machine he had used to write nearly four hundred pages over the past several months. Finally satisfied with the narrative structure of his uniquely twisted story, Costa landed on a title for his manuscript.

He struck the keys with his fingers, typing the word *Resurrection* in bold letters. On the next page, he wrote, "Truth demands courage, and rather than live a life of illusion, together we persistently sought the spiritual truth of life. And our search is only beginning."

He stared down at the thin piece of white writing paper with a grin of satisfaction. He was sure that the book would become a runaway bestseller. He wanted to be remembered not as a killer of young women but as a writer and a thinker who had helped to define the Age of Aquarius for a whole generation of readers. In his mind, this book would also cement his legacy as one of Cape Cod's great novelists, mentioned in the same breath as Norman Mailer and Kurt Vonnegut Jr. Tony Costa then typed his name on the title page, yanked the leather belt from his prison-issued denims, and contemplated his next move.

CHAPTER ONE

Edie Vonnegut was nervous about bringing the boy home to meet her father, who was holed up in his writer's shed off the back of their Cape Cod farmhouse on Scudder Lane. Seventeen-year-old Edie had learned to traipse lightly around her father, Kurt, especially when he was working.

"Wait here," Edie told her date, a handsome young ice hockey player from nearby Hyannis. "He said that he wants to meet you. I'll be back in a sec."

Edie left the boy standing at the edge of Coggins' Pond at the back of the property as she tiptoed toward the wooden door and knocked.

"What?" an exasperated Vonnegut asked. "What now?"

Edie pushed open the door, paused for a moment to calm her nerves, and stepped inside. Standing at the threshold atop a wooden plank that held Thoreau's quote, *Beware of All Enterprises That Require New Clothes*, the daughter saw her father's lanky frame hunched over his Smith Corona typewriter with its space bar indented by his thumb from years of use and self-abuse. His head wore a halo of gray cigarette smoke, and underneath, Edie could see the grimace on his worn and wrinkled face. It was a look that terrified her siblings and on numerous occasions had sent their mother,

Jane, to the laundry room, where she would lock herself inside to cry alone for hours.

The boy heard a rumble of chatter coming from the studio, followed by the slamming of the door as Edie marched out with her arms flailing and her long, brown hair blowing in the Cape Cod breeze. She turned once to flip her father the middle finger and then stomped toward the main house, leaving the boy to fend for himself at the edge of Coggins' Pond.

The boy jogged up the hill just as Vonnegut exploded out of his study and intercepted him on the beaten path back to the house.

"I'm going to say one thing, so let me be perfectly clear," the writer barked. "Don't you fuck my daughter. Don't you dare fuck her!"

Vonnegut's words startled the boy. He had only come over to take Edie for ice cream and a movie, and now he was being subjected to a bizarre, sexual interrogation from the girl's domineering dad.

Scared and confused, the boy simply nodded and picked up his pace toward the main house.

Vonnegut watched him go and hoped that his words would sink in. The writer then retreated back to his studio and continued the daunting work of editing his latest novel, a book that he intended to call *Slaughterhouse-Five*.

Locked away in his study, Vonnegut reached for another Pall Mall and struck a match. After taking the smoke into his lungs, his mind returned to his daughter. She had been a real sweet kid, but now that she was older, she'd become a bitchy little flibbertigibbet.

He felt that he had a right to be overly protective of the teenager. She was beautiful after all. Edie was gifted with a svelte, athletic figure that had turned every boy's head at Barnstable High School. She wore her skirts short and her hair long, parted in the middle with brown curls cascading over her shoulders. Vonnegut knew he did not need to worry much about the boy he had just encountered in the backyard. The kid seemed polite enough. Instead, he fretted over a new crowd that Edie was hanging out with down the road in Provincetown. That group seemed aimless, uninspired, and hungry for only drugs and sex. Hippies were taking over the tip of Cape Cod, and Kurt Vonnegut Jr. feared that his precocious daughter could get washed away with the tide.

Like Edie Vonnegut, Sydney Monzon was fascinated by Ptown, which was only a thirty-minute drive from the place where she grew up but a world away from her parents' stuffy home in the village of Eastham, which ran up the Cape's long, giraffe-like neck. Commercial Street, with its eclectic vibe, was the closest that Sydney could get to the counterculture eruption that was happening in places like Haight-Ashbury in San Francisco and Greenwich Village in New York, at least for now. She had recently told her sister Linda and her closest friends that she wanted a new life, one filled with adventure and exploration. Sydney was a year out of Nauset High School, where she had graduated in 1967. Blessed with a radiant smile and delicate features, Sydney made friends easily, but she was desperate to break away from the ordinary.

In her high school yearbook, she wrote that she was leaving with the belief that "the future holds more valuable hours than has the past." While her classmates waxed their surfboards to tackle the waves at nearby Coast Guard Beach, Sydney, or "Snyd" as she was called, could often be found curled up under a tree with her nose in a book. She loved to read the work of philosophers like Bertrand Russell and quoted them often. Sydney paraphrased Russell in her senior quote: "Some men would rather die than think; in fact, they do," she wrote. Sydney was drawn to intellectuals, which was why no one raised any concern about the friendship she had struck with Tony Costa, a handsome young man in Provincetown whom she called Sire. The pair was often seen riding their bicycles together down the narrow streets and alleyways in the center of town. Sydney had told her sister Linda that their relationship was casual and platonic. She was living with another man, a local fisherman named Roland Salvador, at the time. Still, Linda had her suspicions that her sister had fallen hard for her new friend and that Sydney's relationship with Roland had hit a dead end. On Friday, May 24, 1968, Linda Monzon left her two-room cottage at 25 Watson Court, in Provincetown's historic district, and began walking up the hill toward Commercial Street. At the top of the hill, she noticed a small figure standing next to a car. Linda recognized her sister immediately and smiled. Sydney was tiny: about four feet, eleven inches tall, she weighed less than one hundred pounds. Friends had playfully teased her that she had been the model for the Baby First Step doll, which was hugely popular among little girls at the time.

"Hey, Linda, can you come here?" Sydney shouted. "I need to talk to you."

"I can't, Sis," Linda said, looking at her watch. "I'm already late. I'll just see ya later."

Sydney gave her sister a troubled look. Linda waved it off as some minor boy trouble and made herself a mental note to dig in further when the sisters were alone. Linda kept walking while Sydney got into the passenger seat of Costa's car, a 1963 Oldsmobile, and drove away.

He took his eyes off the road briefly and let them rest on Sydney's body. She wore a pair of white Levi's bell bottoms with cuts above the knees and a sleeveless, pastel-orange blouse that was tucked into her small waistline. Her silky brown hair was parted in the middle and flowed over her shoulders. Sydney caught his gaze and then looked into the back seat where she spotted a pair of gloves, a laundry bag, and a small screwdriver.

"Where are we going, Sire?" she asked nervously.

Costa smiled. His eyelids were heavy.

"We need to get some pills," he told her. "And then I'll take you to a place where a thousand tiny Tinkerbells will descend upon you and carry you to fantasy's domain."

Sydney realized where they were headed: an ancient cemetery near Corn

Hill Beach in North Truro. They had gone there several times before to get stoned. But Costa was now out of drugs and low on cash. They would need to replenish the stash Bonnie and Clyde style. He rolled down his window to let in a gust of damp salt air. The breeze seemed to revive him. They drove past the doctor's office on Route 6A and saw that all the lights were out. The doctor had closed his shop early to enjoy the long Memorial Day weekend, the unofficial start to the busy summer tourist season on Cape Cod.

They waited for nightfall and switched seats. Sydney was now behind the steering wheel. She adjusted the cushion so that her bare feet could reach the pedal.

"All right, love. You can drop me off at the telephone booth over there by the hamburger stand," Costa told her. "When I'm done pillaging the doctor's office, I'll wait for you in the phone booth. I'll just pretend that I'm making a call if anyone shows up."

Sydney nodded. She could hardly imagine what her father, Bertram, a drywall contractor and Navy veteran, would think about the idea that his daughter was about to pull off a drug store robbery.

"I'll hide the dope over there," Costa said, pointing to a row of bushes. "We can pick the stuff up after we see that everything is all right. Then we'll head home, okay?"

"Yeah, I'll drive down the road a ways and will come back in about an hour. Is that cool with you, Sire?"

"That sounds groovy."

Sydney let the young man out and sped off. She drove back to Eastham, back toward her mundane past, where she had once fretted over simple things like decorating for the prom with its "Over the Rainbow" theme and working on the yearbook committee. Sydney had even supplied a baby picture for the Nauset Tides yearbook of her in a dress, balanced against the grill of her father's car. She had been the epitome of the all-American girl until the move up to Ptown. Sydney pulled the car over near the Eastham

Windmill and waited. The giant gristmill, with its large wooden sails, had towered over the town green since 1793. It was the oldest structure of its kind on Cape Cod and a source of great pride for local residents, but for Sydney, it was a symbol of a small town that was stuck too far in the past. She fiddled with the radio and landed on Hugo Montenegro's orchestral from the Clint Eastwood film *The Good, the Bad, and the Ugly*, which was nearing the top of the Billboard charts. She now felt a bit like a desperado herself as she sat in wait for her companion to make his score.

Tony Costa made his way ninja-like to the medical office just as a Truro police officer drove past on his nightly patrol. Stealthily, he crept toward the back of the building and tested a window to see if it was unlocked, but the office was totally secure. He then wedged a screwdriver into the muntins that separated the glass panes and tripped the lock.

Costa climbed into the office, drew the shades, and slid the gloves on both of his hands. He had put together his cat burglar kit in a hurry and realized now that he was wearing two left-handed gloves. The pill closet was located at the front of the building, so he navigated his way slowly through several small offices with locked doors. Costa had carpentry experience, so he easily managed to remove the doors by pulling out their hinges. He did not want to trash the office. His sole mission was to obtain the pills he needed and nothing more, at least not yet. He found the pill closet and examined it with a small penlight.

"Gold mine," he whispered to himself.

Suddenly, the penlight shut off. The battery was dead. He did not panic; instead, he pulled out a book of matches and a tiny glass of denatured alcohol from his laundry bag. Using a piece of clothesline rope for a wick, he lit the end to create a makeshift lantern. He had used the kit to cook up dope and had now transformed it into an alcohol lamp. He trembled with excitement as he gazed into the pill closet. He had never seen such an abundance of drugs before. Reading each label carefully, he stuffed sealed bottles of Nembutal, Seconal, Dexedrine, and so-called black beauties into his laundry bag, filling it to the brim.

Costa found his way back to the open window and slipped out as silently as he came.

He hid the drugs in the woods and strolled over to the phone booth to wait for Sydney. Two cars passed by before she pulled into the parking lot, hugging the steering wheel with her diminutive frame. He opened the passenger door and climbed in next to her.

"What happened, Sire? Where's the stuff?" she asked. "Did you get anything?"

"Did I get anything, love? There's more dope in there than a pharmaceutical warehouse," he replied. "The bag's over there in the pine grove. Let's go get it and get out of here."

Sydney drove over to the wooded area and watched as her companion retrieved the laundry bag.

"Are we headed back to Ptown?" she asked.

"I've got a stash in the woods," he told her. "You know the place. We can sort the stuff out there and put it all into the ammo cans. It'll be safer than riding all the way into town with it."

Costa had purchased several army surplus tank ammunition canisters that were airtight and water resistant. The cans were now buried in a thicket near Cemetery Road. Sydney stepped on the gas pedal, and soon the pair wound their way down the twisting country lane. She gripped the steering wheel tightly around each hairpin turn while her companion increased the volume of the car radio. The local station was now playing "Blue Turns to Grey" by the Rolling Stones, his favorite band.

He sang along with the tune, imitating Mick Jagger.

Sydney kept her focus on the road. The difficult drive was made worse by a heavy rain that began to pelt the windshield. She flipped on the wipers as he guided her off the main road to a dirt track, an old carriage trail, barely wide enough to fit his car. They could hear the bushes and long vines scraping against the sides of the Oldsmobile as they bounced over tiny moguls and deep puddles before coming to a small clearing about a mile into the woods.

"We're here," he told her, smiling.

Costa reached over and wrapped his long arms around her small shoulders. They kissed as droplets of rain rolled down the windshield like tears on a baby's cheek. Sydney moved closer, finally straddling him. He held her tightly, breathing heavy with excitement now, as he ran his hands over her compact body. Sydney met his soft touch with her own delicate caress.

This is perfect, he thought to himself. They were alone in the Oldsmobile, but they were not alone. The young man's split personality, an alter ego he had named Cory, had come along for the ride.

Don't do it, Cory, he urged the alter ego. *She doesn't deserve to die.*

Costa suddenly broke the embrace.

"Love, why don't we sort and stash this stuff now, before we get too involved in each other's bodies and minds and forget what we came here for."

Sydney nodded and adjusted her blouse. They got out of the car, and he grabbed the heavy laundry bag from the back seat. He reached for her hand as they ran through the rain toward a large pine tree at the edge of the clearing. Sydney giggled as the mud squished through her bare toes. She said something to her companion, but he didn't hear it. The young man's inner voice was now raging loudly in his skull.

He set the bag down at the base of the tree and dug through wet leaves until his fingers found one of the canisters. Sydney began rifling through the bag, handing him bottle after bottle. The drugs filled three full ammo cans.

"Are we done yet, Sire?" she asked him. "We're getting soaked to the bone out here."

"We are just about done, love," he responded. "Why don't you head back to the car?"

Tony Costa reached his hand inside a fourth ammo can and felt the thick wooden handle of a large knife.

"You fucked my head up bad tonight, Cory," he muttered to himself as he pulled out the weapon. "Let's leave her alone."

Suddenly, he felt the sharp edge of the blade against his neck.

You'll die too, motherfucker, Cory threatened. *Just like the rest of them.*

Costa looked over at Sydney, who was walking with her back turned toward the Oldsmobile. He jumped to his feet and gave chase, running toward her with the knife

The ancient cemetery in Truro, Massachusetts, where Tony Costa had lured his victims. © Casey Sherman.

held high in his right hand. Sydney heard the rustling of leaves under his feet and then the splash of a puddle as he drew closer. She spun around quickly and could see her companion's crazed eyes, nearly illuminated in the darkness. Her own eyes followed his raised arm as it swung down upon her.

"Sire!" she screamed.

The blade cut into Sydney's shoulder, triggering a fountain of blood that sprayed across the young man's shirt. He lifted the knife and struck her again and again.

CHAPTER TWO

Linda Monzon walked up to the A&P supermarket where her sister had been working for the past two weeks. She noticed that Sydney's bicycle was sitting outside, secured by a padlock. Linda entered the store and headed for the produce counter.

"Where's my sister?" she asked the female store clerk. "Is she taking her break? Can you tell her I'm here?"

"Your sister didn't turn up for work tonight," the clerk replied with annoyance. "I've had to stay and work a double. They're making me cover her shift."

Linda was befuddled. "Snyd's bike is chained up outside. What do you mean she's not here?"

The clerk shrugged her shoulders as she wrapped a head of fresh lettuce for a customer. "Dunno, but tell her that it's not cool to stick me with her shift, especially on a Friday night."

"Maybe she's partying in the dunes with some friends," Linda deduced. "She'll be back for her bike. You can tell her yourself then."

Linda left the market and returned to her cottage. The next day, she visited her sister's apartment on Conant Street, the place she shared with her boyfriend, Roland Salvador.

"Is my sister here?"

"Didn't come home last night," he said and shrugged.

"Aren't you the least bit concerned?"

"No biggie. It's the holiday weekend," he said lazily. "She's probably sleeping on somebody's couch or something."

"Can I come in?" Linda asked.

She was met with another shrug as the boyfriend opened the door. Linda walked through the smoke-filled living room into their cluttered bedroom and over to the nightstand. Sydney's pocketbook was hung over a chair, and a bottle of pills was left on the table.

"She's on a special prescription for chronic palpitation," she reminded Roland. "She'd never leave her pills behind."

Linda coaxed Roland to grab a jacket and join her as they door knocked around the village in search of Sydney. They checked with friends, who opened bedroom doors and lifted blankets to see if the diminutive girl had turned up early in the morning somewhere, looking for a crash pad. They crossed Route 6A and trudged up the dunes and across the rippling sands until they spotted the remnants of a campfire with a few charred wooden logs surrounded by a dozen empty beer cans. If Sydney had been there, she and everyone else were long gone by now.

Linda and Roland headed back into town. The bars lining Commercial Street were now open, haunted by the lingering stench of stale beer and smoke from the night before. The sun was beating down on them, with the cool breeze of Cape Cod Bay choked off by tight rows of century-old buildings lining both sides of the crowded street. They entered the dark confines of the Pilgrim Pub, where the locals drank schooners of beer while arguing about the war in Vietnam, bemoaning their depleted daily catch and gossiping about who was fucking whom in the small town. Linda and Roland moved toward the jukebox where Sydney usually spent her time there, feeding the record machine. The nineteen-year-old had not been seen in the place for days, the bartender told them.

"We'll keep an eye out for the girl," the bearded barkeep promised as he pulled down the tap to serve another thirsty customer.

The pair continued searching and found a glimmer of hope when they spotted Sydney's friend, the one they called Sire, surrounded by a group of hippies who answered to the names Romulus, Barabbas, Speed, Weed, and Fluff, all huddled on the grass in front of town hall. The hippies gathered at Tony Costa's feet like moss, listening intently as he regaled them with stories about his travels to San Francisco and other far-off places. For the long-haired teens stuck living parochially at the tip of Cape Cod, Costa was their only real connection to experiences in the outside world. He was articulate and well read, and he exuded charisma. Young men competed with one another for Costa's attention, while the young women of Ptown fantasized about what it would be like to sleep with him.

They had all anointed him as their king and did their best to please him.

"Do you know where Sydney is?" Linda asked Costa. "I saw you with her last night by your car. I figured if anyone knew where she might be, it had to be you."

"No, I haven't seen her," he answered calmly. "I couldn't imagine where she might be."

He was unsteady on his feet, swaying to the strumming of an acoustic guitar and completely stoned.

Sire looked like he didn't have a care in the world.

Frustrated, Linda and Roland walked off. When they returned to the apartment, Linda grabbed her sister's pocketbook and emptied it on her bed. Sydney's makeup kit spilled out, along with her wallet. Linda picked up a pay envelope from Sydney's supermarket job and discovered that only ten dollars had been taken from the money she had earned during her first week at work.

"Sydney has been saying that she wanted to start a new life and leave this one behind," Roland reminded Linda.

"My sister's not gonna get very far with only ten bucks. She left her medication, her makeup, and all her clothes behind. Sydney wouldn't just skip town like this."

Roland agreed. They continued searching for several more days until Linda ultimately told her parents that Sydney had gone missing. Bertram Monzon immediately filed a report with the police department, but the local cops only gave lip service to the worried father that they would make every effort to find his daughter. In Provincetown, police chief Francis "Cheney" Marshall had more pressing problems to deal with. The drug scene in town was exploding. Over the past year, Marshall's officers had made nearly a hundred arrests, ranging from heroin possession to sniffing glue. That number was miniscule compared to other places, but considering that Ptown covered less than two miles of land and employed only three full-time police officers, Chief Marshall had his hands full. The chief ordered his men to crack down on the mangy-haired hippies who were crowding corners along Commercial Street and driving the tourists away.

"We need informants," Marshall told his officers. "Bust some heads and turn the screws on these freaks, and see what you can find. I'm not overly concerned with grass. Just make sure that nobody's smoking it out in the open. It's the hard stuff that keeps me up at night."

One of Marshall's officers knew exactly where to start. He grabbed a local drug dealer off the street, the one they called Sire, and convinced him to rat out his friends.

Runaways were also the least of Chief Marshall's worries. Nineteen local teenagers had disappeared in 1968, but no one seemed to notice. The prevailing thought was this—the place was transient, which was part of the charm. Young people came and went depending on their whims, some piling into cars or old school buses heading west to California, north to Canada, or south to New York City. Marshall believed that Sydney Monzon had likely joined a caravan on some kind of drug-fueled trip to who knows where.

She would turn up sooner or later when the reefer and pills ran out. At last count, there were more than four hundred runaway girls in New England alone, including a nineteen-year-old named Linda Darlene Drouin.

Like Sydney Monzon, Linda was born in a coastal community some three hours north of the Cape in a place called Biddeford, Maine. Her parents later moved to Milford, New Hampshire, a small manufacturing town that rested along the banks of the Souhegan River and was best known for its annual Pumpkin Festival. Linda's father, Rosaire, had found work in the local construction trades, but money was tight, and that often fueled violence in the home. Rosaire eventually abandoned Linda's mother, Joyce, who later remarried. Linda was a bright student and well thought of by her teachers and classmates. Some called her a "starry-eyed romantic." She even excelled at sports, playing varsity basketball for the Milford Spartans. But the girl never got along with her new stepfather, and she dropped out of school at sixteen and ran away. After spending a few months in Miami, she moved to Boston, where she met a young man and got pregnant. They wed, her second marriage in two years, and she gave birth to a daughter. Over the next few months, the teenager was busted for drugs and split up with her husband. Keeping her married name, Linda Drouin, then known as Linda Kasabian, headed west with her baby on a quest to find God.

Sydney Monzon, the first victim lured by Tony Costa into the Truro Woods. © E-Yearbooks.com.

Back on Cape Cod, Sydney Monzon's disappearance garnered zero media coverage.

There was not a single mention of her in the *Cape Cod Standard-Times*, the newspaper of record for the seventy-mile-long peninsula.

Kurt Vonnegut Jr. liked to read the daily paper while seated behind his desk at his day job as manager and proprietor of a car dealership in a freestanding stone garage near his home in West Barnstable on the corner of Route 6A and Plum Road. Close by, a stone marker commemorated the winding roadway as the Old King's Highway, where British soldiers had once marched crew members from the sunken pirate ship *Whydah* to Boston for their eventual meeting with the hangman in 1717.

With a sense of pride, Vonnegut called himself the first Saab dealer on Cape Cod. This wasn't true, but it became part of his sales pitch. He pushed the foreign vehicle, which he touted as "the Swedish car with air-craft quality," to friends, neighbors, and anyone who drove along the historic route that began at the Sagamore Bridge over the Cape Cod Canal and ended at the tip of Provincetown. Occasionally, a customer would pop in and immediately see the value of owning a foreign car, but it was more

Kurt Vonnegut's former Saab dealership on Route 6A in Barnstable as it looks today.
© *Casey Sherman.*

often than not a hard sell. First, the car needed a fresh quart of oil with each gas fill-up, and the models were grossly overpriced. The part-time writer and full-time car salesman haggled with would-be customers over the cost, which would ultimately kill the sale most times.

As he later wrote, "The Saab then as now was a Swedish car, and I now believe my failure as a dealer so long ago explains what would otherwise remain a deep mystery: Why the Swedes have never given me a Nobel Prize for Literature." While Vonnegut was going for humor in the essay, there is clearly a touch of bitterness in his writing.

Much of that resentment stemmed from his complicated relationship with another Cape Cod novelist, Norman Mailer, who at that point in 1968 was wildly more successful than Vonnegut was. Vonnegut had always felt a deep jealousy of Mailer. They had first met while walking the beach in Provincetown during the summer of 1951. Vonnegut was writing his debut novel, *Player Piano*, while his counterpart had just published his second book, *Barbary Shore*, which was an instant national bestseller.

"He wasn't shy but was quite convinced that he was entitled to be an important literary figure," Vonnegut would later recall about his first impression of Mailer. Vonnegut did not care for *Barbary Shore* but thought that Mailer's debut novel, *The Naked and the Dead*, was an extremely good book, although "too derivative." Vonnegut never shared his thoughts with Mailer but instead let them simmer. After finishing *Player Piano*, Vonnegut had reached out to Mailer, who was quick to volunteer his opinion that although he liked parts of Vonnegut's book, the sociology behind it, about the ideas the world holds about progress, was a little weak.

It was late summer, and the Saab showroom was dead. No one wanted to buy a new car in the dog days of August. Vonnegut sent his one mechanic home for the day while he remained at the garage alone and away from the seemingly constant demands of his wife, Jane, and their kids. He leafed through a stack of notes from his publisher, Sam Lawrence, regarding

Slaughterhouse-Five. Vonnegut did not appreciate heavy-handed editors, but he managed to stomach the notes out of an allegiance to Lawrence, who had bailed him out of countless financial jams over the years.

"The manuscript needs work," he said to himself. "Everything here is so short, jumbled and jangled."

Vonnegut set the notes aside and pulled the day's newspaper closer. Below the fold on the front page ran a story about the upcoming Democratic National Convention, which was about to open in Chicago. He knew that America's greatest journalists and writers were about to blow into the Windy City to cover the most critical political convention of his lifetime. Outside his experiences during World War II, 1968 was the most turbulent time he could remember. The year had begun with the disastrous Tet Offensive in January, which had been broadcast in color to nearly every living room in the nation. Network television cameras captured the chaos and carnage as American soldiers struggled to quell a coordinated surprise attack by North Vietnamese forces against several targets, including the U.S. embassy in Saigon.

In its news coverage, NBC dubbed it, "Viet Cong Terror: A Guerrilla Offensive." Although communist forces suffered nearly forty thousand casualties compared to just over fifteen thousand killed or wounded American-led troops, CBS News anchor Walter Cronkite, the most trusted man in America, recognized the offensive for what it was. "For it seems now more certain than ever that the bloody experience in Vietnam is to end in a stalemate," he editorialized on his evening news program. "But it is increasingly clear to this reporter that the only rational way out then will be to negotiate, not as victors, but as an honorable people."

Thirty-three days later, President Lyndon Baines Johnson announced that he would not run for reelection. As bullets and bombs continued to rain down on Southeast Asia, two gunmen opened fire in Memphis, Tennessee, and later Los Angeles, California, killing a dream and ending any hope for a quick resolution to the war. The assassinations of Dr. Martin Luther King Jr. and presidential candidate Bobby Kennedy were the tipping point of a national rage that had been festering throughout the decade of the sixties. It seemed 1968 was a reckoning for America's past sins. It was a year that would undoubtedly be remembered, analyzed, and debated for generations to come. The words written during this time would provide historians with a bible to recount what it looked and felt like to be living in this period of violent change. The next chapter in the saga was about to unfold in Chicago.

The present is so wide and so deep, Vonnegut reminded himself. *How much of it is mine to keep?*

Incensed, he shouted, "When will my voice be heard? Who the fuck will listen to me?"

As he stewed at the Saab dealership in Barnstable, Vonnegut's contemporaries—writers and thinkers like William F. Buckley Jr., Gore Vidal, and Vonnegut's emerging rival Norman Mailer—were all booking their flights to Chicago.

CHAPTER THREE

Mailer stepped out of Midway Airport into the hazy morning sun of a city that was just waking up or headed for slumber, depending on how its people earned their living. To him, Chicago was not only a great American city, especially compared to Los Angeles, which he described as a constellation of plastic, but it also rivaled faraway places like Prague and even Moscow for its resplendent architecture. The writer had come here just once before, in 1950, but as he rode in a cab to the Hilton Hotel, he noticed that Chicago had not changed all that much. It was still a city of Mafia lands and immigrant lands with women he called "tough, keen eyed ladies."

He stared out the window of the taxi, gazing upon the seemingly endless vista of low-roofed stockyards that he imagined were filled with beasts: cattle, sheep, and the like, huddled together in "an orgy of gorging, dropping and waiting and smelling blood."

It was an ideal metaphor for what he could expect to happen on the smoky convention floor of Chicago's International Amphitheatre, which had the "packed intimacy of a neighborhood fight club" filled with "hecklers, fixers, flunkies and musclemen," and out in the sticky heat of the streets and parks where thousands of protesters had set up encampments, much to the dismay of the city's all-powerful, bullnecked Irish mayor, Richard J. Daley.

Chicago, Mailer thought, was hotter than Miami Beach, where he had just reported on the Republican National Convention and the nomination of Richard Nixon by a sea of white middle-class delegates with "dowager's humps and flaccid paunches." Although Mailer could almost taste, in his words, "the vegetable memories of the exciting jungle that had once covered that land," the GOP convention was a sober, even boring affair populated by "rigidly sexless people who were locked into their belief of an American infallibility blessed by God." As for Nixon, Mailer admitted that he had never written anything positive about the man, but he did recognize the presidential hopeful's subtle transformation from "looking like an undertaker's assistant to an old con seriously determined to go respectable."

Young America was looking for a fight, and there was little doubt in Mailer's mind that blood was about to spill and seep down into the storm drains of Chicago. The anticipation of violence may have led him to bunk with his friend and boxing teacher, José Torres, the former light heavyweight champion of the world turned journalist, who was reporting for the *San Juan Star* in his native Puerto Rico. Mailer needed to ask himself why he was even there.

"I own two homes, I have a beautiful wife, and I have enough kids to cover the infield at Ebbets Field," he muttered. "At forty-five, am I finally too old to write about this young man's game?"

But he had promised himself that he would see it through, that he would not curl up into a tight ball and weep his way into 1969. The murder of his friend Bobby Kennedy just two months before had caused his knees to buckle and his heart to deflate like a punctured balloon. As Mailer later wrote, "Of course the reporter (himself) had been partisan to Bobby Kennedy, excited by precisely his admixture of idealism plus his willingness to traffic with demons, ogres and overlords of corruption." The writer had watched Kennedy age in reverse, almost like the fictional Benjamin Button, from an old/young man to a mature yet youthful idealist.

To Mailer, Bobby Kennedy looked like a boy on the day of his death, hours after he was struck by three bullets from an eight-shot revolver in the kitchen hallway of the Ambassador Hotel with his pregnant wife, Ethel, looking on in horror. The floppy-haired, perpetually grinning forty-two-year-old junior senator from New York exemplified youth. The 1968 version of Bobby Kennedy had been a stark contrast to the earlier model, which Mailer had described "as the kid with a rocky, sharp glint in his eye who had gone to work for Joe McCarthy in his twenties."

Mailer screamed like a wounded pig when he learned that Kennedy had been shot. Always searching for the deeper meaning within himself, the wretched sound reminded him of his long-standing premise that he must balance every moment between the angel in himself and the swine.

America's war was not only being fought in the villages, rice paddy fields, and rat tunnels of Vietnam, it was now waged in stateside cities and slums burned asunder after the killings of peace prophets like Kennedy and MLK.

A year earlier, Mailer had marched on the Pentagon, got arrested, and was slapped with a fifty-dollar fine in an attempt to slow the gears of the U.S. military's meat grinder. At that point, 475,000 American troops were fighting and dying in Southeast Asia. Some observers saw the march as a significant move from dissent to resistance, but the protest was a farce, capped off by an attempt to levitate the Pentagon three feet off the ground to exorcise its demons. The entire country needed a cleansing and a spiritual exorcism. The Kennedy magic was all but gone, buried under six feet of old and fresh dirt in two separate plots at Arlington National Cemetery. Mailer pushed any idea that he was ill equipped for this writing assignment back into the far recesses of his mind. On the contrary, he was at the top of his game. The poet Robert Lowell had called him "the best journalist in America," and an Irish literary critic praised him for his "remarkable feeling for the sensory event."

Mailer had managed to pull together a masterpiece of reportage from the march on the Pentagon, first for an issue of *Harper's Magazine*, which at ninety thousand words was the longest article ever printed in an American magazine, and then in his nonfiction novel *The Armies of the Night*, for which he would later be awarded a Pulitzer Prize and the National Book Award.

Literary awards and recognition were, at this point, far out of Kurt Vonnegut Jr.'s grasp. He yearned to be taken seriously as a writer and even as a journalist. Vonnegut had managed to sell some short stories to magazines like *Ladies' Home Journal*, the *Atlantic*, and *Collier's*. An editor there had once described Vonnegut's work as "superficial, flat and inconsequential" in a scathing rejection letter. The *New Yorker* and *Harper's Magazine* had wanted nothing to do with him. Rejection letters were so common that Vonnegut used each rejection letter as a sort of Post-it note to jot down grocery lists and the like.

Still, he believed that he deserved to be covering the convention instead of traipsing across the six-mile barrier beach at Sandy Neck, just a few blocks from his home in Barnstable, on a deserted island of inconsequence. Vonnegut knew Chicago intimately. He was a Midwesterner after all. He had studied at the University of Chicago and then worked as a police reporter for the Chicago City News Bureau covering criminal trials, stabbings, shootings, fires, and even the occasional foul weather Coast Guard rescue out on Lake Michigan. He was paid two dollars a week then. "Doing that job, surviving it, was like getting a purple heart," he would later say. "I wouldn't have missed it for anything." As a City News kid, Vonnegut would rush to the scene of an accident, such as a guy who got squashed by an elevator car, interview witnesses, and telephone in all the details to a reporter at the bureau. The electric atmosphere had a "front page" vibe to it, which was how Charles MacArthur, another City News kid, came up with the idea for his famous stage play. The bottom line was that Vonnegut knew every police precinct and understood the drumbeat of the city better than just about any other writer, especially Norman Mailer. But he was on the outside looking in right now, and something had to change.

"Dresden, Dresden," he repeated to himself as he plucked a shard of sea glass from the bleached Cape Cod sand and examined it in the sunlight, its edges dulled by waves and time. "This book will change everything. It must."

It was only Norman Mailer's second visit to the Second City, yet he felt at home there because the Chicagoans reminded him of the good people of his native Brooklyn. He checked into his room at the Hilton, which also served as headquarters for the Democratic National Committee, poured himself a glass of bourbon, walked to the window, and stared down at the angry faces gathering on Michigan Avenue.

The republic is hovering on the edge of revolution, nihilism, and the lines of police on file to the horizon, he thought to himself. The protesters were led in large part by Jerry Rubin, Abbie Hoffman, and the Yippies, who called for the immediate end to the war in Vietnam, immediate freedom for all Black people, including jailed members of the Black Panther Party, the legalization of marijuana and all other psychedelic drugs, and even the abolition of money. "Vote Pig in '68," they cried.

Mayor Daley would have none of it. He had seen twenty-eight blocks of his city either burned or looted in the immediate hours after the Martin Luther King Jr. assassination in early April. Daley was frustrated when he learned that his police officers had been told to use their own judgment in their attempts to quell the violence. The next day, he gave his cops specific instructions to shoot to kill any arsonist or anyone with a Molotov cocktail in their hands in *his* Chicago. Now, five months later, police officers were ready to put down this latest protest by any means necessary.

Mailer decided to leave his hotel room perch and stroll over to Lincoln Park. The sky was gray and the air was cool for late August. He walked toward the sound of music, pushing his way through the growing crowd like a boxer entering the ring. Craning his neck, he spotted a singer in the distance whom he described as wearing one giant puffball of hair teased out six to nine inches from his head.

This is a generation that lives in the sound of destruction of all order as I've known it, he thought to himself. *Are these odd, unkempt children the sort of troops with whom one wished to enter battle?*

Mailer would not march shoulder to shoulder with them this time. He felt that the justification was not there, a rationale as he described it, to push himself into actions more heroic than himself. The Pentagon had been a despised symbol for him, a fast-spreading cancer, while Chicago was a benign tumor. He shrugged and made his way back to the Hilton to attend a party for Vice President Hubert Humphrey, the Democrats' presumptive nominee. Mailer was asleep when the first canisters of tear gas were emptied into the faces of the protesters, when the first billy clubs dropped like hammers on their skulls. Everything changed that night. The next day, he saw that the city was "washed with battle." Kids began constructing barricades out of park benches and picnic tables. Mailer caught up with some of his friends and contemporaries, like poet Allen Ginsberg and writer William S. Burroughs, to discuss the evolving situation that was growing tenser by the minute. Mayor Daley's baton-wielding cops made no distinction between these men of letters, the protesters, and even card-carrying members of the press. They were all considered the enemy. Mailer brought his friend José Torres to the park and immediately thought better of it. Torres, a Black man, would undoubtedly become a target for the officers. Mailer feared that the former boxing champion would take out six to eight men if he was touched. Mailer got Torres out of the park quickly before cops began smashing down the barricade. Ginsberg stayed and was tear-gassed with hundreds of others, the chemical irritants blinding them all and scorching their throats.

The counterrevolution has begun, Mailer told himself.

The whole world was indeed watching, and Kurt Vonnegut Jr. was among them, glued to his television set in the living room of his colonial-style home in Barnstable. He found himself missing in action, no more consequential than the staid insurance salesman who lived up the street. Rome was burning, and Vonnegut was more than a thousand miles away from its smoldering embers, a literary eunuch with no impact or personal observations to add to this historic event.

"So it goes," he whispered to the television screen.

In contrast, Norman Mailer leaned into the chaos. Back in Lincoln Park, the writer found himself groveling in the grass as tear gas canisters sailed into the crowd, splitting branches and blanketing protesters under a toxic fog. He felt like a British soldier trapped in the mud-caked trenches during the third battle of Ypres in World War I as eighty-eight tons of mustard gas rained down upon the Allied troops from German shells. Mailer stumbled out of the park and sought refuge in a subway tunnel while the ragged army of protesters fought back, hurling bricks at cops and lighting trash cans on fire. The acidic odor of tear gas flowed in the corridors of the Hilton, which to Mailer resembled an old fort that was about to fall.

Do my loyalties belong to the revolution or to the stability of the country? he asked himself.

At that moment, Mailer transformed himself from UN observer to a philosophical enemy combatant. He took the microphone at the band shell inside Grant Park where fifteen thousand protesters gathered for a march through the city. The charcoal-colored sponge covering the microphone smelled of Mace.

"You're beautiful," Mailer told the bandaged and bedraggled protesters. "This is the beginning of a war that could last twenty years and today's march is one battle in it."

He apologetically told the crowd that he had "finked" and that unlike the march on the Pentagon, he had done his best to record but not engage with the protesters or police in Chicago.

"I cannot march with you today because I am on deadline and can't take the chance of getting arrested," he continued. "But you will all know what I'm full of if you don't see me at other marches."

Mailer paused, unsure how the crowd would react.

"Just write good, baby!" someone yelled.

Applause broke out, and a member of the Black Panther Party took Mailer's wrist and hoisted it into the air with his own hand in defiant solidarity.

CHAPTER FOUR

Sydney Monzon's killer did not own a television set, so he did not keep up with the bloody spectacle in Chicago. But on the town all green in Provincetown, Tony Costa gathered his hippie friends, his so-called disciples, to rail against the bloodshed overseas in Vietnam.

"Our fathers preach peace, but give us war!" he told them. "Peace cannot be obtained through war. Peace can be obtained through peace and only peace."

He did not need to watch the nightly news to express how he felt. The killer also shied away from reading the *Cape Cod Standard-Times* out of fear that police might announce a break in the Monzon case. Sydney was still considered missing and not murdered. He figured that the likelihood that someone would stumble upon her remains was remote, considering the secluded area and sprawling vegetation she was buried under. Costa also believed that his role as a police snitch in Provincetown would give him the opportunity to keep tabs on the investigation, if there was one. Local cops were the worst gossipers in town, he knew.

The killer did not think about Sydney anymore as his focus was now on a new girl. Labor Day was approaching, and the Cape Cod tourism season was winding down. He had enjoyed a good summer, living at the

Crown & Anchor hotel on Commercial Street, where he paid off his room and board by performing light carpentry and plumbing work. Built in the nineteenth century, the seventy-five-room hotel was always in need of some repair, as long as the work did not interfere with the nightly cabaret shows performed by a gaggle of glittering drag queens. But the entertainers, who called themselves the "Wuthering Knights," had packed away their evening gowns and high heel pumps, and the cruising area of Bay Beach known as the "Dick Dock" was deserted once more.

Costa busied himself by winterizing the hotel, repairing toilets, rebuilding the gazebo room bar, and adding a new sundeck.

He met seventeen-year-old Susan Perry one day while pedaling home on his bicycle, the one he called Baby Blue, from the town library. He had a book tucked under his arm: *Manual of Taxidermy: A Complete Guide in Collecting and Preserving Birds and Mammals*. It was a reprint of a textbook written by Charles Johnson Maynard in 1883. The killer devoured books on taxidermy, and he vanquished small creatures like egrets, piping plovers, squirrels, and chipmunks from salt marshes and heath lands along the Cape Cod National Seashore. When he was too tired to hunt, he would scout for roadkill around town. He was diligent in his work, using a sharp knife to carve an incision in a small animal's tail, then pushing the blade up to the head before separating and peeling its skin back and cautiously removing the innards.

Costa hid the book in the back pocket of his jeans as he chatted with Susan in front of the Lobster Pot restaurant on Commercial Street.

"Are you going to stick around this dead-end town through autumn?" he asked her.

She shrugged and smiled, brushing a blond curl away from her face.

"I've taken a splendid job in Boston, building a new home for a client," he told her. "I am going to stay with some acquaintances in the suburb of Dedham. You should visit if you get bored."

"You kinda talk funny, Sire," Susan noted. "You don't speak like the guys around here. You use big words. You remind me of an actor, Cary Grant, I think."

He grinned sheepishly. "If you find that you want to get off the Cape for a period, please let me know."

He continued his bike ride while Susan Perry contemplated the offer.

She told some friends that she was eager to leave Ptown, that spit of sand at land's end, and head up to Boston where everything was *happening*. Plus, Susan did not have enough money to afford a place of her own on Cape Cod, even during the off-season. She turned what seemed to be a casual invitation to visit into a formal proposal to live together.

A friend spotted her a week or so later hanging around the Boston Common, where college kids from nearby Harvard, Boston University, and Emerson College gathered daily to smoke dope and decry the war. Susan carried all her clothes in a big duffel bag. She had also dyed her hair black. The blond pixie was now a spitting image of Sydney Monzon.

"We're living together now," she said to the friend, beaming. "I've slept with him. I hope he likes me now."

Tony Costa soon joined them. He pulled out a hash pipe from his pocket. Its ornate carving showed a female body without arms or legs. The three of them got high and sat in the grass near the Parkman Bandstand at the eastern side of the Common and listened to rock music. After sharing a few tokes of pure Black Gundji hash with a trace of opium, they strolled through the city together. Costa had a small camera and snapped away each time they came across a road sign.

"One Way, Do Not Enter, Detour and Exit, they each have a symbolic significance toward my relationship with someone," he explained to the girls. "For instance, if I hand you a photograph of an Exit sign, it means that you are no longer in my life."

Hearing this, Susan hugged him closer, fearing that he would soon get tired of her.

Later, alone together at the apartment in Dedham, he pulled out three tabs of blue cheer acid and offered them to Susan.

"Do you feel like turning on?" he asked her. "Just let them melt on your tongue. The next thing you will see is a Tinkerbell ballet."

The girl was unsure, but she realized that sex and drugs were the keys to owning the young man's heart.

Susan closed her eyes and parted her narrow lips. She could barely feel the specks of paper touching her tongue.

"It's real *head* acid," he told her. "This will be magical for your mind."

A sudden feeling of warmth spread through Susan's body as her blood pressure rose and her eyes dilated.

The young man walked over to the turntable and let the needle fall on the Rolling Stones' "The Spider and the Fly."

He hummed Keith Richards's bluesy opening chords and sang along to Jagger's lyrics.

With her tiny body almost lost in an overstuffed armchair, Susan stared back at him blankly as he continued.

He stopped singing and looked at her for a moment. He then lunged forward, grabbing the girl's throat. She pulled away, so he reached for her hair and dragged her into the bathroom.

What's happening? Susan asked herself. *Am I tripping? Am I hallucinating?*

But the pain was all too real, and Susan tried to free herself from Costa's tight grip. She felt his other hand grab the back of her collar as he hauled her across the carpet.

There was a sharp knife resting on the bathroom sink. He called it his "pig stabber." He threw Susan to the floor, raised the weapon, and plunged the blade into her chest. Her eyes went wide, and she emitted a gurgling sound as blood formed at the corner of her pink lips and blossomed like a scarlet flower from her shirt. He pulled the knife out and stabbed again, this time keeping the blade inside her chest. Her body went limp, and her eyes were lifeless. Susan Perry had completely submitted herself to him. He stood up and began unbuttoning his shirt. His jeans came off next. Tony Costa covered the dead girl's body with his own, letting her blood smear his bare chest. This excited him. He ran his hands over her nude figure and suckled her breasts. He then pushed her legs apart and entered her. She was still warm. After several violent thrusts, he finished the ritual. He pulled himself off her body and walked back into the living room naked, glistening with sweat and blood. He reached for a book, the one titled *Manual of Taxidermy: A Complete Guide in Collecting and Preserving Birds and Mammals*. With fingers bloodied, he flipped through the pages dedicated to catching prey—he had already succeeded in that—and turned to chapter 2, "Skinning Birds." "A bird had better lie for at least six hours after it has been killed," the author advised. The killer had no time for this. Following further instructions, he inserted the point of the knife under the girl's skin near the sternum and slid it downward, and so on.

He sliced off Susan's breasts and then removed her heart and placed the body parts next to him on the floor. His knife traveled south along her bloodied corpse and located her vagina. Costa made deep incisions in her pelvis and cut out her genitals.

Later, he stumbled into his bedroom in search of Susan's green duffel bag. He expected that all her dismembered body parts would fit into the army surplus bag, but they were too large. He fetched a plastic bag from the kitchen and stuffed the girl's severed head inside. He then wrapped the rest of her body in a blanket, cleaned himself up, shot some speed, and carried Susan Perry's remains out to the trunk of his car.

"This is ghastly, Cory," the young man moaned. "Cutting her up into pieces! Necrophilia? That's so ugly."

We did fuck her, and we did a lot worse than that, the killer's inner voice reminded him. *We had no choice. She's dead. That's a fact. Keep it together, and don't freak out.*

Susan Perry believed that Tony Costa loved her. Hers was the first body recovered from a shallow grave in the Truro woods.
© *Ancestry.com.*

The name Costa had given to his alter ego did not come from a book that he had read or from his own warped imagination. *Cory,* as in Cory Devereaux, was actually the name of a local high school student and friend of Costa's. The killer also believed that Devereaux was his closest rival in the Provincetown drug trade and had built up a certain animosity toward the teen. That animosity had manifested in Costa's dark subconscious. The beast that had burrowed into his soul needed a name. The killer decided that the name would be Cory Devereaux.

He got behind the wheel of his Oldsmobile and began the long drive back to Cape Cod.

"Stay calm," he told himself.

Costa drove down Route 3 to Plymouth and then over the Sagamore Bridge.

"Just a few more miles to go."

Soon, he passed Eastham and wondered if Sydney Monzon's parents kept a candle in the window in the false hope that she would one day return home. He crossed into Wellfleet and headed toward Truro. The speed he had injected earlier was reaching its peak, and his foot was heavy on the gas pedal. This got the attention of a Massachusetts state trooper who was conducting a routine patrol along the remote stretch of highway.

The killer heard the siren wail and gazed into the rearview mirror at the blue lights that were fast approaching. He slowed the car down and pulled off to a soft shoulder on the side of the road.

The trooper, a man in his thirties, stepped out of his squad car and walked toward the vehicle. At that moment, Costa jumped out of the Oldsmobile.

"Is there a problem, Officer?"

"Yeah, you were speeding, and you have a noisy muffler," the trooper replied. "You'll want to get that looked at."

"I'm so sorry about that," the young man said as he continued walking toward the officer. "I will be sure to watch my speed from now on."

"I'd appreciate that. Still, I gotta write you a ticket."

The killer did not argue. "I completely understand, sir. Thank you for keeping our roads safe."

The trooper shrugged as he wrote up the citation. Tony Costa took it, grinned, and walked back to the Oldsmobile. Next stop was the wooded area off Cemetery Road, and then he would continue on to Helltown.

CHAPTER FIVE

"Helltown. The nickname fits this place perfectly," said Norman Mailer as he peered out at Long Point and the Provincetown harbor from the third-floor study of his home at the east end of Commercial Street. Sitting at his desk, he also had a pristine view of the Pilgrim Monument, the 252-foot granite tower looming like a colossal sentry in the distance.

To Mailer, the town in July was "as colorful as St. Tropez on Saturday morning and as dirty as Coney Island come Sunday night."

But it was autumn now, and the leaves were dead. The town was dead too.

Mailer had just returned from Chicago, and he was all alone in his five-bedroom, fifty-eight-hundred-square-foot brick fortress, which sat on more than a hundred feet of waterfront. Beverly Bentley, his fourth wife, was gone. She felt isolated and bored and could not take another winter here. Mailer missed her warm touch and the aroma of her cooking. Beverly made a dish of mushrooms stuffed with duxelles that was to die for. The writer would have to fend for himself now.

Unlike Vonnegut down the road, Mailer worked in longhand and at a feverish pace. Over the next eighteen days, he scribbled his memories and observations from both party conventions down on yellow legal pads, fifty thousand words in all, which were added on top of the twenty-five thousand words he had already committed to paper. It was the job of his secretary, Sandy Charlebois Thomas, to type them up and send them off to his editor. Mailer put in between twelve and fourteen hours a day at his writing desk, and his assistant found it nearly impossible to keep up with the manic author. She understood why he did most of his writing there on Cape Cod instead of New York City.

"Your attachment to this place goes back to writing *The Naked and the Dead* here," she told him. "P-Town's your spiritual home. It embodies a great natural beauty and quality of light and incredible evil."

Inside Norman Mailer's former Commercial Street home where the author once entertained guests at his own personal bar overlooking the ocean.
© Casey Sherman.

Mailer knew what she meant. Despite being surrounded by all the enchantment and artistry that embodied life in Provincetown, it was the darkness that drew him there.

Danger and deceit flowed through the veins of this place. When the pious Pilgrims first dropped anchor in Provincetown Harbor after fleeing religious persecution from the Church of England and later as exiles in Holland, they stole corn from the Pamet Indians before signing the Mayflower Compact and returning to their ship and heading east along Cape Cod Bay to establish a permanent settlement in Plymouth.

Later, the area crawled with pirates, whalers, smugglers, and mooncussers, who lured ships to their doom by raising lanterns high atop the dunes at night, convincing ship captains that a lighthouse and safe harbor revealed themselves ahead. The ships would wreck on the constantly shifting shoals, and the mooncussers would then steal their cargo and occasionally slit the throats of any survivors on board. The ploy only worked on moonless nights, and these outlaws would cuss the moon if its radiance foiled their plans. Helltown was a settlement just south of Hatches Harbor with about thirty dwellings: rooming houses, taverns, and bordellos. When a sea captain was asked why the place was called Helltown, he grumbled, "Because of all the helling that goes on there."

It was a place for those creatures, spit onto the sand, that the sea did not want, and according to Benjamin Franklin's uncle, it also came with a sea monster.

Mailer rested his pencil on his wooden desk and ran his hand across his whisker-free chin.

"Maybe it's time to grow another goatee," he said aloud.

He had worn facial hair years earlier, back when he lived in Greenwich Village. Now he was a suited, tie-wearing, middle-aged fossil. But like most dinosaurs, he was still feared. He loved Provincetown, but most townies did not love him back, at least not anymore. Tavern owners called him a menace, especially now during the off-season, when he would stumble in and out of bars along Commercial Street picking fights with anyone who looked at him sideways. Locals were weary of what they called "the Mailer headbutt," which the writer was quick to employ on his foes. Many considered him a bastard, but at least he was *their* bastard, and his presence added to Ptown's eclectic decor. He fit right in here in Helltown.

Police Chief Cheney Marshall knew him well. Their first run-in had occurred nearly a decade earlier when Mailer and his second wife, Adele, rented out the Hawthorne House for themselves and their two young children. It was shortly after 1:00 a.m. on June 9, 1960, when Mailer, stumbling home from two local joints, Ace of Spades and the Atlantic House, yelled out, "Taxi, taxi!" to a passing squad car. Adele told her husband to shut up and called him a fool. The car stopped, and two cops got out and asked the writer to move along.

"I'll move when you get out of my way," Mailer slurred.

Hearing this, the officers grabbed him and stuffed him into the back of their car.

"Adele, you're my witness," he cried out. "I'm not resisting arrest."

Mailer stayed mute for the quick ride to the police station. A Portuguese American police officer known as "Cobra" pulled him out of the vehicle and pushed him along the pavement. Stubborn and intoxicated, the novelist demanded to walk in on his own accord. That demand triggered a tussle on the steps with Cobra. Mailer ducked, spun, slipped, blocked, and sidestepped the officer's advance until a billy club came crashing down on his head, opening a gash that would take thirteen stitches to close.

"Okay, you happy now? I'm bleeding," Mailer snarled.

A short time later, as he cleaned the wound with a towel in his cell, he got into a verbal joust with Chief Cheney Marshall.

"I coulda beat those two toy cops of yours and you know it, kid."

"Listen, boy, I could take you with one hand," the chief fired back.

"Maybe you could, and maybe you couldn't, but you picked the wrong pigeon this time. You cops are used to dealing with people who can't defend themselves. Well, I'm a writer, and I know how to use words, and boy, I'm going to use them."

Adele brought fifty dollars cash to the police station and bailed him out.

The charge was drunk and disorderly, and there would be a trial with Mailer acting as his own lawyer.

At this time, the writer had plenty of support from his Ptown neighbors. Chief Cheney Marshall had planted his big thumb on the village, and the townies rebelled. He had already arrested Franz Kline, the abstract expressionist painter, for playing records late at night, and he also closed down a number of gay bars on trumped-up charges.

During the one-day trial, Mailer called Officer William Sylvia, the cop known as "Cobra," to the stand. Mailer had a laundry list of questions for him. "Do you know what Cobra means?" he wanted to ask. "Webster defines it as 'any of several very venomous Asiatic and African snakes.'… Are you aware that people in this town believe they have a bullying and brutal police force?… Do you know the nickname for the police here is the Gestapo?"

The judge tossed out these inquiries before they could leave Mailer's lips. Still, the writer did his best to agitate the witness. "You grabbed my arms from behind, isn't that right, Cobra?"

After a stern objection from the judge, Mailer followed with another uppercut.

"Do you ever have bad dreams about violence?" he asked Officer Sylvia.

"Objection!"

Mailer then took the stand in his own defense.

"I have a bad temper," he told the judge. "Maybe they thought I was a dangerous beatnik. I was cocky, sassy, and arrogant."

But he forcefully denied that he could have gotten drunk on only four cocktails, and he certainly was not, in his opinion, disorderly to the cops.

The judge split the verdict, announcing to the packed courtroom that the writer was guilty of drunkenness but not disorderly conduct. He also blasted Chief Marshall for the actions of his Officer Sylvia.

"You police officers are too thin skinned," the judge surmised. "You have to deal with many summer visitors here, but you can't manhandle a man because he says something you don't like."

Mailer claimed victory and celebrated with a few stiff ones down the street at the Old Colony tavern.

That kind of circus was typical of Mailer. He was known as much for his outlandish antics as he was for his authorship. The writer considered himself to be the heir apparent to Ernest Hemingway, his hero, who had taken his own life in 1961. But still, Mailer refused to have his writing overshadowed by his personal transgressions. While working on the book that would eventually be called *Miami and the Siege of Chicago*, he learned that *Armies of the Night* had won the Pulitzer Prize and the National Book Award. Ever weary about good fortune, Mailer shouted, "Gott helfe uns vor dem bösen Blick!" *God protect us from the evil eye.*

News of Mailer's accolades traveled fast through literary circles and found its way to Vonnegut's writing studio in Barnstable.

"It all comes so fucking easy for Norman," Vonnegut grumbled. "Motherfucker exploded out of the gate and has tasted nothing but gravy ever since."

Vonnegut viewed the success of Mailer's debut novel, *The Naked and the Dead*, with a touch of disdain. Mailer was twenty-five years young when the book was published in 1948, and it sold an astounding two hundred thousand copies in the first three months. When he was drafted into the U.S. Army in 1943, Mailer set out to write, in his words, *the* war novel. He was stationed in the Philippines and served as a typist, line wireman, and cook there. He also went out on patrols, as the self-confessed third lousiest guy in a platoon of twelve. Those experiences fueled his creativity, and that combination had produced a masterpiece. It also introduced the word *fug* to the American vernacular, because Mailer's publisher would not allow him to use the word *fuck* in his prose.

The combined sales numbers for Vonnegut's collective works were far less than for his rival's signature novel. Vonnegut had to clear his mind, or he would sink into a funk of depression, and the writing would not come. He had spent much of his adult life parrying and dodging his darkest thoughts. Depression was something that Vonnegut had inherited like a set of polished silver from his mother, Edith, who had swallowed too many sleeping pills, overdosing and dying in her bed when she was fifty-six years old.

Her eldest son was forty-six years old now, looked much older, and was wallowing in artistic and financial misery. The Saab dealership was a disaster, and Vonnegut had five children to clothe and feed. He and his wife, Jane, his classmate since kindergarten, had three kids, including the teenaged Edie. They had also adopted Vonnegut's two nephews after his sister Alice died of cancer in 1958, just two days after her husband, James, was killed in a train wreck.

Vonnegut had given up economic security long ago when he quit his white-collar job as a publicist for General Electric in Schenectady, New York, to pursue his dream as a writer on Cape Cod.

"Don't give up your job and devote yourself to writing fiction," one mentor had advised him. "I don't trust a freelancer's life. It's tough."

But Vonnegut did just that, despite a steady stream of rejection letters, including one from an editor at *Esquire*, who critiqued a short story Vonnegut had submitted this way: "Not a striking plot. Overdramatized—not on our level of interest."

When he did manage to sell one of his stories, the money was not enough in his mind to buy a pack of baseball cards. Instead of tucking the funds away, he and Jane would celebrate by throwing a big party for their friends with lavish food and drink, only to go back to eating plain cereal the next day.

Like the Pilgrims, Vonnegut had chosen Provincetown as his first landing spot when he arrived on Cape Cod back in 1951. He and Jane rented a tiny, shingled home on Commercial Street, close to the place where writer John Dos Passos had once worked in a house built on an old wharf that had been destroyed by fire, ice, and the sea. Provincetown had also been home to Pulitzer Prize–winning playwright Eugene O'Neill, who wrote *Anna Christie* at Masonic Place and had lived for a time at a lifesaving station tucked away in the Sahara-like dunes.

Shortly after their arrival, Jane Vonnegut bumped into a young Norman Mailer on the street and introduced herself. "My husband is a writer as well," she said. "I'd like very much for you to meet him."

The two men gathered over cocktails, and Jane found Mailer to be "a nice guy." Mailer did not think twice about the encounter; it had been a turning point, however, for Vonnegut. Mailer was a boxer, but it was Vonnegut who sized him up like a fighter during a weigh-in for a championship bout. Physically, Mailer did not impress. He was short with curly hair and a barrel chest, and he had ears sticking out of his head the size of Dumbo's. But his eyes, those striking blue eyes, offered Vonnegut a window into his youthful genius. Vonnegut attempted to swat away thoughts that he was not worthy of Mailer's attention or his friendship. They were more alike than one could realize just by looking at them, and this notion settled Vonnegut's nerves.

You're about my age, Vonnegut thought as he stared at Mailer over the brim of his cocktail glass. *You were a college-educated infantry private like me. But you're a world figure because you've published your great war novel. But I've got a story of my own to write.*

Vonnegut would spend the next two decades stopping and starting his Dresden novel. The novel had cost him dearly in money, anxiety, and time. It was the fall of 1968, and Vonnegut, in his words, had "gone broke, was out of print and had a lot of kids."

Something had to happen for him fast. He focused his attention on the Luftwaffe sabre, a memento from the war, with its gold-plated ceremonial handle, standing upright in the corner of his writing shed and went back to work revising *Slaughterhouse-Five*.

CHAPTER SIX

————————

Less than a mile away from Mailer's home on Commercial Street, Tony Costa had his nose in a book. The young killer had returned to his residence in room 213 at the Crown & Anchor and was reading *Steppenwolf* by German writer Hermann Hesse. Focusing on the words typed on each page, it was as if he were staring down at his own personal diary. Like Hesse's protagonist Harry Haller, Costa had entered his own magic theater, one designed "for madmen only." He had swallowed a handful of Nembutal tablets a few hours earlier and was smoking hash to level himself out. Later, he planned to fetch a few tabs of acid that he had buried in a glass jar on the beach.

He recited Hesse's words and made them his own: "I'm a beast astray who finds neither home, nor joy, nor nourishment in a world that is strange and incomprehensible. I am the wolf of the Steppes."

There were now two bodies cut up and buried in the North Truro woods. Costa recalled the looks in the eyes of Susan Perry and Sydney Monzon at the moment when their lights went out. The killer wept. Like Hesse's book, he was engaged in an internal battle with the high, spiritual nature of man and the low, animalistic nature that lived inside the caverns of his soul.

At that moment, Cory's voice reentered Costa's mind. *They died on their own, Sire, and I don't want to say any more about the way they died. They just did, and they had it coming to them. And there were others too.*

The young man blocked his ears, rocking back and forth on his bed.

"But I never intentionally hurt anyone in my life," he told Cory. "For me to needlessly injure someone would be to inflict pain on myself. We've committed a dastardly deed. I curse the night!"

He jumped to his feet and fled the room. He walked across the street to Adams Pharmacy, took a stool at the counter, and asked for a cup of hot water while pulling a tea bag from the pocket of his army surplus coat. He dipped the bag in the cup and watched the contents bleed out. The hot tea calmed his nerves, and soon after, his alter ego retreated once again to the dark corners of his mind.

The front door opened, bringing with it a gust of briny, salt air as a young woman approached the counter. Her name was Christine Gallant, and she appeared disheveled.

"What on earth happened to you, my love?" Costa asked.

Christine told him that her boyfriend had beaten her again. She moved a strand of brown hair off her face to show him the welt bubbling under her right eye.

"If he ever touches you again, I'll teach him something he'll never forget," he said gallantly. "That bastard will wish he never heard my name."

He was attracted to Christine, even more so than the others. She was the most beautiful woman he had ever seen. She was well endowed with a full bosom, and her brown hair, parted in the middle, was lightened by the sun of the previous summer. She reminded him of the actress Ali MacGraw.

"Your eyes burn with a deep fire," he told her.

Christine was taken aback by the compliment but felt secure in his presence. They left the drug store and sat on the grass at town hall where they continued their conversation. Christine had to return to New York City by the end of the weekend to resume her job as a library clerk at Columbia University.

"You should come with me," she told him. "New York is alive, and the Village is amazing. It sure beats Provincetown right now. This place is a ghost town."

Costa had a few carpentry jobs that he still needed to complete at the Crown & Anchor and promised to meet her when he was done. The work was slow because he was getting high most of the time or tripping on acid. He continued to sell pot and pills, which afforded him the money to purchase a round-trip bus ticket to New York City.

During the trip, as the Greyhound bus passed through Massachusetts, Rhode Island, and Connecticut, Costa sat silently in his seat, holding his duffel bag to his chest. The woman in the next seat noticed that he had his eyes closed and was rocking slightly.

Must be having a bad dream, she thought to herself. She could not hear Cory's voice or what he was urging Costa to do once he arrived in New York.

The first couple of days with Christine were sheer bliss. They took in a screening of the Beatles' animated feature *Yellow Submarine* and spent hours talking in coffeehouses and strolling Central Park together. At night, they loved with a passion that neither had experienced before.

It was all going so well. It had to end. Cory wanted it that way.

They sipped Chianti in Christine's apartment in Morningside Heights on the Upper West Side while listening to Bob Dylan's "Chimes of Freedom." She placed her head on Costa's lap with her eyes closed as he ran his fingers through her hair. There was a sense of calm in the room, and Christine had no indication of the powerful urge that was erupting inside him.

With his free hand, he dropped a tablet into her wineglass and watched as it quickly dissolved in the liquid.

No, no, no, he told Cory. *Not Chrissie. I want to invest my whole world, my whole life in her. Every dream, every hope.*

He placed the glass to Chrissie's lips and offered her a drink. She sipped it at first. Then she emptied the glass and soon told him that the room had begun to spin around her. Her brown eyes fluttered, and then everything went black. The killer retrieved his duffel bag and went to work.

After he was finished, Costa hopped on a bus and made his way back to Helltown.

Christine Gallant's body was discovered by her roommate, Cynthia Savidge, the next day.

A reporter picked up the story, and the following headline ran in the *Boston Globe* on November 26, 1968: "DRUGS BLAMED IN DEATH OF EX-BAYSTATE GIRL."

"Blonde, Christine Gallant, 19, who drowned in her bathtub last weekend, apparently had been experimenting with the hallucinogenic drug LSD," the report stated. A newspaper man interviewed the associate city medical examiner by phone. "People who use these drugs are often depressed and neurotic," Dr. Michael Baden told him. "During the past year, we've had 15 to 20 suicides of this type where people have taken their own lives on the heels of an LSD trip. These trips usually end within eight hours, but we've had cases of severe and violent reactions as much as six months later."

Baden, who would later gain international fame for his role in the O. J. Simpson trial and on the HBO series *Autopsy*, also told the reporter that Christine Gallant had taken at least a dozen sleeping pills before getting into a tub full of water. He had also found puncture wounds on her chest but surmised that they were self-inflicted.

Christine's mother, Evelyn, living in Fall River, Massachusetts, was notified by New York City police of her death and was asked to identify her body. She fainted when she saw her daughter lying lifeless on a slab.

Her killer read the *Boston Globe* story with great interest and tore it out of the newspaper. Costa folded the article and stuffed it in his wallet as he dressed to attend her funeral.

"This was the last time," he vowed. "I cannot handle this torment any longer."

He drove off Cape to Chrissie's parents' home in Fall River, a city once teaming with textile mills, located at the mouth of the Taunton River.

The city was made famous by Lizzie Borden, who was tried and acquitted for murdering her father and stepmother with an ax in 1892. Borden was buried at Oak Grove Cemetery, the place where Christine Gallant would be laid to rest.

At the funeral parlor, Costa got one last look at his latest victim as she lay in an open casket, her delicate body still intact, unlike the others. The young man then drove to the cemetery for her burial. On passing the Borden family plot, he hummed the macabre nursery rhyme in his head.

Lizzie Borden took an ax and gave her mother forty whacks.
When she saw what she had done, she gave her father forty-one.

"I am the wolf of the Steppes," he whispered to himself once more.

CHAPTER SEVEN

———

My name is Yon Yonson,
I work in Wisconsin,
I work in a lumber mill there.
The people I meet when I walk down the street,
They say, "What's your name?"
And I say,
"My name is Yon Yonson,
I work in Wisconsin."

Vonnegut recited the recursive poem to himself using a Swedish accent. He had included the verse in the first chapter of his Dresden book. He used the rhyme to symbolize the infinitely repeatable questions that can be found in each man's painful search for meaning. The war had been like that for Vonnegut, as was his writing career.

He had a copy of the publisher's galley of *Slaughterhouse-Five* in his hands. He pulled an old blanket over his shoulders and thumbed through the galley. A harsh wind pulled off Cape Cod Bay and found its way into his writing studio, which lacked sufficient heat despite its wood-burning stove. He had retreated to his work bunker, which was twenty-two feet long and fifteen feet wide, after his wife, Jane, had caught him dialing up an old girlfriend. He used drunkenness as an excuse and was banished to the shed, which sat like a sidecar adjacent to their home. It was late in the evening, and his daughter Edie was still out at God knows where. She was home from college for the Thanksgiving holiday. The village of Barnstable was basically shuttered in late fall, and nearby Hyannis was relatively quiet also. Therefore, Edie and her pals would all hop into someone's car and drive up Route 6A to Ptown to do God only knows what.

Vonnegut chose to settle in Barnstable over Provincetown because it was close to Cape Cod's only airport. He had imagined that he would be jetting back and forth between the Cape and New York City once his literary career took off. It was almost twenty years since he had made that prediction, and he still had not set foot inside the small airport, as his writing career remained stuck on the tarmac. Instead, he peddled short stories. Many of them were nothing more than "miserable crap" in his words. "There must be an eager readership out there wondering why there wasn't more from the pen of Kurt Vonnegut," he told his literary agent Ken Littauer at the time.

"Who asked you to be a writer in the first place?" the agent replied coldly.

Vonnegut thought his first published novel, *Player Piano*, would bust him out of anonymity. The publishing house was Scribner's, the literary home of Ernest Hemingway. Vonnegut dreamed that he would achieve some success by association, but his satire, one that pitted man versus machine, hit a sour note with readers and reviewers alike. Scribner's printed seventy-six hundred copies and sold just thirty-six hundred books. Vonnegut saw a psychiatrist for depression. He formed a group at his local library to explore great books, and he dabbled in theater at the Cape Cod Comedy Club, just a few blocks away from his humorless home. He rattled around the two-hundred-year-old house like an apparition. It had six fireplaces and twelve rooms, and it sent a message to others that Vonnegut earned a healthy living as a writer. But the place was a disaster on the inside, and the furnace was ancient. Vonnegut bought it for a song and had been paying for it ever since with its near-constant upkeep. He yelled at the kids when they were little and playing in their bedrooms. "What the hell are you doing up there?" he would grouse. "Shut the hell up!"

Jane Vonnegut could barely hang on, especially in those early days. She was also suffering from depression, the postpartum kind, and often put her own pen to paper.

"I love him, I could never live with anyone else, this is true. But he hasn't the slightest idea how crazy he makes me," she wrote in her journal. "I have no business being here at all and yet I have to be… He is a genius. I love it. I hate it. It is awful. It will never be good."

Edie could hardly recall any joy in the Vonnegut household as a child. She had fleeting images of her father carrying her home off their boat following evening picnic excursions to Sandy Neck, but that was about it.

Vonnegut parted ways with Scribner after he delivered only six chapters of *Cat's Cradle*, the follow-up to *Player Piano*. He negotiated the rights back and promised Scribner that he would repay his advance of several hundred dollars if it was ever published. He had high hopes for another book, *Mother Night*, his "Nazi book" about a U.S.-born Nazi propagandist turned double agent for the Allies. The book was released as a thirty-five-cent paperback, but it failed to catch the attention of even one reviewer.

Vonnegut responded to the disappointment in his usual way, by lashing out at his wife and kids. Jane took to wearing sunglasses around the house to mask her eyes, which were often swollen by tears. Vonnegut threatened to run away too. He would hop in his Saab and speed out of the driveway without warning. He would then find a motel on the beach and negotiate a fee with the manager before deciding it was too much and drive back home where, in his opinion, the house was always dirty and the roof always leaked.

Vonnegut never understood why he acted this way. He also never discussed his experiences during the war and how they were likely the root of his angry, erratic behavior.

Vonnegut had been assigned to the 423rd Regiment and crossed the English Channel and landed in Le Havre, France, on December 6, 1944, exactly six months after the D-Day invasion. He advanced with the 106th Division toward the front in Belgium before eventually digging in atop a mountain in the Ardennes Forest. Ten days into Vonnegut's combat deployment, German guns began pounding the 106th's position, turning unit command posts into deep craters filled with limbs and blood. For Allied troops, there was no recourse but to surrender or be slaughtered.

Vonnegut was among thousands of captives who were forced to march for two days with little food or water until being transported by boxcar to a POW camp at Bad Orb and eventually on to Stalag IV-B, one of the largest POW camps in Germany, located in the quaint Prussian town of Mühlberg. The journey was hellish, as soldiers were forced to shit thin gruel into their steel helmets and toss the waste out through narrow ventilation slats. The Germans wrote in blue chalk on the outside of each train the number of prisoners inside as if they were moving prized heifers. The tops of the trains were painted black and orange to alert Allied fighters and bombers that the cars were carrying POWs. Still, Vonnegut and his fellow soldiers tightened their stomachs each time they heard a plane's engine roar in the distance.

In a postcard to his parents, per the Geneva Convention, Vonnegut told them not to worry. "I've come through this God awful slaughter without a scratch," he wrote. "This life is not bad at all."

Vonnegut spoke too soon. Due to overcrowding at Stalag IV-B, he was forced on the move again, as he and 150 other POWs were loaded onto a train car and sent to a work detail in Dresden, Germany, the "Florence of the Elbe." Friedrich Schiller wrote the poem "Ode to Joy" in the majestic city on the River Elbe, and Johann Sebastian Bach once performed a recital there.

Dresden was a dramatic place, made even more so by the large, flowing Nazi banners hung in places like the Frauenkirche, a massive baroque domed church, in the city center. The prisoners were housed in a rectangular building that had been used to slaughter pigs before the war. Vonnegut's barracks were commonly known as Schlachthof-Fünf or Slaughterhouse-Five, and it was guarded by a teenage, ferret-looking Nazi the prisoners called "Junior" and a one-eyed sergeant nicknamed "One-Lamp Louie." Vonnegut, with two years of high school German under his belt, served as camp translator. He also labored on a work detail that cleared away rubble from the streets after Allied bombing raids and unloaded bags of grain from boxcars. He was always tempted to forage for any leftover food found in the bombing debris or train cars, but he knew such an act would be punishable by death. With little food to eat and a lack of vitamins, Vonnegut contracted impetigo as white spots bleached parts of his arms and legs. One day, fed up with the abuse he witnessed of a fellow POW, Vonnegut called a German captor a "fucking swine" and was beaten mercilessly for it.

The first signs of impending doom for the city were the magnesium parachute flares that dropped from the sky just before 10:00 p.m. on February 13, 1945, an unusually warm winter night in "the Florence of the Elbe." To most Dresdeners, the flares looked like Christmas trees descending slowly to the ground. The subsequent air raid sirens did not spark a panic, as they were a normal occurrence in those days. Many residents did not even bother to get out of bed. They believed their city to be invincible. Dresden had no military significance, and the Allies surely would not carpet bomb the beautiful baroque city and destroy centuries of Western art and culture. It must only be some kind of reconnaissance mission, thought the majority of Dresdeners, who were ill prepared for an Allied onslaught and had only a few buckets of sand and water on hand to put out any fires.

The flares were followed by the deafening hum of eight hundred RAF Avro Lancaster bombers soaring eight thousand feet over the city. The nighttime sky was suddenly filled with 1,400 tons of high explosive bombs and 1,180 tons of incendiary bombs.

Vonnegut was ordered out of his bunk by One-Lamp Louie and sent with others down into the basement of a nearby storage building sixty feet below the ground.

"Giants stalked the earth above us," he later recalled. "First came the soft murmur of their dancing on the outskirts, then the grumbling of their plodding toward us, and finally the ear-splitting crashes of their heels upon us."

A few blocks away, a twelve-year-old boy named Eberhard Renner was huddled with his family in the cellar of their turn-of-the-century apartment near a Volkswagen factory. A bomb exploded in their garden, blowing the cellar door in toward the boy and his mother. His father screamed, "Well, it's those criminals we have to thank for this!" referring to Adolf Hitler and his murderous mob. The first wave of bombs lasted fifteen minutes, engulfing much of the city in flames. Three hours later, five hundred more Lancasters flew in to finish the job, dropping another thousand tons of explosives on the train station and other key targets while P-51 Mustang fighters flew low, strafing survivors who were trying to flee as the ground melted under their feet.

The next morning, Vonnegut and the other POWs stepped outside to see what was left. They immediately set their eyes on a side of beef that lay on the ground after getting scorched. The prisoners attacked it like a pool of hungry piranhas, jamming meat into their mouths despite protests from One-Lamp Louie. Under armed guard, the POWs were then ordered to clean up the city, or what was left of it. Outside the gates of Slaughterhouse-Five, Vonnegut witnessed the overwhelming slaughter of human beings. One woman looked like she had been pulled from an archeological dig in Pompeii. She was lying on her back with her arms raised like a mannequin, the pattern of her incinerated dress embedded into her thighs. The corpses of children dressed in carnival clothes to celebrate Shrove Tuesday were scattered everywhere. The city zoo was a wasteland. Caged lions were free to roam the streets, feasting on the dead, who numbered more than sixty thousand. Vonnegut was sent into cellars to look for survivors, but he only found their tombs. Those who were not killed by toppled wooden beams and crumbling bricks suffocated in the firestorm. Those victims "looked like a streetcar full of people who'd simultaneously had heart failure," Vonnegut observed. "Just people sitting in their chairs, all dead."

Vonnegut described his search for survivors and retrieval of the dead as a "terribly elaborate Easter egg hunt."

Two POWs stole some food and were then shot in the back by German guards. Vonnegut was forced to dig their graves and dump the bodies inside. "The sons of bitches, the sons of bitches," he muttered quietly. One of the executed prisoners, an older American soldier named Michael Palaia, had stolen a large jar of pickled string beans. Vonnegut vowed to write about him someday, if he was lucky enough to survive this madness.

On April 13, 1945, as news spread of the death of President Franklin D. Roosevelt, Vonnegut's captors evacuated Slaughterhouse-Five and marched the POWs along the Elbe River some fifty miles southeast, ultimately ending up in the remote village of Hellendorf, near the border with Czechoslovakia, and 592 kilometers southwest of Berlin, where Soviet troops were advancing on the dark heart of the Third Reich. Fearing they would be butchered if they surrendered to the Russians, the German captors isolated themselves and their prisoners, hoping they would be discovered by American troops instead. They all stayed hidden for three weeks without food and scarcely any water. Vonnegut and his fellow POWs grazed on grass like cows and ate dandelions to survive. One day, after a Soviet strafing of the area, the Germans fled into the forest, leaving their prisoners behind. Vonnegut and five others, including a GI named Bernie O'Hare, who had become his closest buddy, stole a wagon, painted a white star on its sides, and rode it back to Dresden, where they were later handed back over to the Americans by Soviet troops.

He was examined at a POW repatriation center in Le Havre. Private Kurt Vonnegut Jr. had lost forty pounds during his imprisonment, his teeth were loose from scurvy, and he was nearly crippled by painful ulcers in his legs. But he was alive. He had made it through hell.

But a part of him remained in Dresden, although he doubted that he would ever return there—to the scene of the crime. The writing of *Slaughterhouse-Five* was not only a desperate and perhaps final attempt to achieve the commercial success afforded to authors like Mailer but not to him, it was also an opportunity to confront the psychological wounds he had suffered but that had yet to scab and heal over.

He could not remember, or he had blocked out, much of what he saw in Dresden, especially after the bombings, so Vonnegut reached out to his old war buddy Bernie O'Hare, who was by then a district attorney living in Pennsylvania.

"Listen, I'm writing a book about Dresden," he told O'Hare on the phone. "I'd like some help remembering stuff. I wonder if I can come and see you, and we could drink and talk and remember."

Vonnegut said he had already envisioned the climax of the book—the execution of Michael Palaia for stealing a jar of pickled green beans while thousands of bodies lay strewn across the city.

"It's great irony," he told O'Hare. He had already decided to change Palaia's name to Edgar Derby in the manuscript.

Vonnegut was the kind of writer who outlined his novels ahead of time. He followed this rule with *Slaughterhouse-Five*, writing on the back of a roll of wallpaper using a set of his daughter's crayons to symbolize each character with a different shade of Crayola. O'Hare was willing to meet, so Vonnegut decided to make a road trip of it, packing his eldest daughter, Nanny, and a friend in the back of an old station wagon and heading off Cape Cod. En route to O'Hare's house, they visited the New York World's Fair, saw streams, and jumped off cliffs into rivers. But there was always a feeling of tension in the station wagon as Vonnegut often turned to the back seat and yelled "Shut up!" to the talkative young girls. When they arrived at O'Hare's place, Vonnegut was greeted with an angry stare by O'Hare's wife, Mary. She reminded him that both he and her husband were "babies" during the war, and she feared his novel would glorify combat like it was a John Wayne or Frank Sinatra movie.

"I don't think this book of mine is ever gonna get finished," he told Mary. "I must have written five thousand pages by now, and thrown them all away. If I ever do finish it, I give you my word of honor: there won't be a part for Frank Sinatra or John Wayne."

He also promised her that he would call the book *Children's Crusade*. But Vonnegut's momentum ebbed, and he sat on the project for the next couple of years. It wasn't until he was offered a chance to join the faculty of the University of Iowa to teach a creative writing course that the Dresden book finally came into focus for him. He was a last-minute choice after poet Robert Lowell had dropped out, but Vonnegut accepted the challenge with gusto. He had been frustrated by the fact that most critics had dismissed his work as science fiction since the publication of techno satire *Player Piano* more than a decade before.

"I have been a sore-headed occupant of a file drawer labeled science fiction ever since," he later wrote. "I would like *out* since so many serious critics regularly mistake the drawer for a tall, white fixture in a comfort station."

Vonnegut's thinking was that science fiction books were often hidden in the bowels of bookstores and that he wanted his work to be displayed up front near the cash register. The selling of a book always came down to proper product placement.

He drove out to Iowa City in the fall of 1965. He had borrowed his son's Volkswagen for the trip. Jane Vonnegut welcomed her husband's departure, as the walls had been closing in at their home in West Barnstable, and living with Vonnegut had become unbearable. He taught two classes each day: Form and Theory of Fiction and his fiction workshop, and he wrote and rewrote his Dresden novel at night inside a cramped second-floor apartment close to downtown.

"The place is awful," he told a friend. "But if I can't write in a dump like this, I'm gonna quit."

In the classroom, he urged his students to "steal from the best," especially if they could not come up with interesting characters of their own. At his apartment, without the distraction of kids, dogs, and an angry wife, he wrote at a maddening pace. Jane wrote to him that their daughter Edie was getting in trouble at Barnstable High School for wearing low tops and skimpy skirts. He paid little attention to his parental responsibilities, as he had become distracted by a second-year student named Lora Lee Wilson with whom he had ignited a torrid affair. Sensing trouble, Jane brought Edie out to Iowa City in an effort to stabilize him. Vonnegut treated Edie like a maid, ordering her to clean his messy apartment when he was out teaching classes.

When he finally returned to Cape Cod, he struggled with domestic life and began drinking heavily, martinis being his cocktail of choice. But the Dresden book was in better shape than ever. He needed to go back to the city for one last round of research and secured a Guggenheim grant to fund the trip.

At the same time, he attracted interest from a book editor named Seymour "Sam" Lawrence, who specialized in aiding struggling writers. Lawrence shared Vonnegut's belief that his work had been misread by critics and that he was a serious man of letters. The two men met at Lawrence's office at 90 Beacon Street in Boston and immediately hit it off. Despite being nearly twenty years younger than Vonnegut, Lawrence became something of a father figure to him. He bought back the rights to all Vonnegut's previous books and pushed them back out into the marketplace. Most importantly for Vonnegut, he became an unwavering champion of *Slaughterhouse-Five*.

With his stock finally rising as a writer, Vonnegut's reputation as a faithful husband plummeted at home. Jane had discovered a love letter that he had written to Lora Lee Wilson and confronted him in front of their kids. Vonnegut wanted no part of the conversation.

"Shut the fuck up!" he scolded her.   He certainly did not want an airing of their troubles to be witnessed by their children.

Once the Guggenheim Foundation money came in, Vonnegut fled overseas with his army buddy Bernie O'Hare at his side. They visited Helsinki and even traveled behind the Iron Curtain to Leningrad to witness festivities to commemorate the fiftieth anniversary of the Russian Revolution.

When he arrived in Dresden, in what was then East Germany, Vonnegut found the place as dull as Cedar Rapids, Iowa. The former "Florence of the Elbe" had been reconstructed years after the bombings and was dominated by drab buildings and communist architecture. Vonnegut recalled a quote from a British historian who described Dresden this way after visiting there in the late 1950s: "It was as though a woman reputedly the most beautiful in Europe turned out to be an old hag, wrapped in rags with a cigarette dangling from her lips."

Vonnegut and O'Hare hired a taxi driver to take them to where they had lost their virginity toward violence, a place where the young army scouts had grown old and weary. But there was nothing left of Slaughterhouse-Five now. The ground was flat and covered by weeds, grass, and shards of broken masonry.

The two men stepped out of the cab and took a look around.

"There's tons of human bone meal in the ground," Vonnegut told his friend.

They tried to locate their former Nazi guards, including the teenager they called Junior. But they had no luck. Nobody there wanted to talk about the war or the murderous crimes they had committed while in uniform. The truth about Dresden lay only in its ash-laden soil.

Upon his return to the States, Vonnegut found greater clarity in his writing. To describe the horror he had witnessed during the war, he would tell the story out of context, carving out much of the benign and focusing almost solely on those malignant moments of sheer madness. His protagonist, Billy Pilgrim, was much like him, a character who had become detached from reality after the brutality he had witnessed during the war. In the plot, Pilgrim is treated for mental impairment issues at a veterans hospital and is later abducted by aliens, taken aboard their UFO, and whisked away to their home planet, Tralfamadore.

Vonnegut himself often dreamed of such an escape.

Psychiatrists called it *battle fatigue*, as post-traumatic stress disorder had not yet become part of the nomenclature. Whatever the term, Vonnegut recognized that his experiences as a prisoner of war had changed him drastically. His wife would no longer know the Vonnegut who existed before he had crossed the English Channel with the 423rd Regiment in December 1944, and his children would never get the chance to meet him. Writing *Slaughterhouse-Five* would help him explain his trauma to his family. It was his personal postcard from the edge.

Vonnegut was ultimately satisfied with his Dresden book, which was at the printer and getting bound in hardcover in late November 1968. The publisher, Delacorte Press, had promised an initial printing of ten thousand copies, scheduled for release in March the following year. In *Slaughterhouse-Five*, the author described himself in a note to his readers this way: "A fourth-generation German-American now living in easy circumstances on Cape Cod (and smoking too much), who, as an American Infantry Scout, Hors De Combat, a prisoner of war, witnessed the fire-bombing of Dresden, Germany, 'The Florence of the Elbe,' a long time ago, and survived to tell the tale. This is a novel, somewhat in the telegraphic, schizophrenic manner of tales of the planet Tralfamadore, where the UFOs come from. Peace."

As with each of his books, but especially this one, Vonnegut was melancholy upon its completion. To him, it represented the end of his relationship with the story and its characters. He had too much time on his hands and needed to focus his attention on another topic. The writer was about to discover one close to home and beyond even his wildest imagination.

My name is Yon Yonson,
I work in Wisconsin,
I work in a lumber mill there...

CHAPTER EIGHT

The killer spent the Christmas holidays acting as a psychedelic Santa Claus, pedaling his English racer around Provincetown delivering pot and pills to close friends and acquaintances. Costa's drug stash, hidden in the ammo cans in the North Truro woods, was nearly depleted, but business had been good as of late, since almost everyone he knew wanted to greet the new year stoned and happy. The money earned would help him survive another frigid winter on the outer Cape. He was no longer living at the Crown & Anchor, because the manager there found him pleasant but unpredictable. The young man had to rely on the kindness of friends, his so-called disciples, sleeping on their couches and spare beds until he could find a more permanent residence.

There was little talk around town as to the whereabouts of nineteen-year-old Sydney Monzon and seventeen-year-old Susan Perry. It was as if they had both fallen off the face of the earth. When asked about Susan, Costa shrugged his shoulders and replied, "I haven't seen her in such a long time. I believe she moved to Mexico City as she wanted to watch the Summer Olympic games there."

It seemed odd that Susan would be so adventurous, as the young woman had never traveled beyond Boston before.

"I think it's groovy to think that Susan got to see Tommie Smith and John Carlos raise their fists in a Black power salute. She got to witness true history," he said. "Plus, the weather in Mexico City has to be nicer than the winter doldrums on the Cape."

The killer believed that his secrets would be kept dead and buried under the crusted earth off Cemetery Road. He did not keep to himself; instead he strolled along the barren streets and narrow alleyways of Provincetown with confidence and a sly smile for everyone he met. He frequented Adams Pharmacy during the day, and at night, he would slip into the Foc'sle for a glass of Chianti.

One evening, his English racer was spotted by Provincetown police officer William Sylvia parked outside the tavern on Commercial Street. The cop known as "Cobra" stood under a lamppost across the street, smoking a cigarette and waiting for the young man to emerge. Costa paid his tab and left a healthy tip for the bartender. He turned up the collar of his army surplus jacket and stepped out into the cold night.

Cobra crossed the street and signaled for the young man to follow him. Costa left his bicycle tied up and began walking a few paces behind the officer. On the next block, both slipped into a dark alleyway between two downtown businesses that were shuttered for the season. A married couple enjoying their after-dinner walk noticed their movement. The image of two men sneaking off to find sex in dark places was commonplace here in Ptown, so the couple minded their business and continued their stroll.

"Got something good for me tonight?" Cobra asked in a low voice.

"I've heard some things," Costa replied. "I've learned that someone is peddling bad scag around town."

"I want a name."

The young man pulled his hand out of his coat. "You recall our arrangement."

Annoyed, Cobra dug into his pocket, fished out a twenty-dollar bill, and slapped it down on the informant's palm.

"His name is Cory Deveraux. He attends Ptown high school, and he's into everything. I think you should bring him in before someone overdoses and dies."

The officer grunted. "When did you become such a caring soul? You're going around selling the same shit."

"That's where you are wrong, Officer. I don't play with heroin. I want it kept out of our town just as badly as you do."

"I'll follow up on Devereaux . Keep me posted if you hear anything else."

The killer nodded. "I certainly will do that, Officer. You enjoy the rest of your evening."

They parted ways in the alley, and the young man returned for his bicycle. He had no idea whether Cory Devereaux was selling heroin or not, but now there would be some heat on him. Serving as an informant for the Provincetown Police Department was a great way to earn some extra money and eliminate his potential rivals in the local drug trade at the same time. It also allowed Costa to keep tabs on the cops and their investigations of the two girls who had gone missing from Helltown.

"You're handsome enough to run for office," Pulitzer Prize–winning playwright William Inge wrote to Norman Mailer after seeing his profile adorning the cover of *Newsweek* magazine in December 1968. Inge was not alone. Mailer's friends Gloria Steinem and Jack Newfield were also pushing him toward the political arena. Richard Nixon was president-elect after winning 43 percent of the popular vote and beating Democratic challenger Hubert Humphrey and a third-party candidate, former Alabama governor and rampant racist George Wallace in the 1968 election. Nixon won his home state of California and the thirty electoral votes that came with it. He lost in Massachusetts, a longtime Kennedy stronghold, where Vonnegut's wife, Jane, and daughter Edie campaigned heavily for Minnesota senator Eugene McCarthy in the Democratic primary, Edie going so far as to wear a McCarthy flower power decal on her stomach while sunning herself at Sandy Neck in her bikini.

Mailer had been frustrated by McCarthy, who had the guts to take on LBJ and denounce the war in Vietnam but lacked the passion to build on his base, and Mailer had no use for Humphrey, President Johnson's fawning second in command.

He wrote back to Inge, "The disease of the 20th century is that politics had invaded the heart and polluted our sensibilities and there is no real way out—that one must write about politics as endemically as love."

Mailer owed it to the memory of his late friend Bobby Kennedy to give back in a way that went a step beyond the written word. He had served as a member of the honor guard at Kennedy's memorial service six months before, and that experience had a major impact on him as he watched a human convoy of catharsis, "the poorest part of the working class of New York," make their way slowly passed Kennedy's flag-draped coffin in tribute to the late senator. These people needed someone's help. Mailer was spending more time in Provincetown, because New York City was such a mess. There was an outer borough backlash against liberal Republican John Lindsay, the city's incumbent mayor. The Brooklyn-bred Mailer began to see himself as the perfect antidote to a silk-stocking Manhattanite like Lindsay. But any decision about jumping into the mayor's race would have to be tabled for the time being, as Mailer was making final edits to an upcoming experiential film that he wrote, directed, and produced, titled *Maidstone*.

Fueled by a seemingly never-ending supply of scotch, Mailer shot the movie over five days in the Hamptons on Long Island while grieving Bobby Kennedy's assassination that past summer. The script for *Maidstone* revolved around an assassination plot against an erotic filmmaker turned politician played by Mailer himself. Cinema offered Mailer, as an artist, a new canvas to paint on, and he took to the medium with unbounded energy. He already had two films under his director's belt, *Wild 90* and *Beyond the Law*. *Wild 90* was a heavily improvised movie about three gangsters, including Mailer, hiding in a warehouse, arguing and insulting each other. It had cost him just $1,500 to produce with no retakes and was roundly panned by critics. Writing for the *New Republic*, Stanley Kauffmann described the author/director/actor this way: "I cannot say Mailer was drunk the whole time he was on camera. I can only hope he was drunk."

Unbowed by such criticism, Mailer climbed back into the director's chair for another experimental film set in a New York City police station. Once again, Mailer wrote the script and performed in the lead role as a grizzled Irish detective named Xavier Pope. Mailer explained his goals for *Beyond the Law* this way: "I wanted to get below the reality, beneath the reality, within the reality of an evening inside a police station." In truth, he acted more like a kid making a film with his friends in the backyard and using his parents' home movie camera as his instrument. On the evening of the shoot, he told his buddies, "We're making a movie tonight and you're playing the cops. So eat and drink all you want 'cause that's all you're getting paid."

Mailer did hire one legitimate actor for the film, Rip Torn, a young Texan who had studied under Lee Strasberg at the Actors Studio and had more than a decade of stage and screen experience. *Beyond the Law* lost Mailer nearly $80,000, but it did provide him with some positive reviews for his work. The *New York Times* called it "So good, and tough and entertaining so much of the time that you have to forgive those moments when it becomes unintelligible."

Maidstone was a much bigger production, with a larger cast and dozens of extras, mostly attractive young women.

"I'm interested in sexuality, rampant and resplendent," Mailer told his actresses. "But it has to be in good taste, I cannot bear bad taste."

He had placed all his chips in the middle of the table for this one. The film's budget was a whopping $200,000, and Mailer was forced to sell his shares in the *Village Voice* to cover the costs. He was trying to edit down forty-five hours' worth of footage into a 110-minute film. His friend and cinematographer D. A. Pennebaker urged Mailer to end the movie with an improvised scene that had devolved into a moment of real-life terror. Rip Torn's character, Raoul Rey O'Houlihan, was supposed to make an attempt on the life of Mailer's character, Norman Kingsley. But Mailer could not decide how to approach the scene in his ad hoc script. Frustration spilled over the next day while Pennebaker discussed Mailer's lack of direction with Torn, the thirty-seven-year-old actor from Texas. Instinctively, Pennebaker picked up a handheld camera and filmed the exchange. Torn mumbled something behind a pair of dark sunglasses while staring at the ground. It is clear while watching the footage that the actor had ingested some kind of hallucinogenic drug beforehand. Pennebaker's camera then captured Mailer's wife, Beverly, strolling with their children in tall grass nearby.

"Daddy, Daddy!" shouted Mailer's young son Michael when he saw his shirtless father standing under a large tree. Torn noticed Mailer too. He tossed his sunglasses onto the grass and pulled a small hammer from his sack. Pennebaker continued to shoot, mesmerized by Torn's method approach to acting. His camera zoomed in on the actor's face, capturing Torn's wild eyes and the sinister grin forming at the corners of his mouth.

"Kinda nice out here," Pennebaker said as Torn felt the weight of the hammer in his hand while deciding on his next move. Torn wore the sunglasses once more, and the camera followed him as he approached Mailer under the tree. Both Mailer and Pennebaker were startled when Torn lifted the hammer over his head and swung it at Mailer. Suddenly, each man understood that the unfolding scene was all too real. Torn had broken the fourth wall in a frightening, violent way.

"You crazy fool!" Mailer screamed as the steel hammer cracked the back of his head above his ear.

"You're supposed to die," Torn explained, advancing with the weapon. "Right, Mr. Kingsley? You must die. Not Mailer. I don't wanna kill Mailer, but I must kill Kingsley in this picture."

Torn swung the hammer again, but this time, Mailer wrapped his arms around him and sunk his teeth into the actor's ear, drawing blood—real blood. Both men wrestled and fell to the grass. Mailer had Torn gripped in a headlock.

"You're going to hell!" Mailer shouted. "You're going to hell!"

"No, baby," Torn replied. "You trust me," he said over and over.

"I'll trust you if you let go," Mailer advised, fighting for breath.

"I'm sorry, Dad," Torn apologized. "Now, lemme kiss you."

They began fighting once more. Mailer pulled at a bushel of Torn's curly hair while Torn clutched Mailer's throat with his hands. Still filming, Pennebaker did nothing to interfere or stop the assault. Mailer was fighting for his life. Torn was younger and bigger than the famous writer. Mailer's wife, Beverly, rushed to the scene.

"Oh, shit! What is this?" she shrieked while the two continued tussling on the ground. "What have you done?"

Beverly hauled off and slapped Torn at the top of his head while Mailer's young children watched and cried for their father.

"What have you done, you motherfucker?" Beverly screamed, trying to push the lumbering actor off her husband. "Get off of him, you son of a bitch!"

Beverly Mailer was soon joined by two crew members pushing and pulling and trying to unwind this human pretzel.

By this point, the children's cries were deafening. Mailer finally freed himself and grabbed Torn from behind, choking him. With his opponent vanquished, the writer disengaged while his wife continued to yell.

"Oh my God, look at you, Norman!"

Ever the fighter, Mailer shouted back, jabbing his finger in Torn's direction. "I'm not hurt. He's hurt worse than me!"

Standing on his feet, Torn tried to explain himself. "I had to pull that, Norman. You know that."

Mailer dismissed the actor's premise. "Look at what you did to my kids!"

Torn gave the famed writer some room to comfort his weeping children. Moments later, he approached again. Both men were bleeding.

"Get away from me," Mailer shouted. "Or I'm gonna coldcock you!"

Beverly then stepped in front of her husband and stared right through Rip Torn. "There's gonna be no fight! I'll fucking kill you. I'll kill you!"

She stood her ground like a momma bear and told the actor to go away.

"Just wait. I owe you one," Mailer threatened. "Wait till the day comes, 'cause I'll pull it. I'll pull it."

"The picture doesn't make sense without this," Torn replied.

"You did this in front of my kids. That's what I can't forgive you for. Cocksucker!"

"When, when is assassination ever planned, man?"

"Your dialogue is dull," Mailer responded. "If I was as ugly as you, I'd bury my head in shit!"

A child of Mailer's pleaded with the two men again. "No more fighting," she wailed.

"No more fighting," Torn promised the little one. "It's just a scene, a scene in a Hollywood whorehouse movie, okay, baby?"

The actor turned his attention back to Mailer. "Walk on," he said menacingly.

"Kiss off," the writer muttered in response, with a stream of blood trickling from his ear.

Mailer finally asked Pennebaker to turn off the camera because of Torn's dull talk.

Fade to black.

Months later, sitting in an edit suite, Mailer watched the violent encounter over and over again. He could still remember the metallic taste of Rip Torn's blood on his lips and tongue.

"Violence is the last frontier of literature," he said aloud. He could have killed the actor for what he had done. "Murder offers the promise of quick release," he continued, quoting one of his earlier novels. "It's not unsexual."

Unbeknownst to Mailer, he had a kindred spirit of sorts living within spitting distance of the author's Commercial Street home who felt the very same way.

CHAPTER NINE

Tony Costa sat on a stool inside Adams Pharmacy sipping a cup of hot tea. It was early morning, and a steady snow had begun to smother the street outside. Fishing boats remained hitched to their moorings or tied to the dock at MacMillan Pier as the town's fishermen and most shopkeepers stayed home huddled around their woodstoves, waiting for the winter storm to slowly pass.

He heard the sound of a bell ringing, followed by the stomping of boots at the entrance to the store. Chief Cheney Marshall brushed snow off his cap and the shoulders of his jacket as he walked toward the lunch counter and sat down.

"I greatly appreciate you meeting with me," the young man said. "Especially in this horrid weather."

"It's winter in New England. It snows," the chief reminded him. "What can I do for you?"

"I'm concerned about our arrangement."

"Looking for more money? Sorry, it's not gonna happen. The information you're providing us isn't that good."

"I'm being threatened," Costa said. "Bad people, vicious people know that I've been working with the police. Can you help me in any way?"

"I can't do anything unless the threats are carried out," Chief Marshall replied.

"Can you issue me a pistol permit for my protection?"

The chief laughed. "I wouldn't even give my own mother a permit."

"I'm astonished and I cannot believe your indifference. You will not offer me protection until there is a violent action against me?"

"Watch it, kid. Don't you realize who you're speaking to?"

Don't you realize who you are speaking to? the killer wanted to say. "Sorry, I didn't mean to offend."

"So, are we done here?"

"Yes, Chief. We are done."

Marshall stood up, his long and bulky frame casting a large shadow over the Formica counter. He straightened out his fur-lined police cap and stepped back out into the driving snow.

Costa blew on the surface of his teacup to cool it off and drank. He was alone, but with company.

Cory, his murderous alter ego, began planting more dark thoughts in his mind.

We need a gun. We need a gun to keep our deeds clean, Cory told him. *One shot, two shots, then it's all over, and we can get to our business.*

"But we didn't need any bloodshed with Chrissy," Costa reminded Cory. "Wasn't that clean enough for you? Police still think it was suicide."

She wanted to die, remember? She wanted to commit suicide just like her favorite poetess Sara Teasdale had done, overdosed in a bathtub.

"My God, my God. Why did this have to happen?" the killer yelled out, startling both the counter clerk and the pharmacist working at the back of the store. "My mind is bent! I need a way out."

His stomach convulsed, his brain pounded, and his eyes were red and sore.

Attempting to calm himself, he recited Teasdale's final poem, the one she had written before swallowing all those sleeping pills in 1933.

"When I am dead and over me bright April shakes out her rain-drenched hair, Tho' you should lean above me broken-hearted, I shall not care," he whispered. "And I shall be more silent and cold-hearted than you are now."

———————

A short time later, on January 18, 1969, Costa rode his blue English racer bicycle by a white-shingled Victorian rooming house at 5 Standish Street that advertised for guests by the day or week on a freshly painted sign hung on the side of the building. He hopped off his bike and climbed a short set of stairs leading to the front door and then knocked. He waited for a few minutes outside, stomping his boots against the wooden stair planks to help fight off the frigid cold. He heard the shuffling of shoes inside, and the door opened just slightly. Broad shouldered, thickly bosomed, and wearing a housecoat with her bleached hair in rollers, Patricia Morton, the owner of the boardinghouse, peeked outside.

"Who is it?" she asked.

"My name is Antone Costa," the young man replied. While most people called him Tony, he felt that introducing himself as Antone, his proper name, might sway the matronly landlady in his favor. "I would like to inquire about a room for rent."

Morton had just returned from an extended stay in the Virgin Islands, as noted by her dark tan. The rooming house had been shuttered all winter while she was gone, and she had yet to take in new tenants.

"Where are you from?"

"I live right here in Provincetown."

"I'm sorry, but I don't serve locals here, only transients," Morton replied.

"I'm a carpenter and can help you with any repair work you might have," Costa offered.

There were a few minor jobs still to be done around the house, and Morton liked the calm, eloquent tone of Costa's voice, so she let him inside.

She gave him a tour of the available rooms and asked him a battery of questions about his work history and repair skills. Costa was very knowledgeable about carpentry and acted the perfect gentleman, which put Morton at ease, as she lived alone and was leery of strangers.

"Why do you need a place to stay?"

"Most recently, I've been sleeping on the sofa at a friend's house," he explained. "Patches and his wife, Dolly, are expecting a baby any day now, so they will need all the space they have. I have been staying at my mother's place, but she's getting old and I like to go out nights, which disturbs her rest."

"I don't put up with partiers, druggies, or hippies," Morton warned him. "I run a very respectable place here."

"Oh, it's nothing like that. I spend nights at the library and when the weather is decent, I like to stroll the beach in the evening."

"Okay, that seems reasonable," the landlady replied. "I charge twenty dollars a week and I ask for payment in advance. If I rent you a room, I'll have to open up the rest of the house to other people. Let me know if you can round up more tenants. I prefer boys to girls. They're much cleaner and take care of the place better."

"Thank you, Ms. Morton," the killer replied, smiling. "I will let you know."

Tony Costa shook the landlady's hand gently before departing the rooming house and pedaling off into the night.

He returned to Patricia Morton's doorstep the following week with a duffel bag full of clothes and books and three fresh twenty-dollar bills.

"I would like to pay for most of the month in advance," Costa told her. "I should be able to supply you with another twenty dollars next week when I get paid again."

Morton took the money happily, had him sign his name in her guest ledger, and showed him to his room. Costa smiled at the decor. The hallway floors and stairs were painted blood orange and the walls a dull blue and gray.

"The orange imparts a warm, welcoming glow," Morton said proudly. "While the blue offers a cooling effect for those hot summer days. The house was once owned by the sheriff of Provincetown. It had a big wraparound porch when I bought it, but I had it removed. It was too much upkeep."

For the first two nights, Costa stayed in the "register" room adjacent to Morton's office, which she operated out of her cellar garden living room. But despite the frigid temperatures outside, the room was too hot for Costa because it was so close to the boiler. He asked Morton if he could switch rooms. The landlady thought hard for a moment, as she did not want her best room to be rented for an entire month for a mere twenty dollars a week. But Costa charmed her, and she finally relented, telling him to take his belongings to another room with a double bed on the opposite side of a shared bathroom on the second floor. This room had a large bay window that looked out onto Standish Street. Costa unpacked, neatly unfolding and then refolding a spartan collection of sweaters and jeans before pulling a small stack of 45s from his duffel bag. He was happy to see that the room came with a record player. He placed the A side of a single called "Are You a Boy or Are You a Girl" on the turntable and let it spin. The song was written and performed by the Barbarians, a band that had formed in Ptown a few summers before and scratched the surface of success before flaming out after appearing alongside James Brown and Jan and Dean in the 1964 concert film, *The T.A.M.I. Show.*

Costa knew all the band members and had sold drugs to their teenaged groupies. He played the record at low volume and opened his worn copy of *Manual of Taxidermy,* which was months overdue from the town library, and he began to read Section II—Shooting.

"Although…many valuable species can be secured by trapping, snaring, etc., yet the collector relies mainly on his gun," the author wrote. "For ordinary collectors, a 12-gauge is perhaps better than any other, as such birds as ducks, hawks and crows can be readily killed with it… The student of nature possesses an innate love of his pursuits, which causes him to respect even a dead bird."

But Tony Costa did not fancy himself an "ordinary collector," and he was not hunting warblers, jays, or even golden-winged woodpeckers. The wolf of the steppes had much bigger prey in mind.

Twenty-six-year-old Russell Norton took a swig from his draft beer and checked his watch. He was seated with a buddy inside a booth at Armando's Bar & Grille in downtown Providence, Rhode Island. Norton was waiting for two more friends to show up: Mary Anne Wysocki and Patricia or "Pat" Walsh. After about an hour, the two beautiful young women walked into the dark bar and both immediately apologized for being late. Norton ordered a round of drinks for the group and shared his package of cigarettes with Pat and Mary Anne.

"We're wicked excited for the weekend," Mary Anne announced as she blew a plume of smoke toward a ceiling fan. "We're blowing out of Providence and heading for the Cape."

"We've called ahead and booked a place in Provincetown. I'm gonna call in sick to work on Friday so we can leave early," Pat added mischievously. Pat worked as a second-grade teacher at the Laurel Hill School in Providence. It was not like Pat to just skip school and leave her principal in the lurch on a Friday, but the twenty-three-year-old green-eyed brunette was angry over the inauguration of President Richard Nixon and needed a mental break. Mary Anne was also exhausted from her semester exams at Rhode Island College and from her volunteer work with Progress for Providence, the city's antipoverty program. A change of scenery would do them both good. Norton also wanted in.

"I'd love to go with you guys," he told them. "But I just switched jobs and wouldn't be able to leave until Saturday. I can hop a bus to Hyannis though, and thumb my way up to Ptown for the night."

"Great, you can ride back with us on Sunday," Mary Anne said. "This is gonna be so much fun!"

They raised their beer mugs and toasted the weekend to come.

Two days later, on the morning of Friday, January 24, 1969, Pat Walsh faked a scratchy throat and cough while telling the school secretary that she was too sick to teach class that day. Her performance was convincing enough that the secretary wished her well and hoped that she would feel better soon. Pat hung up the phone and started to pack. It would be a short trip, so she packed light, fitting a change of clothes and other essentials into a small bag. She swung by Mary Anne Wysocki's apartment to pick her up and then filled up the gas tank of her 1968 light-blue Volkswagen Beetle to begin the 120-mile drive to land's end on the outer Cape. Leaving the city limits of Providence behind, they drove southeast past the bleak old textile city of Fall River and the historic former whaling port of New Bedford, toward the town of Bourne, where they crossed the fifty-nine-year-old steel bridge over a wide canal, entering Cape Cod. The young women listened to the car radio and the sounds of Marvin Gaye's "I Heard It Through the Grapevine," which at that moment was the number one song on the Billboard charts and had dominated the airplay at local radio stations. The Volkswagen Beetle chugged along Route 6 through a patchwork of towns that make up Cape Cod, from the commercial hub of Hyannis to the bucolic village of Brewster. Traffic along the Mid-Cape Highway was scarce during this time of year, and Pat Walsh drove well over the speed limit in an effort to fuel the vehicle's force-fed heater. The faster they drove, the warmer it got inside their small car, which was necessary on an ice-cold day such as this one.

Pat and Mary Anne arrived in Provincetown at approximately 10:30 that morning, where, peering out the car windows, they noticed the breathtaking views of Ptown's snow-capped dunes, where artists and writers such as Jackson Pollock, Lillian Hellman, and Jack Kerouac had once spent their summers. Pat flipped on her turn signal and took a left off Route 6A into

Provincetown village toward Commercial Street. The two women were hungry and considered the idea of stopping at the A&P supermarket on Conwell Street, where Sydney Monzon had worked before vanishing a year before, to pick up some snacks for lunch. But instead, they decided to get food somewhere along Commercial Street after checking into their room. Pat Walsh parked her Volkswagen next to the sidewalk at 5 Standish Street and popped the hood to retrieve their travel bags from the front boot.

Perched next to the large bay window of his room, Tony Costa studied the two specimens that were about to be ensnared in his trap. Both looked pretty enough, as far as he could tell.

Pat and Mary Anne knocked on the front door and were greeted pleasantly by Patricia Morton. The landlady showed the women around her house and explained that they would have to share a bathroom with other guests, which Pat and Mary Anne did not seem to mind. They approached Costa's room, and Morton noticed that the door was ajar.

"This is Patricia, and this is Mary Anne," the landlady said, pointing to each of them individually.

"Hi." They waved in unison.

"Girls, this is Antone. He was our first guest this winter. He's a carpenter and also does a few jobs for me here. If you have any complaints, he's the man to see." Morton chuckled. "Just kidding about bringing your complaints to him. They're my department."

The landlady asked Costa for a favor. "I've given the girls the small room upstairs, the one at the head of the stairway. Well, I have all those hippies staying up there using the kitchenette and bath. I was wondering if the girls could use the bath next to your room instead."

Morton did not like renting to hippies, but this was winter on Cape Cod, and their money was as green as anyone's.

"Of course," he replied. "I do not mind at all. The living conditions upstairs are a bit ridiculous to say the least."

He then turned his attention to Pat and Mary Anne.

"Make yourselves at home, girls," he said and smiled. "You will get used to all the hang-ups this place has after a while. So feel free to do your thing and if you need any help finding your way around town, I will be glad to help if I am able."

With that introduction, Morton walked the two women upstairs to their small double room, where they left their overnight bags before returning to the cellar office so that Mary Anne could pay Morton twenty-four dollars for a two-night stay and sign her name in the registration book.

Morton left them alone for the afternoon. Just after nightfall, the landlady decided to go to bed early. She changed into her nightgown and climbed the stairs to the girls' room. She found Pat and Mary Anne sitting up in their beds. Both were fully dressed, and a blanket covered each of their narrow shoulders.

"I'm so sorry it's so cold," Morton told them. "The thermometer just dipped below five degrees."

"That's no worry," Mary Anne said. "We're cozy enough."

"We'll make sure to bundle up when we go out later," Pat chimed in.

Morton said good night and walked back to the staircase. On her way down, she passed Costa climbing the stairs, her tight velour bathrobe brushing against his body. He could feel the side of her large breasts pressing against his arm. The killer was not stimulated though. Patricia Morton was not his type, and if she were, she would be dead by now.

Costa reached the top landing and knocked on the bedroom door.

"Hello, girls, it's Antone. May I come in?"

Pat jumped off the bed and opened the door, welcoming Costa inside. This move appeared to upset Mary Anne, who hugged the blanket tighter around her body to cover her chest and knees.

"Where are you girls from?" he asked.

"Providence, Rhode Island," Pat offered. "Have you been there before?"

"I've been through there, never stayed long enough though. I do not believe in staying too long in one place. I thought you might be from Boston."

Mary Anne raised her eyebrow, annoyed. "What made you think that?"

"I don't quite know," he replied, examining the women once more. "It could be your attire. You're wearing army surplus jackets, bell-bottom dungarees. It's hippie attire. I know many women in Boston who dress as you do. I guess I was just curious. It was just an empty assumption."

"You've got a nice name," Pat told him. "*Antone* sounds so sophisticated, intellectual. You speak well also. Do you read much?"

"I've been reading Hesse," he revealed nonchalantly. "I enjoy the existential writers. Camus is a favorite of mine also."

Feeling more comfortable now, he asked them if they smoked. Pat produced a package of Pall Mall cigarettes and offered him one.

"I did not mean that kind of smoke," he said. "I meant grass or hash. I do not mean to get you so uptight by asking you so bluntly, and of course, if you'd rather not answer, you do not have to. But I have some excellent hash and would gladly share it with you."

"Your offer sort of caught me off guard," Pat told him. "I don't know what to say. I guess I will say that *yes*, we do smoke grass."

Mary Anne jumped into the conversation to correct her friend. "I've only smoked pot once or twice. I don't think I'd like to smoke now, but you two should enjoy yourselves. I'll go take a shower."

Costa led them downstairs to his room. Mary Anne disappeared into the adjacent bathroom, and moments later, Costa and Pat could hear the sound of water running. Walsh sat on the bed while he filled his pipe with hash and cracked a window.

"I've never seen such a large chunk," Pat said, referring to the clump of hash that Costa was stuffing into the pipe. "It smells great. I love the smell of it."

"Yes, I do too," he replied. "It has a fabulous aroma. It is very exotic. It's the concentrated pollen of a marijuana plant. It is about seven to ten times stronger than grass. It is a beautiful high."

Costa then felt the presence of his alter ego. Pat could not see him, but he was undressing her with his eyes.

Look at her, Cory urged Costa. *She's perfect for us. Her long, dark hair reminds us of Sydney.*

Costa glanced over and realized that his alter ego was right. She was perfect.

He lit the pipe, inhaled deeply, and passed the porcelain tube to Pat, who did the same. The smoke affected her immediately, and her head began to spin. She declined another puff, got off the bed, and walked around the room, attempting to stabilize herself. She noticed the dog-eared copy of *Steppenwolf* sitting on the wide windowsill. She picked it up and thumbed through it briefly before spotting another book that was tucked underneath on the sill. Pat grabbed it and studied the cover.

"*Manual of Taxidermy for Amateurs*," she said. "You're reading this stuff?"

"That was left here by the previous tenant," Costa lied. "I haven't opened it."

She opened the book and browsed its table of contents.

"Skinning birds, making skins of mammals? Sounds pretty creepy." She turned to a random page and began reading aloud. "'Peel away the skin from the tail, place the forefinger under its base, and cut downward through the caudal vertebra and the muscles of the back...' I don't know about this stuff, Antone."

He took the book from her hand gently and placed it back on the windowsill.

"I would have to agree with you, Pat. I find those things to be disturbing. I would never harm an animal. I could not even hurt a fly."

In an effort to lighten the mood, Costa focused her attention on his collection of 45s.

"Do you like the Stones?" he asked, holding up the A-side single "She's a Rainbow." "It's from the album *Their Satanic Majesties Request.* Mind if I play it?"

Pat shook her head no. "I like that song too!"

Costa played the disc and began to serenade Pat. "'She comes in colors everywhere, she combs her hair. She's like a rainbow.'"

Pat started laughing as Costa drew closer. The moment was broken up by Mary Anne, who had emerged from the bathroom following her shower with her wet hair tied up in a towel.

"Pat, I'm going to use the hair dryer, and then we should get dressed for dinner," Mary Anne said. "I'm getting hungry."

Pat glanced at Costa and shrugged. "It's been fun, but gotta go."

"Enjoy your evening, ladies," he told them. "And please be careful out there. There is not a lot of craziness here in the off-season, but it's still Ptown."

Pat and Mary Anne thanked him for the advice and returned to their room.

The wolf of the steppes closed his door, collapsed on his bed, and continued to fantasize about what the next hours and days would bring.

Around 8:00 p.m., Pat Walsh and Mary Anne Wysocki decided to go out. Pat wore bell-bottom jeans while Mary Anne dressed more conservatively in tweed slacks, a buttoned-up blouse, and penny loafers. They stepped out of the rooming house, hugged themselves against the biting wind and cold, and walked one block up to Commercial Street, which was nearly deserted. They noticed a lantern beaming over the front door of the Foc'sle and strolled over toward the tavern. When they got inside, the place was warm and inviting with a mix of townsfolk and those tourists hearty enough to travel to Ptown in the dead of winter. Pat and Mary Anne both found the interior decor charming and exactly what they were looking for. Cork flotation rings hung on the walls along with several ornate ship compasses. One half of a weather-beaten dory protruded from a wall as if it had crashed into the pub, while behind the bar, aged fishing nets drooped down from the ceiling like cobwebs. Pat ordered two cocktails, and they both sat down at a long wooden table that faced the street. They soon were joined by two other women, strangers from Hyannis named Irene Hare and Brenda Dreyer.   Pat and Mary Anne wondered if they were giving off the wrong vibe, that they might be mistaken for lesbians. But neither Irene nor Brenda tried hitting on them, as they were also just two single women who were enjoying a night out on the outer Cape. After about fifteen minutes, Brenda introduced herself and Irene to Pat and Mary Anne. They ordered a round of beers and began to talk about their lives back in Providence and also in Hyannis, which was a thriving metropolis compared to Provincetown. They took turns feeding quarters into the jukebox, selecting "Wichita Lineman" by Glen Campbell and "Abraham, Martin and John" by Dion. Pat wished to dance, so she added Dusty Springfield's "Son of a Preacher Man" to their playlist, and she began snapping her fingers and shaking her hips to the beat. Everyone at the bar seemed to be enjoying themselves as they shook off their cabin fever and partied like it was the Fourth of July. At around 10:00 p.m., Irene Hare suggested that they head over to the nearby Pilgrim Club for more drinks and fun. The foursome stayed at the club until last call was announced, and Irene and Brenda walked their new friends back to the guesthouse at 5 Standish Street and said good night.

Tony Costa had also returned to his room for the evening. While Pat and Mary Anne were pub-crawling on Commercial Street, the killer had pedaled his bike to an apartment shared by two attractive girls known as Sadie and Thumper to trip the night away on LSD. The girls were members of his so-called hippie disciple clique. Normally, Costa had plenty of pot, pills, and tablets to satisfy his needs, but the hash he had shared with Pat Walsh was his last. He would have to find some way to get to his ammunition canisters to replenish his stock in the morning. The idea of pedaling his bike all the way to North Truro, especially in icy weather, had zero appeal to him. While tripping on acid with Sadie and Thumper, Costa suggested they head over to the Foc'sle for some excitement. They pedaled their bicycles to the bar and slipped inside the dimly lit shanty. Costa ordered two beers and a glass of Chianti and sipped them quietly at the bar while Thumper and Sadie made the rounds, talking up their hippie friends as well as the local fishermen. He spotted Pat Walsh and Mary Anne Wysocki seated at a distant table with two other women. Neither Pat nor Mary Anne seemed to notice him, so the killer sat in silence, watching Pat sway to the music. His thoughts retreated back to the pages of his taxidermy manual.

"The hunter must be guided by circumstances," he muttered to himself between sips of wine. "A skin is of little value unless it is labelled with date, locality, and sex."

Under the evening's circumstances—the fact that he was without his killing tools and that his mind was muddled by LSD—it would be most difficult for Costa to hunt his prey in his current state. But tomorrow would be different. Saturday was open season. He labelled the skins of Pat Walsh and Mary Anne Wysocki in his mind.

"January 25, Cape Cod, and females," he said to himself.

Soon after, Pat and Mary Anne left the Foc'sle while the killer remained seated at the bar. Sadie and Thumper hooked up with a couple of guys, and they left too. Costa drained another glass of Chianti and heard the clock inside the town hall bell tower chime eleven times. He paid his tab and returned to 5 Standish Street just after 11:00 p.m. Once inside, he went to the communal kitchen and made himself a cup of hot chocolate. He then stood by the bay window waiting for Pat and Mary Anne to return. Costa heard them before he saw them. The women were saying goodbye to their friends and giggling as they walked up the front steps of the guesthouse. Their loud voices lowered to dull whispers as they navigated the staircase to their rooms. The killer's body suddenly tensed for a moment, thinking they may knock on his door for a late-night visit. What if they wanted to hang out? Could he stop the growing urge to kill them both right there inside his room? Fortunately, he did not have to decide just then, as the girls continued on beyond the second floor landing and retreated to their small double room and closed the door. A short time later, Costa scrawled a note to Pat and Mary Anne and pinned it to their bedroom door before returning to his room and picking up his Hesse novel from the windowsill. He collapsed on his thin mattress, turned again to page 7, and read. "A wolf of the Steppes that had lost its way and strayed into the towns and life of the herd, a more striking image could not be found for his shy loneliness, his savagery, his recklessness."

Costa laid the book on his chest and drifted off into a sound sleep.

CHAPTER TEN

———————

The killer felt something grabbing his leg. Lost in an advanced stage of REM sleep, he cried out as he was trapped in the dreamscape of darkened woods, while the hand belonging to the long dead Sydney Monzon clawed at and clutched his ankle from her shallow grave. Costa began to perspire, and soon his sheets were covered by his sweat.

"No!" he yelled.

"Wake up. You're just having a bad dream. It's us."

His eyes flickered open, and he recognized two silhouettes standing at the foot of his bed. Costa reached for his granny glasses, which helped to put the figures into focus.

"Good morning," Pat Walsh said, smiling, with Mary Anne Wysocki by her side.

"Good morning," he replied with a groan. "What an ungodly hour to be awake. What time is it, and what brings you into my room?"

Pat waved her wristwatch in the air. "It's 9:30 in the morning, and we got your note about needing a ride."

It took a moment for Costa to remember that he had left a note on their bedroom door.

"We can give you a ride this morning or later this afternoon if you'd like," she continued. "But after lunch, we're supposed to meet up with a friend who's hitchhiking his way here from the bus station in Hyannis."

"Thank you, ladies. I need to pick up my work check as rent is now due. I don't want to be tossed out of here by Ms. Morton and forced to sleep in fish sheds until I find a more suitable place."

Costa told them that it would take him about thirty minutes to get ready, which would give Pat and Mary Anne time to go downtown to enjoy a quick breakfast. They exited the room while Costa moved his head back and forth and up and down repeatedly in an effort to shake the last remnants of the previous night's acid trip from his mind. A beam of sun from the bay window burned like a laser across the room, revealing tiny specks of dust to his naked eye. He imagined that the particles were miniature planets and that he was observing them as an alien from afar. He took a brief shower to steady his mind and then dressed warmly for the day ahead.

Pat and Mary Anne returned exactly thirty minutes later, their faces reddened by the winter blast outside.

"We just called our friend to see if he's left yet," Mary Anne announced. "He didn't answer, so he's probably on the way and should be here soon."

With this, the killer understood that he had only limited time to make his move.

The three of them jumped into Pat's Volkswagen Beetle and cranked the heat. It took a few minutes for the ice on the windshield to thaw for better visibility. Pat pulled the car off the sidewalk and followed Costa's directions.

"I was supposed to get my check from my boss at his home in Truro, but he gave it to a coworker of mine, who will meet us at the A&P," Costa said. "He'll be riding a motorcycle."

Costa soon spotted the man, twenty-two-year-old James Zacharias, and flagged him down. Zacharias was holding a check for thirty-two dollars made out to Costa for working less than a week on a local construction job before being fired for not showing up. Along with payment, the boss had a message for Zacharias to give to Costa: *Don't come back.* Zacharias hopped off his bike and pulled an envelope out of his jacket.

"Thanks for meeting me, Zeke," Costa said with a wide grin.

"This is for you," Zacharias told him. "The foreman also says that he doesn't want to see you around the work site anymore."

Costa accepted the envelope through the passenger-side window and thanked Zacharias once again.

Driving away, Pat asked Costa why he was now verboten from visiting the construction job.

"I suffered a painful foot injury on the job," he explained. "I could not work for about five days and the boss simply fired me."

"Well, that's just wrong," Mary Anne told him. "Since that took no time at all, we probably have another hour or so to kill before our friend gets here. Are there any cool sites to see?"

"Have you ever been out to the woods of Truro?" the killer asked. "There's an ancient cemetery out there, it dates back to the Revolutionary War. It's kind of spooky and it is supposed to be haunted. I have a marijuana stash not far from there."

Pat and Mary Anne looked at each other and smiled. Both were game for a little side trip out to the Cape Cod wilderness.

Pat turned the steering wheel right and onto Route 6A and kept driving. "How far is it?"

"Not far, I think it's about nine miles. We will be there before you know it."

The ride was made slower, however, due to frost heaves that had buckled patches of the road. The three of them bounced and rattled around the small vehicle as they left the town limits with the mighty Pilgrim Monument growing smaller in the distance. To pass time in the car, they shared stories about their lives.

"I wish I'd brought my camera here," Pat said. "The Cape is so beautiful, especially in winter. I'd love to take some pictures to bring to school to show my class. The little kids would really love it."

"Are you a teacher, Pat?" Costa asked.

"Yes. I teach the elementary grades; the young children. I love them. For me, it's the fulfillment of a dream."

Costa told her that his friend Chrissie Gallant had also dreamed of becoming a teacher and that he had been in a deep depression since her sudden death two months before.

"Her overdose was such horrible news," he said. "I could not handle it then and I am still having difficulty facing the ugly reality of it all. All my hopes and dreams were with her and then they abruptly vanished. They were gone."

This revelation brought out a collective sigh from Pat and Mary Anne. As they entered Truro, Costa told Pat to put her blinker on in anticipation of an upcoming right turn onto Old County Road. Once there, the gray, late-January sky gave way to a canopy of sprawling bare oak tree limbs that interlocked from both sides of the road like fingers folded in prayer.

"Are you ready to go for a little tour of the countryside?" Costa asked. "We'll begin our fantasy journey, our odyssey through time and space."

Both women laughed.

Off to the right, a house appeared on the otherwise barren road. It was painted yellow with white trim and a bloodred door.

"That's Marshall's House," he informed them. "Edward Hopper painted it in water color back in 1932."

Costa's knowledge of art history impressed the women.

"We're basically driving along one of the oldest roads on the Cape," he added. "When we get to the cemetery, I will show you why."

They drove for another couple of miles before taking a right turn onto Hatch Road, which was nothing more than an old wagon-rutted dirt pathway.

"It's very quiet here," Pat pointed out.

"Yes it is, and the dead don't seem to mind at all," he replied.

She parked the car, and they climbed out of the Volkswagen. Costa noticed a full bottle of red wine in the back seat and grabbed it.

"Do you mind?" he asked the women. "Prepare yourselves to imbibe on a few delicately flavored drops of pure ambrosia."

They giggled at Costa's words. Pat and Mary Anne thought of their new friend as handsome, smart, a little weird, but also great fun. He led them on a walk through the forest, past the ammo cans, and over the frozen graves of Susan Perry and Sydney Monzon. The dirt path soon gave way to a gravel road leading into the cemetery.

Costa pulled the cork from the wine bottle with his teeth and handed the bottle to Pat, who took a swig before passing it along to Mary Anne. The cheap wine may not have tasted like pure ambrosia, but it did warm them up.

"Many of the earliest tombstones here have toppled over or have disintegrated after centuries of Cape Cod storms," he said. "But you'll be amazed at the history that one can still find here."

He reached into his coat pocket and fished for a tab of LSD with his fingertip. It was his last hit of acid, and he was not about to share it with his new friends. Surreptitiously, he placed the tab on his tongue and let it dissolve.

For the next hour, while waiting for the acid to fully kick in, Costa toured the cemetery with Pat and Mary Anne, stopping at several gravestones covered by moss, fungus, and frost to read the inscriptions.

"In memory of Atkin S. Rich who died June 1778," Pat recited as she ran her finger over the engraving of one stone. "Aged thirty-five years."

"How about this one?" Mary Anne shouted while pointing at another cracked headstone in the Rich family plot. "Sabra, wife of Richard. Jesus calls and I must go, and bid adieu to all below."

Walking from stone to stone and drinking wine, they marveled at the old Puritan names, such as Deliverance, Elisha, and Thankful, that marked the graves, along with the tragedies that had ended so many of their lives early. Some died from disease; others had been swept out to sea, leaving only a tombstone to cover empty ground.

"It's both beautiful and sad," said Pat.

"Well then, I certainly have something to cheer us all up," Costa announced. "I mentioned that I have some grass hidden not far from here. It's on the way back to the car. I'll grab the pot and we can get stoned while also getting out of this freezing cold."

The women followed Costa as he led them out of the ancient cemetery, but not before they passed an eerie turf-covered tomb with its wooden door ajar.

"Can we have a peek inside?" Pat asked.

"I don't see why not." Costa smiled. He led the way and pulled back the old door, allowing them inside. The space was tiny and could barely fit the three of them.

"Where's the body buried?" Mary Anne asked.

"Under our feet," Costa surmised. "You would be surprised at the number of graves we have all probably walked over completely unaware, during our lifetime."

"You're right, this place is spooky," Mary Anne said. "I'm ready to go now."

Costa nodded and escorted them out of the crypt.

As they walked, they noticed a break in the dark clouds and felt the sudden warmth of a single ray of sunshine washing over them. With the LSD taking hold, Costa thought the sun had exploded, and he felt that his body was melting into the light.

"I need to water the grass," he told the girls.

"Water the grass?" Mary Anne inquired.

"Yes. I must empty my reservoir of all that wine and cause a puddle to form in the ground. Dig it?"

The two women laughed once more at Costa's unusual colloquialisms and kept walking while he searched for a place to take a piss. He stumbled upon a large tree depleted of foliage. Hallucinating, he imagined the trunk of the tree to be a giant human wrist erupting from the ground. He followed the tree upward to its twenty-foot peak, covered by massive twisted branches forming the shape of a claw.

"Sydney," he muttered to himself as he urinated on the tree trunk.

Like his dark dream from that morning, her restless spirit had revealed itself to him once more.

Costa fought to steady himself. He squeezed out the last droplets of piss, folded himself back into his jeans, and zipped his fly.

"This trip is turning into a real bummer," he told himself. "This acid is doing strange things to my head."

This comment woke Cory from his slumber somewhere in the back of Costa's mind. *The acid is freeing us,* the alter ego reminded him. *There's not another soul in sight for miles right now. It's our time to hunt.*

Costa absorbed these thoughts and trotted playfully up to the girls, who were walking a few meters ahead.

"My stash is hidden just around the next bend in the woods," he told them. "I will retrieve some pot and get us all back to the car safe and warm."

"Please be quick," Mary Anne replied, checking her watch. "We've lost all track of time out here. We must get back to town and meet our friend."

"This won't take but a minute."

Costa crouched down by some nearby bushes and brushed away a pile of dead leaves. Pat and Mary Anne were deep in conversation and paid little attention to their new friend's foraging. He found one of the ammo cans and pulled out two weapons: a sheathed knife with a twelve-inch cutting blade and a loaded .22-caliber pistol with a pearl handle. He stuffed them both into the pockets of his jacket, stood up, and scraped the snow and dirt off the knees of his jeans.

The killer turned back in the direction of Pat Walsh and Mary Anne Wysocki. They broke their conversation and watched him as he approached. There was something different about him, something dangerous. His eyes were determined, not playful anymore. Before either woman could say a word, he pulled his hand out of his pocket, extended his right arm, and fired the pistol with dead aim.

The bullet struck Pat Walsh through the back of her neck, embedding itself in her left cheek, snapping her head forward as she fell to the ground.

Mary Anne gasped. She tried to scream, but her vocal cords were paralyzed by fear. Instead, she turned and started to run down the path away from Tony Costa. He fired two quick shots in Mary Anne's direction but missed both times. He then took a few steps to close the distance and fired two more shots as she turned her head back in his direction. The first bullet penetrated Mary Anne's skull just below her right eye. She fell facedown in the crusted snow. Mary Anne was mortally wounded, but she was still breathing.

Costa stood over her body and fired another bullet—a kill shot through the left side of her brain. The three gunshots echoed like thunderclaps through the forest, but it was as if they did not make a sound at all in these remote woods.

The air was cold, but the bodies of Pat Walsh and Mary Anne Wysocki were still warm. This idea aroused Tony Costa tremendously. He put the pistol back in his coat pocket and began to strip each of his victims below the waist. The killer unzipped his pants and climbed on top of their bodies, one after the other. He thrust his hips with unbounded aggression and finished quickly. After ejaculating twice inside the remains of Pat and Mary Anne, he lay with their bodies in the blood-covered snow. Costa then stood up and fished for his other killing tool, the razor sharp blade that he called his "pig stabber."

He tore off the rest of their clothes and went to work. Costa dragged their naked bodies to a tree and hung them from low, thick

Patricia Walsh and Mary Anne Wysocki set out for a weekend in Provincetown, Massachusetts, and were never seen alive again. © Ancestry.com.

branches using a long piece of rope that he had hidden in one of the ammunition cans. He attended to the body of Pat Walsh first, and his initial cuts were frenzied, causing deep stab wounds through the front and back of Pat's legs and buttocks and even the tops of her feet. The lacerations were meant to cause pain, despite the fact that he knew she was already dead. Costa then turned her body over, facing him. He plunged the knifepoint just beneath the breastbone and into her heart. Costa stiffened his arm and allowed his full body weight to press the blade as it sank deeper into her chest. Using the knife once again, he carefully made a T-shaped incision wound at the midline of her chest. Carving vertically, he pushed the blade from the jugular notch of Pat's sternum down to her pubic area. He then peeled her skin back like an open sweater over both sides of her anterior chest wall. He made two more cuts into her liver before turning his focus to her legs. He sawed into the base of her pelvis and through the second lumbar intervertebral disc until the skin and bone became detached from the body. Completely covered in Pat's blood, Costa stepped back with his hand to his chin and admired his work like an artist inspecting his own unfinished canvas. With the left leg amputated, he proceeded to chop off Pat's right as well. He decided to leave both of her arms intact, not even removing the beaded ring from a finger on her right hand.

Mary Anne Wysocki was next.

Costa carved her body into five pieces. First, he sliced the knife across her neck, working the blade continuously until he cut off her head, leaving only the upper cervical spine attached. A geyser of blood erupted from her neck wound, cascaded down her body, and pooled on the ground in the dirty snow as Costa held her severed skull like a trophy in his free hand and droplets of red splattered across his tan work boots. He then made five deep cuts through her chest before inserting his blade across the bikini lines of her hips. Costa chopped off her vagina and anus and carefully stacked the body parts on the ground like a cord of wood.

After nearly two hours of uninterrupted work, the dissections of Pat Walsh and Mary Anne Wysocki were complete. Costa then fetched a small shovel that he had ditched in the woods months earlier. It was time to introduce his latest victims to Susan Perry and Sydney Monzon.

CHAPTER ELEVEN

After digging through ten inches of icy ground and burying the gory body parts belonging to Pat Walsh and Mary Anne Wysocki in two shallow graves that had once been occupied solely by Susan Perry and Sydney Monzon, Costa ran his hands through a clump of snow to rinse off the blood. He then reached for his own neck and squeezed.

You'll die too, motherfucker, just like the rest of them, Cory threatened. *You'll die.*

For several seconds, Costa stood in the woods, trying in vain to choke himself out, just as his alter ego wanted. When that attempt failed, he raised the pistol and pressed the barrel against his temple and cocked the hammer back. It could all end right there.

"You bastard, you're the cause of all of this," Costa cried. "You brought us out here. You forced me to kill them, these two defenseless women!"

Costa pulled the trigger but nothing happened. The gun had jammed. He tossed the pistol to the ground.

"I didn't mean to do it, really I didn't," he wailed. "It's all a horrible mistake. You've got to help me!"

Listen, you little son of a bitch. You'd better get yourself together, Cory told him. *This is national park land, which means the rangers could be out here any minute.*

"If I get caught, that means we'll both go to the electric chair. I'll tell them that you were here with me when I killed them. I'm taking you down with me!"

Ditch the car, and let's get the fuck out of here.

"Just remember that we're in this together now and there's nothing you can do about it!"

Costa covered the graves with a pile of crushed leaves and pine needles. Instead of returning the knife and pistol to the ammunition cans, he buried the weapons at the base of the large tree that he had pissed on a few paces back. He dug a quart-sized hole to conceal his killing tools and covered it with dirt and brush. Now, what to do with his bloody clothes?

The killer had come to the forest prepared. Costa had worn a fresh pair of khakis under his bloodstained jeans and two shirts under his sweater along with an extra pair of socks. He carefully stripped off the bloody outer garb and buried them too. Costa then bolted out of the woods, his hands cutting through the cold air like knives as he ran back to Pat Walsh's VW Beetle. Catching his breath, he climbed into the driver's seat and turned the key in the ignition. The engine sputtered but soon roared to life. He drove back to the main road and looked for a spot to leave the car. Soon, he found a small clearing nearby and abandoned the vehicle there. Night had fallen, and the temperature dropped to ten degrees Fahrenheit. He hugged himself against the freezing cold, walked back to Route 6A, and stuck out his thumb. A delivery truck driver pulled over and offered Costa a ride.

"Too cold to be hitching on a night like this," the driver said. "Where ya been and where ya goin'?"

"I've been on the road for a few days, and I am now headed back home to Provincetown."

The driver offered Costa a cigarette and a light, which he eagerly accepted. He inhaled deeply, and the smoke entered his lungs, settled his brain, and calmed his nerves.

"If you're interested, I've got a little cottage in Truro where we can spend the night," the driver offered. "I have plenty of booze and pot too."

The driver placed his free hand on Costa's knee.

"I'm sorry, my friend, I'm not gay," Costa told him. "But thanks anyway. I would just like to go home now."

Russell Norton was both frustrated and concerned. As promised, he had spent nearly the full day traveling from Providence to Ptown to meet up with Mary Anne and Pat, and they were nowhere to be found. Norton visited every restaurant, diner, boutique, and bar on Commercial Street, hoping to reunite with his friends, but he was having zero luck.

He sat at the Foc'sle nursing a beer, waiting for the girls to show. He remembered how Mary Anne and Pat always ran late for their get-togethers, but several hours had passed, and there was still no sign of them anywhere in Provincetown. Norton bumped into another friend on Commercial Street and spent the night sleeping on the floor of her apartment. The next morning, he scoured the seaside village again before catching a ride back to the bus station in Hyannis and eventually home to Providence.

It had been a busy weekend for Patricia Morton too. Her guesthouse was

Site of the former Foc'sle (now the Squealing Pig), where Pat Walsh and Mary Anne Wysocki were last seen alive. © Casey Sherman.

booked solid despite the bone-chilling weather. She visited each of her tenants, which included two married couples and a college boy from New Jersey, and urged them all to keep their doors open as much as possible for the heat to circulate through the old house. She also reminded them that checkout was at 10:45 a.m. that morning, Sunday, January 25, 1969. Morton stopped by Room #2, which was rented by Mary Anne Wysocki and Pat Walsh.

"Are you both warm enough in there?" she asked through the door. "If not, I can turn the thermostat up a bit more."

Hearing no reply, Morton pushed the door open. The women were not inside. The landlady then noticed a note pinned to the door. It was written in pencil on a torn piece of brown paper bag. She saw that it was a request for a ride from her downstairs tenant, Antone "Tony" Costa. The landlady returned to her small basement office to finish her morning coffee and read the newspaper. The two married couples checked out first, followed by the college student. Morton asked them if they had enjoyed their stay in Provincetown, and each said yes and that they planned to come back in the summer. Since Morton was not strict with her checkout policy, she waited until the afternoon to check on her two tenants from Providence, Rhode Island. She entered their room once more, and this time, all their belongings were gone. Morton found a note on the dresser next to one of the beds.

Dear Mrs. Morton:

We are checking out. We had a nice time. Thank you for your many kindnesses.

Mary Anne and Pat

On Monday, January 27, Pat Walsh's students entered her classroom at the Laurel Hill School, put away their winter coats, and sat patiently at their desks, waiting for their teacher to arrive. The first bell rang, but Pat had not shown up yet. A fellow teacher passed her room and looked inside to find a group of restless children without any supervision. The students told the teacher that Miss Walsh had not come to class, and they asked if she was still sick. The teacher then headed to the principal's office and asked the receptionist whether she had heard from Pat that morning. The secretary said she had not. This was unlike Pat Walsh, but maybe she was bed-ridden with the flu, the teacher thought. The school's first order of business was to find a quick replacement for Pat in the classroom that day with the hope that she would call and give an update on her condition.

Pat Walsh did not call, nor did she turn up in class the following day. Concerned, the school principal telephoned Pat's father, Leonard Walsh, her emergency contact, to alert him to her bizarre absence. The father promised to make some calls to find out where his daughter might be. Leonard Walsh hung up and immediately dialed his daughter, who did not pick up. He then telephoned Pat's friend Linda McNally.

"Have you seen Patricia?" her father asked with growing concern in his voice. "She hasn't shown up for work in two days."

"I haven't seen her, but I did speak with her on the phone before the weekend."

"What did she say?"

"She told me that she was driving to Provincetown for the weekend with Mary Anne, but that's all I know."

"Any idea where she might have stayed?"

The friend could not provide any more information, but at least Leonard Walsh now knew where his daughter may have been last seen. He called Mary Anne's mother, Martha Wysocki, who confirmed that the pair had gone to Cape Cod but that she had not heard from her daughter since Friday, January 24.

Could they have been in an accident? Leonard Walsh thought. He consulted the phone book and found the number to the nearest state police barracks in the town of Rehoboth, Massachusetts, just over the border from Rhode Island. The dispatcher there had no record of a recent crash involving a Volkswagen Beetle.

The worried father then rushed out of his well-kept, two-story home on California Avenue and drove to Providence police headquarters and met with Sergeant Edward Perry.

"My daughter is missing."

"How long has she been gone?" Perry inquired.

"She and a friend drove to Cape Cod last Friday and were supposed to return on Sunday," Walsh said. "My daughter is an elementary school teacher and she hasn't shown up for class in two days."

"Perhaps they extended their weekend?"

"My daughter would have told someone. She loves her job and would not simply disappear like that."

Sergeant Perry ordered another officer to take down information for a missing person report.

"Can you describe your daughter?" the cop asked.

"Yes, she's got brown hair down to her shoulder and has green eyes."

"Height and weight?"

"Um, about five foot nine and roughly one hundred thirty-eight pounds."

Leonard Walsh also provided the officer with a description of his daughter's car.

"Pat has a new, 1968 Volkswagen that's light blue," he said. "It has Rhode Island plates." Walsh pulled a note from his pocket and read. "The registration number is KV-978."

The officer finished the report and delivered copies to the radio room and to the detective division.

"Please find my daughter," Leonard Walsh begged frantically.

Later, a detective called the Provincetown Police Department and shared the father's information.

"The two girls are supposed to be there somewhere," he said nonchalantly. "Give us a call if they turn up."

For the understaffed detective division at the Providence Police Department, there were more pressing matters than the whereabouts of two young women on an extended weekend getaway. The city was dominated by organized crime and ripe with racial strife. Pat and Mary Anne would return home eventually, detectives thought.

Provincetown patrolman James Cook wrote a note about the missing women and handed it over to Chief Cheney Marshall.

"Put this information in the daily log with red ink, so that everybody will be sure to read it," Marshall ordered.

It was noon, so Cook took his lunch over to the school crossing where he made sure the local youngsters got safely across the road to their waiting mothers after morning classes were finished. He then drove his patrol car over to the Provincetown Inn, which was on the ocean, had dozens of rooms and a new indoor pool, and was open year-round. He checked with the front desk clerk to see if anyone fitting Pat Walsh's description had checked in recently. Cook did not have Mary Anne Wysocki's description. The clerk said no one like Pat Walsh had booked a room there, and she had not seen a light-blue Volkswagen in the parking lot.

Officer Cook tipped his cap and returned to his squad car. For the next hour, he drove around Ptown, down Commercial Street and every winding side street he could remember, but found nothing.

When Cook's shift ended at 4:45 p.m., he asked his fellow patrolman George Baker to keep on the lookout for the missing girls. Baker obliged.

Four more days passed, and still, there was no sign of Pat Walsh and Mary Anne Wysocki.

Leonard Walsh felt that he was getting nowhere with Providence police detectives, so he recruited Pat's sometimes boyfriend Robert Turbidy to help. The twenty-six-year-old North Providence native had known Pat Walsh for one year and insisted they were unofficially engaged, despite the fact that he had split his time between Rhode Island and California. Pat Walsh had spent twelve days with Turbidy in San Francisco in December. Most recently, he had her first name tattooed on his arm.

Turbidy was driving cross-country back to New England in his VW camper when he spoke to Pat's father by pay phone and learned that she was missing. He returned to the vehicle and stared at a Christmas card from Pat that had been taped to the dashboard, which read, "I have bought bread, I have been given roses, How happy I am to hold both in my hands, love Pat."

They had met in March 1968 near the campus of Rhode Island College. Both had a love for handmade crafts and Jefferson Airplane albums. A whirlwind romance followed, and Turbidy had made a decision to return to Rhode Island for good and move in full-time with Pat, who rented a small apartment on Prospect Street in Providence and paid the landlord forty-seven dollars each two weeks for rent.

Turbidy barely slept for the rest of the cross-country trip, driving long hours until his eyes blurred and he was forced to pull over for a quick nap. He arrived on February 1, spoke briefly to Leonard Walsh again, and got back on the road en route to Cape Cod.

Turbidy arrived in Provincetown in late afternoon and found his way to the police station at the basement of town hall. Relying on the skills he had acquired as a legal officer in the U.S. Navy, Turbidy grilled patrolman James Cook about the search for his girlfriend and Mary Anne Wysocki.

"I've checked around town, and unfortunately we've come up with nothing," the patrolman said.

"This place is the size of a thumbnail," Turbidy countered. "I find it hard to believe that they've simply vanished."

The insult put Cook on edge. "Well then, feel free to ask around yourself."

Turbidy stormed out of the station and walked Commercial Street armed with two recent photos of Pat Walsh that he had taken of her during a camping trip on Cape Cod the summer before. He showed them to the bartender at the Town House Tavern and to a waitress at the Mayflower Cafe but neither had recognized the attractive brunette. Instead of driving back home, he stayed the night in his camper parked in a lot on MacMillan Pier, racking his brain as to their whereabouts. The next morning, he visited the Portuguese Bakery and flashed Pat's photos to the girl at the cash register. She took the pictures to the backroom. Turbidy heard a conversation in Portuguese before the girl reemerged with a blank look on her face.

"Sorry, but nobody has seen your friend."

He thanked her and stuck the pictures back in the pocket of his winter jacket.

When Turbidy returned to Providence, he called Gerry Magnan, whom he had met only once before. Magnan was dating Mary Anne Wysocki, and Turbidy had helped him move a refrigerator at her place. The two boyfriends decided to meet for a beer while trying to figure out what to do next.

"Providence police are no help, and the cops in Ptown don't give a shit," Turbidy told Magnan.

"Maybe we should hire a private investigator?" Magnan suggested.

Like Turbidy, Magnan was overcome with anxiety and a sick feeling that he may never see his girlfriend again. He and Mary Anne had been dating on and off for six years after meeting at a corner variety store in West Providence where he worked the counter and she came in daily for coffee and cigarettes. They had gone to the prom together when both were seniors at Classical High School. Magnan taught math at Bristol County Community College in nearby Fall River.

The men pooled their money together and came up with $200 to hire a local sleuth to investigate the case. The private detective took the cash and spent the next day gumshoeing around Ptown but came up empty.

"There's no way those girls are in Provincetown," he told Turbidy.

"I feel like a pile of rotten shit," Tony Costa mumbled to himself as he curled into a ball on his bed at 5 Standish Street.

Hunting is our favorite pastime, Cory reminded him. *We love to kill things.*

"I was there when you committed these murders," Costa replied. "According to the law, that makes us equally guilty although I had nothing to do with it."

You had everything to do with it. Their blood is on your hands.

"I'm not a murderer. I didn't mean it. My head just got so freaky. It wasn't my fault!"

To hell with those chicks. They're dead now. We've got to start thinking about us. What are we gonna do?

Costa reached for a pill bottle and emptied several Nembutal tablets in the palm of his hand, opened his mouth, and swallowed.

He then opened a copy of the latest *Mad* magazine and started to read, hoping the juvenile humor would take his mind off the murders of Pat Walsh and Mary Anne Wysocki.

But his alter ego refused to allow Costa to get comfortable.

We need to focus, not screw around with childish things, Cory counseled. *We need to get rid of that car, just drive it to a place that no one will find it. No car, no girls, no case.*

"Just get rid of the car, and?"

Then you'll be scot-free of any hassles. No car, no girls, no case.

Costa set the magazine down and began to think.

On the morning of February 2, 1969, Carl Benson left his home on Cooper Road in Truro with his young son Richard and daughter Penny in tow and climbed into his Jeep to fetch the Sunday morning newspaper downtown. Benson passed a sharp bend in the road and noticed something odd: a

Volkswagen parked about thirty feet up in a clearing. It was not a normal place to leave a vehicle, so Benson decided to stop his car and investigate. After stepping into the clearing, Benson suddenly felt uneasy. He thought he had heard someone running toward him up the snow-covered hill. He jumped back in his car and sped away.

"Daddy, don't drive so fast," Penny cautioned from the back seat.

Benson forgot all about the morning newspaper and instead drove directly to the Truro police station.

"There's a blue Volkswagen that's been abandoned in a clearing off Deerfield Road," Benson told Truro Police Chief Harold Berrio. "There's something odd about it, the way it was left, I mean."

It was a slow Sunday morning, and the police chief had little else to do, so he decided to follow Benson back to the clearing.

Young Penny Benson was the first to notice a fresh track of footsteps in the snow. Someone had visited the Volkswagen while they were at the police station. Carl Benson saw a piece of paper stuck to the windshield on the driver's side.

"There's a sign on it now," he pointed out to Berrio. "That sign wasn't there when we were here before."

On closer inspection, Benson saw that a message had been written in red lipstick on a torn piece of brown paper. It read, *Engine Trouble, Will Return*.

Chief Berrio jotted down the plate number on a small notepad and headed back to the station.

He shared the vehicle information over his police radio with other departments across Barnstable County. There had been no reports of a stolen vehicle fitting the description and tag number.

Thinking this was no longer a police matter; Berrio later went home for dinner and watched an episode of the Smothers Brothers on TV.

At around seven that evening, a mechanic from the Truro Service Center drove that same road, and he also spotted the Volkswagen, but this time, it was not parked on top of a clearing. Someone had moved it to the side of the road.

CHAPTER TWELVE

———

"The Volkswagen has attracted too much attention," Costa told himself. "First, that guy and his two fucking kids, and now a local cop."

His whole world could come crashing down around him at any minute, so the killer made the call to get rid of the car quickly. Costa walked up to Commercial Street and stepped into a telephone booth outside Mother Marion's restaurant to call his half brother, Vincent Bonaviri, who lived in Boston.

Costa's two young friends and drug disciples, Steve "Speed" Grund and Timmy "Weed" Atkins, noticed his bicycle parked outside the booth and stopped to say hello.

Costa smiled and flung open the door.

"Hey, Speed and Weed, what are you fellows doing?"

"Just taking a walk," Grund replied. "We're bored out of our skulls."

"I've got my brother Vinnie on the phone," Costa said, holding up the telephone receiver. "Do you boys want to take a drive to Boston with me? We can visit my brother's place and I'll turn us on to some good dope along the way. I have a car, but it's parked in North Truro right now."

The friends both nodded. Costa told his brother that he would see him in a few hours and hung up the phone. He then returned to his room at 5 Standish Street along with Grund and Atkins.

"How are we gonna get out to Truro?" Atkins asked. "It's past midnight right now."

Costa tried calling for a cab, but no one picked up the phone at the local taxi stand. He then quickly negotiated a ride for the three of them with an upstairs tenant. He gave the guy some pot in exchange for the late-night excursion.

Soon, they piled into the tenant's green Dodge Dart and made their way to North Truro.

"The trip to Boston is going to be about two hours," Costa told his friends. "We are going to need some gas."

He asked the driver to pull over at the American Gas Station in Truro where he paid the attendant for a gas can and five gallons of fuel. Costa placed the can in the trunk of the Dodge Dart and told the driver to continue on.

"Stop the car right here," Costa demanded a few minutes later. "We'll walk the rest of the way."

The driver let everyone out, turned his car around, and motored off while Costa, Grund, and Atkins walked another half mile carrying a gas can until the Volkswagen came into view.

"Not bad, Tony. How did you manage to get this?" asked Grund.

"I'll tell you chaps on the way to Boston."

"I just hope it starts," Atkins added. "I'm freezing my nuts off out here."

At first, they had no idea where the gas should go. Costa opened the hood and fumbled around in the darkness for the gas cap.

"It's here on the side of the car," Atkins pointed out.

Costa filled the tank and then chucked the gas can into the woods.

"So, Sire, did you buy this thing?" Atkins asked as he surveyed the Volkswagen.

"Yes, Weed. These two girls owed me money," Costa lied. "I sold them a pound of hashish and they were supposed to pay me $700. They offered me this car instead. I think I got a pretty good deal."

As Costa fished the ignition key from his pants pocket, Grund weighed in on his story.

"Are you sure this isn't a hot car?"

"Yes, I am positive."

Grund and Atkins were not so sure.

Costa drove the car out of the clearing before exchanging seats with Atkins.

Since Costa did not have a valid driver's license, his friend Weed would drive them all to Boston.

They returned to Ptown briefly to pick up some vitamin B-12 that would keep them all awake for the long drive off the Cape and into the city. Costa also had Atkins stop by the local dump where he had stashed a stolen television set. He placed the Admiral color TV in the back of the Volkswagen, and Atkins headed south on Route 6A.

A Provincetown police car passed, and Atkins panicked.

"Tony, looks like this is it."

"No need to worry," Costa told his friends. "Just be cool. Nobody knows that I have the television set."

The squad car kept going though, and both Grund and Atkins breathed a sigh of relief.

"So, what happened to the chicks?" Grund asked as they passed a joint around in the car.

"They took a plane up to Vermont," Costa replied. "When we get to Boston, I'm going to take a flight and join them there. They got caught up in a dope ring and had to split and leave town. I gave them a couple hundred bucks so they could leave."

The car got quiet as "Speed" Grund and "Weed" Aktins tried to wrap their brains around Costa's logic.

After a few seconds, Costa cut through the silence.

"Do me a favor?" he asked Grund.

"Sure, Sire. Anything for you."

"Don't ask me any more questions."

After driving nearly two hours in Patricia Walsh's Volkswagen Beetle, the bright lights of Boston came into view. Unlike New York, this city was fast asleep. Although lights twinkled from the city's medium-sized buildings and the streetlamps of Boston Common and the adjacent Public Garden, all the bars and restaurants were closed, save for a handful of all-night diners.

"Sire, I hope you know where you're going," said Grund. "Because we sure don't."

"I know this city like the back of my hand," Costa assured them. "We'll follow Charles Street through the park and then take a left onto Beacon Street. My brother's place is not too far from there."

He then told Grund and Atkins that he planned to register the car in his name in Boston and obtain a valid driver's license.

At this point, the two friends barely paid any attention. It was after 3:00 a.m. now, the B-12 pills had worn off, and both men were fighting to stay awake. They arrived at Bonaviri's apartment building and climbed three flights of stairs to his small flat. Costa's half brother opened the door after a couple of knocks and welcomed them inside.

"Do you want me to bring the TV up?" Costa asked him.

"Sure," Bonaviri replied.

Costa went back to the car and lugged the stolen television set up and into Bonaviri's apartment.

"Consider it a gift from me to you," Costa told him as he set the stolen TV on the floor.

"Groovy, thanks."

Grund and Atkins looked around the cramped one-bedroom unit, and both frowned.

"This place is tiny. Where are we gonna crash?" Atkins asked.

Bonaviri pointed them to a vacant apartment across the hall.

"Door's unlocked," he told them. "You guys can sleep there."

Atkins offered to sleep on the floor at Bonaviri's while Costa led Grund to the spare apartment, which was outfitted with a couple of empty beds. The two men soon collapsed for a few hours of sleep.

At 8:35 a.m., Costa shook Grund's shoulder.

"Wake up, Speed. We gotta get you home."

Grund had recently started a new job and could not miss a day of work.

"I've booked you a flight back to Provincetown," Costa informed him. "It's on me. The flight leaves Logan Airport in thirty minutes."

The airport in Boston had been offering direct flights to a small airstrip in Provincetown since the late 1950s. Grund scrambled to get dressed, and Costa drove him to the airport.

"You don't have a license!" Grund reminded him.

"Don't worry, Speed. I am a big boy. And as I said, I know this city like the back of my hand."

They made it to the airport with ten minutes to spare, and Costa handed his friend fifteen dollars for airfare.

Grund thanked him and headed into the airport terminal, completely unaware that he had helped the killer dispose of a key piece of evidence in what would become a shocking capital murder case.

Costa returned Pat Walsh's Volkswagen to his half brother's apartment and parked the vehicle out back.

He grabbed his friend Weed, and the pair walked a few blocks to the bus station, where they purchased two tickets for the next trip back to Provincetown.

On the bus ride home, Costa had an empty seat next to him, while Atkins sat a few rows behind.

The killer closed his eyes and could almost feel Cory's breath on his neck while the bus rumbled along.

We got rid of the car, the alter ego whispered. *Now we need to get rid of the fucking gun.*

———————————

Russell Norton twisted his entire body around when he heard Mary Anne Wysocki's name mentioned by two strangers inside the noisy cafeteria at Rhode Island College. At an adjoining table, two students were discussing her recent disappearance, news that had spread like a brushfire throughout the small campus.

"You know, my roommate Len saw Mary Anne and her friend Pat a couple weekends ago at a rooming house in Provincetown," one student told a friend.

Norton jumped into the conversation and pressed the student for more details. He quickly found out that the roommate's name was Len Mattluck and that he had spoken with Mary Anne and Pat at a guesthouse on Standish Street.

Norton jotted the information down on a napkin and rushed it over to Robert Turbidy, who immediately telephoned Provincetown police. He spoke to Sergeant James Meads, a Navy veteran and churchgoer with deeply set, almond eyes. Meads had grown up in Provincetown and had been serving on the police force there for nine years. The locals considered Meads a town boy who was there for the long haul.

"I have critical information about the two missing girls, Mary Anne Wysocki and Patricia Walsh," Turbidy said excitedly. "I just learned where they were staying. It was a guesthouse located at 5 Standish Street."

Meads recognized the address immediately. The house belonged to Patricia Morton, who referred to herself as "Mrs." although she never mentioned, and no one had ever seen, any husband. Meads took down Turbidy's information and dialed Morton's place, where the landlady confirmed that both women had recently stayed at her home.

"They signed the register, but there weren't any dates included," Morton informed him. "I believe they arrived on January 24 and left that Sunday."

The landlady also mentioned that Mary Anne and Pat had planned to meet a friend the following day, but she did not know whom. Meads surmised that Morton was talking about Russell Norton.

"And one more thing," Morton said. "There was a note addressed to the girls and pinned to their door from Tony Costa."

Meads knew the name. He had been one of the officers who had recruited Costa as a police informant. The police sergeant had also stepped in on Costa's behalf when he was jailed for nonpayment of child support to his wife, Avis, whom he had married when she was just fourteen years old, and their three children. "Only through his [Costa's] efforts were we able to apprehend drug pushers and get a conviction on these people," Meads had written at the time.

He knew that Costa was divorced or in the process of getting a divorce and that he had several girlfriends around town. Meads also knew that Costa was very close to his mother. He called her at her home at 9 Conant Street.

"Mrs. Cecilia Bonaviri?"

"Yes," she replied timidly.

"I'd like to talk to you about your son."

"Is my Tony in trouble?"

"No, but there are two girls missing," Meads told her. "I hoped that Tony could give us some information as to where they went after leaving town."

"Well, I have no idea where Tony is," she replied defensively. "But if he calls, I will share your message with him."

The next day, Mary Anne's mother, Martha, filed her own missing person report on her daughter's behalf with the Providence Police Department. Like Leonard Walsh, Martha Wysocki was directed to speak with Sergeant Edward Perry. Choking back tears, the distraught mother gave Perry a physical description of her daughter and told him that she was wearing a green coat and blue pants when she left Providence two weeks prior. While Martha Wysocki was on the phone with Perry, Mary Anne's boyfriend, Gerry Magnan, was headed to Provincetown with Robert Turbidy and a friend of theirs named John McNally.

They reached the guesthouse at 5 Standish Street at 3:45 p.m. and introduced themselves to Patricia Morton.

"I spoke to you on the phone about my girlfriend Pat Walsh," Turbidy told the landlady. "Do you mind if we come inside?"

Morton led the three men to her basement office and shared with them information about the note left by Tony Costa.

"Where is he now?" Magnan asked. "We must speak with him?"

Morton shrugged her shoulders. "He's gone. He removed his clothes little by little and then he just disappeared without leaving any forwarding address."

"When was the last day he stayed in his room?" asked Turbidy.

Morton checked her ledger. "I think it was Tuesday, February 4. Somebody slept in his room that night but I don't know if it was Antone. He did leave his hair dryer and some clothes behind."

The landlady told the men that Costa's mother had called demanding that she return the hair dryer.

"I gave her a flat, no! I wasn't gonna give back the hair dryer until her son returned the keys to his room."

"Did the mother also ask for Tony's clothes?" McNally inquired.

"No, she was only focused on the hair dryer and getting it back."

"Mrs. Morton, can we check out the room where the girls stayed?"

"Absolutely."

The landlady took the men upstairs to the small room that had been occupied by Pat and Mary Anne. Turbidy lifted the mattress and looked under the bed while Magnan and McNally checked the drawers. They found nothing. They asked Morton if they could inspect Costa's room, and she agreed. Turbidy, Magnan, and McNally entered the room with the large bay window and began scouting around. In the room itself, there was nothing to the naked eye that connected Costa to their missing girlfriends. The room had been cleaned, the bed was made, and the floor was swept. Morton had even dumped out the wastepaper basket.

Magnan then opened the closet door and spotted a brown case made of faux alligator skin with a leather handle, which held a hair dryer inside.

"Is this the hair dryer that Costa's mother wants back?" he asked Morton. She nodded.

"Well, this hair dryer doesn't belong to Costa," he added. "I know for a fact that it belongs to Mary Anne."

Next, Morton took them to an adjoining room where she kept a pair of Costa's boots and three sweaters that he had left behind.

Turbidy examined one of the sweaters, a white turtleneck, and brought it close to his nose and sniffed. The smell of Pat Walsh's perfume lingered on the collar.

"This belongs to my girlfriend," he informed the landlady.

Magnan asked if they could use the telephone, and he quickly dialed the Provincetown Police Department.

As the phone rang, Morton mentioned something else that she found strange.

"When I dumped out the waste basket, it was full of notes," she said. "One of the notes read, 'There is no hope without dope. Long live LSD.'"

CHAPTER THIRTEEN

Patrolman James Cook and his partner, Steve Silva, were dispatched to Patricia Morton's guesthouse to pick up Costa's work boots and sweaters, including the turtleneck belonging to Pat Walsh. They inspected the boots and found dirt caked between the treads of the rubber soles.

"The girls had become friendly with Antone, who was also staying here at the house," the landlady told the officers. "He asked them for a ride to Truro on that Saturday morning. I know this because he left a note on the door."

She handed them the note along with a torn-up letter that she had pieced back together with Scotch tape.

"This one mentions that he was sitting around his room stoned on hash and downers," she pointed out with a tone of frustration. "I always tell my tenants that if they're doing something illegal—don't do it in my house."

The letter was signed *Anthony of Rome*, and it featured a handmade drawing of a hypodermic needle.

Silva took the items back to the police department, tagged them, and went home for the day, while Cook decided to take a drive down to Truro to see if he could find any sign of Costa or the missing women.

As Cook entered the village, he passed Truro police chief Harold Berrio driving in the opposite direction. The patrolman flagged Berrio down and approached his vehicle.

"Hey, Chief, I'm looking for two girls that went missing about two weeks ago. They were driving a blue VW. Any sign of them or the car?"

Berrio's eyes lit up. "I found a car fitting that description parked in the woods a few days back. I asked for a stolen vehicle record but it came back negative."

"Can you take me to the car now?" Cook asked.

"Sure, follow me."

Chief Berrio led the way back to the clearing where the car had been abandoned, but the Volkswagen was gone. The two men got out of their vehicles and walked around a bit. Berrio noticed tire tracks in the snow, while Cook found an empty gas can in the bushes.

"When did you first find the car?" Cook asked.

"It was here on Sunday, February 2, Groundhog Day. There was a note on the car too. It said something about engine trouble."

The police chief invited Cook to the station house to discuss the missing car further over a cup of coffee. Like Cook, Harold Berrio was a native Cape Codder, and he wore that distinction with pride. He was born in Wellfleet, the next town over, and had built Truro's small police department twenty years before. Berrio had the face of a bloodhound and a nose for digging for the truth. He was upset with Cook over the fact that Provincetown police had not shared any information with him regarding the missing girls.

"We've lost a lot of ground here," he scolded the patrolman. "I might run a department the size of a broom closet but I've been at this far longer than you."

"Look, Chief, we just learned about the connection here to Truro," Cook pointed out. "We really didn't know where these girls were or if they were truly missing. They're young and free-spirited. They could be anywhere."

Berrio telephoned the Massachusetts State Police barracks in Yarmouth, about thirty-five miles away. Thanks to the missing person report filed by Martha Wysocki, state police investigators had also begun to inquire about the whereabouts of Mary Anne and Pat. State trooper Robert Sylvia was ordered to rendezvous with Berrio and Cook in Truro. An hour later, all three men were back at the clearing, scouring the area for clues. They spread out, walking down a small dirt road surrounded by scrub oak about a mile from where Berrio said the car had been left. At another small clearing, Patrolman Cook spotted a sprinkling of debris trapped in the frost-covered bramble. As he bent down, he saw what looked to be a torn yellow sales slip. He brushed off some flakes of crusted snow and made out the name printed at the top of the slip—*Patricia H. Walsh*.

The slip was from Kent County Motors in West Warwick, Rhode Island. Next to it were other crumpled-up papers, including two Aetna Casualty insurance receipts made out to Patricia Walsh and her 1968 Rhode Island registration card.

"Holy shit," Cook whispered under his breath.

———————

Tony Costa sat in a booth at Mother Marion's restaurant on Commercial Street waiting for a friend to show. The joint he had smoked an hour before had begun to wear off, so he sipped a glass of Chianti in an attempt to settle his nerves. Several minutes later, as he emptied the glass, Costa saw his buddy James Steele enter the small eatery and make his way to Costa's booth.

"How are ya, man?" Steele asked, smiling. "When you said you wanted to meet, it put me in the right groove. I hope you've come bearing gifts because I haven't had a good high in weeks."

"That's not why I called you here," Costa said softly. "Do you remember the gun I showed you, the twenty-two with the pearl handle?"

"Sure I do. I really dug that pistol."

"Would you like to buy it?"

"Yeah, man, I'd like to have that gun as my own. But I just landed a stock-room job at Brigham Hospital in Boston, and I won't get paid for a while."

Costa shook his head. "That does not work for me. I need to sell the gun right away. I need money to leave town."

"Can I buy it on layaway?"

"I wish you could," Costa replied. "But I need money now. If you can scrape up some cash in the next couple of days, let me know."

"Do you have the piece on you?" Steele inquired. "I'd like to check it out again."

"No, I have it buried. If you find the money, I'll bring it to you."

Costa shook his friend's hand, threw down a few dollars to pay the tab, and hurried out of the tavern.

———

Patrolman James Cook returned to the Provincetown police station in the early afternoon. He had given Trooper Sylvia Pat Walsh's identification papers along with the gas can for fingerprint analysis.

Something has definitely happened to the girls, he thought. *Something bad.*

He also believed that Tony Costa could be the key to solving this growing mystery.

Cook drove around town looking for the young drug informant but could not find him anywhere. Investigators dialed Costa's mother, Cecilia Bonaviri, once again.

"We need to speak with your son," Trooper Syliva told her. "We believe that he has knowledge about two girls that have gone missing."

"He's not around," the mother said. "I believe he moved up to Boston to look for a job."

She slammed the phone down, and the line went dead.

With the mother uncooperative and Costa out of the picture, at least for the moment, it made sense for police to return to the Truro woods to look for more clues. This time, Cook and Sylvia were joined by Massachusetts State Trooper Edgar "Tom" Gunnery and Lieutenant John Dunn, who both were on temporary assignment with the district attorney's office for the Southern District, which had jurisdiction over Cape Cod and the islands of Martha's Vineyard and Nantucket. Dunn had spent twenty years as a motorcycle cop with the Boston Police Department before joining the DA's office. He had three young children and a sick wife at home. Criminal defense attorneys gave him the nickname "All Dunn" because of his tenacity. If he was assigned to investigate a case, that often meant that the suspect was "all done" and would swiftly be convicted and carted off to jail. Tom Gunnery was younger than his colleague, just thirty-five years old with a baby face, but he felt up to the task at hand.

They all met up at the Pamet Road exit off Route 6A in Truro, and Cook and Sylvia then led the investigators into the wooded area near where the car was found. This time, it was Tom Gunnery who made a startling discovery. He found a Volkswagen owner's manual in the bushes bearing the name *Patricia Walsh*, along with her address. Nearby, he retrieved a memo and datebook notepad, a Rhode Island Automobile Club membership card, a purchaser's tax return with Walsh's signature, and a gray driving glove.

That evening, Gunnery and Dunn questioned Patricia Morton at her guesthouse. She shared with them the same story she had given Provincetown police and the missing girls' boyfriends.

"It's like Antone just vanished, along with the girls," Morton told them. "He took his books, a drawing board and protractor, and even the small record player that I had here for guests. It's all gone."

———

The killer navigated a confusing collection of one-way streets until he reached Embankment Road along the Charles River and then Storrow Drive. Tony Costa was behind the wheel of Pat Walsh's blue Volkswagen Beetle, and he was driving alone. He followed a sign for Interstate 93 and downshifted into second gear, which allowed the small vehicle to gain the traction needed to climb the highway ramp near the Boston Museum of Science. Through the rearview mirror, he could see the city's 749-foot Prudential Tower, which reminded him of the Pilgrim Monument back home in Helltown, where the police were on the hunt for him. Costa drove through the night on a highway of darkness with only a worn road map to guide him. Occasionally, he would pull off to a rest area to study the route under the flame of his cigarette lighter. He was sober and clear headed, driving the speed limit to avoid getting pulled over by the cops. Costa had no driver's license, was driving a stolen vehicle, and was wanted for questioning in the disappearance of two young women.

If a cop pulls us over, just act cool, Cory advised him. *If he asks too many questions, we'll just kill the pig.*

"With what, my lighter?" Costa asked aloud. "We don't have a gun. We don't have a knife."

And soon, we won't have this fucking car if you just do as I say.

Once Costa reached Concord, New Hampshire, he turned onto Interstate 89 North, which was popular with skiers at this time of year. Illuminated by the moon, steep mountains cast ominous shadows over the terrain as the killer entered Vermont just past the town of Hanover, New Hampshire. He felt like the wolf of the steppes once more. Early the next morning, Costa pulled off the highway during a snow squall and rode into the city of Burlington, Vermont. He stopped at a gas station on Pearl Street and asked a station attendant named Wayne Blanchard if he could rent a space in the service station yard for overnight parking.

"We have some room," Blanchard said. "Just fill out the registration slip and pay the seven-dollar fee."

"I'm sorry, but I do not have any money," Costa told him. "I will have money though in a day or two when my wife arrives in town."

Costa signed an IOU and parked the Volkswagen on the north side of the gas station and walked away. He strolled from street to street, looking for lodging. The killer was exhausted and had only slept for a few minutes at a time since burying Pat Walsh and Mary Anne Wysocki thirteen days before. Costa found shelter at a rooming house at 30 Winooski Avenue. He paid the landlord, Stella Smith, fifteen dollars, which ensured him a room through February 12. Smith led him to Room #2 on the north side of the building and showed him inside. The killer smiled at the landlady and thanked her for the hospitality. He then closed the bedroom door, collapsed on the comfortable mattress, and drifted off to sleep.

Costa slept for most of the day and only left the rooming house at nightfall. He returned to the service station and removed the Rhode Island license plates from the VW Beetle and hid them under a floor mat in the trunk. He then found a bookstore downtown and purchased a copy of the *Physician's Desk Reference* and the latest issue of *Hush-Hush News*, which featured an article titled "Eat Raw Flesh at Virgin Sacrifice" and an advertisement touting "Red Devil Pills for Men: The Most Exciting Thing Since Adam and Eve Discovered the Apple." He brought the magazine and reference book back to his room at Stella Smith's guesthouse and placed them side by side on top of a small desk. Costa then reached into his duffle bag to retrieve his copy of Charles Johnson Maynard's *Manual of Taxidermy for Amateurs*.

Burlington was a college town after all, home to the University of Vermont, St. Michael's College, and Trinity College for women, and Tony Costa had some time to kill.

CHAPTER FOURTEEN

The next morning, February 8, 1969, Trooper Gunnery raced up the Mid-Cape Highway from the state police barracks in Yarmouth to the one-lane stretch of road entering the town of Harwich known ominously as "Suicide Alley." He sat uneasily behind the steering wheel of his squad car, his one cup of coffee balanced between his legs and amplifying his nerves. Gunnery woke up with a strange feeling about what the day might bring, especially after the evidence he had discovered the day before. It was the same premonition he'd had when he arrived for guard duty at the Kennedy compound on that fateful gray day in late November 1963. Gunnery could still hear the wails coming from the big house on the bluff when Joe Kennedy and his nurse learned that the president had just been shot in Dallas.

Gunnery had protected JFK at his summer home in Hyannis Port, aiding the Secret Service detail in their duties to keep nearby roads and waters clear of potential threats. He wished he had been there at Dealey Plaza instead of patrolling the grounds of the family estate on that tragic afternoon. *Maybe, just maybe there would have been something I could have done*, Gunnery thought. He realized such a notion was ludicrous. What could he have seen that the president's Secret Service agents had not in November 1963? Still, he lived with a pang of guilt for not being there when President and Mrs. Kennedy had needed him most. These thoughts kept him company as he drove through the outer Cape villages of Orleans, Eastham, and Wellfleet and up the peninsula where the small spit of white sand spiraled into a defiant fist.

Gunnery pulled off Route 6A in Truro and traveled along a winding road toward the Old Truro Cemetery. He then joined seventy-five local men, including Air Force personnel from the radar station in North Truro, for a search of the thickly wooded area, which was accessible only by a dirt road and rarely visited except by hunters and berry pickers. He could hear the buzzing of a small twin-engine plane on loan from the town of Barnstable conducting aerial surveillance overhead. This desolate area was pressed up against the bayside of Cape Cod, far away from the taffy shops, clam shacks, and soft sand beaches that drew tourists from all over the world every summer. This was the "real Cape Cod," where the dunes flowed like liquid sand surrounded by barrens and heath lands.

As the search team fanned out, Gunnery navigated the terrain slowly, managing not to slip on the slick bed of frozen leaves blanketing the hidden trails. By late morning, police and volunteers had still found nothing, and the search plane headed back to the airport in Hyannis.

"My side's clear!" hollered Truro Police Chief Harold Berrio as he strolled along Cemetery Road.

Gunnery stood on an embankment on the opposite side of the ancient dirt path. He surveyed the woods and spotted a depression in the earth that was about four feet long, two feet wide, and eight inches deep. There was a piece of green cloth sticking out of the frost. Upon closer inspection, Gunnery smelled a foul odor emanating from the ground. He used a pickax to puncture the icy crust, eventually reaching the soft sand below. Gunnery yanked the cloth free and scraped away the dirt to reveal white stenciling that read *U.S. Army*. He freed the rest of the green duffel bag from the earth and looked inside.

It was empty.

But Gunnery spotted what he believed to be dried blood on one of the straps, so he kept digging. Next, he found a piece of white bone.

"Probably belongs to a deer," he said aloud.

Gunnery knew that the area was popular with hunters. He was quickly relieved of this notion when he pried the bone free. It was connected to a human foot. Gunnery continued to dig. What came next was a leg, and then two arms severed at their sockets. One of the hands held a diamond ring attached to the third finger. The body was cut into eight sections and belonged to a woman. Under the severed appendages was a bag. Gunnery picked it up and examined it through the clear plastic. Staring back at the trooper was the blue, discolored face of the victim herself. Her head had been cut off just below the jawline, her left cheek was swollen, and her nose had been beaten flat. The body parts were badly decomposed, which meant they did not belong to either Mary Anne Wysocki or Pat Walsh.

Gunnery returned to the state police barracks just before dinner. Despite the cold, the trooper kept the windows rolled down in the squad car, as he was sweating. He had been replaying the day's horror over again in his mind. Never in his career in law enforcement had he witnessed this kind of evil. Gunnery maintained a cool demeanor through the long day in the Truro woods but felt he was about to break inside. Supper that night was rare roast beef. As the plate was served to all the on-duty officers in the barracks lunch room, Gunnery took one look at the bleeding roast, leapt from his chair, ran to the toilet, and retched.

The body parts of the unidentified victim were taken by ambulance to Carlson's Funeral Home in neighboring Wellfleet, where Dr. George Katsas would perform the autopsy. Katsas, a forensic pathologist who worked at the Department of Legal Medicine at Harvard University, was given a police escort from Cambridge, Massachusetts, to Cape Cod for this gruesome assignment.

When Dr. Katsas took one look at the makeshift examination area, which was housed in a shed adjacent to the funeral home, he refused to inspect the body. The shed was unheated and illuminated by a single light bulb hanging over a chipped enamel table. He ordered that the remains be transferred to the mortuary at Boston City Hospital. Once there, in a more professional and sterile environment, Dr. Katsas went to work clearing away the sand and gravel that were caked on the remains. The pathologist then made six initial, terrifying observations about the victim:

1. Mutilation of the body in eight distinct portions.
2. Postmortem degeneration (breakdown of brain, heart, lungs, liver, kidneys, and muscles).
3. Incised wounds to lower extremities and the diaphragm.
4. Pelvic evisceration with removal of internal genitals.
5. Amputation of the heart.
6. Amputation of the breasts.

Dr. Katsas then began examining the detached head, which was sharply cut just below the jawline. The neck organs were missing. The victim's eyes were sunken into the orbits, and Katsas could make no distinction as to their color. She was missing several teeth, which could have been the result of a blow to the skull.

Next, the pathologist focused on her chest cavity, which was essentially an empty vessel. The heart and liver were completely gone. When this section of the body had been lifted from its shallow grave, there was a pair of blood-soaked pink panties with the embroidered label *Thursday* stuffed inside the chest cavity. The skin had been peeled off, and the mammary glands, including the nipples, were missing. The victim's sex had also been stolen from her. The unidentified woman's uterus, ovaries, and intestines had been cut out with a sharp blade.

In the thirty years that Dr. Katsas had been performing autopsies, he had never seen anything like this before. To him, it was as if Jack the Ripper had been resurrected to prey on women in the Cape Cod woods.

Based on the findings of Dr. George Katsas, the Massachusetts State Police issued this bulletin:

IDENTIFICATION WANTED FOR UNIDENTIFIED BODY: Identification wanted for a dead body of a white female age 16 to 19 years, 5 feet, light brown shoulder length hair, Exact color of eyes not certain but might be blue. Body dismembered, head in a plastic bag. Torso was wrapped in a large white cotton bag.

The bulletin also stated that the victim had worn a fourteen-carat gold wedding ring with five small diamonds on the middle finger of her left hand. The ring was manufactured by Leaf Brothers in New York City. State police also lifted a partial fingerprint from the little finger of the murder victim's right hand.

———————

Kurt Vonnegut was enjoying his second cigarette of the morning along with his third cup of coffee. His hands were stained by nicotine and ink dust from the thick morning edition of the Sunday *Boston Globe*. The front page of the newspaper barely held his interest. There were stories running above and below the fold about overspending by the U.S. military in Vietnam, the fact that Massachusetts taxes were the fifth highest in the nation, and a gas explosion that left fifteen thousand customers in the Boston suburbs of Waltham and Weston without power. Vonnegut smoked and sipped as he flipped from one page to the next through a minefield of advertisements, ranging from Singer's "Why Wait" sale on sewing machines, vacuums, TVs, and stereos, to a Zayre department store promotion of a local appearance by Bud Dietrich, a nationally known "exponent of humor and hocus pocus." Vonnegut, a former advertising man, chuckled at all the commercial hype. But tucked away toward the back of the newspaper was a story that shook the writer to his core. The headline at the top of page 39 read, "Dismembered Body Found in Lonely Truro Grave." Vonnegut set his smoldering Pall Mall in an ashtray and began to read further.

"The dismembered body of a middle-aged woman was found in a shallow grave in an isolated section of this quiet, lower Cape town yesterday," *Globe* staff reporter William A. Davis wrote. "The woman's arms and legs had been severed from the torso and stuffed in a hole about four feet wide and deep."

The reporter went on to write that the Barnstable County Medical Examiner, Dr. Daniel Hiebert of Provincetown, had determined that the victim was between fifty and fifty-five years old and that the body had been in the grave as long as a year.

"The grave might have remained undiscovered for months—perhaps forever if a search had not been made through the area for two missing Providence, R.I. girls... The district attorney's office and the state police have entered the case. One of the few remaining unspoiled Cape Cod towns, Truro has a permanent population of only 1,000 residents."

Vonnegut knew this was a big story, and he was shocked that it wasn't splashed across the front page.

It appeared that news editors placed little importance on a woman who had clearly been viciously murdered and buried in a pristine section of Cape Cod. The grave site was less than forty miles away from Vonnegut's home. He contemplated driving to the scene that day, but there was more snow in the forecast, and he had to answer letters from his publisher about his forthcoming novel, *Slaughterhouse-Five*, which was just a month away from publication. Vonnegut fetched a pair of scissors and clipped the *Boston Globe* article for future use.

"Who would want to kill and dismember an old lady, and what happened to the Providence girls?" he asked himself. "So it goes."

What Vonnegut did not know was that the victim's age had been misreported by the medical examiner, Dr. Daniel Hiebert, who had inspected the body at the funeral home in Wellfleet before George Katsas stepped in. Because the woman was missing some teeth, Hiebert concluded wrongly that she must have been middle to advanced age.

Vonnegut placed the cut-out article in his desk drawer and closed it. He then picked up a letter of encouragement from his editor, who had high hopes for *Slaughterhouse-Five*. Vonnegut knew that he had swung for the fences with this novel, and he hoped for a smash hit, or at least enough critical acclaim to secure him a writer-in-residence position at the University of Michigan, for which he had recently applied. His old war buddy Bernie O'Hare spoke highly of the novel after reading an advanced copy. O'Hare's wife, Mary, initially a critic of the project, loved it too. The style of writing in *Slaughterhouse-Five* would free him from the shackles of the ill-conceived notion that he was a science fiction writer with a humorist bent. Now, he would be seen as a moralist, which was what critics and readers, especially those on college campuses, were hungry for at that moment with the war raging in Southeast Asia. Vonnegut was ready to rise above the din of his contemporaries, whom he saw as nothing more than bombastic entertainers. He was pleased to learn that his editor had not cut out his dig against Norman Mailer that appeared in chapter 9 of *Slaughterhouse-Five*, in which his protagonist, Billy Pilgrim, is mistaken for a literary critic in a discussion about whether the novel was dead.

"One of them [critics] said it would be a nice time to bury the novel, now that a Virginian, one hundred years after Appomattox, had written *Uncle Tom's Cabin*," Vonnegut wrote. "Another one said that people couldn't read well enough anymore to turn print into exciting situations in their skulls, so that authors had to do what Norman Mailer did, which was to perform what he had written."

It was Vonnegut's subtle way of describing the dancing monkey that he believed his literary rival had devolved into. In truth, Vonnegut hungered for the kind of attention paid to Mailer by nationally syndicated talk show hosts.

For Mailer's part, he appeared disinterested in fighting with his lesser-known neighbor living in Barnstable. Literature bored him. He aspired to be a filmmaker discussed in the same breath as John Cassavetes, the actor turned director, whose 1968 independent film, *Faces*, scored three Academy Award nominations. Mailer still had to edit down forty-five hours of film for his movie *Maidstone*. He was thrilled about securing the rights to three Isaac Hayes songs, including the bluesy ballad "I Just Want to Make Love to You." But Mailer was still undecided about including the unscripted, bloody attack perpetrated against him by Rip Torn in the final cut of the film. Cinematographer D. A. Pennebaker urged the director to keep the scene intact.

"The scene and the film reflect the time we're living in," Pennebaker argued. "There's a peculiar thing in the air, a darkness, and since this is quasi-documentary filmmaking, you need to remember that the movie is never over and that's what we captured here with Torn. Now you've got something real in your film."

"I'm gonna drop it all out," Mailer replied, still angry with the actor over the bloodletting and, most importantly, terrifying his wife and children. "It's all going to go."

"This film has burst into a flower in front of you," Pennebaker countered. "The scene between you and Torn, although unscripted, keeps the film alive."

Mailer the husband and father abhorred the idea, but Mailer the director knew that his cinematographer was right. He would have to find a way to keep the scene in the film. While Kurt Vonnegut Jr. was eager to birth his new novel *Slaughterhouse-Five* into the world, Mailer was just as anxious to share *Maidstone* with moviegoers. The director was in early talks with both the Venice and London film festivals to screen the film, which would take place after a more intimate showing in Provincetown.

While Vonnegut was digesting the day's story about the butchered body in Truro, Mailer's estranged wife, Beverly, called her husband, who had not had a chance to pick up a copy of the *Boston Globe*. She read the article to him over the telephone. Mailer knew the area surrounding the grave site well, as he liked to drive his Jeep through the winding roads of Truro when he needed a break from writing. He also recognized the name of the medical examiner quoted in the article. Dr. Daniel Hiebert had stitched up the deep gash on Mailer's head after his notorious scuffle with the Ptown cop known as "Cobra."

The details of the *Boston Globe* story were particularly grisly and something one might read in a New York City tabloid. The fact that it happened within miles of Mailer's Commercial Street home, his safe place, gave him a sudden chill. Beverly Mailer relayed more specifics from the article, including information that the victim's naked body parts were wrapped in a white sheet inside an army duffel bag, the fact that Pat Walsh's car was found abandoned nearby, and that neither Pat nor her companion Mary Anne Wysocki had been located as of the reporter's deadline.

"Do we have a vicious killer on our hands?" Beverly asked Mailer.

Mailer pondered the possibility. The term *serial killer* had not been coined yet, but the murderous hunting of women both young and old had become a frightening reality in America, especially for those living in Massachusetts. Just seven years before in 1962, a killer or killers began systematically strangling women in the greater Boston area in a kill zone that stretched thirty-five miles from the city neighborhood of Dorchester to the dreary mill town of Lawrence. The victims were young and old, Black and white. Some of the women were sexually assaulted, while others were not. The oldest victim was a seventy-five-year-old widow named Ida Irga, who was murdered in Boston's West End, a predominantly Jewish neighborhood. The youngest victim was nineteen-year-old Mary Sullivan, who was strangled with a scarf and a nylon stocking inside the apartment she shared with two other women at 44-A Charles Street, in Boston's tony Beacon Hill section. Sullivan had also been raped and assaulted with a broomstick. The wooden handle was found protruding from her vagina along with a greeting card propped against her left foot, which read *Happy New Year*. Mary Sullivan was not only the youngest victim, she was also the last.

Sullivan was a Cape Cod girl who had been raised in Hyannis, just a short distance away from the Kennedy family compound. Her killer was never positively identified, although police had zeroed in on a Boston University student as the prime suspect. A year later in 1965, a handy man from Chelsea, Massachusetts, named Albert Henry DeSalvo confessed to Sullivan's murder and the other ten unsolved homicides attributed to the Boston Strangler. DeSalvo added two more murders to the tally, but he was never formally charged with any of the crimes due to a lack of evidence, and many investigators found his confession to be riddled with holes. DeSalvo was incarcerated at the time for unrelated sexual assault charges at Walpole State Prison, where he worked as a jewelry maker selling "choker" necklaces to visitors at the prison gift shop. He had also recorded a pop song called "Strangler in the Night."

The Boston Strangler case had terrified the region. Women living alone armed themselves with switchblade knives for protection and cleared out local animal shelters of stray dogs. They slept with glass bottles against their bedroom doors, and some even kept pointed ski poles under their mattresses in case the killer or killers came calling in the night.

Did the cut-up body unearthed in Truro and the search for Pat Walsh and Mary Anne Wysocki signify a return to a time in all too recent memory when no woman felt safe? Norman Mailer contemplated this idea, as did those men who were investigating the bizarre case.

CHAPTER FIFTEEN

––––––––––

The wolf of the steppes was trapped by a winter storm that blew through town, dropping more than a foot of fresh snow on Burlington, Vermont. He had the urge to kill, but local shops were shuttered for the day, and the streets were abandoned. He also knew better than to leave bloody footprints in the snow.

Trapping was the first order of business for any hunter, according to the manual, but it was the killer himself who felt ensnared by forces beyond his control. As heavy snow pounded the windowpane of his guest room at 30 North Winooski Avenue, Costa sat on his bed fantasizing about death. For a brief moment, he thought about cutting his landlord, Stella Smith, into small pieces.

It would be so easy, Cory told him.

But the killer could not rationalize it. Costa had signed his own name in her guest book, and there were other boarders in the house who would be alerted to her screams. Most importantly, Stella Smith did not fit his profile. She was middle-aged and had confided to him that she was being treated for cancer. Tony Costa decided that he would let the disease run its course. He left his room, walked downstairs, and found the landlady in the kitchen, bringing a pot of water to a boil.

"Would you like a cup of tea?" she asked.

"No, thank you. May I use your phone? I have an urgent call to make."

Smith directed him to a telephone in the hallway.

"Just make sure it's not a long-distance call."

He smiled at her as he backed out of the kitchen and into the corridor. Costa grabbed the phone and dialed the long-distance number for the Provincetown Police Department. Sergeant James Meads picked up the line.

"Good day, Sergeant. This is Tony Costa. My mother informed me that you would like to speak to me."

"Tony, the reason we'd like to talk to you is because two girls have gone missing and their parents are very concerned about them," Meads said. "Their names are Patricia Walsh and Mary Anne Wysocki. Did you have any conversations with them about where they were headed after staying at Mrs. Morton's place?"

Costa paused. "I would rather speak to you in person. It's a very sensitive subject. I wish to clear some things up."

"You'll want to talk to Chief Marshall," Meads advised. "When can you get here?"

"I can probably make it in tomorrow."

Costa ended the conversation and looked out the window. Snow was still falling, but it was lighter now.

He placed another call to the local bus company and left the boardinghouse.

"I had a wonderful stay," he told the landlady. "I'm so sorry that I have to leave so abruptly. But I promise to visit again soon."

The killer walked three blocks to the bus station and bought a one-way ticket to Boston. Costa traveled 353 miles that day, switching buses only once in Boston for the final trek to Ptown. He arrived at his mother's home late that evening. The next morning, he was awakened by the rapping sound of Sergeant Meads knocking on the front door. Costa quickly got dressed and welcomed the officer inside.

"Good morning, Tony. The state police are in town and Chief Marshall is at the station. If you want to clear things up, I suggest you come with me."

Costa gave his mother a knowing look. She hugged her son tightly and refused to let go. The killer pried himself away from his mother's bulky frame, stepped out into the morning light, and climbed into the passenger seat of Meads's squad car.

"Tony, you and I have known each other for a while now and I've always done right by you," Meads said as he backed the police car out of the driveway. "If you have any idea where these girls are, tell me so we can find them and relieve their parents of worry."

"Jim, if I could help you I would," Costa replied. "The only thing I know is that the girls told me they needed money for an abortion. I bought Pat Walsh's Volkswagen for $900. The girls asked me if they could use the car for a few more days and I agreed. They took the car to Vermont instead."

"So, the girls are in Vermont right now?"

"I think they're in Canada. They were scheduled to meet with a doctor in Montreal, so that Pat could have her situation taken care of."

They arrived at the police station a short time later. Meads escorted Costa into the outer lobby of Chief Cheney Marshall's office where they were met by the chief, John Dunn, and Tom Gunnery.

Trooper Gunnery had the gift of instant recall for just about anyone he had ever met. The skill came in most handy in his job as an investigator. He took one look at Tony Costa, and his jaw almost hit the floor.

Costa sported a thick, black mustache and matching hair that he parted to the side. He was fine boned and even featured. With a pair of granny glasses straddling his angular nose, he resembled a Portuguese John Lennon. Gunnery rifled through his memory bank and quickly landed on the moment the two had previously met.

I pulled you over back in September. You were speeding and had a noisy muffler, the trooper thought to himself. *You acted funny, but I didn't think much of it at the time.* Gunnery kept the information to himself until he could be 100 percent sure it was him.

If Costa had remembered the encounter, he certainly did not show it. He looked right through Gunnery and Dunn toward his old pal, Chief Marshall. Costa wondered if Marshall had told the state police investigators that he had served as a paid drug informant for the Ptown police.

"I would like to have a word with Mr. Costa privately," Marshall told Gunnery and Dunn before leading Costa into his small office and closing the door.

The chief informed Costa of his Miranda rights and told him that he could leave at any time. Instead, the killer offered a smug smile as he settled into a chair and folded his arms. Marshall despised the young drug dealer and felt a sudden urge to reach across his desk and smack Costa across the face. But both men decided to play a gentlemanly game of verbal chess instead.

"I'm not gonna press dope with you today. We got bigger problems," Marshall said. "Just tell me about the girls."

"There were some drugs involved," Costa claimed. "Hashish and a tiny bit of heroin. They bought some off me last summer and failed to pay. When I saw them again two weeks ago, Pat Walsh offered me her car instead. She's pregnant. They've both gone to Montreal so that she can get an abortion."

The police chief tried to connect the dots in his head, but the story did not make sense to him, so he switched gears.

"Did you get that gun you were looking for?"

"Do you mean, after you refused to offer me protection unless someone hurt me?"

They stared across the table at each other, and neither man said a word.

Finally, Costa broke the silence. "You boys don't lift a finger for anyone unless a violent act takes place under your noses. You don't have a shred of evidence that something bad has happened to those girls, so why are you giving me a hard time?"

"I'll give you some advice, Tony. If I were you, I'd get myself a damn good lawyer."

Chief Marshall led Costa out of his office and into the adjacent interrogation room where Gunnery and Dunn were seated along with fellow state police detective Bernie Flynn. Lieutenant Flynn had served in the U.S. Coast Guard during World War II and was a longtime New Bedford street cop before joining the state police, where he graduated at the top of his class in 1966. He was also a skilled interrogator and took the lead in questioning Costa.

"First of all, I want you to know that you aren't a suspect in any crime," Flynn said, hoping to put the young man at ease. "Because if the girls did leave and go somewhere voluntarily, this was their right as both girls are over twenty-one years old and they can come and go as they please. Had you ever met the two girls before they registered at Mrs. Morton's rooming house?"

"No."

Costa's answer caught Chief Marshall by surprise. Costa had just told him that he had met the girls the previous summer. The chief said nothing and let Flynn continue with the interview.

"Did you see them again?"

"Yes, I met them that night at a bar in town called the Foc'sle. I sat at a table with them and we drank and talked until about midnight. Pat told me that she needed money and wanted to sell her car."

"What kind of car was it?"

"It was a light blue Volkswagen. I have the bill of sale here."

At that moment, Costa reached into his jacket pocket and pulled out a piece of neatly folded lined yellow paper and handed it to Flynn, who opened it and read its contents out loud.

"Sold to Anthony Costa for the sum of nine hundred dollars, my blue 1968 VW model number 118088538, type 117, engine number H5036528. January 17, 1969. Signed, Patricia Walsh and undersigned by Antone C. Costa."

Flynn tried handing the note back to Costa.

"You can keep it if you want it. I just wanted to show you that I owned the car."

"Did you give Patricia Walsh the nine hundred bucks, after you received this bill of sale?"

"No, I didn't."

Flynn leaned in. Costa could smell the stale cigarettes on his breath and the investigator's aftershave on his neckline.

"You want me to believe that the Walsh girl, a girl you just met that day, signed her 1968 Volkswagen car over to you without receiving any payment for it?"

The killer remained calm. "I told the Walsh girl that I would pay her the next morning. I had six hundred dollars saved up in my room, and my brother Vincent loaned me the other three hundred dollars."

Flynn then asked Costa about the note that was pinned to the door of their room. Costa said that he had written it and that he asked them for a ride to pick up his work check.

"The girls then drove me into the woods in Truro and pulled the car into a clearing. Pat told me that she was going to use the car for a week and when they brought it back, they would leave the car in the woods, where I could pick it up."

The story was illogical, but Costa's delivery was impeccable. As Tom Gunnery listened to the young man's ludicrous story, he could not help but be impressed by his demeanor. Costa had acted erratically when Gunnery stopped him speeding on the highway six months back, but today, he was pure silk.

Flynn continued to press. "Wait, after paying the girls nine hundred dollars, you still let them take the car away with them?"

"Yes, I wasn't worried," Costa replied calmly. "I trusted them. It's what we hippies do. We love one another unconditionally. Money means nothing to us."

"Don't you think nine hundred dollars is a small amount of money to pay for a 1968 Volkswagen?"

Costa shot a look at Chief Marshall before answering. "Well, to be honest, I didn't pay the girls nine hundred dollars. I had seen both girls sometime in August of last year," he explained to Flynn. "They bought a pound of hashish from me at that time. I sold the hashish for seven hundred dollars, but the girls didn't have any money. They sold me the car in payment for the money they owed me."

"You're telling me now that your first statement is false?"

"Yes, I was covering up for myself," Costa replied sheepishly. "I did not want you to know that I was selling drugs."

Cheney Marshall kept silent.

"So when did you see the girls again?" asked Flynn.

"I saw them in Burlington, Vermont. I took a bus from Provincetown to Boston and another one headed north. I went to the Burlington airport and my car was parked there. I drove my car into town and got a room. Then I saw Pat and Mary Anne walking through town. They told me that they were running away from home to Canada. I drove them back to the airport and they boarded a flight to Montreal."

Costa's story kept going around in circles. He also told Flynn that the girls had taken off to California to get an abortion. The interrogator needed to put a pin in this line of questioning. He reached under his seat and placed a pair of dirty work boots on the table in front of Costa.

"Are these yours?"

"Yes, they are my boots but I don't want them. You can keep them or throw them out. You can keep the sales receipt too."

"Tony, do you know where the girls are?"

"I told you, they're in Canada."

"Yes, but you've changed your story so many times, it seems a bit confusing."

Costa's eyes narrowed. "Are you trying to say that I killed them?"

Flynn shook his head. "No, Tony. I never mentioned anything about the girls being dead, but I think you know where they are."

"They're a long way off." The killer smiled. "And I doubt that you'll ever find them."

Flynn thanked Costa for his time and allowed him to walk breezily out of the interrogation room. After Costa left the station, Flynn shared his concerns with Gunnery, Dunn, and Chief Marshall.

"I want that man under twenty-four-hour surveillance," he told them.

CHAPTER SIXTEEN

Bernie Flynn relayed Costa's jumbled alibi to his boss, George Killen, the lead investigator for the Bristol County district attorney. Killen had a hot temper and was stoutly built. He was a walking monolith whose nickname around the DA's office was "Stoneface." But he was considered a good administrator, and the investigative team was in need of a solid coach. Killen took Flynn's information and then called the Burlington Police Department and spoke to Detective Lieutenant Richard Beaulieu.

"I've got a report of a stolen car that might be in your area," Killen told him. "It's an urgent matter."

"I don't see why we need to drop everything we're doing to help you look for a stolen vehicle," Beaulieu replied with a trace of a French-Canadian accent. The Burlington Police Department was small, and the officers there were grappling with the illicit drug trade that was exploding in nearby St. Albans.

"The car was last seen in an area where a dismembered body was found, and it belonged to two girls who are now missing."

"Okay, now I'm listening."

Killen asked Beaulieu to check out Burlington Municipal Airport.

"That's where the suspect in this case, Tony Costa, says the car is now parked."

Beaulieu raced over to the airport, which was relatively small, just over one thousand acres, and served as a hub for Mohawk Airlines. A black-and-white photograph of John F. Kennedy hung in the terminal. It was taken during a campaign speech he gave there just one day before he won the presidency in 1960. Beaulieu spoke with a clerk for Mohawk Airlines and asked him to check the passenger list for the names Patricia Walsh and Mary Anne Wysocki.

"It's believed that they took a five o'clock flight to Montreal," Beaulieu informed the desk clerk.

"That cannot be true," the clerk replied. "We have only one flight to Montreal each day and it leaves at 12:15 p.m. According to our manifest, neither woman had boarded a flight to Montreal over the past two weeks."

Beaulieu left the terminal and scanned the parking lot for the missing car but found nothing.

He returned to the station and called Killen.

"Sorry, Detective, but we just learned that Costa has changed his story again," Killen said. "Now he claims that the Volkswagen is parked at a Gulf gas station at the corner of Pearl and North Winooski Avenue. We want the car located and impounded but not processed. This could be a key piece of evidence in what may be a double homicide."

Beaulieu got back in his squad car and drove to the station. He quickly located the Volkswagen parked in a space at the far end of the lot. It was covered with six inches of snow, and the registration plates were missing.

"Do you remember who left this car here?" Beaulieu asked attendant Wayne Blanchard.

"Yup, it was some hippie fella," Blanchard recalled. "He went by the name of Costa. I wrote it down on a slip for the rental." Blanchard dug the slip out of a drawer. "It says Antone Costa, seven dollars, which is the monthly rate for the space."

Beaulieu had the Volkswagen towed to the police station and then began knocking on the doors of several rooming houses on North Winooski Avenue. Stella Smith was startled when she saw the uniformed police officer standing on the front porch of her two-story home.

"Ma'am, I'm wondering if you've had a recent tenant named Costa?"

"Yes, as a matter of fact, I have," she replied. "He was a sort of hippie-type young fellow. But he had very nice manners and seemed pleasant enough."

The landlady welcomed Beaulieu inside, where she presented him with a handwritten note that had been left in Costa's room. "He told me that he was leaving, but he also left this letter on his bed."

Dear Mrs. Smith,

I have to return home because of an illness in the family.
I will return as soon as possible. Please hold onto the things in the top drawer for me.

Anthony Costa
Please hold any mail
that comes for me.
Thanks again.

Smith then led the detective up a flight of stairs to Costa's room. The landlady struggled with each step, as her breathing was labored.

"He slept most of the day and only went out at night," she said. "He never had anyone else in his room."

She believed that she had seen him arrive in a car with two girls and possibly a boy in the back seat but soon corrected herself. "Sorry, it must be the medication I'm on. As I recall, he came here alone and he was on foot."

Beaulieu entered the bedroom and began to look around. He found some shirts hanging in the closet along with a duffel bag and a smashed peace sign pendant on a broken chain. The detective inspected the wastepaper basket and pulled out a crumpled note. It was a handwritten bill of sale for the blue Volkswagen.

The detective took the note back to the station for processing. His focus was now on the vehicle. Beaulieu called in Agent John Curran from the local office of the FBI, and together they searched the Volkswagen. In the glove compartment, they found two road maps, a red magic marker, and a book of matches. They lifted the hatch to the trunk, and at first it appeared to be empty except for a snow brush. Agent Curran then pulled up the floor mat and found the license plates hidden underneath. Beaulieu called George Killen and delivered the news.

"I'll send two of my men to Burlington straight away," Killen promised.

Tom Gunnery had made dinner plans with his wife but had to cancel. Instead, he and John Dunn found themselves on the highway headed for Vermont. They visited the Burlington police station on Thursday morning, February 13. Gunnery brought with him photographs of Pat Walsh and Mary Anne Wysocki.

"Costa's landlady said that she saw him with two young women," Beaulieu informed them. "She corrected herself, but you may want to press her again on it. She's a sick old woman. Show her the photos. They may register something. I also spoke with the landlady's neighbor who says two young women had stopped him on the street and asked for directions. This city is only about a hundred miles from Montreal. It wouldn't take much effort for Costa to drive them both across the border to Canada."

Gunnery and Dunn next met with Stella Smith, who had some new information to share.

"I just received a call from Mr. Costa," she told them. "He wants me to put his duffel bag and clothes on a bus to Boston."

He had left behind a corduroy sport coat, a plaid lumber jacket, and zippered dress boots. Gunnery also found an application to register the

Volkswagen with the Vermont Department of Motor Vehicles. He would later learn that Costa had sent a check for thirty-two dollars to the DMV to register the car and to apply for a Vermont driver's license.

Gunnery questioned Stella Smith again about whether she saw Costa in the company of two women. He showed her the photos of Pat and Mary Anne, but the landlady did not recognize them. Gunnery also shared the pictures with the neighbor, but he couldn't place their faces.

The two investigators grabbed Costa's belongings and then returned to the police station, where Dunn sent a teletype to the state police barracks on Cape Cod:

"WILL RETURN FROM BURLINGTON EARLY AM 2-14-69. SHOULD ARRIVE BARRACKS 1600 HRS. 2-15-69. MISSING GIRLS WERE PROBABLY IN BURLINGTON WEEKEND OF 2-8-69 to 2-9-69."

When the message reached George Killen, he hit the roof.

He called Dunn just before they checked out of their motel.

"Those girls are dead!" Killen yelled. "Stop sending information verifying that they're alive. There's only one boss in this fucking office, and that's me! Do nothing. Don't even take a piss unless I give you the go-ahead."

Killen slammed the phone down. Dunn got the message loud and clear. He and Gunnery drove back to the Cape separately, with Gunnery leading the way in Patricia Walsh's light-blue Volkswagen. The trooper fidgeted with the car radio to take his mind off the idea that he wasn't driving a VW Beetle; instead, he was driving a hearse. Like his boss Killen, Trooper Gunnery feared that Pat Walsh and Mary Anne Wysocki were both dead.

It had been six days since the dismembered body parts belonging to a young woman had been pulled from a makeshift grave in Truro, and investigators still had no idea as to the identity of the victim. The macabre story was all anyone on Cape Cod was talking about in waterfront bars, coffee shops, and beauty parlors.

Helen Andrews heard about the gruesome tale from a friend, and her heart nearly sank. She immediately thought of her daughter Susan Perry, whom she hadn't seen or heard from in six months. Andrews was estranged from most of her five kids and had lost custody of them during a bitter divorce from their father, a local fisherman. She called Provincetown police and filed a missing person report and spoke directly to Chief Cheney Marshall.

"Why did you wait so long to report your daughter missing?" he asked.

"I had heard she'd run off to Mexico with some hippie friends," Andrews replied. "The way kids are today, you don't know where they are most of the time."

Tony Costa turned up at the police station again later that morning. No one had asked him to come; instead he had some "urgent information" that he wanted to share with investigators.

He met with Chief Marshall and George Killen, who had basically taken up residence in the small police station.

"I want to talk to you about the missing girls," Costa told them. "I want to help you find them so I can clear my name."

"Look, Tony, as far as I'm concerned, you're in big trouble," Killen warned him. "You are a suspect in the disappearance and probable murder of Pat Walsh and Mary Anne Wysocki and the larceny of their car."

"I won't leave until you hear what I have to say," Costa demanded. "First, I didn't steal the car. I bought it from Pat Walsh and paid her nine hundred dollars so that she could have an abortion. The girls are all hopped up on drugs. They are major users of heroin and hashish."

"We have found absolutely nothing to substantiate that claim. One girl teaches little kids. They're not wild hippies. When did you last see the girls?"

"I last saw Pat and Mary Anne when they drove me back to Provincetown on January 25."

Killen then asked him how Mary Anne's hair dryer and Pat's sweater ended up in his room at 5 Standish Street.

"They were there when I rented it."

"Tony, that's nonsense," Killen said. "Here's what we have so far that connects you to their disappearance. You were the last person to see them alive. You were in possession of Patricia Walsh's car, and their personal belongings were found in your room. If I were you, I'd stop talking to us and start talking to a lawyer, one that can handle a murder case."

Costa walked back to his mother's home on Conant Street, and despite the cold, he was sweating profusely.

We need to stop talking to the pigs, Cory demanded. *We're giving them the rope to hang us with.*

"But we're smarter than they are," Costa insisted. "We've covered our tracks."

You dumb shit. You led them to Vermont. You led them to the car. We need to get rid of everything we have that might connect us to the murders.

Cecilia Bonaviri stood at the front door with her arms folded as her son approached the stone driveway of her home at 9 Conant Street and waved him inside. Built in 1850, the four-bedroom house was outfitted with Cape Cod–style cedar shake shingles. The upstairs had been converted into a one-bedroom apartment, where Cecilia had been living alone for the last ten years. The house was set on a small hill with street views of the ocean. It was a nice place to live, and the owner wanted to keep it that way. The landlady thought of herself as a good Christian woman and did not want any young hippies hanging around her home. Costa had confronted the woman once, tearing off a calendar portrait of Jesus Christ from the kitchen wall of Cecilia's apartment and throwing it down a flight of stairs at her feet.

"There, you goddamned hypocrite," he shouted. "Take a look at that long haired freak. He's the hippie that you trot off to church every morning to worship. Someday soon, he's going to walk up to you and *ZAPPOROO*, it will be all over for you. Just like he changed water into wine, he'll change you into Sisyphus, and you'll be punished forever, forced to roll that rock up a hill. But even that would be too good for you. You'll burn in Hell. You're a fine, righteous woman whose hand Satan is waiting to kiss!"

Costa was banned from the property after the tirade. But the landlady was out of town, and he had nowhere else to go, so Cecilia sneaked him upstairs to her small flat.

"You're in trouble again, aren't you?" she asked while preparing his favorite dish, chicken smothered in spicy tomato sauce, on her small cooktop.

"I am just trying to correct a set of bizarre coincidences," he told her. "It will all be fine, I promise."

But nothing had ever been *fine* for her firstborn son.

Tony Costa was born and raised just north of Boston in the city of Somerville, home to the notorious Winter Hill Gang and battleground for one of the bloodiest mob turf wars in American history, where fifty-seven gangsters were gunned down, stabbed, or ice-picked to death in a three-year period in the early 1960s. Costa had managed to steer clear of the Boston underworld, but he learned to kill at an early age. A curious boy with a high IQ, Costa devoured everything he could read about taxidermy and vanquished small creatures like pigeons, squirrels, and chipmunks from his neighborhood. His prey got bigger as he grew older. When household pets began to disappear, the finger of blame was pointed at young Tony. Neighbors had no definitive proof that their cherished toy poodles and cats were stuffed and hidden under Costa's bed, so they told their children to keep away from the odd boy.

Costa's parents were concerned for their son, especially when he confided to them that he saw ghostly spirits in his room. The boy was convinced that his biological father, Antone Fonesca Costa, a U.S. Navy carpenter's mate who was killed while trying to save a fellow sailor in WWII, regularly visited him in the night. Still, his mother and stepfather, Joseph Bonaviri, saw great promise in their son and allowed him at age thirteen to manage the finances of his stepfather's budding masonry business. They worked to keep the boy focused, but young Tony could not contain his dark urges.

In 1961, when Costa was seventeen years old, he broke into a nearby apartment, dragged a teenage girl named Donna Welch out of her bed, and tied her up. Fortunately, the girl's parents came home and caught Costa in the act. Officers from the Somerville Police Department were called, and Costa was placed in handcuffs. Of course, when the teenager was questioned by police, he offered a much different story.

"I met Donna Welch on Thursday, November 16, 1961, and she gave me a key to her house and told me to come to her bedroom the next night," he claimed at the time. "After I entered the house from the backstairs, I walked up to a bedroom on the second floor and saw a girl on the bed. I was not sure it was Donna. I had a flashlight and flicked it on to make sure it was her. I tapped her on the shoulder and she jumped quickly, her head hitting my elbow. She told me that she was glad to see me, but I felt that I shouldn't have been there and said so. I began to leave and she started to scream. I got scared and ran out of the house."

A Somerville police detective then asked Costa if he had tied the girl up.

"It's a game that we play together," he replied. "On many occasions, I have tied her hands with rope. Then I pull her underpants down just to look at her. She never hollered before."

Investigators did not believe his story, and young Tony Costa was indicted on counts of assault and battery and breaking and entering with the intent to commit a felony. He was brought before Middlesex County Superior Court Judge Charles Fairhurst, who found him guilty on all counts. Costa was sentenced to a year in juvenile detention, but his mother pleaded with the judge for mercy.

"I'll send him away from Somerville," Cecilia told the judge. "My son just needs a fresh start somewhere else. Please give my boy a second chance."

Judge Fairhurst relented and instead imposed a suspended sentence and placed Costa on three years' probation.

Cecilia sent her troubled son to live with a relative named Mary Perkins, who lived at 4 Carver Street in Provincetown, and she enrolled Costa in high school.

Costa's violent actions and bondage fantasies toward Donna Welch and other girls had grown out of his complex relationship with his mother. In the teenager's mind, she should have never remarried following the death of his father, whom he never knew but idolized for his bravery. Costa had to fight for her affection with two unwelcome rivals: his stepfather, followed by Vincent, his younger half brother. Cecilia had been taken away from him; therefore, somebody had to pay.

When Costa entered Provincetown High School, he kept to himself and was considered a strikingly handsome but brooding outsider. The only photo of Costa in his high school yearbook, *The Long Pointer*, is a group picture of the cast of the senior class play *Made to Order Hero*. Costa stood in the middle of the back row with a sly half smile and flattop haircut. He had all the makings of a leading man but chose to serve as a stagehand on the production instead. At night, Costa drove along the narrow streets and up to the towering dunes of Ptown in search of roadkill to take home, stuff, and add to his menagerie of petrified animals.

His frightening behavior put a strain on his mother's marriage, and she soon divorced her husband and moved to Cape Cod to be with her son. Initially, they shared a room at 158 Commercial Street, which had once been the home of abstract painter Fritz Pfeiffer. There, finally, Costa could have her all to himself.

Now, nine years later, her son still felt an unnatural attraction to her. Cecilia had lost her beauty, she wore dark circles under her eyes, her face was lined with wrinkles, and her black hair was streaked with gray. But her son felt safe in her arms, even aroused. He knew that she could not survive another scandal, so Costa made the effort to purge anything that would trigger more suspicion among investigators who were searching for the missing girls. After nightfall, he slipped out of his mother's home and strolled down to the edge of MacMillan Pier. Sitting alone on the dock, he pulled out Maynard's *Manual of Taxidermy* and read the author's inscription one last time. "I trust the present little work may aid others who are entering the fairy land of science, to prepare lasting mementoes gathered by the way."

Costa tore out the page from the book and dropped it into the ocean. He then ripped out page after page, chapter after chapter, and dumped them all into the sea along with the well-worn cover. The tide soon carried away his guidebook for murder, washing away his past sins.

CHAPTER SEVENTEEN

Tom Gunnery felt that Cecilia Bonaviri had something to hide. He had learned from Patricia Morton that Costa's mother had tried in vain to obtain Mary Anne Wysocki's hair dryer from the guesthouse at 5 Standish Street. The trooper had also reviewed the 1961 police report about the incident in Somerville.

"He's a bad seed, and the mother knows it," he told Bernie Flynn and John Dunn. "If we can't get Costa to crack, let's start pulling in the people around him. Who else is this guy close to?"

"I heard that he's got a wife, or had one," said Dunn. "He's got some kids too. He was thrown in the can last year for failing to pay child support."

The estranged wife, twenty-year-old Avis Costa, lived in a shabby upstairs apartment at 364 Commercial Street with their three young children: Peter, Michael, and a daughter they called Nico, which was short for Nicole. Avis was tall but waifish, with bony shoulders and small breasts. She wore her dark hair parted in the middle and down to her shoulders. Avis maintained a crooked smile, but she was considered attractive and alluring to most. She was a child when she first met Costa during his senior year at Provincetown High School. They began having sex when Avis was just thirteen years old. The young girl relinquished her virginity to seventeen-year-old Costa, who taught her everything he knew about sex. They dated for a year and were inseparable. Costa and Avis skinny-dipped at nearby Pilgrim Spring and drank wine together at the town dump. The couple wanted to get married right away, but Avis's mother rightly rejected the idea. After all, the girl was only in the eighth grade. But Avis and Costa had a plan. The following year, as Avis breezed through high honors classes as a high school freshman, Costa got her pregnant. He schooled her on the rhythm method so she could track her menstrual cycle. During ovulation, they had sex before and after Avis finished school, anywhere they could, which was usually in the apartment Costa shared with his mother and younger brother when neither was home. When Avis's mother learned of the pregnancy, she wanted to go straight to the police and charge Costa with raping her daughter. But since there was now an unborn child involved, Avis forced her mother to consent to their marriage. They exchanged vows on April 20, 1963, when the teen bride was four months pregnant with a boy they would later name Peter.

Upon learning the story, Gunnery could hardly believe it, as he had young daughters of his own.

"She was thirteen years old when Costa began having sex with her? What kind of sick individual are we dealing with here?"

The killer kept his composure during his recent visits with Avis and the kids. He tried to play the doting dad, although he barely lifted a finger to help his struggling ex-wife. He never mentioned to her that he was being hounded by the local cops and state police. There was nothing that she could do for him anyway, unlike his mother, who would go to any length to save her son. Cecilia reached out to her brother, Costa's uncle Frank Bent, who was well respected in Provincetown and served as town treasurer and tax collector.

"I know an attorney that may be able to help," Bent told Cecilia. "His name is Maurice Goldman, and he runs a law office down on Bradford Street."

Bent met with Goldman and brought him to a construction site where Costa had just been hired to perform some carpentry and electrical work to help convert garages into new apartments. Costa was paid only three dollars an hour. There was no way he could afford a lawyer, but Goldman owed Bent a favor and offered to have a word with his nephew. The attorney, squat and mole-like, looking ill fit in his suit and tie, listened passively while Costa explained his situation.

"I am being harassed for no reason," he said. "I'm being accused of killing two girls who were friends of mine. We all lived in the same house. I even volunteered to help the police find them."

"Are you sure they're dead?" Goldman asked.

"To my knowledge, they've returned to Providence," Costa lied.

"Well then, you should have nothing to worry about. But please, no more conversations with police for right now. They are not on your side, and you don't have to answer any questions without a lawyer present."

"But, sir, I don't have a lawyer."

"If the police bug you again, just send them my way."

Bernie Flynn had long been a proponent of victimology, the idea of understanding the active personalities of victims and their relationships with others. He always thought it best to start with the person at the center of each case and then create concentric circles around them and examine everyone in their lives in an effort to uncover any abnormalities and potential motives. Although George Killen was convinced that Pat Walsh and Mary Anne Wysocki were dead, Flynn felt he owed it to the missing girls and their families to retrace their steps, so he drove down to Providence and began asking around.

On February 14, he interviewed Russell Norton at Providence police headquarters. Norton told Flynn that he wished he had gone to the Cape with Pat and Mary Anne as they had asked him to.

"I blame myself," Norton said. "I really do."

"Did either Mary Anne or Pat offer any indication to you that they weren't returning home after their trip to Ptown?" Flynn asked.

"No way. They were definitely coming back to Providence. If they were gonna leave home for any reason, Mary Anne would've told me. We are pretty close."

"What about drugs? Do you have any knowledge that the girls may have sold narcotics?"

"You've got to be kidding me," Norton replied. "They're about the straightest girls I know."

"Okay," Flynn said. "I get it. This next question is a bit sensitive. Did Mary Anne or Pat ever confide in you that either of them needed to have an abortion?"

"No way," Norton replied adamantly.

Flynn had to ask the tough, uncomfortable questions. It was part of the job. He thanked Norton for his cooperation and promised to stay in touch with any new developments in the case. He left police headquarters and drove to Parade Street in Providence, near the city's historic armory, where Gerry Magnan was waiting to be interviewed at his mother's house. Mary Anne's boyfriend sat at the kitchen table with a list of handwritten notes to share with the investigator.

"I want to point out a few things to you," he told Flynn. "First, there's no way that Mary Anne would leave town like this. We had just talked about the courses she's selected for her next semester of college. She was super excited. Also, my girlfriend washed her hair every day. There's no way that she'd leave her hair dryer behind. She barely had any money, so to imagine that she's out there somewhere right now on some kind of long vacation is just ridiculous."

Flynn found both Norton and Magnan to be convincing, unlike Tony Costa.

Next, he spoke with Pat Walsh's boss, Ronald Karnes, the principal of the Laurel Hill School.

"We all miss her," Karnes said, choking back tears. "It's been a difficult three weeks. She is well liked by the faculty here and loved by her students."

At that moment, the school bell rang, and the students filed out of their classrooms toward the cafeteria for lunch. Flynn wondered how many of the kids were taught by Pat Walsh and left confused by her long absence. A female teacher also spoke highly of her and told Flynn how proud Pat was to own a new Volkswagen.

"She's still making payments on it through the Teacher's Credit Union," the teacher said. "She loves that car and is always washing and vacuuming it. The Beetle was spotless."

An hour later, Pat's boyfriend, Robert Turbidy, handed the detective the jacket for the Beatles' *White Album* during a tour of Pat's apartment, decorated in bohemian chic, on Prospect Street in Providence.

"Pat loved music. I gave this album to her at Christmas. She also listened to Dylan, Richie Havens, and Jefferson Airplane," Turbidy pointed out to the detective. "She read Steinbeck, but her favorite book is *Summerhill*, which is about a new approach to child rearing and learning."

"Why are you telling me all this?" Flynn asked.

"Because I want you to see her as more than just a *missing person*. She is a *person* who is missing."

"Is she a person who dabbles in drugs?" Flynn pressed.

Surprisingly, the question did not offend the boyfriend. "Look, she smoked grass with me on occasion," he sighed. "But by no means was Pat a 'pothead.'"

Flynn reached into his coat pocket and pulled out a piece of distressed jewelry and dangled it from his fingertips.

"Do you recognize this?" he asked.

"It's a peace sign pendant that I gave to Pat," Turbidy replied. "Where did you find it?"

"A detective seized it as evidence from a boarding house in Burlington, Vermont, close to where we found her car."

"Who rented the room?"

"That I can't tell you yet, but you'll find out soon enough."

"Was it Tony Costa?"

Flynn said nothing, but his dour expression told Turbidy all that he needed to know.

"That fucking guy is responsible for all this," the boyfriend said angrily. "I don't know how or why, but he's responsible."

"It's our job to figure those things out."

"I gotta be honest, Detective. I haven't had much faith in investigators doing their job and finding out what really happened to the girls."

That same day, Bernie Flynn also visited Mary Anne's parents, Walter and Martha Wysocki. The soft-spoken mother described a blue Pan-Am bag that Mary Anne had collected during a trip to Bermuda three years before.

"She brought the bag to Cape Cod," Martha Wysocki mentioned somberly. "It was filled with three pairs of slacks. Mary Anne also took thirty dollars and her hair dryer. My daughter would never leave home without telling us. She cares for people. Mary Anne volunteers for Progress for Providence and teaches inner city children."

Flynn's heart broke for the parents, who looked and sounded completely lost without their daughter.

The detective had three girls of his own from his first marriage and two sons. He could not imagine what he would do if something terrible happened to his own children. Flynn pushed those thoughts toward the back of his mind and powered on.

His meeting with Pat Walsh's parents took a much different tone. Catherine Walsh was combative toward Flynn and his line of questioning from the outset.

"My daughter would never sleep with a man before marriage," the heavy-set mother contended. "And she would never have an abortion. She's a good girl of the highest morals. Why are you here badgering us with outrageous questions when you should be out there looking for my daughter?"

The detective apologized. "We're doing everything we can to find the girls."

Catherine Walsh lifted her large frame from the couch and reached for a photograph of her daughter from the mantelpiece. "I hate the picture of Pat that's running in the newspaper. She looks like some hippie."

She was referring to a photo that Robert Turbidy had given reporters, which showed his girlfriend in a smoldering pose wearing a multicolored, psychedelic dress, black tights, and long, zippered boots.

She handed another photo of her daughter to Flynn. "Use this instead."

He took hold of the framed photo, which had been taken for Walsh's high school yearbook. In that picture, Pat's hair was cut short, her smile was wide, and her eyes were sparkling with hope.

She looks like Mary Poppins, Flynn thought to himself.

While Flynn was adding flesh and bone to the images he had created in his mind about the two missing women, Tom Gunnery kept his focus on the prime suspect in their disappearance. He returned to Tony Costa's vacated room at Patricia Morton's guesthouse and examined the space for anything he or others might have missed. This time, he discovered a rope hidden in the back of the closet. He brought it to the state police barracks in Bourne, on the opposite side of Cape Cod, where state police chemist Melvin Topjian was conducting benzidine tests on the interior of Pat Walsh's VW. The chemist found miniscule traces of blood in several areas inside the car: on the steering wheel, the passenger-side seat belt and door panel, and the back seat.

Gunnery handed over the rope, which stretched out to twenty-three feet across. Topjian conducted a similar forensic test and found the presence of blood along with several brown hairs from an unidentified female.

"The work boots you gave me also had traces of blood on them," the chemist told Gunnery. "These were found on the tops and soles of the shoes."

Topjian also discovered brown human hair and heavy blood stains on the top right shoulder of a fleece-lined, brown corduroy jacket and on the lower left sleeve and cuff of a plaid sports shirt. Both items had been taken from the closet at the boardinghouse where Costa had stayed in Burlington, Vermont.

There was zero doubt among investigators that the young man was responsible for the disappearance and likely the murders of Pat Walsh and Mary Anne Wysocki. The Costa connection could also lead to a major embarrassment for the Provincetown Police Department.

"This guy's been on our payroll," Chief Cheney Marshall reminded Sergeant James Meads and Special Patrolman William "Cobra" Sylvia. "If the press gets wind that one of our drug informants killed these girls, all hell is gonna break loose, and we need to prepare ourselves for that."

"There's no way around it," Meads pointed out. "I wrote a letter asking the judge for leniency when Tony was put behind bars for being a deadbeat to his wife and kids. It's on record."

Sylvia didn't say anything. His clandestine meetings with Costa had always been off the books. "Cobra" was never much for small talk. When Sylvia wore his uniform and tourists asked him for directions, he would fold his arms and tell them he was from "outta town."

"His lawyers will try to use it against us," Marshall added. "I guess we'll have to figure it out when the time comes. But right now, let's do all we can to collar this asshole."

At that moment, Chief Marshall's phone line rang. It was Tony Costa on the other line.

"I demand that you return all the belongings that you took illegally and without a search warrant from my room in Burlington, Vermont. My lawyer will be in touch. You are all in big trouble."

"I don't know a damn thing about your stuff. The district attorney's office probably has that information, so don't try to threaten us," Marshall replied angrily. "Ya know, Tony, one day, we're gonna find those bodies."

"I have no idea what you are talking about," Costa insisted before he hung up the phone.

––––––––––

Truro Police Chief Harold Berrio had a hunch. Investigators were still baffled about the identity of the cut-up body found in the woods on February 8. Berrio searched through his records and came upon a report for a missing girl that had been filed nearly nine months before.

"Sydney Lee Monzon from Eastham," Berrio muttered as he reviewed the report. "She was young and petite, just like the girl we pulled from the ground. It's gotta be her."

Monzon was last seen alive by her sister on May 24, 1968. Berrio located Linda Monzon and introduced her to George Killen.

"Did Sydney ever tell you that she wanted to leave Provincetown, leave Cape Cod?"

"She mentioned it once or twice," Linda told Killen. "She talked about heading out to California and starting a new life out there."

Killen then asked Linda Monzon for details about her last conversation with her sister.

"She was standing on top of a hill beside a car. Sydney was terribly upset and wanted me to go up there and talk to her, but I told her that I was in a hurry, and that I'd catch up with her later," Linda told the investigator. "Sydney then got into the car with someone. He's a local guy named Tony Costa. He's a shady character, real heavy into drugs and everything."

Killen wrote Costa's name down on his notepad and circled it. *Funny how his name keeps coming up*, he thought.

Later, Killen obtained Sydney Monzon's fingerprints. As an elementary school student, Sydney had taken part in a civil defense program where children across Cape Cod were fingerprinted in the event of a natural disaster or nuclear attack. Her fingerprint was compared to the one lifted from the pinky finger of the dead girl's right hand, but it did not match.

Was Sydney Monzon enjoying a new life in sunny California? Or was she still buried somewhere in the North Truro woods? Killen believed that he knew the answer.

On Friday, February 21, Killen led Gunnery, Flynn, and Chief Marshall back to the clearing where the Volkswagen had been spotted before it ended up in Vermont. They fanned out on a two-mile search of the area before meeting up again at the Old Truro Cemetery. Gunnery explored the aboveground crypt but found no evidence of foul play inside. They walked the edges of a nearby pond and also came up with nothing.

"This fucking guy continues to play games with us," Killen said in frustration. "We know Costa murdered those girls, and probably Sydney Monzon too. But with no bodies, we got no crime."

"We have a body," Gunnery reminded him. "If we can ID her and connect her to Costa, he's all done."

"Keep working," Killen told them all.

When Killen returned to the state police barracks in Yarmouth later that afternoon, there was a telegram from the FBI waiting for him on his desk.

"An examination of the bill of sale for the Volkswagen, 1968, Blue, bearing Rhode Island registration #KV-978 which bears the signature of Tony Costa is identical to the handwriting on Costa's identification card," the memo read. "However, the signature of Patricia Walsh was not prepared by Patricia Walsh."

Killen called the FBI field office in Boston and spoke to the special agent in charge.

"So you're telling me that the bill of sale is a forgery?" Killen asked.

The FBI special agent was not willing to go that far. "We're gonna need some additional samples of Walsh's handwriting if we are going to make a positive declaration beyond our report," the agent replied.

Killen had Bernie Flynn contact Pat Walsh's parents, who brought one of her college essays, a seven-page paper titled "Psychological Research Methods," to the state police barracks in Rehoboth, Massachusetts.

Flynn then asked Provincetown police if they had any handwriting samples from Tony Costa. Somewhat reluctantly, Sergeant James Meads turned over a letter Costa had written to him while he was incarcerated at the Barnstable House of Correction for failure to pay child support.

Dear Jim,

I have a special favor to ask of you. I would appreciate it greatly if you would send me, or the parole board, a recommendation for my release on parole as soon as possible. In here, I am only wasting my time, and am of no use to anyone. The state holds the entire burden... I was wrong in not paying the welfare people, I realize it now.

Sincerely, Anthony C. Costa

CHAPTER EIGHTEEN

───────

Tom Gunnery had his hands on both knees, and he was gagging. Close by, Bernie Flynn and Chief Cheney Marshall chuckled at the sight. The investigators were gathered in the backyard of Cecilia Bonaviri's apartment house at 9 Conant Street. They were there following a tip from Bonaviri's landlady, Mary Roderick, who was also Cecilia's distant cousin. Roderick had been struggling to keep up the house since her husband, Arthur, a trap fisherman, was killed two years before when he collapsed while repairing fishing nets on a dory in the middle of the harbor. His body was taken to MacMillian Pier, where Dr. Daniel Hiebert pronounced him dead of a heart attack.

His widow had just gone to the Provincetown police station to complain about problems with her plumbing.

"Tony Costa's mother lives at my place," she told Chief Marshall. "Family or no family, I don't like him sneaking around the house. Now my upstairs toilet is running, and I think he's been trying to flush things down the loo."

The next day, Marshall got a local company to pump the cesspool. Gunnery and Flynn wore rubber gloves and boots and spent an hour sifting through human waste while Cecilia Bonaviri watched with suspicion from her upstairs window.

Massachusetts State Trooper Tom Gunnery, who discovered the bodies and the murder weapons used in the Costa case. © Tom Gunnery.

"This could be something," Gunnery yelled as his gloved hands caught something unusual. He placed it on the grass and cleaned it up with a hose. He nearly fainted due to the noxious smell. It appeared to be a torn piece of a black-and-white photograph. Gunnery found several other pieces close by. Setting the sections close together, he could tell that it was a picture of a young female. The woman had her back toward the camera, and she was nude.

"Could it be Walsh or Wysocki?" asked Gunnery.

"Or what about Sydney Monzon?" Flynn added.

At that angle, it was impossible to tell. They gathered the evidence and placed it into a bag. As Gunnery was leaving the backyard, he caught the mother's eye watching him from her apartment window. The trooper nodded. Cecilia had a vacant expression on her face. She shook her head and closed the blinds.

The following morning, Gunnery and Flynn drove into Hyannis to check out the Samurai Motor Inn on busy Route 132. The name of the motel had been inscribed on a book of matches found in the glove compartment of Pat Walsh's Volkswagen. The investigators were hoping to find out if either Pat Walsh or Mary Anne Wysocki had ever checked in there. The motel was located in the grimy, industrial part of town, far away from its sun-splashed beaches and waterfront restaurants. It was more of a flop house than a motor inn, and tenants rented by the week or by the hour, depending on their vice and choice of company.

"I can't see these girls staying in a shithole like this," Flynn told Gunnery.

The desk clerk opened the registration book and searched for their names.

"I can't find them here," the clerk said. "But most of the names in this ledger are fake anyway. That's the kind of place this is. Look around. You're standing in the lobby of the No Tell Motel."

Flynn showed the clerk the photos of Pat and Mary Anne.

"Nope, I ain't seen 'em. And trust me, I'd remember those two chicks. But they haven't been around this place."

Flynn could only imagine the arrests they could make with a quick raid of the rooms. But he was going to do nothing to jeopardize the search for Pat Walsh and Mary Anne Wysocki.

They returned to Gunnery's car and heard the crackle of the radio dispatcher.

"Suspect Tony Costa is about to board a bus at the Hyannis depot," the dispatcher alerted them.

The bus station was about two miles from the motel, so Gunnery flipped on his lights and siren and circled a roundabout from Route 132 onto Barnstable Road. They caught up with Tony Costa in the parking lot of the bus station. The suspect was carrying a duffel bag and a portable record player. Flynn tapped Costa on the shoulder as he was about to step onto the bus.

"I need a minute," Flynn said, flashing his badge in Costa's face. "Let's have a little chat in the car." He grabbed Costa tightly by the arm and moved him away from the bus.

"I don't want to get into the car," the suspect pleaded.

Costa struggled, but Flynn pushed him along toward Gunnery's state police vehicle.

The lieutenant opened the back door and shoved the young man inside.

"Listen, you son of a bitch. At the very least, I can bust your ass right now for grand larceny of a stolen vehicle. But we both know the real game here, don't we?"

"I bought that car fair and square," Costa countered. "You've got nothing to hold me on."

Flynn nodded at Gunnery, who reached into the back seat for Costa's duffel bag.

"This is bloody outrageous," the young man yelled as he held onto the bag's nylon strap.

Gunnery pulled hard and gained control of the duffel bag and placed it next to him on the front passenger seat.

"This is illegal," Costa continued. "My lawyer is going to hear about this."

"Listen, fucko, you are the prime suspect in the disappearance and likely deaths of Mary Anne Wysocki and Pat Walsh, and who the hell knows who else," Flynn shouted. "I'm not just gonna let you skip town on me. Where are you off to?"

"I'm headed up to Boston. I don't like it in Provincetown anymore. Nobody wants to speak to me, and it's all because I'm getting hassled by the police. My friends think I'm a narc."

"But you are," Flynn reminded him.

As the detective inched closer in the back seat, the butt of his pistol revealed itself from his shoulder holster. Costa's eyes grew wide.

Reach for it, Cory urged. *Let's go out, right here, right now in a blaze of glory. Then ours will be the last body they find. We'll be martyrs. They'll burn all the pig styes to the ground, and kids will chant our name in the streets.*

Costa fought hard to suppress the voice of his alter ego. *I can beat them,* he thought to himself. *I am beating them.*

"Hey, kid, look at me," Flynn demanded. "I lost you for a second. Here's the straight shit. I wish I could buy your lies. I wish the girls went off to Montreal as you said for their parents' sake. But you and I both know what you did to them, and I can't wait till one of us gets the chance to slap the cuffs on you. I hope to God it'll be me!"

"I've told you everything I know about those girls. Are we done here?" Costa asked. "You can't keep me here. I know my rights."

Instead of antagonizing Costa like Flynn was doing, Gunnery figured that he would play along with the suspect, the good cop to Flynn's bad cop.

"Tony, if you hear from the girls, I hope you'll let us know. Their parents are worried sick about them. You can be a big help to the investigation." Gunnery then zipped up the duffel bag and threw it into the back seat. "He's clean."

At that moment, the last bus to Boston rolled out of the terminal.

Flynn and Gunnery smiled.

"Looks like you're not going to Boston after all," Flynn told him.

Undeterred, Costa walked to a nearby restaurant on Main Street in Hyannis and called a cab.

He took a taxi from Cape Cod to Boston and got out at Park Square in front of the Greyhound Bus Terminal. He paid cash for a one-way ticket to Canada, boarded the bus without hassle, and took a front row seat behind the driver. As the bus pulled out of the depot, the killer was already asleep. He arrived in Montreal the next morning and booked a five-dollar room across the street from the bus station. Once inside, Costa kept the room dark. He closed the heavy blinds and turned off the desk lamp. He placed two tablets of LSD on his tongue and let them dissolve before washing the drugs down with a glass of water.

He turned on the black-and-white television and watched an American TV program dubbed in French. Costa twisted the volume to its highest setting and sat down on the edge of the bed, waiting for the hallucinations to take over. He started flipping through the channels in his mind until he came upon a setting he found familiar. There was a tall tree casting shadows over dense woods, and underneath, there was a fresh mound of dirt. Costa's thoughts directed the scene. He knew what was about to happen next. First, he saw Sydney Monzon's arm punch its way out of the ground. The arm was holding Mary Anne Wysocki's severed head. Blood cascaded down Sydney's forearm while gun smoke billowed from the bullet hole in the back of Mary Anne's skull. Soon, another hand crawled like a spider out from the shallow grave. The hand, belonging to Susan Perry, wore a diamond ring on its middle finger. Other body parts followed, including the flayed legs and feet of Patricia Walsh.

The remains regenerated, stacking themselves on top of each other like a Jenga puzzle to form a human body, one body to represent all the women Costa had buried in two shallow graves. Mary Anne Wysocki's maggot-infested jawbone began to move, and out of it came a chorus of screeching voices belonging to the dead.

"Why did you kill us, Tony? We trusted you. Why did you rip us all apart?"

"I have a sickness of the soul," he cried. "It's a neurosis of a generation. I chose you all, not because you are worthless and weak. You are all so very beautiful. I selected each of you because you are strongest in spirit and richest in gifts. I am the wolf of the steppes!"

Costa reached his arm into the television set and touched Susan Perry's ringed hand. With the force of not one but four victims, she yanked him through the TV screen and into the grave with them. Soon, his voice joined their symphony of screams. He locked eyes with Mary Anne Wysocki and watched her dirt-covered face transform into that of his mother, Cecilia. She was young and desirable now, how he had remembered her when he was a child.

"It's my love that you've wanted and could not have," Cecilia whispered. "It's my body that you crave. It's my body that you want to see buried in these graves."

"You should have loved me and no one else," Costa moaned. "Was I not enough for you?"

The killer then blacked out; the hallucination proved too traumatic for him to bear.

The following morning, Costa woke up groggy. The small television set had toppled off its stand, and the power cord was ripped from the wall. He showered quickly, got dressed, and left the room before anyone could inspect the damage.

He visited Toronto and then Niagara Falls, where he lodged on the New York side of the falls at a run-down place called the Villa Nova Motel on Chippewa Street in Buffalo under the name Jonathan Cabot. On this day, he stayed off drugs.

Costa kept his mind alert, only allowing his alter ego to invade his thoughts sparingly.

How long are we gonna play this maddening game? Cory asked.

"Until they stop hassling me," Costa replied.

The pigs will never stop coming. They're hunters, just like us.

The killer hiked the 500-foot crest elevation of the Bridal Veil Falls and stared down over the wooden barrier to the 181-foot drop below. The ferocious sound of the rushing water penetrated Costa's eardrums and drowned out the chatter in his head. His fingers gripped the wooden railing, and he braced himself to jump. It would be so easy to end it all here, without ever having to face his mother, his ex-wife, and their young children over the horrors he had committed. There was still a sliver of humanity in his dark soul. But any desire for mercy was overwhelmed by the constant baying for fresh blood.

He was the predator, not the prey.

After a moment, Costa released his hands from the railing and stepped back. He was breathing heavily.

Today would not mark the end of his journey. Perhaps it was only the beginning.

He returned to the motel and telephoned his brother Vinnie Bonaviri, asking him to wire some money for bus fare back to Boston. Bonaviri obliged Costa's request. Costa arrived at his brother's apartment at 364 Marlborough Street just before midnight. He was grinning when Bonaviri opened the door.

"Good news. I just heard from Mother," Costa told him. "She's received a telegram from the girls, and they are both alive and well in New York City."

CHAPTER NINETEEN

―――――――――

Cecilia Bonaviri burst into the Provincetown police station waving a telegram high over her head and demanding to speak with Chief Cheney Marshall.

"Where is he? I have proof that my son is innocent. Where is he, I say!"

Costa's mother marched into the chief's outer office and passed Marshall's secretary without breaking her stride. She flung open the office door and slapped the telegram on his desk.

"I want you to read this out loud for everyone to hear!"

Chief Marshall adjusted his eyeglasses and picked up the telegram.

"It says, 'What happened? We waited as planned. Is everything alright? Will meet you as scheduled. New York City. Call Chuck first. Love, Pat and Maryann [sic].'" Marshall took off his reading glasses and looked up at Cecilia. "So what does this mean?"

"Well, as you can see, it means that those two girls are in New York and that my boy is innocent!"

The chief urged Costa's mother to go back home while he and his men checked out the veracity of the telegram. Cecilia turned on her heels and walked triumphantly out of the office and through a row of desks where officers were smoking cigarettes and manning phones.

"You'll all be sorry that you harassed my Tony!" she warned as she stormed out of police headquarters.

After the dust settled following Cecilia's dramatic entrance and exit, Marshall gave the telegram to Bernie Flynn.

The detective returned to his temporary desk and dialed the number for Martha Wysocki.

"Has Mary Anne ever mentioned a friend named Chuck to you before?" he asked her.

"Sorry, Detective Flynn, but that name doesn't sound familiar. Do you have any new information about my daughter's disappearance?"

Flynn was careful not to offer any false hope. "Nothing to report yet unfortunately. We're just following up on a random tip from New York City. I'll let you know if it leads anywhere."

The detective asked the same question of Pat Walsh's mother. She did not recognize the name either but added that her daughter had too many friends to account for. Later, Flynn huddled with Dunn and Gunnery in the small interrogation room.

"Do you think it could be true?" Dunn asked. "Is there any chance that the girls could still be alive and hanging out in New York?"

"Nah, I think Costa is trying to send us down another rabbit hole," Gunnery theorized. "I'd be willing to bet that he sent the telegram himself somehow."

Flynn agreed. At that moment, Chief Marshall walked into the room, shaking his head.

"The crafty bastard just called me, collect, from his brother's place in Boston. He asked me if I was satisfied that Walsh and Wysocki were all right. He also said that he planned to meet the girls in New York City as they'd arranged."

"We need to find those bodies quick, for their parents' sake," Gunnery said. "He's just gonna keep fucking with us because he thinks he can. Let's tighten the noose a little more. We need to pull in some of those young hippies who follow the guy like he's the Pied Piper."

The investigators had compiled a list of local teenagers they believed had purchased drugs from Costa. Flynn jotted down a few of the names and took them to Provincetown High School principal George Leydon, a man with an easy smile, thick jowls, and a lazy eye.

"Pull these students out of class pronto!" the detective demanded.

Flynn and Gunnery commandeered the principal's office as Leydon went classroom to classroom with the list of names.

The first student interviewed was Larry Andresen, a thin, pimply, and ponytailed seventeen-year-old who lived with his grandmother just down the hill from the school on Bradford Street.

"Tony's been really nice to me," Andresen told them. "He's nice to all us kids. He likes to rap about philosophy and peace and love. He's quite gentle."

"When did you see him last?" asked Gunnery.

"Just a couple days ago. I bought a camera from him for twenty bucks. He said he needed money because he was skipping town."

"Did he give you a reason?"

Andresen shifted in his chair. "Well, we all know that he's getting hassled by you pigs, I mean cops. I'd probably bail on this place too if I had the chance."

"Anything else? Does he have a girlfriend currently?" asked Flynn.

"Tony hooks up with a lot of chicks. We all call him Sire, because he's like the king of Provincetown. But there's one girl who he's really into. Her name is Marsha Mowery. Just don't tell her where you got that information."

The detectives sent the student back to class and called for Mowery, who was dismissed from a math exam by the principal. When the girl entered the office, Flynn swore to himself that she looked like a slightly younger and more petite version of Pat Walsh. Mowery sat nervously in a chair opposite

Flynn and Gunnery and placed her books down on the table between them. Gunnery took the lead on the interview. His tone was soft and gentle.

"First, I would like to tell you that you are not in any trouble today. Do you understand?"

Mowery nodded.

"I am just going to ask you some questions that may help us in a police matter. Can we begin?"

"Yes, sir."

"How old are you?"

"Seventeen," the girl answered meekly. "I live with my mother at the Waterfront Apartments at 535 Commercial Street. My grandfather owns the building. I'm a junior here at the high school."

"Do you know Tony Costa?"

Her body stiffened at the mere mention of the name.

"I've known him for three years. Yes, I think three years."

Taking over the questioning, Flynn leaned in, almost whispering. "Did you ever go out to the Truro woods with him?"

She paused before answering. "The first time I went out there with him was to go to his drugs, his marijuana plants. We went in his red and white Pontiac."

"Did anything unusual happen?"

Mowery reached for the back of her shoulder and began rubbing, as if to soothe a phantom pain.

"One time when I went out there with him, he had arrows—a bow and two arrows," she said. "He wanted to shoot the arrows off in the woods."

Gunnery scribbled the words *bow and two arrows* in his notepad and circled them.

Flynn continued. "Can you describe where this marijuana patch is?"

Mowery took out her notebook, opened a page, and began to draw. "As you come to the road from the old cemetery, it's just over the hill and into the road a little farther."

She showed Flynn the drawing.

"Is that where the marijuana patch of Costa's is?" he asked again.

"Yes, we picked the plants and were bringing them back to the car. We had walked through the woods and then on the road. Just as we came out of the woods, Tony said that he was going back to shoot the arrows off. I said that I'd meet him back at the car."

Mowery suddenly stopped talking. She reached for her books and held them tightly to her chest and let out two deep breaths. Gunnery handed her a Dixie cup filled with water, and she gulped it down.

"Are you okay to continue?" he asked.

The girl nodded nervously. "I started walking back to the car, I was halfway between him and the car and all of a sudden, an arrow hit me!"

Mowery told the investigators that Costa came running over and asked if she was okay and whether she needed to go to the hospital.

"The arrow hit me in the back. I had a heavy coat on that day so it didn't kill me."

"That coat took some of the force of the arrow?" Gunnery asked.

"Yes, it just felt like a hard blow to the back. That night, when I was getting ready for bed, I noticed a big hole in my back. I had my mother take me to Doctor Hiebert. I thought it was just an accident, but we still had to report it to the Truro police."

"There's a record of this with the Truro police?"

"Yes, sir."

Why the fuck didn't Berrio tell us this when Costa's name was first brought up? Gunnery asked himself. He then asked the teenager to continue with her story.

"Well, the next time I went out there with him, I went with two friends. This time he had a big blue car. My friend Robbie Parnicious found a gun in the glove compartment. She took it out and was looking at it. She commented how it matched her outfit."

"What did the gun look like?"

"It had a black-and-white handle. It was small and pretty."

Flynn jotted this information down and underlined it twice.

"Did you notice the caliber?"

"I would not know that," she answered. "I'm not familiar with guns."

The following morning, Marsha Mowery led Flynn, Tom Gunnery, and Chief Marshall to the area she had described in her drawing. At first, she was reluctant to go, claiming that she did not believe Costa had anything to do with the disappearances of Pat Walsh and Mary Anne Wysocki. But in truth, she was terrified. After all, Costa was still a free man, and she feared that she could be "disappeared" as easily as the others. They drove Mowery and her father to the site, which was close to where Gunnery had discovered the unmarked grave several days earlier. The hole was now filled with water, and a wooden shovel was sticking out of it. The forecast had called for snow, but the temperature crept up a few degrees, and the rain was falling sideways when they stepped out of the police car. Mowery tucked her arm under her father's elbow for comfort as he shielded her with a sturdy black umbrella that he held in his other hand. The teenager trudged through the wet thicket, her eyes darting through the trees to see if Costa was hiding somewhere in the forest, studying her every step. A clap of thunder cracked through the sky overhead, causing Mowery to jump. Her father held her closer, and they continued through the woods with Flynn, Gunnery, and Marshall falling in close behind. About three hundred yards into the damp woods, they came upon a slope that led to a small clearing. It was virgin territory for the investigators, as they had not searched this area previously.

"Tony's marijuana patch was right here," she announced.

The clearing was shaped like a bowl, with the tree line beginning again on its outer edges.

The wind picked up, lifting winter leaves from their slumber, creating a tiny funnel cloud. The investigators pulled their wool hats tightly over their ears and began walking the grid. They hoped to find evidence among the swirling debris but came up empty. The rain was torrential now, making it impossible for the group to continue. Still, Gunnery believed that this little field trip was not a fool's errand. "Something's out here," he muttered to himself. "I can feel it."

Soaked to the bone, they all returned to the squad car where Gunnery fired up the engine and turned on the heater. The teenager's father spoke up from the back seat.

"My daughter has something else to tell you all."

Marsha shot an embarrassed look at her father.

"It's okay. There's nothing to be shy about. Please tell the officers what else you know."

The high school junior braced herself and then began. "I know Tony's wife, or ex-wife, Avis. She told me that he used to do really perverted things to her. The first thing she started to tell me was that she almost died one time. She had taken some sort of medicine, the kind they use to put animals to sleep."

"Was it chloral hydrate crystals?" Gunnery asked.

"Yes, that's it. That's what she took. Tony liked to make love to her when she was unconscious. She also used a plastic bag to knock herself out. He used to tell her that's what he wanted. She told me about all the other things that he did to her and she did to him."

"Such as what?" Flynn inquired.

"He had her beat him with a heavy belt. He also had a hook hanging from the bedroom ceiling. He used to hang himself by his feet from the hook and they had sexual relationships that way. Most of the time though, he would hang her from the hook."

The investigators tried to digest the teenager's twisted story on the ride back to Provincetown.

"He's a real Jekyll and Hyde," Gunnery told Flynn and Marshall when they returned to the station. "How could someone be so charming and yet so depraved?"

"Remember where you are, Trooper," Chief Marshall reminded him. "This is Provincetown. Residents let their freak flag fly around here. If we investigated everyone's sexual predilections around town, Lord knows what else we'd find."

The teletype machine began clicking and clacking as it spit out a bulletin from the state police barracks in Rehoboth, Massachusetts, close to the Rhode Island border.

"TWO MEN TO BE ARRAIGNED IN NEWPORT R.I. DIST. COURT ON MONDAY AND BOTH ARE CHARGED WITH CUTTING UP A GIRL IN ROGER WILLIAMS PARK IN PROVIDENCE R.I. AND PUTTING PARTS OF HER BODY IN PLASTIC BAGS AND BURYING SAME IN PARK."

Marshall nodded to Flynn, who grabbed his coat and flew out the door.

Jesus Christ, if the girl turns out to be either Pat or Mary Anne, that means Costa's been telling us the truth this whole time, Flynn told himself. *No matter how fucking crazy his alibi sounds.*

Later that day, the detective learned the truth about the latest case, which left him feeling both relieved and sickened. The body belonged to neither Mary Anne Wysocki nor Pat Walsh. This told him two things: one, that there were other men out there depraved enough to mutilate young women, and two, that the bodies of the missing Providence girls were likely buried in the Cape Cod woods and that their killer was still roaming free.

The following day, March 4, 1969, the weather cleared and the search resumed in the spot identified by Marsha Mowery. Ray Kimpel joined the search party. He was a long way from home, but the Milwaukee, Wisconsin, native knew the Truro woods better than anybody. He had spent the last two years serving as a National Park Service ranger for the expansive sixty-mile stretch of sand dunes and dense forest that made up the Cape Cod

National Seashore. Kimpel lived in Truro with his wife, Emilie, and their two kids, and he had spent hundreds of hours patrolling the wooded area off Cemetery Road. Ranger Kimpel joined Flynn, Gunnery, Killen, and Marshall in their inspection of the area. As they were preparing to hike into the woods, Kimpel came across a quart-sized plastic jug in the bushes where he had parked his car. The jug had some soil on the outside of it. Kimpel picked it up and handed it to Killen, who placed it on the hood of his car. The investigators then lined up in formation and followed the overgrown trail with a hunting dog named Cookie leading them.

"If there's anything to be found out here, my Cookie will sniff it out," the dog's handler, State Trooper William Waterhouse, said proudly.

But the dog seemed as anxious as a new puppy and found a new tree to urinate on every five yards.

"Don't stand still," Flynn joked to Gunnery. "If you do, that fucking dog will piss down your leg."

Cookie's nose was as useless as its bladder. The dog raced up the trail and beyond an important piece of evidence sticking out of the snow. Fortunately for investigators, the hound tripped over it and tumbled into some nearby bushes. The dog yelped, and that got Kimpel's attention. The park ranger bent down and scraped aside some leaves to find a shallow hole about five inches in diameter. He reached his gloved hand into the hole and pulled out a brown suede handbag that was covered by mud and clay. The bag had a twisted leather strap and lacing on the sides. Kimpel unzipped the pouch and saw that it contained several identification cards. He handed it over to George Killen, who inspected the contents. He pulled out Pat Walsh's Rhode Island driver's license, her social security card numbered 036-30-1433, a 1966–1967 Rhode Island College student ID card, a membership card for Local 958 Providence Teachers Union—AFL-CIO, and a ticket stub for a screening of *Bonnie and Clyde* dated December 26, 1968. The bag also contained a change purse with sixty-five cents and four one-dollar bills, along with several makeup products, including a tube of Maybelline "Velvet Black" mascara.

After combing the dense forest for another hour and finding nothing, Killen brought Pat Walsh's handbag back to the parking area. The investigators were satisfied, as it was a critical piece of evidence to suggest that her body was probably buried someplace close by. Before returning to his vehicle, Ranger Kimpel spotted some discoloration at the base of a tree in the parking area. It looked to be a mound of clay and sand, which did not belong there atop the crusted leaves. Kimpel walked about thirty feet to the tree and peeked down inside another shallow hole, which contained another handbag; this one was brown leather with the texture of alligator skin. Inside the handbag were two Juicy Fruit gum wrappers and an identification card that had been ripped in half. Kimpel placed the torn halves together and saw the face of Mary Anne Wysocki smiling back at him. Next, he found her birth certificate, a bus schedule, a Providence library card, and a note listing her mother Martha Wysocki as her emergency contact in case of "an accident or serious illness."

Kimpel dug further and pulled out a receipt that read "$24.00-Fri. & Sat. 5 Standish Street, Guest House, Charming *Clean*Comfortable Rooms, Center of Provincetown, Mass. MRS. PATRICIA MORTON, Phone 487–1319."

CHAPTER TWENTY

The killer needed inspiration. Tony Costa did not travel down to New York City as he had promised Chief Cheney Marshall. Instead, he was hiding out with his half brother, Vincent Bonaviri, and his girlfriend at their apartment on Marlborough Street in Boston. Costa had spent the past several days getting high and eating stale pizza while watching TV on his brother's secondhand couch. Cecilia Bonaviri called the apartment to report that Marsha Mowery was seen riding in a police car headed out of town.

We should have killed her when we had the chance, Cory told him. *Had she not turned around so quickly, that arrow would have gone straight through her back. And what did you do, you little bitch? You rushed to her aid instead of feeding the bow with your last arrow and finishing her off.*

This time, Costa did not argue with his alter ego. He knew Cory was right. He had allowed the teenager to lead the pigs to the place where he had created his masterpiece: the dissection of four beautiful human specimens.

Costa felt wolflike once again. He was hungry for human flesh, and that hunger needed to be satiated. The killer left the dark apartment and stepped out into the sunlight. The first day of spring was just two weeks away, and the piles of snow stacked up on city streets were slowly giving way to the thaw. Costa walked a full block before taking a left onto Exeter Street toward

Copley Square. He soon found himself on the steps of the Boston Public Library. An architectural homage to Paris's Bibliothèque Sainte-Geneviève, the library's facade was decorated with large, resplendent arcade windows flanking a set of massive bronze doors. Costa stepped inside, and it was as if he had been transported back to the Victorian age. He wondered whether Jack the Ripper had ever ventured away from his killing fields in the streets of Whitechapel to enjoy the grandeur of the National Gallery. As he walked under John Singer Sargent's mural cycle, *Triumph of Religion*, his focus shifted from art and architecture to the beautiful bodies that passed within inches of his grasp. It seemed that everywhere he looked, there were pretty young women all around him. He smiled at the steady stream of girls from nearby colleges who were there to take advantage of the thousands of books that were available to them for free with a library card.

Costa asked the librarian where he could find the collected works of Hermann Hesse and was then directed to a row of towering book stacks nearby. Someone had checked out the library's only copy of *Steppenwolf*, so he thumbed through *Siddhartha* and *Journey to the East* before settling on the 1930 Hesse novel *Death of a Lover*. He pulled the hardcover off the shelf and carried it into Bates Hall, the basilica-like reading room, where he settled into a wooden chair under a green reading lamp. Costa opened the cover and let Hesse's words wash over him. Costa was unfamiliar with this particular work and was stunned at how similar the narrative was to his own unfolding life story. It was as if Hesse had dipped his pen into the future to preordain every abnormal trait in Costa's behavior through *Steppenwolf* and now *Death of a Lover*. In this story, the killer's life mirrored that of Goldmund, a handsome "seeker" in medieval Germany, who was separated from his mother and forced into a monastery because of her life of sin. Like Costa, Goldmund sexualized his mother in his dreams, making all other intimate contact with women a cruel exercise, full of lust and bloodthirstiness. But there was also redemption in the novel, as Goldmund fights off a rapist who has bitten Helene, Goldmund's lover. It was the same battle waged in Costa's fragile mind against Cory, his murderous alter ego. As the killer read on, he reached a moment in the novel when Goldmund is threatened with the gallows.

Imprisoned in a wine cellar, bound at the wrists, and awaiting his final confession, Hesse's protagonist envisions his mother and expresses the love they could not share. "In parting, all of life's beautiful confusion shone once more," Hesse wrote. "From the misery of his heart, a sigh, an imploring complaint rose: 'Oh mother, oh mother!'"

Costa recited the words out loud and wept softly in the chair. He closed the book, not wanting to learn of Goldmund's ultimate fate, fearing that it could foreshadow his own.

He gained his composure before returning the novel to the shelf.

The killer exited the library and walked north on Boylston Street and across the Boston Public Garden and the Boston Common until he found himself in the heart of the Combat Zone, the city's red-light district, where streetwalkers plied their trade in the open and flashing neon signs lured desperate men into dark, cavernous places like the Naked i Theater and the Pussycat Lounge. He paid a quarter and caught a screening of the porn film *Lucretia Enjoy Nude* at the Pilgrim Theater, which offered "stark realism" for adults only. Costa sat in the back row behind a sprinkling of young and old men; seated either far apart from each other or dangerously close. Costa could hear the faint sound of pants unzipping, and he did the same while watching a group of attractive young women and men engaging in a wide range of sexual acts as they frolicked through the forest. The setting reminded him of the North Truro woods. He closed his eyes and masturbated while remembering the look in the eyes of Sydney, Susan, Pat, and Mary Anne at the exact moments of their deaths. Costa moaned loudly as he ejaculated over his knuckles before wiping his wet hand on top of the seat in front of him. He left the theater satisfied but still wanting more. After applying for a counter position at a liquor store next to the theater on Washington Street, he walked another two miles to Massachusetts General Hospital. He entered the lobby through a set of glass doors and scanned a listing of job postings on the wall opposite a set of elevators. The bulletin also included directions to the employment office, so Costa memorized them and then took the elevator to the second floor. He walked confidently into the office and asked to speak to the job recruiter, who turned out to be an attractive blond in her late thirties.

"I'm interested in a career in medicine," Costa told her. "I'd like to apply for a laboratory position. I'm not squeamish. I've worked with bodies and organs before."

"Where are you studying currently?" the recruiter asked.

"I'm saving money for medical school," he smiled. "But it's truly my passion."

"Do you have a résumé and references?"

"I need to gain experience for that, which is why I am here."

The recruiter frowned. She would have ended the interview right there, but there was something very interesting about the young man. He exuded grace, charm, and unbounded confidence.

"I would love to help you, Mr. Costa, but without a résumé, the best we can do right now is to get you a job in the kitchen as a helper, but unfortunately those positions are all filled right now. But I'd be happy to keep your name on file."

"That's very kind of you. Thank you."

"In the meantime, you may want to check out some of the other hospitals in the city. We have a lot of them, you know," she reminded him.

Costa shook the recruiter's hand and let the gesture linger a bit. She beamed and allowed her fingers to touch his for a moment longer before slowly pulling away.

The killer was aroused again. He left the job office and began searching for relief. The hospital barely had any security and staff members; patients and visitors moved about the large facility as freely as they pleased. Mass General was also teeming with medical students working on rotation in various departments. Costa swiped a white lab coat from the locker room and fell in with a group of interns making their way to the pathology department. He was in luck; the students were crowding themselves into a conference room to observe an autopsy. The killer stood with seven others, who were roughly his age, in front of a large viewing window that overlooked an L-shaped dissecting table. No one questioned whether he belonged. Costa pulled a small notebook from the pocket of his lab coat along with a Bic pen as the students did the same. The pathologist, short and rotund, turned toward the window to address the class.

"We perform three hundred and fifty autopsies each year," he said. "This equates to about thirteen percent of all hospital deaths. We are also called to perform autopsies for Cambridge Hospital and several community hospitals. Today, we will work on the body that was brought to us as a drug-related fatality. We shall see if that is truly the case here."

The pathologist pulled the sheet back to reveal the specimen.

She is perfection, Costa thought to himself. The body was that of a twenty-two-year-old Black female with close-cropped hair, long legs, and a flat torso. There were no visible scars on her body, and a casual observer might think she was only sleeping. The pathologist took his scalpel and made a Y-shaped incision in the woman's chest, with the two arms of the Y running from each shoulder joint, curving the blade around under the breasts to meet at the midsection. Because the body was cold, there was very little blood.

Costa's palms grew sweaty and his mouth watered. He could almost smell her through the glass. He hungered to be inside her, to devour her. He was an apex predator. He was the wolf of the steppes. "The next step is to examine the organs *in situ*, which of course is Latin for *in place*," the pathologist explained as he traded his scalpel for a rib cutter. He then cut the boundary between the ribs and the cartilage connected to the breastbone. The pathologist then removed the chest plate, freeing the intestines.

With her skin peeled back, the woman's naked body was completely open. The killer leaned closer to the glass, and his mind drifted back to the North Truro woods.

Tom Gunnery stabbed at a chunk of steak, ran it through the yellow ooze of an egg yolk, popped it into his mouth, and chewed. He had woken up on the morning of March 5 with a strong belief that the missing girls would be found that day. He kept this thought to himself and didn't mention it to his wife, Jane, as she served him up an oversize plate of steak and eggs. Gunnery wolfed the food down quickly while standing at the kitchen counter and sipped his cup of steaming hot coffee carefully so as not to burn the roof of his mouth. He had dressed for the weather, wearing a pair of thermal underwear beneath his dark trousers.

After breakfast, Gunnery drove directly from his tidy split-level house in the village of Centerville straight to the wooded area in North Truro without stopping first at the state police barracks in Yarmouth. He rendezvoused with Flynn, Killen, Marshall, and Ranger Ray Kimpel just after 9:00 a.m. They followed Marsha Mowery's directions once again, marching through the forest until they arrived at the small, bowl-shaped valley. The investigators fanned out, with Gunnery inspecting the tree line. Nothing appeared to be out of the ordinary until he spotted the cracked limb of a large pine tree on the far edge of the clearing. The branch was still connected to the tall tree, but just barely. The damage did not appear to have been caused by wind. Gunnery took a closer look and discovered pieces of rope wrapped around the limb. The fibers were stained with a dark substance. At the base of the tree, he also spotted a plastic tablet container, a glass vial, and a razor blade.

Gunnery began kicking up the snow and dirt around the perimeter of the pine tree. Soon, he noticed a tiny object shining through a layer of frozen crust. It was a gold earring attached to a black onyx.

"Here we go," he whispered to himself.

He expanded his view around the earring and noticed traces of a recently dug hole. Gunnery then raised his hand and yelled to the others, "I need a shovel over here!"

Flynn rushed over and handed him a pointed-edge digger shovel. Gunnery wrapped his gloved hands around the shovel and drove it into the frozen ground. The earth refused to yield, so the trooper placed his boot on the back of the shovel and pressed his weight against the handle with enough force that the blade broke through the crust. The investigators huddled around Gunnery as he continued to dig, often hitting the roots of the towering pine. After creating a hole more than three feet deep, Gunnery threw the shovel aside and started scooping the dirt with his hands. His heart was pounding. "There's something else down there," he shouted.

Something stabbed him through his gloved hand, and he drew his arm back instinctively. He looked closer and saw that it was the sharp edge of a turquoise ring attached to a human hand. Flynn jumped into the hole with Gunnery. He reached deeper inside the hole and found a clump of soiled brown hair. Flynn tried to lift it, but the strands of hair peeled easily away from the scalp. He knew that he had found a human head. As he looked closer, he realized that it had been cut off at the jawline. Using both hands, the detective cradled the severed skull and brought it to the surface. He brushed the grime away from the eyes and mouth. He recognized the face immediately from the photographs that he had been carrying in his pocket. It belonged to Mary Anne Wysocki.

George Killen took out his pistol and fired a shot in the air to alert other members of the search party. The men rushed to the sound of gunfire and then stood silently watching while Flynn and Gunnery continued to work.

Gunnery grabbed the shovel again and dug around the outline of Mary Anne Wysocki's body. He pulled her headless torso from the shallow grave. Her skin was peeled back, and her chest was wide open. Each one of the hardened police officers stood in utter shock around the makeshift grave site.

"Dear God in Heaven," Gunnery said aloud. "This is as bad as it gets."

"There's no God here, Trooper," Chief Marshall added. "Only the Devil."

Next to the torso, Gunnery found a cut-up pair of knee boots along with twenty feet of bloodstained rope.

Ray Kimpel's attention was then drawn to a sandy area about two hundred feet away from Mary Anne Wysocki's grave.

"Check over here!" he called to the others.

Gunnery and Flynn lifted themselves out of the hole and raced over to Kimpel's position. Covered in dirt, Gunnery worked the shovel, penetrating two feet of frozen earth. The sharp edge of the shovel then grazed something soft. The trooper pulled the tool back, allowing Flynn to reach in with his hands. It was another set of human remains. This time, the body parts were stacked one on top of the other. He pulled out the lower portion first, followed by the legs, which had deep slash marks from the upper thighs to the toes. The upper part of the body came next; this time, the head was attached. Lying under the upper body was a severed pelvis, hacked and dislocated at the bikini lines. Folded between the cuts of flesh were a white cable-knit sweater drenched in blood, a pair of slacks, and a pair of bell-bottom jeans. Flynn collected the clothing from the hole. Gunnery handed him a faded army jacket with the name *Turbidy* printed on the inside label, along with another piece of rope.

There was no question that the dismembered remains belonged to Pat Walsh.

"Is that it?" George Killen asked as he bent over the ditch.

"Not sure," Gunnery replied. "There's something else, and it stinks to high heaven."

He and Flynn kept digging until, under another two feet of dirt, they found the source of the terrible stench. It was another body; this one was in heavy decay. The face was black and unrecognizable. The body parts, severed like the others, had given themselves to the earth and were in a grotesque, advanced stage of decomposition. The investigators surmised that they had found Sydney Monzon, who had gone missing nearly a year before.

At last, the killer's full masterpiece was unveiled for the world to see.

While Gunnery and Flynn remained at the crime scene, George Killen and Chief Marshall drove to the police station in Provincetown, where they telephoned the state police barracks at 1010 Commonwealth Avenue in Boston. Killen spoke to Detective Lieutenant Richard Cass and ordered him to arrest Tony Costa.

"We believe he's staying in an apartment on Beacon Street," Killen told Cass. "Round up your best boys and go grab the son of a bitch!"

CHAPTER TWENTY-ONE

With the information provided by George Killen, state police dispatched detectives William White and James DeFuria to 415 Beacon Street but were told that Costa's brother, Vincent Bonaviri, no longer lived there. A tenant informed the investigators that Bonaviri worked at Macy's Liquors on Canal Street near the Boston Garden. Next, the pair drove to the liquor store and questioned the brother about Costa's whereabouts.

"Tony's back in Provincetown," Bonaviri told them. "I haven't seen him in about ten days."

William White, the older cop, asked him to write down his new address and phone number, should they need to get back in touch.

"I can call my mother in Ptown," Bonaviri offered. "Maybe she knows where he is."

"No worries. We just have a few routine questions for him. If you hear from Tony, have him give us a call," White said leisurely.

Not believing Bonaviri's story, they hurried over to the brother's new address at 364 Marlborough Street.

Costa had showered and shaved and was enjoying a heavy pipe full of marijuana along with two tablets of acid. While smoking, he gazed out the large bay window of his brother's apartment down onto the street below. He saw an unmarked car pull up to the curb. Two men in trench coats got out of the vehicle and flew up the front steps.

Costa then heard the loud sound of the buzzer.

"What the fuck should we do?" he asked his alter ego.

You've been playing them, and now they're about to play you! Cory replied.

The killer ran around the apartment, looking for a potential escape route. The window leading to the fire escape was sealed shut. He thought about smashing the glass, but he looked down at the alleyway and saw one of the trench-coated cops, the young one, waiting for him there. It was time for one last act of deception.

Costa opened the front door and walked casually down the flight of stairs where he met Detective White as he approached the second landing.

"Is this Costa's apartment?" White asked.

"No, this is the hallway," he replied.

"What's your name, kid?"

"I'm Vincent Bonaviri. I live here."

The cop stared back. He was smiling. "Funny, we just talked to Vinnie down at the liquor store. You're a fucking liar!" The detective turned him around and slammed him against the wall. "I'll ask again. What's your fucking name?"

"Antone Costa. Antone Charles Costa."

"Well, Mr. Costa, you're under arrest for larceny of an automobile, a Volkswagen."

White wrapped a pair of handcuffs tightly around the killer's wrists and led him downstairs.

"What am I being charged with again?"

"Larceny of an auto, a stolen car," White repeated. "Police from Cape Cod are on their way here to pick you up. We'll take you down to the station and book you first."

So they have us for Walsh's Volkswagen, that's it! the alter ego told Costa. *We*

*need to play it cool right now. Let's just be
sure to keep our fucking mouth shut!*

When they got to the street, Costa's
pipe fell out of his pocket and smashed
on the sidewalk.

Detective DeFuria leaned down to
pick up the broken tube but was pulled
back by his partner.

"Leave it there," White advised.
"It's of no use to him now."

He was right. The marijuana had
already taken its effect on Costa, and the

*Costa is flanked by Massachusetts State
Police Detective Bernie Flynn shortly after
the killer's arrest in 1969.*
© *IMGN.*

two hits of acid were beginning to blur his mind. He was shoved into the
back seat of the unmarked police car for the ten-minute ride to the state police
barracks. The detectives drove in silence, but Costa heard several voices, female
voices, shouting angrily at him as the LSD took hold. They were the voices
of the dead. He rocked his head back and forth and let out a terrifying howl.

"Maybe we should take him to the hospital," DeFuria suggested. "Looks
like he's having a seizure."

"Nah, he's just hopped up on something," White replied. "If he grabs at
you, just crack him one!"

At the barracks, the detectives took Costa under each arm and whisked
him into the station and up to the third floor, where he was photographed
and fingerprinted.

Detective Lieutenant Richard Cass called Killen and told him that
Costa was in custody. "We expended a lot of resources here to hunt down
your stolen car suspect. What gives?"

"The man you're holding is now the suspect in at least two murders,"
Killen replied. "I've written up the warrants and will have my men serve
them at the barracks."

"Lemme get this straight. We bring this guy in on a bullshit stolen vehicle warrant, and you guys get all the glory for the murder charge?"

"My men have earned that collar!" Killen shouted.

Killen handed the warrants to Tom Gunnery and Bernie Flynn and ordered them to Boston. "Knowing Cass, he'll call every fucking reporter he knows," Killen told them. "If the cameras are there, I want you both front and center surrounding Costa. This is our case. This is our arrest."

Gunnery and Flynn arrived at the barracks two hours later, and the lobby was teaming with reporters. They pushed their way through the horde of media and crammed into the small elevator with Cass and another state police official. When they reached the third floor, Gunnery and Flynn were led to the interrogation room where Costa was seated and handcuffed to a desk. Flynn reached into his coat and pulled out four pieces of paper and waved them in his face.

"We have four warrants here," Flynn told him. "Each one is a murder charge, a first degree murder charge."

"Well, there's that then," Costa shrugged.

"Tony, did you kill those women?" Gunnery asked. "Did you murder Sydney Monzon, Pat Walsh, and Mary Anne Wysocki?"

The room grew silent as the names of the victims hung in the air.

"Did you kill Susan Perry?" Flynn asked. "We believe that she's the other girl who was buried in the Truro woods."

When Costa finally spoke, he was defiant. "I don't have to answer to either of you. A higher power than man has made that decision for me, and if you think either he or I will play your silly games, you are wrong. If you think you can prove that I committed these horrible crimes, then take me to court and prove it. I've got nothing else to say."

"We found the bodies today, just a few hours ago," Flynn informed him.

"What does that have to do with me?" Costa asked.

"You are under arrest for murder."

Costa demanded his one phone call. Flynn slammed the telephone down in front of him.

The killer called attorney Maurice Goldman but could not reach him. He called his half brother instead.

"Vinnie, I'm under arrest for the murders of the girls," he said without emotion. "Get Goldman and tell him to be ready."

After the call ended, Gunnery stood the suspect up while Flynn searched his coat pockets. In Costa's wallet, he found a classified ad for a liquor store position, a receipt for a personal money order from Burlington Savings Bank to the Vermont Department of Motor Vehicles, and a neatly folded article clipped from the New York *Daily News* with the headline "CHRISTINE'S TRIP TO THE MORGUE: WHAT A WASTE AT 19." Written underneath was the New York City telephone number for Christine Gallant.

Gunnery and Flynn then led the shackled suspect off the elevator onto the first floor as the sound of flashbulbs crackled through the lobby. Bernie Flynn stopped to address reporters.

"Antone Costa is a suspect in a double murder involving two girls missing from Providence, Rhode Island, since January 25," he said. "We have no more information at this time."

The killer made no attempt to cover his face. He seemed to enjoy the attention.

Costa's cuffed hands were attached to a restraining belt tied to his waist. He moved slowly toward the front door of the barracks, trying to take the moment in. Gunnery squeezed his triceps and ushered him out the door to the parking area where a convoy of police vehicles waited with their lights flashing. The killer smiled as he was placed in the back seat of the second cruiser.

"This is quite a spectacle," Costa said aloud. "I wonder what reception I'll get when I return home to Cape Cod?"

Gunnery got behind the wheel, slid the key into the ignition, and began the long drive back to Helltown. When Bernie Flynn returned to his home in Falmouth that night, his wife, Jacqui, was waiting for him.

She had watched the impromptu press conference on the evening news. Jacqui met him at the front door with her arms wide open. The detective pulled back from the front step. Flynn was trembling as tears formed in the corners of his eyes.

"Don't hug me," he warned her. "I smell like death."

———————

The bodies of Sydney Monzon, Mary Anne Wysocki, and Pat Walsh were brought to Nickerson Funeral Home in Provincetown where their limbs were reassembled on an examination table. Dr. Dan Hiebert and the pathologist, Dr. George Katsas, carefully placed Mary Anne Wysocki's severed head atop her upper extremities before recording six initial findings.

1. Mutilation of the body in five distinct portions.
2. Postmortem degeneration.
3. Gunshot wounds to the right occipital and left temporal area of the head.
4. Incised wounds of lower extremities, right chest wall, and right inguinal area.
5. Incised wounds of anterior chest with peeling off of the skin.
6. Presence of spermatozoa in vagina and rectum.

Upon further inspection, they discovered an extensive hemorrhage beneath the gunshot wound in the undersurface of the twenty-three-year-old victim's scalp where two bullet fragments were found. The second bullet had entered Mary Anne's skull on the left side of her head, slightly behind the left ear. The bullet's trajectory traveled through the base of her brain from the left entrance wound and embedded itself in the right petrous bone.

Dr. Katsas removed the bullet and placed it on a metal tray beside the body. Attached to Mary Anne's head were the first four cervical vertebrae. Her chest showed a long, vertical wound, three inches deep, from the jugular notch of the sternum to its lower end. The skin had been peeled off with five incised wounds penetrating the soft tissues.

"The victim's pelvis was sharply cut along edges corresponding to the outline of panties," Hiebert and Katsas observed in their report. "The vagina contains a small amount of whitish, viscid material. Spermatozoa are found in large numbers in the rectal smears and in small numbers in the vaginal smears."

At this point, the medical examiners had not determined whether Mary Anne was raped before she was murdered or whether her killer had desecrated her body after her death. Her legs were cut off at the hip joints, and they showed deep cuts along her calves and feet. It looked as if the woman had been attacked by a great white shark.

"This woman wasn't just murdered," observed Katsas. "She was mauled."

The autopsy of Pat Walsh came next. The initial findings were as follows:

1. Mutilation of the body in two distinct portions.
2. Gunshot wound to the back of the neck: with laceration of the left carotid artery and bullet in left cheek.
3. Presence of spermatozoa in vagina and rectum.
4. Incised wounds of buttocks and lower extremities.
5. Incised wounds of anterior chest and abdomen with peeling off of the skin.

Like Mary Anne, Pat Walsh's body parts were covered in sand and gravel. Dr. Hiebert spent several minutes cleaning the remains before the examination could truly begin. George Katsas recorded that Pat Walsh's left cheek was swollen and bluish with a massive hemorrhage caused by a bullet that was lodged in the left side of her jaw. Once again, the projectile was extracted and set aside for investigators. The killer had also carved a deep wound from the jugular notch of her sternum to the pubic area. Pat's skin was peeled back at her breasts. There were several other cuts to her chest, which suggested a frenzied attack. Katsas made note of a beaded ring worn by the victim that was still present on her right ring finger.

As gruesome as the top half of Pat Walsh's flayed body was, it could not compare to the butchering of her severed lower half. Katsas recorded a gruesome collection of seven-inch cuts on the buttocks and the backs of her legs. The killer had used a sharp instrument to penetrate the victim's underlying muscles at different angles, zigzagging across the backs of her thighs and cutting vertically down her calves. There was also a deep wound to her rectum.

"Spermatozoa are found in the vaginal smears and in small numbers in the rectal smears," Dr. Katsas and Dr. Hiebert noted in their official report.

The autopsies of Mary Anne Wysocki and Pat Walsh had taken several hours to perform, and the work was not done yet. Katsas and Hiebert finally turned their attention to the decayed remains of Sydney Monzon. As with the other autopsies, the forensic examiners took photos and X-rays of the victim's body parts. A fingerprint was also taken, which would ultimately match the remains to the nineteen-year-old Eastham girl. Sydney's body was cut into four pieces, and her right leg was chopped off and missing. Her left leg had also been amputated at the femoral shaft, and her kidneys were gone. Because of the advanced postmortem degeneration of the body parts, Dr. Katsas found it nearly impossible to perform a pathological evaluation. Sydney had been buried for ten long months in the North Truro woods. Most of the soft tissues of her left hand were destroyed, and the existing bones were kept together by only the remnants of tendons. "The lungs are markedly decomposed and contain many cystic spaces filled with gas," Katsas and Hiebert noted in their report.

CHAPTER TWENTY-TWO

With the arrest of Tony Costa, Bristol County district attorney Edmund Dinis smelled an opportunity. After failing three times in his bid to become mayor of New Bedford and getting trounced in a run for Congress, the Azores-born lawman believed that his political ship had finally arrived. Dinis had watched as the state's African American attorney general Ed Brooke manipulated the media covering the Boston Strangler case to catapult himself into an open seat in the U.S. Senate three years before. Now, with any luck, the serial killer from Cape Cod would help the forty-four-year-old Dinis resurrect his stagnant legislative career. He decided that Costa would be held at the state police barracks in Yarmouth and not at the police station in Provincetown, as it did not have enough parking for reporters and news photographers. Dinis drove from his office in New Bedford to Cape Cod, where he was met by George Killen and Bernie Flynn.

Both Flynn and Gunnery had sifted through a Pan-Am flight bag that was seized from Vincent Bonaviri's apartment on Marlborough Street. Inside the bag, they found a blues harmonica, several handwritten pages of vocabulary drills, torn-out pages of a Webster's dictionary, which described the most common synonyms and antonyms, a paperback copy of Maharishi Mahesh Yogi's *The Science of Being and Art of Living*, a scuba certificate indicating that Costa had completed an underwater diving course, more than a dozen photographs of Christine Gallant, and an application for the Northwestern School of Taxidermy and J. W. Elwood Supply Company in Omaha, Nebraska.

"Where is he?" Dinis asked in a deep baritone voice as he entered the barracks. "I want to see the suspect. I want to look in his eyes."

Flynn guided him to a holding cell where Costa was sitting on a steel bed with his arms folded.

"We've got evidence that you killed those girls, Tony. We know you did it. You might as well tell us all about it now," Dinis urged.

"I didn't do anything," Costa replied, yawning. "I liked those girls. I had nothing to do with killing them. I'm innocent, and that is where I'll stand. I don't wish to discuss it anymore."

Dinis left and Detective John Dunn approached the cell.

"There's quite a circus happening outside," Dunn told Costa. "I've never seen so many newsmen gathered in one place before. What do you think of all the attention you've attracted?"

Costa stood up from the steel cot and walked slowly toward Dunn, wrapping his hands around the bars of the cell while pressing his face against the cold iron.

"What do I think? I think that there is a maniac loose somewhere out there!"

Edmund Dinis did not hear Costa's comment, as he was busy in the men's room running a comb through the thick locks of his gray-streaked, charcoal hair. He could hear the commotion in the other room as journalists jockeyed for position in preparation for the impending news conference. It was almost showtime. Dinis delivered his lines in the mirror once more, making sure to overenunciate the most titillating words of his press statement. Satisfied with the rehearsal, the lanky district attorney straightened his regimental tie and brushed the lint from the lapels of his navy-blue suit coat. He walked out of the bathroom and into the brightly lit interrogation room where several microphones were set up at a small lectern. He sat down and addressed reporters.

"I'm here to announce the discovery of the bodies of Patricia Walsh, Mary Anne Wysocki, and an unidentified female in an area of woods near the old Truro Cemetery," Dinis said. "The bodies were dismembered and found in the vicinity of where another mutilated corpse was recovered back on February 8. The victims were all found nude."

He paused to allow reporters time to scribble their notes. They were hanging on his every word.

"The hearts of each girl had been removed from the bodies and were not in the graves, nor were they found," Dinis added.

Standing in the back of the room, Gunnery and Flynn shot curious looks at each other.

"Well, that's bullshit," Flynn whispered under his breath.

Dinis continued. "A razor like device was found near the graves. Each body was cut into as many parts as there are joints. There were some instances in which there appeared to have been an axe or meat cleaver used. A definite pattern was repeated in all four cases of dismemberment. Whatever method was used, the evidence points to an extreme degree of abnormality. It was purely maniacal, insane. Sections of the body bear teeth marks and other evidence of having been chewed. Simply said, these are the most bizarre murders in the history of Cape Cod."

"Could you be specific as to where the girls were bitten?" asked one reporter. "Was it the ear, the arm, or the leg?"

"Well, just generally," Dinis replied. "I wouldn't want to be more specific than that."

Both Flynn and Gunnery had spoken with the medical examiners, and there was no evidence to support Dinis's theory in their initial findings.

"Are we talking about a Cape Cod vampire?" another newsman asked.

Dinis confirmed with a stern nod while inside, he was flushed with excitement. He was the center of attention and ready to milk the moment for all it was worth, facts be damned.

"We feel that the conditions surrounding these murders could have continued," he added. "The age of the decomposed bodies may go back six months, eight months, nine months. We don't know what took place during this time. There are at least two or three thousand missing females in the United States and we don't know how many are buried out there in the Truro woods."

Dinis paid lip service to the work of his investigators, although at first, he did not mention them by name. This was *his* show after all.

"My men were drawn to the makeshift grave sites by some strands of rope that were found at the base of a tree. The rope might indicate the girls had been tied up before they were butchered, since one of them had a rope around her face."

Flynn elbowed Gunnery. "There goes the fucking case," he muttered.

The district attorney made it clear that the murders were not the result of a robbery gone awry, as cash and jewelry were discovered near the graves. In this, he was correct.

"The evidence indicates that the Walsh girl was attacked first. Her companion then ran for her life, only to be caught, dragged back and killed."

"So who did this?" a reporter shouted from the back of the room.

"We have a suspect in custody right now," Dinis announced. "His name is Antone Charles Costa and he's twenty-four years old. Costa is a handyman-carpenter and an amateur taxidermist."

The taxidermy angle was another Easter egg to drop in the news conference in Dinis's effort to further sensationalize the case.

"Is Costa cooperating?"

"He has refused to submit to a polygraph examination," Dinis replied.

Following the press conference, the murder suspect was shaved, ate two pieces of toast, and washed them down with a glass of water before he was escorted from the holding cell by armed guard and led to the back of the police barracks, where a squad car would take him to his murder arraignment in Provincetown. A gang of reporters fought with one another to get a closer look at the so-called Cape Cod vampire.

Costa looked relatively clean-cut, wearing a blue turtleneck, white chino pants, and black-framed eyeglasses.

Boston Globe reporter Richard Powers described the killer in his notebook this way: "of slight build, and dark complexioned…black, neatly trimmed mustache, sideburns and semi-mod hairstyle."

Lieutenant George Killen had stood in support behind his boss, Edmund Dinis, during the press conference and was now getting called out for that subservient display by Bernie Flynn in the parking lot, away from reporters.

"I guess we arrested Count Dracula," Flynn mocked. "These murders were gruesome enough. Why did Dinis have to lie about them?"

"Yeah, that was the goddamnedest stuff I ever heard," Killen replied.

"You shouldn't have allowed him to go that far."

"What was I gonna do?" Killen shrugged. "I couldn't correct him in front of all that press."

"Well, the kid has Maurice Goldman for an attorney," Flynn reminded him. "Once he gets a hold of the autopsy reports, he's gonna eat Ed Dinis alive, and the five weeks we've spent out in the cold woods and all over the fucking place will be for nothing and the sicko could walk."

Costa sat quietly in the back of the cruiser during the ride to Provincetown, occasionally staring out the window at spectators lined up along Route 6A in the hopes of catching a brief glimpse of him as he rode past in a high speed convoy.

We're immortal now, Cory told him. *Our name will echo through eternity like a god.*

Costa was bemused by his alter ego and this time did not try to shut him out of his mind.

Provincetown Town Hall, where Tony Costa was arraigned for the murders of Patricia Walsh and Mary Anne Wysocki, as it looks today.
© *Casey Sherman.*

Look at their faces. They are smiling at us. We're famous now, and it's only the beginning.

Soon, the top of the Pilgrim Tower came into view in the distance, and Costa knew that he would be coming home, possibly for the last time, back to Helltown.

Once in Provincetown, he was taken to a cell at the police station as he waited for his arraignment at the Second District Court, which was located upstairs inside town hall.

Dozens of residents packed the courtroom, including many of his female followers, such as Sadie and Thumper, all adorned with flowers in their hair. Downstairs in the dingy holding cell, Costa was introduced to a tall, middle-aged attorney named Justin Cavanaugh.

"Maurice Goldman sent me here. I will be representing you at your arraignment."

Costa stared blankly back.

"I will be instructing you what to say and what not to say during these proceedings."

Costa remained motionless. Cavanaugh was getting frustrated.

"Nod if you understand what I just said to you."

Finally, the murder suspect acknowledged the attorney's presence. "I understand you perfectly," he replied.

There was no private set of stairs leading from the police station to the courthouse, so Costa was escorted outside and through a gauntlet of gawkers and up the front steps of the town hall.

"We love you, Tony!" Sadie shouted.

Costa's mother, Cecilia, and his ex-wife, Avis Costa, joined the crowd, but they said nothing to reporters. Other villagers were eager to express their views.

"To think such a demon lives among us," one local woman told a newsman. "Even though they have arrested a man for those awful things, I won't be able to sleep at night. It's worse than the Boston Strangler!"

Another woman nodded in agreement. "It makes us believe that some of us can be possessed by the devil. I couldn't eat my breakfast this morning, thinking about those cut-up bodies, and yet I couldn't stay away from the courthouse. I need to see the killer."

Once again, reporters and photographers huddled around Bernie Flynn and Tom Gunnery as they whisked Costa inside the building. The killer could hear the planks of the wooden floor creak under his feet as he shuffled passed two oil paintings, *The Crew of the Philomena Manta* and *Fish Cleaners*, both painted by local artist Charles W. Hawthorne in 1899 as an homage to the town's proud Portuguese fishermen. The murder suspect offered a middle finger to the media from his manacled hand before entering the crowded courtroom. Special Judge Gershom D. Hall, nicknamed "God Damn" Hall by prosecutors and defense attorneys alike, took the bench in a flowing black robe covering his long, lean body. The courtroom was standing room only, and Hall had not seen this much interest in a local case since he presided over Norman Mailer's drunk and disorderly trial nearly a decade before. The balding, seventy-three-year-old judge whispered something to probation officer James Cordeiro, who then shared it with everyone in the gallery.

"There will be no photographs allowed per Judge Hall's order!" he declared in a booming voice.

Those spectators who were fortunate enough to get seated in folding chairs stirred impatiently as a matter regarding an unpaid laundry bill was brought to the judge's attention. Their eyes were communally fixed on the young killer, who was also seated with his shackled hands folded on his lap. After more than an hour of settling petty disputes, Judge Hall asked the clerk to read the murder charges against Antone C. Costa.

"We have a signed complaint from Truro Police Chief Harold Berrio which alleges that the suspect, Mr. Antone Costa, did assault and beat Patricia H. Walsh with intent to murder her by stabbing her several times with a knife and by such assault and beating did kill and murder Patricia H. Walsh," the officer announced. "We also have a signed complaint from Lt. George Killen of the Massachusetts State Police which alleges that Mr. Antone Costa did assault, beat and murder Mary Anne Wysocki. Wysocki was also stabbed with a knife. These complaints also indicate that Walsh and Wysocki were the victims of a fatal gunshot."

Both the judge and the murder suspect sat quietly while the dead air was filled with the incessant murmurs of gathered townsfolk, all providing color commentary to one another about the shocking charges they had just heard.

"Will the defendant please stand," ordered the judge.

Costa lifted himself off the wooden chair and stood before the court.

"I would like to offer a plea of not guilty on behalf of Mr. Costa," Justin Cavanaugh told the judge.

"Do you represent the defendant?"

"Yes, Your Honor. I have been retained by Mr. Costa's mother, Cecelia Bonaviri."

"All right, counselor. My initial order is that the defendant undergoes thirty-five days of psychiatric observation at Bridgewater State Hospital." Judge Hall then pounded his gavel on a wooden sound block. "This arraignment is adjourned."

Uniformed state troopers created a wall around Costa as he was led out of the courthouse by Bernie Flynn and Tom Gunnery.

"We're with you, Tony!" Thumper shouted. "We love you, Sire!"

The killer smiled as he fought against the shackles, raising his right hand slightly to form a peace sign. The curtain closed briefly on Tony Costa as he was driven ninety-seven miles away to a prison-like mental facility in the leafy town of Bridgewater, Massachusetts. It was the same place that self-confessed Boston Strangler Albert DeSalvo had staged a daring, daylight escape just two years before in 1967. Would security be tight enough to hold the wolf of the steppes? The killer could hardly wait to find out.

For Edmund Dinis, the day's spectacle was not over yet. The district attorney offered Justin Cavanaugh a tour of the grave sites in North Truro, and he extended invitations to reporters to tag along.

It was Dinis's first visit to the crime scene, but he presented himself as an expert of the terrain, leading Costa's lawyer and a group of newsmen through the dark woods. Dinis took a wrong turn and found himself momentarily lost in the forest until Bernie Flynn quietly led him back on course. It was comical retribution for the district attorney's grandstanding and outright lying to reporters during the morning press conference back at the Yarmouth barracks. Standing over the dug-out holes, Edmund Dinis held court once again.

"The attention of the police originated here," he said, pointing down at the site where Susan Perry's body was discovered weeks before. "This was the first grave that was found. It was an area which indicated some depression in the ground and after probing we found the unidentified remains of the body of a girl."

The lawman in his resplendent top coat vowed to continue to search the area for more victims.

"I expect more bodies to be discovered," Dinis predicted.

CHAPTER TWENTY-THREE

Kurt Vonnegut Jr. felt agitated, and his family chalked up his dark mood to pre–book launch jitters. He was always difficult to be around, but in the days leading up to publication, he was absolutely unbearable.

He stood in the kitchen of his home, stirring his first cup of coffee of the day. Upstairs, he could hear his wife, Jane, on the phone, telling a friend that Vonnegut had promised to build her a new bookshelf and she didn't know if and when it would ever get done. She wasn't complaining. Jane was only sharing a bit of the reality of being married to a writer.

"They're all like professors," she told the friend. "So focused on their work that they forget to put their shoes on."

It was a witty line, and Vonnegut smiled for a moment. Then he took the spoon out of the coffee cup and threw it into the sink, making a loud clanging noise. He set the cup down and walked to another other room where several small numbered pieces of white wood were stacked neatly, ready to be assembled. Vonnegut gathered the pieces in his arms like kindling and stomped upstairs to their bedroom. Jane had just finished her call when her husband burst into the room and dropped the pieces of wood on the floor beside their bed.

"You want a fucking bookcase?" he shouted, pointing at the pile. "There's your fucking bookcase!"

Vonnegut left his wife crying and returned to his morning coffee.

To take his mind off her wailing, he grabbed the newspaper and studied the front page. The headline of the *Boston Globe* was bold and dramatic— "Cape Pushes Probe in Murder of 4 Girls. Two Victims Unidentified and There May Be Others." The story was accompanied by a black-and-white close-up photo of the alleged killer from his murder arraignment. Under the photo ran this description: "Suspect—Antone Costa, held in Cape murders. Police describe him as an amateur taxidermist, odd jobs man."

Vonnegut recognized the suspect's name as someone his daughter Edie had mentioned in passing. He read every gory detail of the reporting, including the district attorney's claim the victims were bitten and their bodies cut up with a razor-like device. He also read the sidebar stories that quoted friends of the victims. "Pat Walsh was quiet, but always willing to work," said her former high school classmate John Foley, who went on to describe Mary Anne Wysocki as a "lively girl" and "a leader in the movement to bring more casual dress to school."

So it goes, Vonnegut thought to himself. But he recognized immediately that the case had weight. There had not been another series of murders like it since Richard Speck had tortured and killed eight nurses in Chicago in 1966. Those crimes became a national story, and this one would be too. Vonnegut had just heard that Norman Mailer had won the opportunity to write about the upcoming Apollo 11 mission to the moon planned for July for *Life* magazine.

"Shit comes so easy for Norman," Vonnegut said and sighed. "What the fuck does he know about the space program?"

Normally, Vonnegut would stew over such a question for days, falling into an even deeper funk than usual. But he had *Slaughterhouse-Five* on the horizon, and its success would give him the cachet to compete with his rival on an even playing field. The North Truro murders were perfect fodder for an article in a major national magazine.

"Fuck Mailer," Vonnegut said to himself. "I can write the shit out of this story. Hell, I'll even out-Capote *In Cold Blood*."

He drafted a handwritten note to his agent with four words underlined and in capital letters: GET ME LIFE MAGAZINE.

But Vonnegut needed a hook for the story. He spoke to an editor at *Life* and told him that he had an authenticity by proximity to tell this story better than anyone else, since the murders had taken place so close to his home on Cape Cod.

"Jack the Ripper is alive and well and living in Provincetown," Vonnegut said cheerfully. He then described the grisly murders of the four young women, as he had read in the *Boston Globe*, and promised that he had another unique pathway into the prose. As he had done in *Slaughterhouse-Five*, Vonnegut would write the tale from his own personal perspective.

"The killer is a guy named Tony Costa, and he's friends with my daughter Edie."

The *Life* editor was sold on the macabre story, especially because of Vonnegut's approach to the bizarre narrative through his teenage daughter, who might very well have fallen victim to Tony Costa's charm and his blade if fortunes were reversed. The magazine editor promised Vonnegut that he would reserve space in the July 25 issue for his special report.

———

Norman Mailer was not concerned at that moment with his own pending story for *Life* about the Apollo 11 mission to the moon; instead he was focused on his decision whether to run for mayor of New York City. He had gathered several of his confidantes, including José Torres, Pete Hamill, Jerry Rubin, and Jimmy Breslin together for a meeting to discuss the viability of his candidacy.

"I'm ready to take all my fame and awards and fling them on the gaming tables of life," he told them.

When pressed about his lack of legislative experience, Mailer insisted to the group that his candidacy would not be considered a farce. "It's 1969. The real has become more fantastic than the imagined," he said. Breslin, a celebrated columnist for the New York *Daily News*, became an immediate convert, pledging to run alongside Mailer for president of the city council. Jerry Rubin scratched the unkempt, curly mane on his head, wondering why the author would run as a Democrat since he thought the two-party political system should be flushed down the toilet altogether. But he was struck by Mailer's passion for the challenge.

"You know something?" he said to the group of fellow attendees afterward. "That fuckin' bum is serious!"

Mailer was deadly serious, and he needed isolation to contemplate his final decision. He left the awful din of the city and retreated back to Provincetown to think. He also promised himself to lose some weight so that he would be in fighting shape for the possible campaign ahead.

When he settled into his home on Commercial Street, he found the tiny seaside community buzzing over the arrest of Tony Costa. Mailer felt uneasy over the fact that the suspected killer had lived just 1.2 miles away at a rooming house on Standish Street. Like Vonnegut, Mailer was also the father of a teenage daughter. Susan Mailer spent part of her summers with her father and her younger half siblings in Provincetown. The nineteen-year-old Barnard College student was the same age as Sydney Lee Monzon and just a bit older than Susan Perry when they were cut up and buried in the North Truro woods.

Susan Perry's remains were positively identified in late March thanks to a fingerprint that was lifted from the dermal layer of skin on her right little finger. Ed Dinis made a formal announcement, making sure to reemphasize all the ghoulish details, including the facts that her heart had been cut out and that she was decapitated by her killer, who stuffed her severed head in a plastic bag.

Mailer was in the middle of drafting his first policy paper when he got bored, poured himself a tall glass of bourbon, and collapsed on the couch of his spacious living room. He turned on the television and watched a news report from WNAC-7 in Boston. The day's lead story focused on what local reporters had dubbed "the Truro Murder Case." The anchorman interviewed noted local psychiatrist Dr. Robert Mezer, the author of a book called *Elements of Psychiatry for Nurses*, about whether a sane man could have committed such a crime where the victims were not only killed but also dissected.

Mezer doubted that the killings were done by a "normal individual." Answering a follow-up question about a possible sexual connotation to the crimes, Mezer replied, "In normal people, we see that sex follows love. In people who commit this type of crime, we see that sex follows violence, or violence follows sex."

At the end of the interview, Mezer editorialized about the notion of temporary insanity: "This business of these individuals getting into institutions and serving three years after committing a murder, then going out to commit it again, just isn't right."

Mailer pointed the remote control at the television set and flicked it off. The author looked down at his coffee table and was surprised to find that he had written down several notes from the interview. If he was going to run for mayor of New York City, he had more than sixteen million people to worry about, so why had he allowed his mind to drift toward Tony Costa?

It was because Norman Mailer knew Tony Costa better than the accused murderer knew himself.

The suspected serial killer was at this point in the confines of Bridgewater State Hospital, where he was given a physical examination and deemed to be in good health. Costa was also forced to submit to an entrance interview where a doctor found him to be "free of delusions" and not tempted by suicide.

Mailer had gone through a similar battery of physical tests and psychiatric analysis nearly a decade before in November 1960, when he was committed to Bellevue Hospital in New York for three weeks of observation after stabbing and nearly killing his second wife, Adele, during a dinner party in their apartment.

At that time, the relationship between Norman and Adele Morales Mailer had already been exposed to major cracks in its foundation. Their marriage had been one of white-hot passion and blinding fury. Mailer wed the Spanish and Peruvian beauty in 1954 after breaking up with his first wife, Beatrice Silverman. The writer had once slapped Adele across the face so hard that it sent her eyeglasses flying across the room. She had pointed a loaded pistol at her husband during a drunken exchange at the Copacabana nightclub after she had asked the bodyguard of Sammy Davis Jr. to inspect his firearm. They had a fistfight during a party that was attended by their friends Jason Robards and Lauren Bacall. Together, they were the definition of a hot mess. The idea of fidelity was also lost on the couple. Mailer slept around while Adele took several lovers of her own.

Their personal war of roses came to a frightening head on the evening of Saturday, November 19, 1960, at a birthday party the couple hosted for a friend at their apartment at 250 West Ninety-Fourth Street. During the soiree, Mailer had planned on announcing to their partygoers that he was going to run for mayor of New York. He leaned on his friend and fellow writer George Plimpton to help pack the room with two hundred guests, including notable figures like Allen Ginsberg, bandleader Peter Duchin, and actor Tony Franciosa. Mailer drank bourbon and smoked marijuana for much of the day. By the time the party was in full swing at around 10:00 p.m., the author was outside on the street, challenging guests to fist fights. In the wee hours of the morning, the number of party guests had dwindled down to twenty or so drunken, weary survivors. Mailer separated them into groups of those who supported him and those he declared were his enemies. Adele was in the enemy camp. By then, after hours of brawling, Mailer had a black eye and blood spilled on his jersey, a white matador shirt he had worn for the special occasion. Adele laughed at the spectacle that was her husband.

"*Aja toro, aja,* come on you little faggot," she taunted. "Where's your *cojones*? Did your ugly whore of a mistress cut them off? You son of a bitch!"

Mailer grabbed a penknife, one with a two-and-a-half-inch blade that he had used to clean his nails.

"Here you think you're tough?" he snarled. "Well, I'm tougher!"

Adele began walking away, and Mailer jabbed her in the back with the blade. His wife turned her body toward him, and he struck her again, this time piercing the upper abdomen, narrowly missing her heart.

The knife did penetrate the pericardial sac, the double-walled sac containing the heart and the roots of the great blood vessels.

Adele collapsed on the floor, her blood spilling onto the carpet of their apartment. As she bled out, Mailer stood over her body.

"Don't touch her," he told his shocked guests. "Let the bitch die!"

Fortunately, the horrified partygoers did not listen. One guest took quick action and rushed into their bedroom and retrieved a mattress, which he dragged into the living room for Adele to lie down on. All the while, Mailer stood in the corner in a "zombie-like" state. "I don't think he's fully aware of having stabbed her," said his friend and eyewitness to the assault Harold "Doc" Humes, who was also the creator of the *Paris Review* literary magazine.

An ambulance was called, and Adele was taken to nearby University Hospital and whisked into surgery.

A psychiatrist was called to the apartment, but Mailer refused to let him in. A short time later, he visited the hospital to check on his wife. Adele was still being operated on.

Mailer returned home, put on a suit, and had a few drinks at his neighborhood bar. He arrived back at the hospital to see Adele in the recovery room. She opened her eyes and saw the dark circles around his swollen eyes. He looked manic. He looked insane.

"Do you know that I watched you being wheeled into the operating room? You never looked so beautiful," he told her. "Do you understand why I did it? I love you and I had to save you from cancer."

Mailer wept and his wounded wife wept along with him. He left her in her hospital bed and went to a friend's home for the night.

"I need to get outta here," he told the friend. "Maybe I'll rent a fishing boat out of Provincetown and sail down to Cuba to join Castro's revolution."

New York City police detectives tried twice to interview Adele. The first time, she was sleeping and was too ill to talk. Later, she claimed to investigators that she had fallen on a broken bottle, but eventually, she admitted to them that her famous husband had stabbed her. Mailer was already on the police department's radar. A week earlier, he had been arrested at Birdland after attempting to pay for drinks with his credit card, which was against the rules at the famous jazz club. The following day, Mailer studied an open letter that he had been working on to Fidel Castro. "In Cuba, hatred runs into the love of blood," he wrote. "In America, all too few blows are struck into flesh. We kill the spirit here. We are experts in that. We use psychic bullets and kill each other cell by cell."

He even made time for a previously scheduled television interview with Mike Wallace, all while Adele was recovering in the hospital from his near-fatal attack and listed in critical condition. She asked a nurse to move her to another room because she was afraid that her husband would come back. Adele was placed into a secluded postoperative cardiac room where she was watched closely by the nursing staff.

Mailer met a friend for dinner and drove back to the hospital, where detectives waited to place him under arrest. The writer was dazed and pleaded to speak to Adele, but she did not want to see him.

"I refuse to answer your questions," he told police as he was being slapped with handcuffs and charged with felonious assault.

During Mailer's arraignment in felony court, two days after the armed attack on Adele, Magistrate Reuben Levy read aloud a letter from Dr. Conrad Rosenberg of University Hospital. "In my opinion, Norman Mailer is having an acute paranoid breakdown with delusional thinking and is both homicidal and suicidal. His admission to a hospital is urgently advised."

The defendant spoke up, arguing against hospitalization, claiming that he had had only a passing conversation with Dr. Rosenberg while visiting his wife's bedside.

"Naturally, I have been a little upset, but I have never been out of my mental faculties," Mailer told the magistrate. "It's important for me not to be sent to a mental hospital, because my work will be considered that of a disordered mind. My pride is that I can explore areas of experience that other people are afraid of. I insist I am sane."

The judge stared down at Mailer from the bench and saw a disheveled figure wearing a dirty raincoat.

"Your recent history indicates that you cannot distinguish fiction from reality," Magistrate Levy told him. "In your interest and the public interest, I have to commit you."

Mailer was ordered to Bellevue Hospital and was incarcerated in the facility's violent ward. His friends in the literary world wondered if he was insane at all or if he was simply testing the limits of evil within himself. The writer kept a diary during his three weeks at Bellevue, which he called his Kafkan nightmare. In it, he penned a short poem: "So long as you use a knife, there's some love left."

Now, nearly nine years later, in the late winter of 1969, Adele was long gone. She survived the attack but was out of Mailer's life, along with the wife who came after. Beverly had still not filed for divorce, which he took as a good sign. Like Adele, though, Mailer was also a survivor. He had weathered a scandal that would have destroyed most literary careers, and he escaped jail time after Adele had refused to testify against him out of concern for their two young children, Danielle and Betsy. His political aspirations, once derailed by his explosion of violence, were also back on track. The mayoral seat of the greatest city on the planet was not out of his grasp, despite his turbulent past. He stared back at the notes he had taken during the television news segment about the Truro murder case and wondered whether the accused killer was keeping a diary of his own while undergoing psychiatric evaluation.

At Bridgewater State Hospital, a psychologist put Tony Costa through a series of mental tests and determined that "his good intellectual energies generally compensate effectively for his impulsivity, as he is able to almost immediately recover from aggressive, acting-out behavior."

The shrink also noted that Costa appeared to be "a narcissistic, inadequate, somewhat depressed man who had difficulty maintaining reality."

Inside Ward F, the maximum-security unit of the hospital, the accused killer had also taken to writing poetry, as Mailer had done. Staring out the iron-mesh-covered window of his small cell, Costa wrote a sonnet that he titled "Sundown."

> *Fleece-lined lavender clouds,*
> *Suspended in a turquoise sea of milk.*
> *The chirping of the birds outside,*
> *Their voices made of fine silk.*
> *All God's colors before my eyes,*
> *An artist's brush cannot duplicate.*
> *Free me Lord from unjust hands,*
> *Don't make these prison walls my fate.*

CHAPTER TWENTY-FOUR

Operation Purple Martin put American troops through the meat grinder in March 1969. Since the beginning of the month, the Third Battalion of the Fourth Marine Regiment had come under heavy mortar fire while trying to clear out enemy positions around Elliot Combat Base, better known as the Rockpile, and located a few miles south of the DMZ. One hundred U.S. Marines were killed in just eight days of fighting and shelling. Another three hundred casualties would be recorded in the following weeks. The carnage triggered more protests at home as vandals ransacked a Selective Service office in Silver Spring, Maryland, destroying hundreds of draft records, while another antiwar group poured blood on files, destroyed furniture, and smashed glass at the Dow Chemical offices in Washington, DC.

Young Americans were looking for a fresh voice to lead them away from the abyss, and the timing of the publication of *Slaughterhouse-Five* could not have been more perfect. Ten thousand first-edition copies of Vonnegut's antiwar novel were printed, and all were sold in just a matter of days. Multiple reprints followed, and soon, Vonnegut celebrated his first major *New York Times* bestseller.

It was the big kaboom for the writer after toiling for decades in near obscurity and financial failure. The *New York Times* praised the novel. "Mr.

Vonnegut pronounces his book a failure 'because there is nothing intelligent to say about a massacre.' He's wrong and he knows it," the *Times* reviewer wrote. "It is very tough and very funny; it is sad and delightful; and it works... Kurt Vonnegut knows all the tricks of the writing game."

Reviewing *Slaughterhouse-Five* for the *New Republic*, a twenty-six-year-old medical student and aspiring novelist named Michael Crichton called Vonnegut's work "beautifully done, fluid, smooth and powerful." Crichton ended the review with an examination of the writer himself. "One senses that underneath it all, Vonnegut is a nice man, who doesn't really like to have to say this, but...his description of one character might stand for all mankind in his view: 'She had been given the opportunity to participate in civilization, and she muffed it.'"

Describing Vonnegut's unique style, Susan Lardner of the *New Yorker* wrote, "The short, flat sentences of which the novel is composed convey shock and despair better than an array of facts or effusive mourning" but also warned readers that Vonnegut's "deliberate simplicity" caused him to skid into fatuousness, while Christopher Wordsworth of the *Guardian* called the Dresden book "devastating and supremely human."

The phone rang almost nonstop at Vonnegut's Cape Cod home as reporters clamored for interviews.

"Let others bring order to chaos," Vonnegut told a journalist during one of dozens of interviews about his new book. "I will bring chaos to order. If all writers do that, then perhaps everyone will understand that there is no order in the world around us, that we must adapt ourselves to the requirements of chaos instead."

Reporters and literary reviewers who had paid little or no attention to him now hung on his every word. Hippies flocked to his Barnstable home, hoping to capture a glimpse of the great Vonnegut in his driveway. They camped out in sleeping bags on his lawn. Starry-eyed fans even urged him to run for president. With the publication of *Slaughterhouse-Five*, Vonnegut had eclipsed his goal of becoming a commercially successful writer. To the younger generation, he was a rock star and an oracle. Some called him the heir to Mark Twain, and Vonnegut's hometown newspaper, the *Barnstable Patriot*, had even compared him to the crucified Christ. It had taken him more than twenty years to become an overnight success, and the feeling overwhelmed him. Sitting and smoking inside his writing studio, Vonnegut pulled two wartime mementos from his desk drawer. One was the Purple Heart he had received for frostbite during the war. The other was a letter that his father, Kurt Vonnegut Sr., had sent him in 1945. It was returned by the U.S. Army to the elder Vonnegut with a note stating that his son had gone missing in action on January 7, 1945. When Kurt Jr. finally came home from the war in July of that year, his father handed his namesake the letter. In March 1969, the envelope still had not been opened, and Vonnegut had no idea what his father had written to him over two decades ago. All the horror he had witnessed and had kept sealed in his mind since the war finally spilled out of him in the pages of *Slaughterhouse-Five*.

"So it goes," he mumbled once more.

He had reached the summit of the literary Mount Olympus and felt that he did not have to write anymore if he did not want to. That notion gave him a sense of freedom, but it also scared him. Vonnegut knew that if he did not keep working, he may never publish anything again. It took a killer like Tony Costa to get the writer out of his momentary funk.

Vonnegut telephoned his daughter Edie, who was finishing her freshman year of college at the University of Iowa, and pressed her about her relationship with the young murder suspect.

"My experience with Tony Costa was so brief and remote that in retrospect, I'm not even sure it was him who I met," she told her father. "If I did, it was for two minutes on the meat racks of Provincetown. There's another guy in town who I think may be the killer. He compulsively washes his hands and he spooks me."

Vonnegut did not like what he had heard from his nineteen-year-old daughter. In the writer's mind, Edie *knew* Tony Costa, and that was that. A mere brush with infamy would not titillate his readers as much as a fully formed relationship, one where the accused killer might even have invited her to the North Truro woods.

Vonnegut jumped into his car and drove to the crime scene on the outer Cape. His adrenaline was pumping, and he felt like a young reporter again. There was still plenty of police activity in the forest as investigators had yet to find the murder weapons. Vonnegut walked around the area, taking mental snapshots of the leafless trees and brambles and the comings and goings of police cars that he would later bring to life in his prose. He drove out to Provincetown and noticed graffiti spray-painted in blood red on the side of a laundromat on Shank Painter Road that read *Tony Digs Girls*. Vonnegut interviewed a local businessman who joked that a car salesman had offered Costa a new El Dorado at a steep price—an arm and a leg. "Costa said, 'Deal!'" the businessman chuckled.

Vonnegut was surprised by the gallows humor, especially since families were in the midst of burying what was left of their daughters. The funerals for Pat Walsh and Mary Anne Wysocki fell on the same day in early March and just hours apart. Mourners celebrated high mass for Mary Anne Wysocki at St. Mary's Church in Providence at dawn and then migrated over to nearby St. Paul's Church to pay their last respects to Pat Walsh.

Vonnegut had missed the services, but he was not going to pass on an opportunity to interview District Attorney Ed Dinis. They met for a cup of coffee at a café near the courthouse in Barnstable, and Vonnegut dangled the false narrative that his daughter was friendly with the murder suspect.

"Really, what does she have to say?" Dinis asked.

"If Tony's really the murderer, it's a surprise to Edith," Vonnegut replied. "She never suspected it. But then again, she isn't very old. Up to now, she hasn't suspected that much evil in anybody. She always felt safe."

The writer lit a cigarette and waited for the lawman's reaction.

"What did she say—*exactly?*" asked the district attorney eagerly. "Were those her words?"

"She said, and this was on the telephone from Iowa City where she goes to school now: 'If Tony is the murderer, then *anybody* could be the murderer.' This was news to her."

After the meeting with the district attorney, Vonnegut remained seated at the small table in the coffeehouse. He studied the notes he had taken during the course of the day and began to form the narrative spine of his special report in his mind. During Truman Capote's research for his true crime novel *In Cold Blood*, he'd had the opportunity to interview killers Richard "Dick" Hickock and Perry Edward Smith behind bars. Vonnegut needed face time with Tony Costa. The writer was already thinking beyond the article for *Life* and to the possibility of a book about the sensational case, which could be his eagerly awaited follow-up to *Slaughterhouse-Five*.

He ordered another cup of coffee and fished another Pall Mall out of the cigarette package. The waitress and some of the locals paid him no mind, as he had been coming to the café for years. But tourists, stopping in for coffee and sandwiches to take along on their antiquing sojourn on picturesque and historic Route 6A, gawked at the author and bothered him for his autograph.

This is what it must feel like to be Mailer, he thought to himself, smiling.

Ed Dinis was also awestruck by Vonnegut and thankful that the newly minted celebrity had taken such an interest in the case. The idea that his name would also be prominently mentioned in *Life* magazine excited the district attorney even more.

As Kurt Vonnegut's star rises, so will mine, Dinis thought to himself.

Reporters, with Edmund Dinis's help, were now referring to Costa in the press as "the Provincetown Vampire." The prosecutor did nothing to refute the story or dissuade newspapers from printing sensational headlines. Dinis also fielded calls from reporters at *Time* and *Newsweek*. During interviews with both magazines, he never bothered to correct himself and state that Pat Walsh's and Mary Anne Wysocki's hearts had not been cut from their bodies. Dinis also let it slip that Costa had Polaroid photographs of at least a dozen women in his bedroom, that investigators were now cross-referencing those pictures against lists of missing persons, and that the suspect had a blank application for permanent residency in Canada among his effects. These statements were patently false. Dinis also fed information to a writer for *True Detective*, a salacious true crime magazine that boasted scantily clad women in various stages of duress on its cover along with headlines such as "Being Wed to a Sex Goddess was Murder!" and "Riddle of the Trussed-Up Nudes on the Beach." The district attorney told his detectives Killen, Flynn, and Gunnery to cooperate with the reporter for a double-length feature story titled "He Butchered the Beauties Before Burying Them!"

"It's sort of hard to put into words," George Killen told the tabloid journalist. "But it's kind of like finally reading the last chapter of a horror story that you started a long time ago but never finished."

Ed Dinis continued to keep the media pressure on, telling reporters that he expected more bodies to be unearthed in the North Truro woods. This speculation frustrated many in law enforcement, including Truro police chief Harold Berrio.

"He's talking about the possibility of finding more bodies, but I don't see him going through the underbrush looking for them," Berrio complained to a friend.

By this time, Chief Berrio, Bernie Flynn, and Trooper Tom Gunnery were being deluged with calls from parents of missing girls across the country. Letters also poured in from as far away as Australia and South Africa. Volunteers with shovels and curiosity seekers began tramping through the woods around Cemetery Road, looking for signs of a sadistic murderer.

Park Ranger Ray Kimpel was called back in to cordon off the area with chains. One local newspaper columnist wrote that she was startled by "this encounter with a strangeness of which the town had no previous experience… Drugs, death, horror moved upon the little town beloved by inhabitants to make it a focus of evil." According to the columnist, first, there was a sense of shock and bewilderment among local residents, followed by "resentment and a rising anger that the town's remote places have been desecrated and defiled, made the scene of some Witch's Sabbath."

Costa's lawyer Maurice Goldman rushed to court, seeking a gag order against the district attorney. "We've got to shut Ed Dinis up and try this case in the court instead of the newspapers!" Goldman told his small legal team. The defense lawyer pleaded with the judge. "With Tony Costa's life at stake, it is not too much to ask this court to order the district attorney to try the defendant in an atmosphere undisturbed by so huge a wave of public passion," Goldman argued. "Ever since Mr. Costa's arrest, venomous and incriminating publicity about this defendant and the murder of two, three, four, or possibly more girls has made this case notorious. Statements by the District Attorney and his staff, as well as the medical examiner in the Provincetown area have been fraught with images of sexual perversions, mutilation, and diabolic mischief with suggestions of occultism."

But Ed Dinis had the media in his corner. He leveraged his relationship with the editors at WEEI Radio 590, the most influential talk radio station in the region, to generate an op-ed praising his work.

"Barnstable County and the Town of Truro are currently investigating the most bizarre and grisly murder case in recent Cape Cod history," WEEI's general manager stated in an editorial. "The killing and butchering of at least four young women has attracted news attention from all over the nation… As WEEI sees it, the Truro case has already become a remarkable example of how a murder case should be handled. For in spite of the fact that every day of investigation has uncovered shocking and bizarre evidence, the investigators have revealed to the public nothing more than the public has a right to know… Too often in such cases, a politically ambitious prosecutor will feed ravenous journalists with statements, insinuations and rumors that make a fair and impartial trial impossible... But not this time. From what we have learned so far, these are dreadful crimes. They may prove to be even more bloodthirsty and terrifying than the acts of the Boston Strangler. Justice must be served. WEEI believes that the Truro murder case sets a fine example of how such news should be handled. This is good law enforcement, for it upholds the law on both sides."

Trooper Tom Gunnery listened to the radio editorial on his drive to the DA's office in New Bedford. He entered the lobby and was escorted up a flight of stairs to Ed Dinis's outer office. At the top of the staircase stood a life-size portrait of the local lawman that would rival any painting hung in a presidential library. Gunnery was kept waiting for fifteen minutes until his boss hollered at him from behind a closed door.

"Come in!"

The trooper entered the spacious office and saw the district attorney seated behind a large mahogany desk under several rows of framed photos, including one of Dinis with JFK.

My new boss thinks he's got the same magic as my old boss, Gunnery thought to himself.

"What are you here for, Trooper?" Dinis asked.

"I just wanted to update you on some of the interviews we've conducted on the Cape."

"Have you found Costa's murder weapon yet?"

"No, sir."

Dinis let out a sigh of frustration. "I need that gun. I need that knife or ax or whatever he chopped up those girls with."

"Well, we interviewed a nineteen-year-old hippie named David Nicholson," Gunnery told him. "He's a friend of Tony's. Nicholson told us that he accompanied Costa to the woods in Truro in February and that the suspect was carrying a long bayonet-style knife in his coat."

"Go on," Dinis urged. "Where does he believe the weapon is now?"

"Nicholson believes Costa took it with him back to Provincetown, so we're also searching there. Another friend named Christopher Silva claims that Costa and Sydney Monzon were dating as he had seen her come and go from the suspect's room at the Crown and Anchor shortly before she disappeared."

"Any connection between Costa and the Perry girl?"

"Flynn and I spoke with a kid named James Steele who saw Susan Perry with Costa up in Dedham before she too went missing. He also told us that Tony tried to sell him a .22-caliber revolver at Mother Marion's restaurant in Ptown. Steele thinks that Costa has it buried somewhere. Steele also mentioned that Costa carried around a twelve-inch knife that he called his *pig stabber*."

"Well, hell, Trooper. Stop briefing me and go back to the Cape and continue digging," Dinis ordered.

Gunnery left the office, and Dinis dialed his new friend Kurt Vonnegut to update him on the case.

CHAPTER TWENTY-FIVE

State police Lieutenant Bernie Flynn had just entered the barracks in Yarmouth for what would be another long, slogging day on the case when he was handed a letter sent from Bridgewater Hospital and written by the accused killer himself. Tony Costa was now pleading for a meeting with investigators.

"I have done much thinking concerning this ugly crime I am accused of," Costa wrote. "I have some information which will be of utmost importance to both of us. There is a maniac running loose out there. We may both benefit since you want the correct man and I want my freedom. God Bless. Go in Peace. Tony Costa, 10910 F-Ward."

When Maurice Goldman learned about the correspondence, he was furious. The defense attorney drove to the mental hospital for the first face-to-face meeting with his client since the two had been introduced at Costa's job site weeks before. Goldman was joined by his colleague Justin Cavanaugh, and despite their outrage, the two men tried to remain cordial when speaking with their new high-profile client.

Cavanaugh recorded the first formal interview session with Costa, while Goldman led the questioning.

"Would you tell us what you said in the letter?" Goldman asked.

"I simply requested that Flynn come and visit if he had the chance because I wanted to find out if he had, you know, either been investigating some of these other people or just dropping this whole thing in my lap," Costa replied. "I would refer them to you people of course so that he could get information from you or whatever necessary to continue this thing rather than just stopping it here because there is someone else out there, that's a maniac or something, and this has happened many times, this crime, and what's to say this isn't going to happen again if they do nothing, if they just sit still, and you know, don't do a damn thing about it. That has bothered me. It got to me, so I had to write it."

Goldman shifted in his chair and loosened his tie. The heat was stifling inside the small office they had been given by the warden. Yet Costa remained cool, both physically and mentally, and detached from the horrors he had committed.

"Well then, your inquiry was for a determination to what the district attorney's office was going to do with respect to *try* to find out who's committing these horrible crimes out there. Is that the sole purpose?"

"That's the only purpose, yes," Costa replied. "Just to see if they were doing anything, so that this thing won't happen again, because I didn't do it. I know for a fact that there's someone else out there that did do it. You know, there's a, God forbid, it may happen again. And you know I just don't want to see it."

"That's the reason I'm asking to record this, Tony, so we'll know exactly what it is, so I can tell 'em in response. Uh, when you say that terrible thing, you mean the selling of dope or do you mean the death of these girls?"

"The death of these girls."

"Do you feel that I should reveal some of the information that I have in my files to the DA, if I in my judgment think I should?"

"That, Mr. Goldman, depends on yourself. You are my attorney, so you just do what you think is right and proper for the case."

"I certainly appreciate the confidence you have in both Mr. Cavanaugh and myself, and we want to be absolutely certain that we're doing the right thing for one person only, namely Tony Costa, let there be no doubt about that. That's where our loyalty lies, that's our oath of office, and that's what we're bound to do as lawyers."

The suspect smiled. "I've got loads of letters, and every one of them says that you're out there working hard, so I am really happy to hear it. It really boosts my spirits."

"Well, I'll tell you, Tony, what we've got," Goldman went on. "In addition to, we have one, two, three, four, we have four investigators that are out checking every little bit of information to help you. And they're not ordinary people. For example, the head of our staff, so called, in the role of head of our staff, is a former newspaper reporter, a crime reporter, and he ended up as editor of the *Boston Daily Post*. In the midst of that, we have a former expert police officer who is now running an independent detective agency. One of his partners is a beatnik, so you might as well know it, in style, dress, and action."

Costa pointed to Goldman's associate. "Haha, Mr. Cavanaugh?"

"Jeez, I've been called a lot of things, but not a beatnik," Cavanaugh countered.

"I mean a genuine beatnik, Tony. He dresses that way, he acts that way. He also was a former official investigator, and he is in our corner too, interviewing people. And for example, he spent Sunday night investigating around Provincetown, and no one would know either by dress or style or manner or speech or anything."

"He could fit right in, in other words," Costa added.

Goldman reached into his satchel and pulled out several press clippings about the murders and handed them to his client. "The district attorney has already made up his mind about you."

"It seems like a lot of bull," the suspected killer said as he reviewed the newspaper articles. "It's all trash. He has circumstantial evidence and nothing else. They've found no murder weapon. Mr. Dinis must be really desperate, saying the hearts are missing and the bodies were chewed. That guy's really sick. It's so gory, it's unreal."

But what was truly unreal was Tony Costa's alibi. Goldman was concerned about his client's convoluted story, and the attorney tried his best to gain some clarity. "It's the car situation that's disturbing Mr. Cavanaugh and myself. And then the money situation bothers us as to when Patricia Walsh comes back and what she did with the money. What happened to the money and why didn't you get the stuff and you ended up only with the car. You see, she got your nine hundred dollars. Now, all you've got is a car that isn't worth any more than nine hundred dollars, probably not even that much, I don't know, maybe about the same, I don't really know what the value is. We're checking through that thing too. We just don't get it, figure out in our minds how the car supplements, takes place, of the quarter of a pound of heroin."

"We need a little work in that area," Cavanaugh said. "I'll get you a paper and pencil, and what I suggest, Tony, is that you concentrate on this area of the story. Just write it all down when you have a good chance to think."

Goldman then shifted the conversation to Sydney Monzon and Susan Perry. While the evidence in the murders of Pat Walsh and Mary Anne Wysocki appeared strong, there was only hearsay to connect his client with the older crimes.

"They're both town girls, weren't they?" Cavanaugh asked.

"Yeah, well, Sydney was in town for a little while in the spring. She was from Orleans, I think."

"Says here she was from Eastham," the lawyer corrected him.

"I will take your word for it," the killer replied nonchalantly.

"Did you ever go out with either of them?" Goldman asked.

"No, I didn't. I never had the occasion to."

"Not even Sydney?" Cavanaugh pressed.

"Uh, no, I used to hang around with Sydney. I'd meet her at the Pilgrim Club and talk to her or something, once in a while, or ride through town on our bikes. But she was going with…she was living with a guy named Roland Salvador at the time."

"Did Sydney use dope of any kind?" Cavanaugh asked.

"Sydney was a speed person," Costa replied. "She was always using speed, a tremendous amount as far as I know."

"What about Susan, was she on dope of any kind?"

"Susan, as far as I know, she was just getting into LSD. She wasn't on any, she wasn't using a needle or anything, but she was using LSD and speed also. I knew her for a while when we were in town, not as friends but as an acquaintance, I knew her. Then, during this summer and the summer before, I knew her as what you would call a friend. You know, she was hanging out with some other people. And through town, just sitting around, I knew her. We would gather together all my friends and everybody, and she was among the crowd. We would get together."

"Did you ever sleep with her?" Goldman asked.

"Uh, yes. Yes, I did."

"Don't be ashamed to tell us."

"Yes, I did sleep with her."

"How many times?"

"Approximately two nights."

"When we use the expression did you ever sleep with a woman, that means, cleverly stated, did you ever have sexual relations with her in any form," Goldman pointed out. "Whether you practice fellatio on one another or whether you practice cunnilingus or any form of sexual relations. So we use *sleep* in its all-inclusive term. Now I ask you again, did you ever sleep with Susan Perry?"

"Uh, no," Costa replied. "We only shared a bed. Susan was a bit too young for me. She was a young girl, and she was small, you know, she only stood yea high."

Neither Goldman nor Cavanaugh pointed out the contradiction regarding Susan Perry's age, as Costa had begun having sex with his ex-wife Avis when she was only thirteen years old.

"You went to bed with her but you didn't sleep with her, all right. Did you ever sleep with Sydney?"

"I never even got near a bed with Sydney," Costa claimed. "Ours was more or less just a friendly relationship on the street."

Goldman ended the interview session soon after. Costa was sent back to his cell while the attorneys were escorted to the parking lot.

"Dinis is gonna give us one helluva battle with the two Providence girls," Goldman told Cavanaugh. "But I think we can fight against the indictments in the murders of Susan Perry and Sydney Monzon and just maybe keep Tony Costa out of the electric chair."

CHAPTER TWENTY-SIX

After fourteen days of contemplation at his Provincetown oasis, Norman Mailer decided to officially announce his candidacy for mayor of New York. Feminist Gloria Steinem got swept up in the author's fervor and joined the Mailer-Breslin ticket and ran for city comptroller. Together, their campaign slogan was *Throw the Rascals In!* Mailer's vision was bold. He promised to fight to make New York City the nation's fifty-first state and build a monorail around Gotham. Mailer also advocated for the prison release of Black Panther Party cofounder Huey Newton, which made him popular among African American voters. But as always, Mailer served as his own worst enemy. He showed up stumbling drunk at campaign events where he told off-color jokes and insulted his guests. During the campaign, he also tried to reconcile with his estranged wife, Beverly, but even she kept her distance from what was fast becoming a political train wreck.

When asked how he would prevent a snowstorm from paralyzing traffic in the city, Mailer said, "I'd piss on it!"

Jimmy Breslin compared his running mate to the controversial poet Ezra Pound and threatened to drop out of the race just about every day.

"Aquarius is in a depression," Mailer confided to friends. "It's a curious depression full of fevers and forebodings."

Mailer soon lost the Democratic primary, finishing fourth in a field of five candidates with just forty-one thousand votes. He returned to Provincetown and committed his focus to his next writing projects, the Apollo 11 story, and the Tony Costa case, which was continuing to unfold. Mailer believed that the Truro murders had all the makings of a great novel. He reached out to a local newspaper columnist named Evelyn Lawson, who had been writing about the case since it broke. Lawson was a popular theater critic with no hard news experience, but she had studied witchcraft and demonology and therefore considered herself to be an expert on the case. Mailer drove to Lawson's small cottage in Hyannis, and together they sipped tea in her small den. The walls of the den were covered with old playbills from the Cape Playhouse, and Mailer could feel a young Eva Marie Saint staring down at him from one of the black-and-white posters as he drank his cup of Earl Grey. Lawson was as theatrical as the productions she wrote about. The woman was in her late fifties, and her woolly hair formed the shape of a beehive on her head. She was heavily made up, not for afternoon tea but for the stage. She flung her arms wildly as she talked.

"I firmly believe two things about the murders," Lawson told Mailer. "First, they are the work of a coven of witches. And second, the coven is a front for a large narcotics group. There are other forces at work here. The mutilation implies ritualistic murder. Did you know that one of the girl's heads was cut off and stuffed in a plastic bag?"

Mailer had not heard that information before. He began scribbling notes as Lawson continued to theorize. She told Mailer that she had gained her wealth of knowledge about witches while living in Los Angeles in the early 1960s.

"I was working on a screenplay for Vincent Price," she said. "I had researched ancient volumes on the ritualistic rites of the black arts. I found detailed accounts, including human sacrifice, practiced by the witch cults at the four or five times a year when Satanists hold their Sabbath. Tony

Costa was born on August 2, the day after Lammas. That's one of the major annual festivals representing a distinct phase in the tide cycle of the Wiccan calendar."

If what Lawson said was true, then Costa wasn't the only killer out there. Were the murders in the North Truro woods simply a precursor of darker things to follow? What if a group of killers invaded Mailer's Provincetown home? Could he protect his family from harm?

He debated that question while driving his Jeep back to Provincetown. Mailer was always up for a fight, and he believed that he had bettered Rip Torn during their bloody encounter on Long Island months before. But if Costa wasn't just a lone killer but the head of a witch-worshipping drug cartel, how could Mailer defend his home from multiple attackers?

The writer did not mention his conversation with Lawson to his wife Beverly that night during dinner. There was still plenty of tension in their marriage, and Mailer chose to keep their conversations on the lighter side. Each had a few cocktails and retired to bed early that evening.

At around midnight, Beverly awoke to the screams of her husband on the other side of the bed. She turned on the light and shook Mailer, who was sweating and panting with his eyes closed.

"You're having a nightmare, Norman. Wake up!"

He tossed and turned before opening his eyes and shooting upright in their bed.

"What was it? What's the matter?"

"It was awful," he cried. "I dreamed that I was stumbling around in the woods at night and came upon a hole in the dirt. Inside, there was a plastic bag. Inside that plastic bag, I saw your head!"

The next morning, Mailer got up early. The lack of sleep coupled with the gruesome nightmare made him jumpy and irritable. He left his home and walked north on Commercial Street toward the Mayflower Cafe where he could sit undisturbed and enjoy his morning coffee with a plate of eggs and bacon. Mailer's perception of Provincetown had changed since the night before. He now viewed every young person he saw with suspicion. As he reached the Lobster Pot restaurant in the center of the village, he saw three young women pedal past him on their bicycles. The girls all looked blankly in his direction, their dark eyes staring right through him. They offered crooked smiles and knowing giggles. Mailer felt spooked. He stared back at the girls but kept walking as they turned left up Standish Street. The girls pedaled their bicycles up to Patricia Morton's guesthouse. It was a particularly warm morning, especially for early spring, and the landlady was outside sweeping the front step with her broom.

"We'll fix you for talking about Tony!" Sadie threatened.

"Susan Perry is alive and living in Boston," shouted Thumper.

"You didn't see anything, and you don't know anything," said the third hippie chick, known as Strawberry Blonde, jabbing her finger in the air toward Morton. "Got it, bitch?"

The landlady sized up these waifish intimidators. She needed to stand her ground.

"One swing of my broom, and I'll knock your asses off those bikes," Morton warned.

The girls giggled fiendishly.

"Okay, old bitch," Sadie said. "Whatever you say. You've got a nice place here. It'd be a real shame if it burned to the ground with you inside. But accidents do happen. Just keep your cunt lips shut about Tony Costa!"

Morton gripped the broom and raised the handle over her shoulder, prepared to strike. The girls did not flinch. They laughed once more and then pedaled away, the bells on their bicycles ringing as they continued up the hill toward the Pilgrim Monument.

Mailer spotted them again as he reached High Point Hill Road. He had decided to forego breakfast and get some exercise instead. As he walked up the steep hill, he stopped and turned, both fists clenched.

"Are you ladies following me?" he shouted.

The girls straddled their bikes and did not say a word.

"Mute, huh?" Mailer taunted. "Well, I suggest you allow a man to get his morning workout in and fuck off!"

The girls rode away. Sadie began singing lyrics to the Rolling Stones' song "Paint It Black," which was one of Tony Costa's favorites.

"I look inside myself, and I see my heart is black," she screeched. "I see my red door, I must have it painted black."

Mailer felt uneasy, but he shook it off and kept marching up the hill toward the granite tower. Once there, he entered the monument and began climbing. He did not use the handrail as he took each of the 166 steps to the top of the 252-foot-tall structure. Mailer was perspiring through his hooded sweatshirt, and his heart rate was high. The space became more confined the higher he climbed. When he finally reached the observation floor, Mailer felt he could walk no more. He placed his hands on his knees and watched a bead of sweat slide off his nose onto the granite floor. He then lifted himself up, stretching his body, and stood on the balls of his feet like a prizefighter. He gazed out the open windows, which offered a 360-degree view of the village below. He spotted his brick house in the distance and peered southeast to the rolling dunes and forest on the opposite side of Route 6A.

"Is that where the witches live?" he asked himself. "Will they crawl across the road, slink down to Commercial Street, cross the threshold of my home, and murder us all in our sleep?"

The questions truly terrified him. Mailer leaned his upper body out and over the observation deck and vomited.

———————

Trooper Tom Gunnery did not read Mailer, or Vonnegut for that matter. When he took a vacation, he usually stretched out on the hammock in the backyard of his Centerville home with an Ian Fleming spy novel. But there would be no time off for the young investigator any time soon. He was tasked with building a stronger case against Costa for the Sydney Monzon and Susan Perry murders so that Ed Dinis could prosecute him for those additional crimes. He also had to track down the murder weapons used to kill and dismember Pat Walsh and Mary Anne Wysocki. Gunnery interviewed a desk clerk at a marine supply store on Commercial Street who told him that Costa had purchased two watertight containers shortly before his arrest. Might he, in an effort to destroy the evidence, have sealed the gun and the bloody knife in one of the containers and tossed it into the sea?

"We need to get justice for these women, and we need to find the murder weapon," Gunnery said to himself.

The trooper pulled Steve Grund off the street and questioned him about the ride to Boston in Pat Walsh's stolen VW and also about the missing gun used in her murder and the killing of Mary Anne Wysocki.

"He asked me if I wanted to buy his twenty-two-caliber pistol," Grund said. "I said, 'No, it's hot.' I knew it was hot and had no use for it. Tony told me that he had it hidden in the Truro woods."

Grund also mentioned that Costa kept a small sack with him. "He called it his *suicide kit*. Tony was sick of the hassle you cops are giving him. The bag contained twelve pills in all, including two Rainbows. If he swallowed 'em all at once, it would definitely be an overdose."

Gunnery then joined Bernie Flynn during an interview with a twenty-year-old friend of Costa's named William Watts Jr., who had known the suspect for at least six years.

"The first time I met him, he was dissecting a fish," Watts said. "He had taken different parts of the fish out. He said that he wanted to be a doctor and go to medical school. He was always reading books about abortions and operations."

Watts told them that he had seen Costa with a .22-caliber pistol adorned with a black-and-white handle. The witness also mentioned that Costa had once borrowed a German military shovel from Watts's mother but never brought it back.

Trooper Gunnery returned to the North Truro woods and zeroed in on the bases of several towering pine trees in the area where the bodies of the four women had been unearthed several weeks before. He got down on his hands and knees and began sifting through dirt where he had previously discovered three expended .22-caliber short shells. He found a rusted lock and an old carpenter's apron in the thick brush but nothing else, so he walked back to the parking area and the site where Ray Kimpel had previously found a handbag belonging to Mary Anne Wysocki. Gunnery began searching the bases of several trees lining the clearing. Soon, he found a depression in the soil and lifted the loose turf with his gloved hand.

"There's something here," he said aloud as he scooped dirt into a small pile. Moments later, he felt foreign material in his hand. He pulled slowly. It was a plastic bag covered in debris, and inside it was a small gun with white grips on its handle. The investigator could hardly believe his eyes or his luck. He got on his knees and swept his hands through the dirt and felt another object under a bed of wet leaves. It was a hunting knife with a red-striped handle secured in a leather snap sheath. Gunnery had found Costa's "pig stabber." He placed the weapons side by side and photographed them. He then brought the gun and knife to his superior, George Killen, for analysis. State police chemist Melvin Topjian was able to restore the gun's serial number—549086—which had been filed off, while the knife showed a presence of blood.

Maurice Goldman soon got word that investigators had recovered major evidence from the crime scene. The attorney relayed the troubling news in a meeting with his client.

"We have a strong suspicion that the gun is already in the possession of the police," Goldman informed Costa. "We believe they got it within the last three or four days."

"Are you sure they have it?" Costa asked.

"When I last saw Flynn and Gunnery, the look in their eyes said, *We've got the bastard good now!* Did they find the gun? We don't know. But they did find something. For God's sake, tell us everything you can. We have faith in you. Did you put a gun out there?"

"Yes," Costa finally admitted. "The gun itself is at the base of the biggest tree by the parking spaces. I was in a state of uptightness and panic. I knew there was a body discovered on that road. I put the gun beside the tree because it was given to me and I didn't know what to do with it."

"Who gave you the gun?"

"A man named Chuck Hansen. He knew the girls."

Chuck was the name Costa had written down in the phony telegram from New York.

"Will the gun have your fingerprints on it?" Goldman asked.

"Yes, I'm pretty sure it will. It wasn't wrapped in anything. It was just in the ground in a plastic bag."

"What about bullets? How many were in there?"

"There should be none. I never carried it with anything in it. I don't believe in the use of firearms. When it was given to me by Chuck, it was empty."

"Where is the gun exactly?"

"The gun is in the other direction from the woods. That's where I put the gun and the knife."

"Wait a minute," Goldman said, catching his breath. "There's a knife out there too?"

"Yes. It's like a Bowie knife. It has a long blade and has a reddish type handle."

At that moment, their conversation was interrupted by attorney Justin Cavanaugh, who entered the room and handed Goldman a piece of paper.

"Police just spoke to someone who claims that he sold you the gun," Goldman announced. "His name is Cory Devereaux."

CHAPTER TWENTY-SEVEN

Mailer was riding in his Jeep along Route 6A heading back to Provincetown from a meeting in Boston when he noticed a familiar figure standing on the side of the road with her thumb sticking out. It was Evelyn Lawson, and she was hitchhiking. Mailer pulled to the shoulder and swung open the passenger-side door.

"Hop in, stranger," he called.

Lawson looked inside the Jeep and revealed a painted-on smile. She hoisted her sturdy frame into Mailer's military surplus vehicle and patted him on the shoulder.

"Drive," she ordered.

"It's a bit dangerous to be hitchhiking out here, don't you think?" Mailer commented. "You told me yourself that there are more killers in *them thar woods.*"

"My car broke down in Wellfleet," Lawson said. "I've got friends who are work-shopping a new play in Provincetown, and I need to show my support."

"Seems to me that you're heading into the belly of the beast," Mailer replied. "It's not the Provincetown you think you know anymore. The place is spooky."

"So why haven't you left?" Lawson asked.

"I'm interested to see how this whole thing plays out," he told her. "I'm an existentialist who believes there is a God and a Devil at war with one another."

"Which side are you on?"

"I'm definitely not evil. Unquestionably wicked, yes."

"Well, there's wickedness all around us," Lawson claimed. "Ed Dinis is a dope, and he doesn't want to admit that the Cape is crawling with witches and drug fiends. He and others believe that if word gets out, it'll drive the tourists away. But witches have called Cape Cod home long before any vacationers came here. Did you know that the *Whydah* pirate ship sank somewhere off our coast as its captain was returning to his love, Maria 'Goodie' Hallett? She watched his ship go down from the dunes and adopted witchcraft thereafter. Hallett has cursed this area since 1717."

"Okay, I'll play your game," Mailer said. "I've encountered some strange girls in town. They made the hair stand up on the back of my neck."

"They belong to a coven," Lawson insisted. "Witches exist here. But who believes it? The fact that people don't believe in witches is one of the strongest factors that cults have going for them, leaving them free to practice their ceremonies."

"And by that, you mean the murders of those girls?"

"Take Costa for example. Could one man sustain so diabolical a series of activities?" Lawson asked. "Or could these crimes have been the work of an organized group bent on ritualistic murder?"

"And you feel that the district attorney is covering all this up?" Mailer asked.

"Of course! Narcotics are always involved in ritualistic murder. Cannibalism is a feature of these rites too. The timing of the murders also seems to fit an ancient pattern. February 8 is the date designated for the witches' winter conclave. The other three dates when cultists hold their rituals are in May, when Sydney Monzon disappeared, August 2, and Halloween night. Didn't the medical examiner suggest that Susan Perry was murdered and buried sometime in October?"

Mailer mulled over the theory as they arrived in Helltown. He dropped Lawson off at a gallery on Commercial Street.

"Be safe," he told her as she exited the vehicle. "How do you plan on getting back home?"

"I'll stay the night here with friends," she said.

"Okay, just make sure that you sleep with the light on."

District Attorney Ed Dinis did not have witchcraft on his mind when he met with his famous new friend Kurt Vonnegut Jr. at his temporary office inside the Barnstable Superior Courthouse. Vonnegut walked there from his home, which was only a few blocks away. The two-story Greek Revival building stood gallantly on top of a hill facing the Barnstable section of Route 6A. With a paper cup filled with hot coffee in one hand and a notepad in the other, Vonnegut strode the granite steps leading to the courthouse and passed the large bronze statue of local patriot James Otis Jr., sculpted by renowned artist David Lewis. The courthouse itself was built in 1831, but it was not the first building of its kind constructed on this stretch of land. It had replaced the original courthouse, which was built in the 1700s with monies donated by the British crown. Founding father John Adams had once argued a case here when he was a young lawyer. There was indeed much history here. But that rich history would soon be overshadowed by a ghastly series of events that would be adjudicated inside this courthouse.

Unlike the treatment of subordinates such as Tom Gunnery, Ed Dinis did not keep Vonnegut waiting. The lawman met the writer with a big smile in the lobby of the courthouse and ushered him into his office.

"There is so much work to be done in this case that it made no sense for me to commute from New Bedford each morning," Dinis explained. "I've decided to put up shop here for the duration, which we hope will culminate in Costa's trial and conviction."

"Why did you call me here this morning?" Vonnegut asked.

"Well, I wanted to inform you that this is a national story."

"I already know that. The news coverage has been insane."

"No, I mean that Costa has killed other young women around the country."

Vonnegut took out his notepad, licked the tip of his pencil, and got ready to write.

Dinis flipped open a thick manila file and handed a stack of investigative notes to Vonnegut.

"Our investigators have learned that Costa had driven two women, described by hippies in Ptown as dirty, down-and-out diggers, west to California last year," Dinis said. "Their names are Bonnie Williams and Diane Federoff. Costa told his ex-wife that he ditched the girls in Pennsylvania because he was afraid of crossing state lines with a minor. Williams is only sixteen years old. Costa then changed his story and confided to friends that he had dropped the women off in the town of Hayward, just outside San Francisco. But detectives have found no sign of them there. Their families have not heard a word from Bonnie or Diane in months. The women have simply vanished."

"Or they're buried out west in the desert or somewhere in Golden Gate Park," Vonnegut surmised.

"It seems that the women around Tony Costa either die or go missing or both," Dinis added. "Costa had a girlfriend named Christine Gallant who turned up dead in a bathtub in New York City. At first, the medical examiner thought she OD'd or committed suicide. But there were injuries to her body. Now we can probably add her to Costa's kill list. Coupled with Williams and Federoff and the bodies buried in North Truro, which makes seven victims so far. And I wouldn't be surprised if there were more."

Vonnegut spent the next few minutes writing up his notes.

"All this is on background for now," Dinis told him. "I will give you a proper quote when the time comes. Just make sure you spell my name correctly."

Trooper Gunnery and Bernie Flynn were intrigued by the idea that Costa may have left a trail of bodies behind him during his trip to California and his stay in San Francisco in 1967. They learned that Costa had first lived at 1667 Haight Street, the epicenter of America's counterculture movement. There he had met a young mother named Barbara Spaulding. She was recently divorced from her husband and was caring for the couple's two-year-old child. Costa and Spaulding bonded over their mutual love of drugs. Costa had no money, and Spaulding was living week to week on meager welfare checks. He moved into her apartment on McAllister Street, which was nothing more than a third-floor bedroom with a small kitchenette, and together they enjoyed a brief bohemian paradise. In the early morning hours, Costa would sneak out of the apartment and poach cartons of milk and other dairy products from the doorsteps of neighbors. He raided local vegetable gardens for lettuce, carrots, and cucumbers. He learned how to sift through dumpsters and garbage cans for day-old bread and pastries. Costa lived with Spaulding briefly before he was ordered back to Massachusetts to face charges of nonpayment of child support to Avis for their three children. After he left San Francisco, Barbara Spaulding mysteriously disappeared. Her sister Grace reported her missing, and her car was also abandoned on Cole Street in the Haight-Ashbury district where it was left untouched for five months.

CHAPTER TWENTY-EIGHT

After spending thirty-five days under psychiatric evaluation at Bridgewater State Hospital, Tony Costa was declared mentally fit for trial and was transported in shackles to the Barnstable House of Correction, located at the top of a steep hill overlooking the superior courthouse and Cape Cod Bay.

Maurice Goldman wanted to learn more about the relationship between his client and Cory Devereaux. They met in a large room inside the prison, and they were not alone. The room was crowded with inmates serving minor charges, nonviolent offenses such as drunk driving and drug possession, who were visited by their girlfriends and lawyers. Tony Costa was the only prisoner wearing handcuffs.

"Did Deveraux sell you a twenty-two-caliber pistol?" the attorney asked Costa as they sat opposite each other at a small wooden table.

"It's much more than that," the suspected killer replied. "I just heard that the autopsy report on the Walsh girl has come in."

"Yeah, so?"

"I didn't shoot her," Costa declared.

"Then tell me who did?" Goldman urged.

"Cory Devereaux shot her, and this is a fact that I plan to prove one way or the other!"

Hearing his name, Costa's alter ego awoke from his slumber in the recesses of the killer's mind.

I thought we were in this together? Cory shouted. *Now you're pinning these murders on me alone? What happened to our plan? We were gonna blame Chuck Hansen, right? They'd never find him because he doesn't fucking exist. But now you want to put me at the scene of the crimes? Fucking turncoat!*

"Did you play any role in the murders at all?" Goldman pressed.

"No, I didn't," Costa pleaded. "I simply cannot stand the sight of blood. I get physically sick. I had nothing to do with that. My part in this whole deal was getting rid of the car. I took that as my obligation. That was the extent of my goings-on in this case. I did my part and Cory did his part, and now I'm stuck with the rest of it. The only difference is that I'm stuck in here and he's out there. We need to do something about my counterpart."

At that moment, Costa doubled over in pain. He could feel his abdominal muscles tighten as if someone had just slugged him in the gut. He dropped to the floor and cried out.

See that, motherfucker? Cory chided him. *You think I'm just gonna let you send me to the gallows?*

Another sharp pain pierced Costa's stomach, and he wailed loudly.

A guard rushed over with his baton out in case it was some ploy.

"He needs an ambulance!" Goldman shouted.

"We can get him to the hospital quicker," the guard said.

He and another corrections officer lifted the prisoner to his feet and led him out of the back of the building to a waiting police car. Costa, still manacled, lay down in a fetal position in the back seat. He moaned continuously during the eight-minute drive to Cape Cod Hospital in Hyannis.

"My kidneys hurt terribly," he told the ER doctor upon his admittance. "I feel like I'm dying!"

Accompanied by the two armed guards, Costa was given X-rays that showed that his kidneys were of normal size, shape, position, and function.

"I haven't been able to urinate for several days," he complained to the physician, Dr. Keith Rapp. He was given a catheter. The X-rays showed that he had a considerable amount of fecal matter in his colon.

"We've identified your problem," Dr. Rapp told him.

My problem is Cory Devereaux, Costa thought to himself.

"We'll give you some meds and some antibiotics, and that should clear things up for you in no time," the doctor added.

"I plan to go to medical school one day," Costa said. "I want to be a doctor, just like you."

Dr. Rapp looked over at the armed corrections officer standing at attention by the door of Costa's room and decided to leave the comment alone.

Costa spent two days at Cape Cod Hospital before he was sent back to his cramped jail cell.

At the same time, Cory Devereaux, the *real* Cory Devereaux, was sitting down for his first interview with Trooper Tom Gunnery and Lieutenant Bernie Flynn at the Provincetown police station. Devereaux was accompanied to the interview by his mother, Nora Welch. Devereaux was tall and lean with long, curly, brown hair and a thick beard that traced his jawline. He was also asthmatic, and the anxiety of the whole experience caused labor in his breathing.

"What's your name?" Flynn asked.

"Cory Bond Devereaux."

"How old are you?"

"Seventeen."

Devereaux told Flynn and Gunnery that he was currently a junior at Provincetown High School and that he had become close friends with Tony Costa.

"We've received information that you were in possession of a firearm last summer," Gunnery noted.

"I got the gun while visiting my grandmother in Bluefield, West

Virginia," Devereux explained. "It was a twenty-two-caliber, six-shot revolver, and it had a pearl handle. I think it was made in West Germany."

"Did Antone Costa inquire about buying the gun at some point?" Gunnery asked.

"Yeah, he said that he needed a pistol for protection. Seems that some people were pissed off when they found out that he was a police snitch. He paid me twenty bucks for the gun."

"Did you have at least two or maybe more occasions to go out to the North Truro woods?" Flynn asked.

"Tony took me out there to show me his stash of drugs," Devereaux replied.

"After we began the investigation and discovered the graves, you saw that location. Isn't that true?"

"It was dark when I went out there."

"You saw the graves?"

"Yes. It was close to the spot where Tony had hidden a big can full of pills."

"Did you ever see Antone Costa with any type of a machete knife?"

"A long one," Devereaux replied. "It was razor sharp, sharp enough that if you held it an inch above your finger and it fell, it would cut."

"Did you have a conversation with him about his trip to California or any girl he might have met?"

"He had a girl out there. He was in love and said that she was gonna come down here and live with him. About two weeks later, he thought she died."

"What was her name?"

"Barbara."

"Did you ever talk to Antone Costa about his philosophy on death?"

"Yes, he thought it was better than life," Devereaux answered. "He believed in the life after death philosophy. He was really strong on it. He thought that the life you had after death was so much better than the life you knew. It's supposed to be beautiful."

Gunnery took over the questioning.

"Look, we have learned through Costa's attorney that he's blaming you for the murders of Pat Walsh and Mary Anne Wysocki."

Devereaux was stunned. "That's insane."

"Well, we're just trying to cover all our bases," Gunnery assured him. "We'd like you to take a polygraph test."

The teenager's knee began to bounce as he squirmed in his chair. "This stuff makes me nervous, but I'm happy to take a lie-detector test. I'm completely innocent of this."

George Killen drove Cory Devereaux up to Boston where they met with a state police polygraphist.

Devereaux had with him a signed permission slip from his mother, as he was underage.

The teenager was hooked up to the polygraph machine, which would record his breathing rate, pulse, blood pressure, and perspiration.

"I have asthma," Devereaux informed the officer.

"Thanks for alerting me to this. It may affect your respiratory responses. Did you tell the police all you knew about the girls' murder?" the polygraphist asked.

"Yes," Devereaux answered.

"Did you have any part in killing any of the girls?"

"No."

"What day is it?"

"Sunday," he replied.

"Were you present when Susan Perry was killed?"

"No."

"Did you have any part in killing Sydney Monzon?"

"No."

"Did you bury either one of these girls?"

"No."

"Did you shoot either the Walsh or Wysocki girl?"

"No."

"Are you wearing a wristwatch?"

"Yes."

"Did you assist in burying either one of the Providence girls?"

"No."

"Did you tell the truth to all the questions on this test?"

"Yes," Devereaux replied emphatically.

Tony Costa voluntarily submitted to his own lie detector test inside the medical suite at the Barnstable House of Correction. His examiner was George Zimmerman, who had emigrated from Frankfurt, Germany, in 1949 and spoke with a thick Hessian accent, which reminded Costa of Hermann Hesse. Zimmerman had worked on the Boston Strangler case and was a frequent lecturer at Harvard Law School.

"Do you know who killed these girls, Tony?" Zimmerman asked while keeping a close eye on the polygraph chart read out.

"Yes I do," Costa replied strongly. "It is one person who is responsible for the deaths of all four girls. It's Cory Devereaux and he's a good friend of mine. He told me what he had done to Susan Perry and then he spoke of Sydney's murder and how he had gone and killed two other girls from Rhode Island."

"Was Cory familiar with the area in the woods where the girls were buried?" Zimmerman asked.

"Yes. I took him out there quite a few times," Costa claimed. "He knows the spot well. Cory had tried to buy heroin from Pat Walsh but she wouldn't sell him any so he completely flipped out. He said that he took my gun from its hiding spot and he used it. He'd seen me leave the pistol in the ammo can so Cory knew exactly where it was. There was a knife out there also."

"Whose knife was it?"

"It had to be Cory's."

Costa was returned to his cell while Zimmerman and an associate examined the results of the polygraph. They studied five chart readouts, which ran between three to five minutes each. The examiners noticed that the accused killer had heightened reactions to nearly every question that was asked during the test.

"What do you think?" Zimmerman asked his colleague.

"I would say that Costa has some problems."

Zimmerman delivered his results to Maurice Goldman.

"These tests do not support Tony's story," he told the lawyer.

The polygrapher who had performed a similar examination on Cory Devereaux had different news for George Killen and the investigative team.

"The young man is telling the truth," he said. "There is no way that he had any involvement with the murders of those young women."

CHAPTER TWENTY-NINE

Vonnegut parked his Saab in front of the Mayflower café on Commercial Street and made his way over to the town hall green. The author turned crime reporter needed to harvest more elements for his *Life* magazine piece. His daughter Edie had spent the previous summer in Provincetown studying oil painting. He floated her name around among the longhairs, all of whom offered a hazy nod of recognition.

"She's a cool chick," Sadie told him as she leaned her bicycle against a tree before stretching out on the grass. "I didn't know she had a famous father. We have a writer here too. Know Mailer? He's a real asshole."

"I'm working on a story about the Truro murders," Vonnegut told her.

Sadie shot a conspiratorial glance at her friend Thumper, who stood straddling her bike.

"Fuck you, old man," Sadie said. "Tony Costa didn't kill those girls. You're all piling on an innocent man. You're trying to extinguish his light."

"Did you know that he has a 121 IQ?" Thumper added.

Vonnegut nodded his head and scribbled something on his notepad.

"First of all, I am not writing this solely on the presumption that he's guilty," he told them. "He could have been framed for all I know. I've heard that he was playing both sides of the street, selling drugs and ratting out those who sold drugs. That's suicide to me. It's a very tribal thing to seek revenge and justice against someone like that."

Sadie and Thumper said nothing. Vonnegut pulled a package of cigarettes from his coat pocket and gave each of them an unfiltered Pall Mall. The girls took the peace offering and placed the cigarettes to their lips while the author struck a match and leaned in. The girls coughed as the smoke entered their lungs.

"What I need to know is this," Vonnegut said. "If the person who committed the Truro murders was high on something when he killed, what drug do you think he swallowed? I mean, these girls weren't only shot, they were butchered and left in shallow graves."

"Speed," the two girls said in unison.

"I've seen guys hopped up on speed do some crazy things," Sadie clarified. "But I've never seen Tony hurt anyone. He's all about love. He's been preaching that to us since the day we met him. Arresting someone like Tony is bad for all of us freaks."

Vonnegut jotted down more notes while the girls enjoyed their cigarettes.

"You're pretty groovy after all. Not at all like that shit who lives at the end of the street," Thumper told him, referring to Mailer. Vonnegut smiled and laughed.

He returned to his Saab and drove back to Barnstable. Inside his writing studio, he compiled his notes from that afternoon and compared them to his interview with the district attorney. The story was coming together, but it was still missing a major piece. He needed to gain access to the accused killer himself.

Vonnegut dialed Maurice Goldman's law office and was directed to speak with Lester Allen, a former newspaper reporter turned private investigator. He had been hired by Goldman after a story ran in the *Cape Cod Standard-Times* that alleged that Tony Costa burned his then wife Avis so badly that she required hospitalization. Goldman tasked Allen with separating the facts from fiction in this extraordinarily bizarre case. For Lester Allen, it was a plum job that paid ten dollars per hour plus six cents for every mile he drove. Allen's formal title was "chief investigator," and he had beaten out private detective Phil DiNatale for the position. DiNatale had investigated the Boston Strangler case a few years before and served as a consultant on the film starring Tony Curtis and Henry Fonda. Actor George Kennedy played DiNatale in the movie. But the word on DiNatale was that he was a lazy, dim-witted glory hound, so Allen was considered to be the smarter, safer choice.

Allen agreed to meet Vonnegut at a local bar in Hyannis called the 19th Hole. The writer entered the dimly lit tavern and navigated his way around the pool tables and dartboard toward the oak bar where Allen was seated, sipping a beer and watching a Boston Bruins game on the small black-and-white television fastened to the wall overhead.

"That Bobby Orr is something, ain't he?" Allen observed as he watched the all-star Bruins defenseman rush from end to end before dumping the puck behind the New York Rangers' goalie for a score.

"We had a kid around here that could move like Orr," Allen said. "Skated for the high school team. Jimmy Sherman, his name was."

"I know. My daughter Edie dated him. I scared him off my property once. I don't watch much hockey," Vonnegut admitted. He looked around the bar. "Kerouac used to drink here when he lived in Hyannis."

"Yeah, here and everywhere else," Allen laughed. "I hear he's not in good shape."

"I know the man well. We've spent time together at my home," Vonnegut confided. "And sadly, you're right. Kerouac is all alone now. I'm not sure he'll be sticking around for the long haul. He's pissed off that he lost a fortune from the TV show *Route 66*, which we all know was based on his novel, *On the Road*. Writing is a sad business."

"Isn't that why you wanted to meet?" Allen asked. "You're writing about our client, Tony Costa?"

"Just a magazine profile is all," Vonnegut told him. "I understand that you've spent some time with him in jail."

"I have, and it's our job to keep him out of the electric chair. I've witnessed seven executions, including three in one night. It's barbaric punishment."

"What can you tell me about Costa?" Vonnegut asked.

Allen gazed back at him suspiciously over the rim of his beer mug. "You working on a book about this case?"

Vonnegut shook his head no.

"Good, 'cause I am," Allen stated. "When all this is over of course. I got more than a thousand pages of transcripts based on our conversations so far."

"And what do they tell you?"

"There's not the slightest hint of how or even why the murders were done."

The investigator was lying to Vonnegut. Lester Allen wasn't about to share much inside information with the famous author.

"I can tell you that he enjoys reading Hermann Hesse and that he despises authority for all the pot busts and what he calls the cruel stupidities of the Vietnam war."

"Sounds like every other young freak," Vonnegut replied.

"Exactly. Tony Costa's no different from any other hippie. Everybody that's related to this case has had some experience with drugs, except for the lawyers of course, and the police."

"Are you saying that the victims were involved with drugs?" Vonnegut asked.

"I'm not saying that," Allen clarified. "But our boy Costa certainly is."

"I'd like to meet him. I'd like to speak to him myself. Is that possible?"

Allen shook his head. "Not a chance unless you go through me or Goldman."

"Can you get me inside?" Vonnegut asked.

"I'll make a deal with you," Allen said and smiled. "I'll get you in, but I want your name on my book."

"You mean as a coauthor?"

"Nah, but a blurb from the great Kurt Vonnegut will help me sell a ton of copies."

Normally, Vonnegut would have declined such a request. But this offer was too good to turn down.

He struck out his hand, and Allen took it. They shook and the deal was sealed. Vonnegut would finally get a chance to meet the suspected killer he had only read and heard about.

––––––––––

Lester Allen conducted another interview with Tony Costa on June 26, 1969, at the Barnstable House of Correction as a follow-up to Dr. Zimmerman's polygraph test. Despite Costa's poor performance during the lie detector test, his legal team had not given up hope that he was telling the truth about the murderous affair. As lead investigator, Allen needed to know whether Costa was the lone killer of the women or merely an accessory after the fact.

"I wanna talk to you about what you discussed with Zimmerman, and let's take it right from the top. The actual dismemberment of the two bodies took place right at those two graves?"

"I can't answer that totally," Costa replied. "They were partially dismembered when I arrived. They were in halves when I arrived."

"Cut in half? Where, Tony?"

"I'd say at the waist. It seemed to be at the waistline. There were two bodies in one pile. They were cold and stiff."

"Which body did you then help to cut up?" Allen asked.

"Mary Anne," Costa said flatly.

The investigator wanted specifics. "And you had to do what? Dismember the legs? Take the legs off? Or what?"

"Yes, just the legs and the head. That was it."

"Did Cory assist you with Mary Anne?"

"We brought the upper section of her body out. It was in some bushes, and we dragged it onto the ground and Cory just stood on it to make it more stationary. From there, I dug a hole and we put the upper section into the hole."

"What was the reason for removing the head?"

"Just to get the depth," Costa said matter-of-factly. "Just to stick it into the hole."

Lester Allen then moved the discussion to the other two victims buried in the North Truro woods.

"The motivation for Cory Devereaux killing Susan and Sydney Monzon isn't too clear unless there's some very far-out sexual hang-up that he has," Allen pointed out. "Was he hung up on dead bodies?"

"I think it has something to do with a fetish involving clothing," Costa claimed. "Cory had a pair of underwear that belonged to a girl that he carried around for some reason."

"Did Cory threaten you?"

"He just told me that I had better keep things quiet," Costa answered. "The indication that I got was that someone else was involved because it was not only Cory alone that I had to worry about. He stated that there were other people that we had to be concerned with and that we'd better watch out what we were doing."

Lester Allen shared his observations with Costa's lawyer.

Dr. Harold Williams drove to Cape Cod from his office at Harvard Medical School at the request of Tony Costa's lawyer Maurice Goldman. Unbeknownst to Costa, the attorney was shifting his strategy to an insanity defense. Goldman had little doubt that his client had murdered the four young women whose bodies were unearthed in North Truro and possibly others too. The suspected killer had already been analyzed and overanalyzed by professional headshrinkers, but Goldman had nothing definitive about Costa's mental state that he could present to a jury. Costa received good marks on the Wechsler Adult Intelligence Scale, scoring in the bright-normal range, although the clinical psychologist who administered the test suggested that he had disorganized thinking and appeared suspiciously overcautious. Another expert suggested that Costa showed no signs of an overt psychosis, while still another diagnosed him as being at least partially schizoid.

Dr. Williams peeked his bald, serpent-like head into the medical room at Barnstable House of Correction to see that Costa was seated at a small table, staring up at the ceiling and having a conversation with himself.

"We should've kept quiet about Vermont," Costa said aloud. "They'd still be searching for the car right now had you not led them right to it! We'd be free instead of caged in this shithole and headed for the electric chair."

Dr. Williams entered the room and introduced himself. "Who are you speaking to?" he asked.

"I'm just talking to myself," Costa admitted. "I like to verbalize situations and scenarios. Is that odd?"

"Not at all," Williams told him. "Millions of people do it every day."

The psychiatrist took a chair opposite Costa and got comfortable.

"Tony, Mr. Goldman would like us to discuss your relationship with Cory Devereaux. Is that all right with you?" Dr. Williams asked.

Costa's face immediately contorted in pain, and he held his stomach.

"Does the name cause you discomfort?"

"He causes me great discomfort, yes. Cory is the reason why I am in this place and not at home with my mother and my family."

"Are you saying that Cory killed those women?"

"Well, let me take you back a bit," Costa said. "Cory is a few years younger than me, and I have a deep compassion for all of my young associates. I suffered as a result of not having a father. I felt alone and deprived. I have developed my own fatherly instinct, and being a father figure to Cory fulfilled a need in me. When I first entered the police station, I intended to relate exactly what I knew about the crime, but under no circumstances would I involve Cory."

"You were trying to protect him?" Dr. Williams asked.

Costa nodded. "God's law commands me not to speak against my brothers and never to judge them. Judging Cory and speaking against him is God's sole responsibility, not man's!"

"But you have now reconsidered this?"

"I have to tell the truth. Cory Devereaux murdered and cut up those women. It was an ugly horrible nightmare, in which I was a victim of circumstance. I had to run. I ran from myself, from life and from reality."

The psychiatrist transcribed the conversation on a yellow notepad.

"My mother predicted all of this," Costa pointed out. "We are very much alike in the head. We don't take good advice. She told me that the only people I listen to are friends like Cory, and that they would get me in a hell of a mess."

After their meeting, Dr. Williams summarized the encounter during dinner with Maurice Goldman.

"Your client is harboring a great rage toward women, and I think it is borne from his relationship with his mother," he told the attorney.

"That's hardly enough to show insanity," Goldman replied.

"Well, I did observe Costa's personality transform when we discussed Cory Devereaux. I think he's created an altered state of consciousness in which he bears no responsibility for his crimes. The *good* Tony becomes an innocent bystander while his alter ego, in this case, Cory Devereaux, performs evil acts."

"Is there a clinical definition for this?" Goldman asked.

"There certainly is," the psychiatrist answered. "It's called ego splitting. It arises from early trauma, such as the death of Costa's father. It's a concept that was developed by Freud. It's a psychological defense. The alter ego that Tony has called *Cory Devereaux* will allow him to act on hideous and abhorrent impulses that Tony's conscious mind would not allow."

"But what would make the Cory Devereaux part of Tony's personality want to kill and rape those girls?"

"Ahh, I have been giving that much thought," Dr. Williams replied. "He talked a great deal about his mother Cecilia. It's my belief that, by killing those women and having sexual intercourse with them after death, your client was acting out a terrible drama of incest and matricide in which he sought a reunion with his mother in the ideal state of bliss and comfort that he had as a child."

"So he sexualized his mother and did the same with his victims?" Goldman asked.

"He also showed hate toward his mother," the psychiatrist added. "He hated what he loved because he could not get from her what he needed. The cutting out of his victims' genitalia made them sexless, pure and perfect, the way he was as a child. The murders were only foreplay to the grand union of death. By having sex with their corpses, Costa joined his victims before they were immortalized. The girls became his forever. They could not betray him as his mother had."

When Goldman arrived at his law office a couple of days later, he had a letter from his client waiting for him on his desk.

Mr. Goldman,

It is now my pleasure to inform you that I now spoken (the) entire truth concerning my implications in the demise of the girls of Providence. It took a tremendous load off my mind and has left me barren, desolate. I truly regret not disclosing this information sooner, but I regret even more my attempt to cover up his hideous crime. In the beginning, I went to the police with the sole intent of telling them what I knew, but once there I lost my courage. I became frightened. The police knew I was shielding someone, but due to my own implications, I failed to confide in them. Every night since my involvement in this, I have asked God for the strength and courage to endure. I have asked for a guiding light. I believe I have it. Would it be rational to confront Mr. Dinis with the knowledge we possess, and possibly allow me to testify for the state? I must impress upon you that I am not intent on reducing any sentence I receive. I am simply concerned with the fact that Cory may never reach trial, then our case is lost. Cory said he's guilty of all 4 deaths. As you know, I have helped the police before and I shall gratefully do so now if they will allow me to, and will offer protection. Please advise me as to whether you believe this would be a wise idea. Always,

Tony

CHAPTER THIRTY

Norman Mailer woke up before dawn and took his morning coffee while sitting in his Jeep, parked at the foot of Ant Hill, located deep in the heart of the Provincetown dunes. He could see the pink orb of the morning sun rising slowly over the Atlantic Ocean. Mailer got out to stretch his legs and get a better glimpse of the sun's diffused light casting long shadows over the windswept dunes. This was a place of solitude for the writer, and he needed it on this particular morning. The previous night, he had dreamed once again of finding his wife's severed head in a plastic bag, but this time, he had managed to muffle his screams, which allowed Beverly to sleep soundly beside him. Still, he could not shake the image from his mind.

"Who could be capable of doing such a thing?" he asked himself. "Could I be capable?" He had almost killed his second wife, Adele, and was fearful that he already knew the answer to his own dark question.

Mailer hiked up a path of bleached sand toward the top of Ant Hill. It was summertime now, but still the morning air was cold. He cradled the paper cup of coffee in his hands for warmth. Mailer trudged farther up the hill, his calf muscles tightening as his tennis shoes sank in the soft sand, which made for difficult footing. At the top of the hill, he could see three gillnet vessels motoring in the distance, their crews fishing the waters for cod and haddock. Mailer looked to the east where the sun was low on the horizon. The pink orb had turned blood orange as droplets of molecules in the atmosphere caused its light to scatter out and change directions and color. The view was breathtaking, and Mailer inhaled deeply, capturing the salt air in his lungs. He took his last sip of coffee and stuffed the empty cup into the pocket of his windbreaker. The writer abhorred littering, especially in a place as beautiful as this. His blue eyes scanned the sand and sea grass around him, and he noticed deep grooves in the dune.

"Someone was here last night," Mailer said to himself.

He traced the lines in the sand and recognized that they formed a particular pattern, a circle with the remnants of a five-pointed star in the middle.

"That's a pentacle," he whispered.

Lying on the sand inside the pentacle were several small polished black stones, which to Mailer looked like chocolate-covered almonds. He bent down and scooped the stones with his hands, placing them in his pocket along with the empty cup.

Mailer hiked back down Ant Hill and jumped in his Jeep. He was satisfied that the vehicle had enough gas to take him to Hyannis. He started the engine and drove to Evelyn Lawson's cottage some fifty miles away.

He arrived there an hour later, catching Lawson in her housecoat, enjoying her morning tea on the patio in back of her cottage. Mailer waved to her and let himself onto the property through a small iron gate.

"Good morning, Norman," she said and smiled. "What brings you here this bright and early? Just cruising the neighborhood, or were you out all night, drinking at the Mill Hill Club?"

"I'm stone sober this morning," he told her as he sat down next to her at her small picnic table. He unzipped his pocket, reached into his jacket, and pulled out the five small stones. They made a clattering sound as he dropped them on the wood table. "I found these in the dunes of Provincetown this morning," he told her. "They were left inside a pentacle that was carved into the sand."

"Last night was Litha, the shortest night of the year and a very sacred date on the Wiccan calendar," she explained. "It looks like you were standing right in the center of a witches' conclave."

"What does it mean?" he asked.

"The inverted pentacle represents the male energy," Lawson told him. "These witches pray to the gods of the forest, like the horned god Cernunnos or Pan, protectors of trees, flowers, and even marijuana plants."

"Do these witches believe that Tony Costa is a god of the forest?"

"Yes, I believe they do," she said and nodded. "And they are praying for him."

"I've had terrible dreams about him," Mailer confided. "And about his girls."

"What kind of dreams?" Lawson asked.

"There is no mercy in a dream," he told her. "Dream logic is strong and central. You can dream about fucking, and you can dream about killing."

"Fucking and killing are so vastly different," Lawson countered.

"That's not true," Mailer said. "Fucking is penetration. Murder is penetration. They're equal. You can express the best and the worst in yourself."

He had gotten far off topic. Mailer then pointed to the stones.

"What are those?" he asked.

Lawson held one of the stones in her hand and inspected it closely.

"This stone, like the others, is inscribed with a character. They are called rune stones, and they go back to about the fifth century AD," Lawson explained. "Rune means secret. The stones are an ancient alphabet first used by Vikings and Nordic tribes. They are very important symbols for a coven of witches, as they are used to foretell future events."

Lawson placed the stones side by side and then changed their order again and again until they finally revealed their secrets.

Her eyes went wide, and she pushed herself back from the table.

"What do you see?" Mailer asked her.

"I see more blood spilled in Helltown."

———————

Mailer returned to Provincetown and immediately called a local locksmith to fortify his home. While he packed for the next day's trip to Houston, Texas, to cover the moon mission for *Life* magazine, the locksmith and his helper installed double-bolt locks on both the front and back doors of his Commercial Street estate and secured every window. The noise and the sudden swirl of activity made his wife nervous.

"Why are we doing this?" she asked him.

"We are doing this because I will be gone for a few weeks in Texas, and that means both you and the children will be home alone until I get back," he told her. "I want you to be safe."

Mailer was referring to the couple's young sons, three-year-old Stephen and four-year-old Michael.

"Are you worried about the Truro murders? I mean, I'm not a teenage girl. I'm a mother with two kids. No one is going to lure me to their marijuana patch. Besides, isn't the killer locked up behind bars right now?"

"He is, but *they* aren't," Mailer replied. "Those murders may go beyond just one madman. This entire community has gone crazy. It's hard to complain about a little extra protection."

"Are you still having bad dreams?" she asked.

"I am," he admitted to her. "I dream of nightmarish things. I dream of a beautiful face wrapped in a death mask of plastic. I dream of body parts stacked upon one another. There's an evil to this wonderful place, and it sticks to my collar like sweat."

She pulled him toward her bosom and hugged him. Beverly could feel her husband's tears as they moistened her blouse.

Hours later, as darkness fell on the village, Mailer retreated to his third-floor writing studio with its views of the harbor and the Pilgrim Monument, illuminated in the distance. All was quiet now in the Mailer household as Beverly had put their two young boys to bed and had retired to the master bedroom with a book while he pored over research materials that had been sent to him by the publicists at NASA. He had the window in his office cracked open just enough to allow the cool summer breeze to circulate around him. The street below was quiet, unlike the other end of Commercial Street, where jazz musicians serenaded restaurant goers and the nightclubs were just opening their doors to summer revelers. All Mailer could hear were the waves running against the shore and the occasional chirping of cicadas, which after a seventeen-year absence had infested Cape Cod like locusts. He sipped bourbon while studying a document that explained how mathematicians had calculated the predicted flight path of the Apollo 11 Saturn V rocket using something called the Schmidt-Kalman filter. Mailer had planned to absorb all the science related to the mission before discarding it and allowing the story to come to him. During a pause between cicada chants, or singing as it were, as the male insects vibrated their back wings to attract females, Mailer thought he heard the sound of a bicycle bell coming from the street. One bell rang, and then another and another. Mailer peered out his window to see the silhouettes of what looked to be three young women straddling their bikes in front of his home. He raced downstairs to the kitchen and pulled a large carving knife out of a drawer. It was much bigger than the weapon he had stabbed Adele with years earlier. This time, Mailer wasn't drunk, drugged, or crazed. He was on a mission to defend his family. He crept out the back door and slithered through the side yard as if he was on army patrol. He then ran out into the middle of Commercial Street with the large knife held tightly in his right hand. By this time, the girls had turned around and were pedaling away from Mailer's home. They were ringing their bicycle bells, and they were laughing.

"Stay the fuck away from here," Mailer shouted. "I'll cut each of your fucking throats. I swear to God I will!"

He brought the knife to bed with him that night. Beverly was turned away from him and sleeping soundly. Mailer slid the weapon under his pillow and waited for the nightmares to come.

As Mailer boarded a plane to Houston the next morning, Vonnegut was preparing for his jailhouse meeting with Tony Costa. He walked the salt marshes of Sandy Neck and looked up past the flock of soaring geese to a massive brick jailhouse sitting ominously atop a nearby hill where Cape Cod's most notorious killer now resided. Vonnegut had not conducted a news interview since the days that he worked as a cub reporter in Chicago. Mostly, he had interviewed grieving widows and the like. He had never sat across from a suspected serial killer before.

"I shouldn't feel nervous meeting with the murderer," he told himself. "I've already witnessed the very worst that the human condition has to offer."

Vonnegut had not been privy to the autopsy photos of Pat Walsh, Mary Anne Wysocki, Sydney Monzon, or Susan Perry. If he had, he may have thought differently about the impending encounter.

The morning sun gave way to afternoon thunderclouds, which was typical weather for Cape Cod in the summertime. The sky spit rain onto the windshield of Vonnegut's Saab as he pulled into a lot in back of the superior courthouse. He stepped out of the car and jogged up the hill to the jailhouse, where he found the two girls he had interviewed in Provincetown, Sadie and Thumper, along with Strawberry Blonde. Sadie held a portable radio while the other two girls danced in the rain to the song "Aquarius" by the 5th Dimension, which was soaring up the Billboard charts. A group of prisoners pushed and pulled each other to gain a better view of the show out the small windows of the jailhouse.

"This is for you, Sire," Sadie shouted as Thumper and Strawberry Blonde rocked their hips and pressed their bodies together, swaying to the music.

"Let the sunshine, let the sun shine in, the sun shine in," the trio sang in unison.

By this point, the floor show had caused quite a ruckus in the jailhouse as prisoners hooted, hollered, and pleaded with the girls to strip naked. Thumper began to lift up her sundress but was stopped by a prison guard who had emerged from the jail.

"The show's over, girls, unless you want to be arrested for indecent exposure," he warned.

The prisoners all booed as the women were ordered off the property.

Vonnegut chuckled at the spectacle as he followed the guard back inside, where he was asked to hand over his car keys before getting buzzed into the jail's reception area.

"Which prisoner are you here to see?" the guard asked.

"Costa, Antone Costa," he answered. "My name's Vonnegut. It should be there on your list."

The guard scanned the manifest, and his dour expression gave way to a slight smile.

"My wife is a big fan of your books," the guard said. "Mind if I get an autograph?"

Vonnegut happily complied and scribbled his signature on a piece of paper. The guard then led him into the visitor's room and told him to wait.

"We'll summon the prisoner," the guard said.

A few minutes later, Tony Costa appeared. He did not look like the photograph that Vonnegut had seen in the newspaper. The accused killer's hair was longer now and unkempt. He had also grown a dark beard.

"Mr. Vonnegut?" he said and nodded.

"Mr. Costa." Vonnegut waved back.

The two men settled in at a small table in the back of the crowded room. Once again, Costa was the only prisoner forced to wear handcuffs. Vonnegut took out his notepad and a pencil.

Costa saw this and shook his head. "That will not be necessary," he told Vonnegut. "Our conversation today is strictly off the record."

"That wasn't the deal I made with Lester Allen," the writer argued.

"He doesn't make my deals," Costa replied. "I do. If you do not wish to speak, I will go back to my cell."

"Fuck it, I'm here," Vonnegut said with a shrug. "Let's talk."

He offered Costa a cigarette, but the prisoner declined. Vonnegut struck a match to a Pall Mall and blew a stream of smoke over the prisoner's head.

"That was quite a cancan show out there. Did you order your girls to do that?"

"I give no orders to anyone," Costa replied. "They did it out of their love for me."

"My daughter Edie is about their age. She studied painting in Ptown last summer and ran with the hippie crowd. Did you know her?"

"Yes, her name sounds very familiar to me. I'm sure we bumped into each other from time to time."

"What would you like to talk about, Tony?"

"First of all, I am not a vampire," Costa told him. "I have never bitten anyone. Ed Dinis has made a mockery of these crimes."

"Are you a killer?" Vonnegut asked.

"You mean like those soldiers in Vietnam?" Costa said, deflecting the question.

"No, I mean like the madman who chopped up those women and left them in shallow graves like buried rubbish."

"Those murders were abominable. I had nothing to do with them. But my lawyers and I are going to expose the real facts of this case and who was responsible."

"You said that there's a maniac on the loose out there," Vonnegut reminded him. "Who are you referring to?"

"I'm referring to the *real* killer," Costa replied. "His name will come out in court and then in a book I plan to write."

Vonnegut twisted the end of his mustache with his fingers. "You fashion yourself a writer?"

"More so than a criminal. I've got one of the greatest untold stories that you'll ever read," Costa said. "I'm the most famous prisoner in the country right now. And that's what I truly am, a prisoner. You would not understand."

"Oh, I think I would, Tony. I've been a prisoner also. I wrote about that in my latest book."

"Well, here I have witnessed perfectly, the cockroaches crawling about in throngs, the mice running across the floor, and the filth of the jail itself," Costa explained.

Vonnegut could not help but chuckle. "I've witnessed that too," he noted. "I've also seen a lion, escaped from a zoo, maul someone before my very eyes."

"That sounds ghastly," Costa replied.

"So it goes."

"Where were you a prisoner?"

"Dresden, Germany, during the war," Vonnegut pointed out.

"My favorite writer is German. Do you like Hermann Hesse?"

"I think that *Steppenwolf* is the most profound book ever written about homesickness," Vonnegut observed. "Hesse speaks to young readers. He speaks to the essence of youth and offers hope. He's a bit like J. D. Salinger in that way. Does he speak to you, Tony?"

Costa leaned forward and whispered, "I am the wolf of the steppes."

A chill ran down Vonnegut's spine. At that moment, he knew that Tony Costa had butchered those women. He could only imagine what would have happened to his daughter if she had accepted his invitation to see his marijuana garden. He shuddered at the thought but kept his composure.

"I've been doing some writing of my own," Costa went on. "Mr.

Goldman is brokering a book deal for me right now. We'll split the proceeds. That is how I am paying him. There will no doubt be a movie in this whole affair as well, just like *The Boston Strangler*. Only my story is much better. As I said, there is nothing else like it. I'm not John Q. Sucker. I know there's a boatload of money to be made here."

"Writing is hard work," Vonnegut said. "But so is killing, I would imagine."

Costa would not take the bait. "I have no idea about that." He reached into his shirt pocket with his manacled hands. A jail guard approached the table.

"You know the rules, Costa. There will be no exchange of materials with visitors."

"I'm not giving him anything," Costa explained. "I'm merely going to recite a poem that I wrote to my esteemed guest. It's not every day that you get a chance to meet someone like Kurt Vonnegut."

The guard shrugged but gave the okay. Costa opened up a folded piece of writing paper and read aloud.

"I call this 'Guardian of the Forest,'" he said proudly. "You stand in the vast expanse of distance. Stopping to look back, as a warrior queen surveying the land she has left, charred, barren, conquered. What you have destroyed you can no longer repair. The grass will not grow. Flowers will not bloom amidst the garbage. The dead must die. Don't look back. You are a plague. A dark and hideous plague. And me? I taught you all I know."

Costa folded the paper and tucked it back into his pocket.

"What do you think?" he asked Vonnegut.

"Who's the plague, Tony? Who is the dark and hideous plague?"

Costa did not answer. He only smiled. "The writings of Antone C. Costa will one day appear side by side with those of Kurt Vonnegut Jr. Who would imagine that?"

"Yeah, Tony," Vonnegut replied. "Who would imagine that?"

CHAPTER THIRTY-ONE

Norman Mailer arrived in Texas with two things on his mind, and neither of them had to do with reporting on the greatest technological achievement in the history of the human race. There were potentially more killers on the loose in his backyard at the tip of Cape Cod, and his marriage was beyond repair. Beverly Bentley, his fourth wife, had grown tired of his criticism, especially about her acting, and had grown even more tired of him as a husband. Beverly had taken a lover and jetted off to Mexico with him while the kids were cared for in Provincetown.

Mailer had burned something in his soul during his tumultuous run for mayor of New York that spring, and he had nothing left to give Beverly except for a husband that in his own mind was a mildly depressed, somewhat used up, somewhat disembodied spirit.

Adding to his frustration was the Apollo team's refusal to meet with him ahead of their launch. Mailer penned a letter to Neil Armstrong, Buzz Aldrin, and Michael Collins requesting an interview. "You wouldn't let a commercial pilot fly Apollo," he argued. "Why not let someone who is recognized as one of the better journalists meet you in order to write about you?"

Armstrong responded, calling Mailer's plea "lucid" and "convincing" but that the answer was still no. In other words, America's space heroes were telling Mailer to fuck off.

His spirits were lifted when his agent, Scott Meredith, brokered what was reported to be a million-dollar advance for a book on the moon landing. The staggering number was only smoke and mirrors, however. Mailer was paid $300,000 for the hardcover and paperback rights while the agent predicted that foreign rights would send that price rocketing over seven figures. Still, it was a princely sum for Mailer, and the bullshit story that he was a million-dollar writer added to his growing legend while causing other authors, like Vonnegut, to become even more jealous of his success.

Mailer got a good look at the NASA Manned Spacecraft Center in Houston where the returning astronauts would be quarantined. He then flew to Huntsville, Alabama, to inspect the Marshall Space Center, where scientists had developed the Saturn V launch vehicle, before ultimately arriving at the Kennedy Space Center in Florida.

On the morning of July 16, 1969, Mailer stood breathless and shoulder to shoulder with journalists from around the world at NASA's press site to witness the historic moment, one he had hoped would live up to his grand expectations.

"Thirty-five seconds and counting," came the announcement from mission control. "We are still go with Apollo 11. Thirty seconds and counting. Astronauts report it feels good. T-minus twenty-five seconds. Twenty seconds and counting. T-minus fifteen seconds. Guidance is internal. Twelve, eleven, ten, nine, ignition sequence start, six, five, four, three, two, one, zero, all engines running. Lift-off. We have lift-off, thirty-two minutes past the hour. Lift-off on Apollo 11."

The moment did not disappoint Mailer or most anyone else watching it televised live across the globe. He could not hear the final countdown from Mission Control as the rocket motors ignited with a ferocious roar that almost blew out his eardrums. The engine's flames were equally as dramatic.

To Mailer, they looked like two enormous wings of a yellow bird of fire flying across an open field. As he would also later describe in his writing, the epic feat had little to do with mechanics. The launch was pure magic.

Mailer had been to war and had witnessed three political assassinations in his lifetime as well as the near nuclear annihilation of the planet during the Cuban missile crisis. Much of the news of the twentieth century unfolded on his watch. Still nothing could compare to the fire and fury of the godlike launch of Saturn V.

"Oh my God, oh my God," Mailer repeated over and over again.

But he could not decide whether it was the work of God or the devil.

"If it's the devil, then the devil is beautiful indeed," he told himself. "If it's the work of God, in that the notion that man voyaged out to fulfill God's vision, the heavens were now being violated by a ship of flames on its way to the moon."

Back in Provincetown, at Race Point beach, Sadie, Thumper, and Strawberry Blonde grabbed pieces of driftwood and began carving the triple goddess symbol in the sand. They drew the three phases of the moon in tandem: the waxing crescent moon connecting to the full moon with the waning crescent on the opposite side. They danced around their creation while the Apollo 11 crew soared forty-three miles above Earth, traveling at a velocity of 4,047 feet per second. Tony Costa watched the launch on a small black-and-white television set in a crowded cafeteria at the Barnstable House of Correction. Cory was once again plaguing his thoughts.

We need to kill, the alter ego urged him. *It's been far too long since we had blood in our fingernails. But instead, we're caged with animals. The wolf of the steppes yearns to be free.*

"Free we will be," Costa promised him. "You now have to begin listening to me. I have a plan to rid us of this mess."

A few blocks away, Vonnegut stewed over the space spectacle. He had just written a full-page essay for the *New York Times* that was highly critical of NASA's mission. Vonnegut was frustrated by the fact that the U.S. government had spent $19 billion on the space program while refusing to clean up its filthy colonies here on Earth. "Excelsior! We're going to the Moon! Excelsior," he wrote. He compared the mastery of a new environment like space to the Spaniards' mastery of the New World. "I think of their masterful torture of Indians," he added. "I think of White America's mastery of the South by the imaginative use of kidnapped Africans."

Unlike the 1968 Democratic National Convention, Vonnegut would not remain on the sidelines of this gigantic story. He had finagled an invitation to the launch but could not attend, but Vonnegut was front and center a few days later when Apollo 11 astronaut Neil Armstrong became the first man to step onto the surface of the moon. Despite his acerbic view of the space program, or perhaps because of it, Vonnegut was invited to the CBS news studio in New York City to witness the event with anchorman and Martha's Vineyard resident Walter Cronkite and a panel of talking heads that also included Gloria Steinem. All watched a live television feed from Mission Control in Houston as Armstrong and Buzz Aldrin landed the lunar module *Eagle* on the cratered surface of the moon. The initial moments were fraught with danger as Armstrong was forced to manually pilot the module past an area of jagged boulders. This act depleted much of the ship's fuel. The *Eagle* had only thirty seconds of fuel left to make the landing. Biosensors in Armstrong's customized spacesuit, made up of twenty-one layers of neoprene rubber and metalized polyester, recorded his heart rate at 160 beats per minute. The spacecraft finally touched down on an even surface, landing on the moon four days, six hours, and forty-six minutes after lift-off from Florida.

"Tranquility base here. The *Eagle* has landed," Armstrong said calmly into his mic.

"Roger, Tranquility, we copy you down," said fellow astronaut Charlie Duke at Mission Control. "You had a bunch of guys down here about to turn blue."

With half a billion people watching on Earth, Neil Armstrong climbed down the ship's ladder and jumped onto the moon's powdery terrain.

"One small step for man. One giant leap for mankind," Armstrong announced to the world.

To Norman Mailer, the Apollo 11 astronaut had just joined the ranks of the forever quoted, bumping Patrick Henry's words, "Give me liberty or give me death," from the highest peak of orations. Vonnegut, however, was less impressed by the moon landing.

"Putting space exploration ahead of eradicating poverty is morally untenable," Vonnegut commented to Cronkite before a national television audience. "For that kind of money, the least NASA can do is discover God."

The CBS news anchor was furious at Vonnegut, but he managed to keep his cool on air.

"He was really sour," Cronkite later told his producer. "He just set the wrong mood, a big downer."

Most Americans agreed with Cronkite. Angry letters flooded the mailroom at CBS News. Many called Vonnegut's appearance unpatriotic and even un-American. He was also blasted by his hometown newspaper as "a man who has something bad to say about everything."

Mailer did not view the moon landing as a colossal waste of taxpayer dollars. To him, it represented something much bigger, much darker. He saw it as a rip in the universe and a work of art designed by the devil. Mailer had recently taken to calling himself by the name Aquarius, which was his birth sign. He called his estranged wife, Beverly, by her own zodiac sign, Gemini. He believed that her growing anger toward him was a derangement brought about by Apollo's usurpation of the moon.

CHAPTER THIRTY-TWO

———

Edgartown, Massachusetts, Police chief Dominic "Jim" Arena ran his hand through his dark, thinning hair as he stood near Dike Bridge, a narrow crossing about fifteen feet wide on the east side of Chappaquiddick Island. It was 8:30 a.m. on July 19, 1969, and his day was just beginning.

He was joined by a middle-aged woman named Sylvia Malm, who lived less than a mile down the dirt road. They were both staring down at a car that was overturned and submerged six feet deep in the waters of Poucha Pond. The nose of the vehicle was at a slight angle and pointing toward the bridge. The left rear tire was sticking out above the waterline. There were scuff marks on the bridge indicating where the car had careened off.

"Did you hear anything this morning?" Arena asked her.

"Not this morning," the woman said. "But I heard a car engine last night."

"Do you have a spare bathing suit?"

She nodded. Arena walked over to his squad car and radioed for a diving team. Knowing that it would take an hour or more for any diver to reach this remote section of Martha's Vineyard, he changed into a pair of borrowed swim trunks and climbed into the murky water.

Arena swam out to the car and dove twice. He tried to get under the vehicle to see if anyone was inside, but the current was too strong and kept pulling him back no matter how hard he swam. Frustrated, Arena returned to his police car and waited for the divers to get there. A short time later, he was sitting on the trunk of the car surrounded by water up to his chest. Arena was holding one end of a rope that was attached to diver John Farrar, who was searching underwater and inside the submerged car. The police chief soon felt a tug on the rope, and he began to pull Farrar to the surface. The diver was carrying the body of a young woman over his shoulder. A small rowboat was dispatched into the pond to retrieve the body. Holding the dead woman in his arms, the police chief noticed that she was wearing a white long-sleeved blouse, a pair of dark pants, and sandals. There were no noticeable injuries. Her body bore no blood, bruises, or contusions. Farrar found a gold necklace and a pocketbook in the back seat. Arena looked through the pocketbook and found an identification card for Rosemary Keough, an employee of the U.S. Senate.

The woman's body was brought to shore, placed on a stretcher, and covered with a blanket. Arena then ordered his men to place her in the back of his squad car until the medical examiner got there.

"What's the story?" Dr. Donald Mills asked when he arrived at the scene.

"Somebody found this overturned car," an officer said, pointing to the submerged vehicle. "We sent a diver down, and he came up with a body, the body of a girl. We need a ruling on what to do with her. What should we do next?"

Dr. Mills instructed the officer to take the body out of the back seat and bring it around to the front of Chief Arena's police cruiser, where he could have sufficient privacy to examine the victim without exposing her to too many people, as a crowd of islanders had gathered at the bridge. Mills pulled away the blanket covering her body. He noted that she was a well-developed, very attractive, nicely dressed girl probably in her midtwenties. Dr. Mills surmised that the woman was between 115 and 125 pounds and of average height. Her hair was upswept, and she had a ring on her right hand. He saw no broken bones. The physician ran his fingers through her matted hair and found no swelling of her skull. The only bruise that Mills could find was a little scuff mark on her knuckle. The victim's color was pale, and she was in full rigor mortis.

"The body is almost as solid as it was made of stone," the medical examiner told Chief Arena. "She also has a fine white froth coming from her nose and mouth." Dr. Mills pointed to a tiny cobweb of blood in the foam around her nose. "This indicates that she has much water in her respiratory tract. There's water in the bronchial tree, the trachea, and her nose and throat," he stated. "I'd say she's been dead at least six hours or more. It's a clear case of drowning."

"There still may be another body in the pond," Arena told him. "We can't seem to locate the driver. If that's the case and we don't find it quickly, the tide from the pond will carry it out to sea."

Crews used a winch to pull the car, a 1967 Oldsmobile Delmont 88, out of the water. The windshield was shattered, the car window on the driver's side was rolled down, and two windows on the passenger side were smashed out. The roof had a big dent in it, and there were dents on the vehicle's right side.

Chief Arena got the license plate number for the car, L78–207, and asked one of his officers to get a listing on it.

The vehicle was registered to U.S. Senator Edward M. Kennedy of Boston, Massachusetts, the prince turned patriarch of America's most powerful political family.

When the island mortician arrived at the scene, Dr. Mills told him, "Take this young lady back to your funeral home and do not do a thing until you hear from me again."

Chief Arena told his officers to find Kennedy, who had been seen that morning at the Edgartown ferry landing. He used the telephone at Sylvia Malm's house on Dike Road to call his office.

"Senator Kennedy is here at the station, and he wants to talk to you," Arena's secretary informed him. She then handed the phone to Kennedy.

"I'm sorry, Senator, but I have some bad news," the chief began. "Your car has been involved in an accident."

"I know this," Kennedy replied.

"Did you know that anyone else was in the car?"

"Yes," the senator replied softly.

"Do you know if they're in the water?"

"No. Could I talk to you? Could I see you?"

"Yes, Senator. Do you want to come over here?"

There was no way that Kennedy was returning to Chappaquiddick Island, to the scene of his crime.

"I'd like you to come over here," Kennedy told Arena.

The police chief got a ride to the police station, which was located inside the Edgartown town hall, to find Kennedy and his friend Paul Markham waiting for him in his office.

"I'm so sorry," Arena told him again.

"Yes, I was the driver," Kennedy said, his voice shaking. "What do we have to do?"

The senator provided a handwritten statement, which Arena typed up. Together, they read the typed version to ensure that it had captured Kennedy's own words verbatim.

"On July 18, 1969, at approximately 11:15 p.m. in Chappaquiddick, Martha's Vineyard, Massachusetts, I was driving my car on Main Street on my way to get the ferry back to Edgartown. I was unfamiliar with the road and turned right onto Dyke [sic] Road instead of bearing hard left on Main Street. After proceeding for approximately one-half mile on Dyke [sic] Road I descended a hill and came upon a narrow bridge. The car went off the side of the bridge. There was one passenger with me, one Miss Mary Jo Kopekne [sic], a former secretary of my brother Sen. Robert Kennedy. The car turned over and sank into the water and landed with the roof resting on the bottom. I attempted to open the door and the window of the car but have no recollection of how I got out of the car. I came to the surface and then repeatedly dove down to the car in an attempt to see if the passenger was still in the car. I was unsuccessful in the attempt. I was exhausted and in a state of shock. I recall walking back to where my friends were eating. There was a car parked in front of the cottage and I climbed into the backseat. I then asked for someone to bring me back to Edgartown. I remember walking around for a period and then going back to my hotel room. When I fully realized what had happened this morning, I immediately contacted the police."

The police chief read the victim's name. It did not match the identification cards that were pulled from the wreck.

"Who is Mary Jo?" Arena asked him.

"Her name is Mary Jo Kopechne," Kennedy replied. "She worked for my brother Bobby."

Arena examined the statement again. "Is that the correct spelling of her name?"

"I have no idea."

Kennedy exited the police station, leaving more questions than answers behind.

"Why had it taken so long, nine hours, for him to report the accident?" the police chief asked himself. "Was Kennedy telling the truth when he said that he'd tried to save the girl's life?"

John Farrar, the diver who had recovered Kopechne's body, showed up at the police station in Edgartown to share his concerns.

"Look, Chief, I believe that the girl was alive for some time in that car," Farrar confided to Arena, privately in his office.

The police chief pushed his chair back from his desk, got up, and walked over to the office door and locked it. He then drew the shade on the window.

"What the fuck are you telling me?" Arena whispered.

"When I found her, she was in the back seat and had positioned herself to breathe in the only available air pocket," Farrar replied. "Remember, the car was on its roof, so the trunk was dry. There was air. She didn't drown. Kopechne suffocated. I think she'd be alive right now if only Kennedy had called for help. But he didn't have the guts or gumption to save her."

"What other evidence do you have to support your theory?" Arena asked.

The twenty-nine-year-old Farrar was no average diver. He was the captain of the fire department's search and rescue dive team.

"When they pumped her chest, she exuded blood froth, not water," Farrar explained. "Blood froth is consistent with suffocation."

"Look, you don't mention a word of this to anyone," Arena ordered. "We need to get our hands around this thing and fast."

Jim Arena had only been the police chief in Edgartown for two and a half years. The former U.S. Marine realized immediately the enormity of the situation, and he called District Attorney Ed Dinis for help.

"There's been an accident here on the island," Arena told Dinis over the phone. "A car went off a bridge, and a girl is dead."

"If it's an accident, why are you calling my office?" the district attorney asked with a trace of annoyance in his voice.

"The driver of the car was Ted Kennedy," the police chief replied. "And his story isn't adding up."

Ed Dinis's blood ran cold, but he maintained his composure. "One of my men will be in touch with you shortly. Do not make any statement to the press."

The DA set the phone back on its receiver. "Fuck, fuck, fuck!" he yelled.

The eruption startled Dinis's secretary, and she spilled a hot cup of coffee on the green carpet of the outer office.

This news was the worst case scenario for the lawman, and it could not come at a worse possible time. All his attention and that of his investigators was focused on building a successful murder case against Tony Costa. He would have the eyes of the world upon him as he prosecuted the so-called Cape Cod Vampire. Greatness was close to his grasp. But now, since Martha's Vineyard was in his jurisdiction, Dinis would be forced to lead the Kennedy probe. If the car wreck had happened in any place outside Massachusetts, a district attorney would salivate over the opportunity to investigate one of the most powerful men in America. But this was the heart of Kennedy country, and Ed Dinis was stuck in a no-win situation. If he attempted to whitewash the incident, he would be viewed as weak by the national media and his fellow lawmen across the country. But if he went up against the mighty Kennedy political machine in Massachusetts, he would be committing career suicide.

There would be no innocent explanation to all this. The Kennedys had been guilty of all sorts of crimes and misdemeanors over the years. From minor transgressions such as wrecking sailboats on jetties during drunken excursions in Hyannis Port to capital crimes like stealing the 1960 presidential election through the efforts of Joe Kennedy's mobster friends, Ed Dinis had heard it all and seen much of it. Weighing his options, there was only one pathway forward that made sense to him. He was in survival mode. Dinis was elected by a constituency that was predominantly Roman Catholic. His voters had framed photos of Pope Paul VI and JFK on the walls of their living rooms. For the district attorney, it was in his own best interest to try to de-escalate the crisis and make it go away.

Ed Dinis picked up the telephone once again and dialed George Killen, his right-hand man, and told him to begin making discreet inquiries around the island. Within minutes, Killen learned that the body of twenty-eight-year-old Mary Jo Kopechne of Wilkes-Barre, Pennsylvania, and 2912 Olive Street NW, Washington, DC, had been taken to the local funeral home in Vineyard Haven. He called the mortician, Eugene Frieh, and asked that the victim's clothing be turned over to him as a representative of the Massachusetts State Police.

Killen flew from Cape Cod to the Vineyard at approximately the same time that Kennedy's legislative aide K. Dun Gifford was making his way to the island from a family reunion on Nantucket. The thirty-year-old Harvard graduate was considered the perfect candidate to help navigate the senator through this evolving crisis. Gifford had faced overwhelming challenges before. He had survived the sinking of the Italian luxury liner *Andrea Doria* off Nantucket more than a decade earlier when fifty-one people perished after the ship collided with a Swedish passenger ship. Gifford had also helped wrestle Sirhan Sirhan to the ground in the pantry of the Ambassador Hotel after the fatal shooting of Bobby Kennedy.

After landing at the County Airport in Vineyard Haven, Gifford took a taxi to the funeral home and huddled with Eugene Frieh to coordinate the transportation of Kopechne's body back home to Pennsylvania. The weather was bad, and there was a low ceiling, so a flight off the island on a chartered airplane would take some time for approval from the airport control tower. During this time, Gifford filled out a stack of forms and examined the death certificate.

"The official cause of death was due to asphyxiation by immersion? What does that mean?" he asked Frieh.

"It means that she drowned," the mortician told him.

"How do we know this?"

"The medical examiner, Dr. Mills, made the finding."

"But there's been no autopsy," Gifford pointed out. "Should we put a hold on the flight until an autopsy is performed?"

"I agree with you, but it's out of my hands."

While Kennedy's aide was grilling the mortician at the funeral home, Ed Dinis was on the phone with Dr. Don Mills.

"Well, Mills, you're quite sure of your diagnosis, aren't you?" Dinis asked.

"I certainly am," the medical examiner replied.

"I don't think an autopsy is necessary. Do you?"

"I do not. And I'm sticking to my guns on that."

The overconfident Mills proved to be the perfect foil for the DA's plan. Bypassing an autopsy would erase any further questions about Kopechne's death, such as how long Kopechne may have been alive in the back seat of Kennedy's Oldsmobile. Was she pregnant at the time of death? Did she die of respiratory depression or even manual strangulation? There was no way to know this, as Dr. Mills had never fully disrobed her body during his examination.

"Questions like this could make an ugly situation even uglier," Dinis said to himself.

George Killen was then ordered to the funeral home to oversee the embalming of Kopechne's body. Frieh injected two liters of embalming fluid into her carotid artery and monitored the process as the fluid was evenly distributed throughout her body. The mortician made a startling discovery during the embalming, however. He saw that there was very little moisture in Kopechne's lungs, which was most peculiar for a drowning victim. Frieh did not mention this to Killen, but he made a note of it later, in case he was called in front of a grand jury.

Following the procedure, Mary Jo Kopechne's remains were placed in a body bag and driven to the airport, where the skies were clearing.

"So no hold on the body? No autopsy?" K. Dun Gifford asked the mortician upon arrival.

"Like I said, it's out of my hands," Frieh replied.

Gifford accompanied Kopechne's body to Pennsylvania for her funeral, which was attended by Ted Kennedy, who was wearing a neck brace despite no previous report of an injury. He was accompanied by his thoroughly embarrassed wife, Joan Kennedy. Unlike Pat Walsh, Mary Anne Wysocki, Sydney Monzon, and Susan Perry, Mary Jo Kopechne's secrets would be buried with her.

The Chappaquiddick case was unfolding in the wake of the Apollo 11 mission. Suddenly, the national media had two major stories to cover. But it was Norman Mailer himself who tied both events together. "Next morning [after the moon landing] came the news of Ted Kennedy's accident at Chappaquiddick," he later wrote. "Dead was the young lady who had been driving with him. How subtle was the voice of the moon?"

Back in Massachusetts, protesters crowded outside Dinis's office, holding signs that read *Leave Our Teddy Alone* and *The Kennedys Have Suffered Enough*. The district attorney pushed his way through the mob and entered his office, where a stack of mail awaited him from people all over the country. Their prevailing attitude was much different from that of the locals. A woman from Stockton, California, wrote Dinis a note in bold letters: "WHAT HAPPENED TO HER IS ALMOST BEYOND BELIEF AND INEXCUSABLE. THIS IS MANSLAUGHTER!" Singer Rudy Vallee also weighed in from his home in Hollywood. "There are many persons out here watching the Kennedy case," he wrote the district attorney. "We are all wondering if you are going to be persuaded to whitewash this case?" Still others questioned Dinis's true motives in the case. "Would you still interest yourself in this accident if it involved a man named John Doe, instead of Senator Edward M. Kennedy?" a woman from Norfolk, Virginia wrote. "Would not the winning of this case promise you, a small town prosecutor, much fame and even fortune?"

She was right about his ambitions but she was dead wrong about the case. Dinis saw Tony Costa, not Ted Kennedy, as his ticket to a higher office. There would be no sympathy for a devil like the "Cape Cod Vampire." But with a man like Kennedy, Ed Dinis found himself caught in a vice, and he was trying desperately to think his way out of it. To show those critics like Rudy Vallee that he would treat Kennedy like any other suspect in a criminal case, Dinis petitioned the court in Pennsylvania to exhume Kopechne's body for an autopsy. The district attorney knew the family would object and that his request would be shot down by the court. He also brought the case to a grand jury but made little effort to push for manslaughter charges. Many jurors felt they were stymied by Dinis from fully investigating Kennedy's actions. Police Chief Jim Arena filed the only charges against the senator that ever stuck. Arena charged Kennedy with failing to report an accident. The senator pleaded guilty and was given a two-month suspended sentence.

As family and friends mourned the tragic loss of Mary Jo Kopechne and others offered their sympathy toward Ted Kennedy, Tony Costa sat in his jail cell on Cape Cod, and he was smiling. He would benefit from the young woman's death. Ed Dinis's legal and political career was in tatters for touching the third rail that was the Kennedy family dynasty. His attack on the senator would no doubt cloud a juror's mind in Costa's murder trial, which was originally scheduled for September but now had to be pushed back because of Chappaquiddick. This would allow Costa and his lawyers to spend more time on his defense and more time to negotiate a deal in Hollywood.

"There's no story like mine," Costa told his lawyer Maurice Goldman. "People will be talking about my case for decades to come!"

CHAPTER THIRTY-THREE

When Vonnegut's *Life* magazine special report on the Tony Costa case hit newsstands, the reaction among Cape Codders was similar to his Apollo 11 commentary: most people hated it. The cover of the July 25, 1969, issue of *Life* showed a smiling and waving Neil Armstrong under the headline "Leaving for the Moon." The cover story was written by Loudon Wainwright because Mailer was still compiling his notes for his own feature story, which was set to run in August with a photo of Mailer himself, not the space heroes on the cover. Vonnegut's story was titled "'There's a Maniac Loose Out There': Novelist Probes the Tale of Four Horrible Murders on Cape Cod." The article was accompanied by several black-and-white photographs, including a crime scene picture of one of the shallow graves in North Truro along with photos of the victims and the accused killer himself being led to court in handcuffs by Bernie Flynn.

Vonnegut opened the piece with an observation about Jack the Ripper from an old story in the London *Times* in 1888 in which the reporter complimented the unknown killer for his dissection skills. "Now, Cape Cod has a mutilator," Vonnegut wrote. "Whoever did it was no artist with a knife. He chopped up the women with what the police guess was probably a brush hook or an ax." Vonnegut laid out the "horrible and pitiful and sickening" details as he had learned them from Ed Dinis and Lester Allen. He then described Tony Costa as a gentle, quiet six-footer who had married his ex-wife Avis when she was just fourteen years old. Vonnegut told his readers that she was prepared to testify to his innocence. He continued his special report with his own personal anecdote about his daughter Edie. "She met him [Costa] during a crazy summer she spent on her own in Provincetown," he wrote. "She knew him well enough to receive and decline an invitation he evidently extended to many girls: 'Come and see my marijuana patch.'"

This tantalizing part of the story was not true of course. Edie Vonnegut had told her father that she may have met Costa in passing in Ptown but was not 100 percent sure. Vonnegut did not believe that he had to color in the lines of true journalism. He was sure that Capote had used poetic license while writing his true crime masterpiece, *In Cold Blood*. The made-up details about Edie's supposed relationship with the accused killer were aimed at hooking the reader, and hook them he did.

His description of Provincetown centered on his conversations with Sadie, Thumper, and Strawberry Blonde. "Freaks," he called them. "Freaks are worth money to the businessmen on the narrow streets of Provincetown," Vonnegut wrote. "Thousands of tourists come in the summertime to gawk at them—and to gawk at all the shameless, happy fags and at the painters and Portuguese fishermen too… When the bodies were found late last winter, tourists arrived off-season. Many brought kiddies and shovels and picnic lunches. They wanted to help dig." Lester Allen had told him that one enterprising young businessman was selling packages of sand from the shallow graves for fifty cents per pound.

Vonnegut quoted Ed Dinis and described the district attorney as a "large, grave and earnest man who has never married." The line was a not so subtle nod to the rumors that were swirling about Dinis's sexuality. Vonnegut also accused the lawman of stretching facts by adding the word *cannibalism* into the Costa equation. Vonnegut's questioning was justified, and both Bernie Flynn and Tom Gunnery had smiled when they read it. Dinis, on the other hand, shook with fury and felt that he had been betrayed by his famous writer friend.

Vonnegut did keep his word to Costa that their conversation would stay "off the record." Still, he sprinkled information throughout the article that could only have come from the accused killer himself. Vonnegut wrote how Hermann Hesse was thought to be a "great writer" among the young. He also floated the idea that Costa could have been framed for the murders as retribution for tipping off Ptown cops to local drug activity.

"But who would chop up four nice girls to frame one small canary?" Vonnegut asked.

As for the victims—Pat Walsh, Mary Anne Wysocki, Sydney Monzon, and Susan Perry—Vonnegut offered a simple bon voyage. "Young women in America will continue to look for love and excitement in places that are dangerous as hell. I salute them for their optimism and their nerve."

Vonnegut finished the piece recounting another conversation that he had had with Edie about a young hippie who told her from time to time that he wanted to kill her. "'Edith— that guy who kept saying he was going to kill you. Was his name Tony Costa?' 'No, no,' she said. 'Tony wouldn't say anything like that. Tony wasn't the one.' Then I told her about Costa's arrest."

If Edie Vonnegut was displeased about the *Life* magazine article, she

Kurt Vonnegut struggled for decades as a writer until the publication of Slaughterhouse-Five *and his* Life *magazine article about Tony Costa. © Archive PL/ Alamy Stock Photo.*

did not express it to her domineering father. Local reporters, however, argued that Vonnegut, with his laid-back approach and throwaway style, had been miscast as a crime reporter and was ill suited to chronicle the brutal murders in the North Truro woods. He also received plenty of angry looks from his neighbors at the coffee shop in Barnstable village. Just days after publicly smearing JFK's legacy and his promise to land a man on the moon by the end of the decade, Vonnegut cannibalized the Cape Cod community by glamorizing the blood and gore in the place they all called home. Gone was the version of the Cape that had been romanticized by Patti Page just a decade before.

> *If you spend an evening, you'll want to stay*
> *Watching the moonlight on Cape Cod Bay*
> *You're sure to fall in love with old Cape Cod.*

Tony Costa loved the article, although he believed that he could write it even better. Still, the attention brought to his case by a writer as well known as Kurt Vonnegut could only help his chances to cash in on the crimes with lucrative book and movie deals. With his legal bills mounting, the accused killer took his focus off his own defense and applied it to what he hoped could be a promising Hollywood career.

If Goldman does his fucking job and we get sprung, I say we head to LA and meet with the movie studios, his alter ego suggested. *We'll be the toast of the town. Fuck Tony Curtis and the Boston Strangler. We can get Brando, Burton, or even Jon Voight to play us, larger than life on the big screen. While we're out in La-La Land, we can trap new prey. Pretty little runaway girls arrive on buses every hour, too many to keep track of. Lots of deserted, empty spaces to choose from.*

"Yes, Cory, I would like that," Costa muttered to himself. "Hollywood loves horror stories."

Linda Drouin, now Linda Darlene Kasabian, walked down the driveway of Dennis Wilson's house at 14400 Sunset Boulevard, trailing behind her new friends Patricia Krenwinkel and Ella Jo Bailey, who had picked her up hitchhiking just a few minutes before. Wilson was hosting a Fourth of July party, and Kasabian was excited to meet the Beach Boys' drummer and check out the old hunting lodge, once owned by Will Rogers, that Wilson had converted into his plush bachelor pad. Her young daughter Tanya was now living with Linda's parents in New Hampshire. But Linda was pregnant again. She had all but given up her on her quest to find God, until he appeared to her standing next to the backyard pool. His name was Charlie, and he was surrounded by beautiful young women. Kasabian took one look at him, resplendent in his buckskin jacket, and thought she was staring at Jesus Christ. She edged closer to him and stayed by his side throughout the night. Kasabian was then invited to join Charlie's "family" at an old western movie set known as Spahn Ranch in the Santa Susana Mountains.

"We live there," he told her. "And we are free."

Once there, Kasabian met a girl who called herself Gypsy.

"This is our hole in the earth. This is our paradise. We all assume new names once Charlie allows us to live here," Gypsy told her. "We're known as the witches."

"What does Charlie call himself?"

Gypsy stared back vacant eyed. "He's just Charlie. He's Charlie Manson, and we're all in love with him."

"What should I call myself?" Kasabian asked.

Gypsy thought for a moment. "From now on, you'll be known as Yana the Witch."

Kasabian had sex with Charlie in a mountain cave during her second night at the ranch and soon gave birth to another daughter.

"You have a father hang-up," Manson told her when they had sex.

This idea impressed Kasabian, as no one had ever told her that before.

"I have no father," she replied. "I hate my stepfather."

With that conversation, Kasabian convinced herself that she had finally found a home, one that was far away from New England.

Later, Manson taught her how to panhandle, steal dune buggy parts, sew, and scavenge for food for the family, often diving in supermarket dumpsters for discarded cartons of eggs and produce. Kasabian was also ordered to wear dark clothes.

"It allows you to creepy-crawl and move at night," Manson told her. "We can move in silence so that nobody sees or hears us."

Kasabian thought nothing of it at the time. Soon, though, she was going out on nightly patrols with other family members to break into nearby homes searching for money, drugs, and food to take back to Spahn Ranch.

Shortly after midnight on August 9, 1969, Linda Kasabian joined Krenwinkel and two other Manson followers, Susan Atkins and Tex Watson, on a ride to 10050 Cielo Drive in the Hollywood Hills, where acclaimed director Roman Polanski lived with his pregnant starlet wife, Sharon Tate. The house had previously been occupied by actress Candice Bergen and Terry Melcher, the son of Doris Day, who was also a successful music producer. Melcher had auditioned Manson but had decided not to offer him his own record deal. Although Melcher had moved to Malibu, the house on Cielo Drive represented failure and rejection to Manson, and for that, someone had to pay. Manson had ordered Kasabian to bring a change of clothes, her driver's license, and a knife.

"It's time to commit Helter Skelter," he told her.

Kasabian knew what this meant. Gyspy had warned her about the coming race war that Manson had dubbed Helter Skelter, after the hard-rocking hit by the Beatles.

After getting lost on Mulholland Drive, the foursome arrived at Cielo Drive in a four-door Ford painted yellow and white. They parked on a side street and climbed a gate surrounding the home. A car, a 1965 Rambler Ambassador, rolled down the driveway, and Tex Watson emerged from the bushes and yelled, "Halt!"

Watson ran to the driver's window and pushed his pistol against the driver's head.

"Don't shoot me. Please don't shoot me!" the driver, eighteen-year-old Steven Parent, begged.

Instead, Watson slashed Parent with a bayonet. When the teenager raised his left hand to defend himself, Watson fired his .22-caliber revolver. It was the same caliber weapon that Tony Costa used to kill Pat Walsh and Mary Anne Wysocki in North Truro six months earlier and three thousand miles away. Parent was struck and killed by three bullets, one to the left cheek and two in the chest. The murderers then creeped toward the home. Roman Polanski was not there. He was fresh off his smash hit *Rosemary's Baby* starring Mia Farrow and was working on a new film in Europe. Polanski had left his beautiful young wife in the care of friends, Jay Sebring, hairdresser to the stars, Polish screenwriter Wojciech Frykowski, and his girlfriend, coffee heiress Abigail Folger. Watson ordered Kasabian to stay with Parent's car and keep a lookout at the front gate. Tex Watson cut a screen in the window and climbed inside the house. He then opened the door for Atkins and Krenwinkel. Watson found Frykowski asleep on the couch. The screenwriter was startled awake with a kick to the head.

"I am the Devil," Watson told him. "And I'm here to do the Devil's business."

Susan Atkins and Patricia Krenwinkel searched the home for more victims. They found Sebring, Folger, and Sharon Tate, who, nine months pregnant, struggled down the stairs. When Sebring complained about how they were treating her, Watson shot him and stabbed him seven times.

"Totally destroy everyone. Be as gruesome as you can," Manson had instructed his killers earlier that night.

Abigail Folger was stabbed twenty-eight times. Her boyfriend was sliced fifty-one times and left virtually unrecognizable and saturated with blood. Sharon Tate pleaded for the life of her unborn child, but the murderers showed no mercy. She was stuck with a knife repeatedly before dying along with her baby.

Susan Atkins smeared the word *Pig* on the front door of the house in Tate's blood.

Kasabian heard horrible screams coming from inside the house, and she ran up the driveway.

"I wanted them to stop," she later testified. "I knew what they had done to that man [Parent] and that they were killing those people."

Kasabian wanted to call the police, but she didn't. Instead, she fled the scene with Watson, Atkins, and Krenwinkel and got rid of the weapons.

Two more people would be killed in similar fashion by Manson and his followers the next night.

Linda Kasabian had not fulfilled her quest to find God after all. Instead, the girl from the small New Hampshire mill town had forged a pact with the devil.

The following day, the headline on the front page of the Los Angeles Times screamed "'Ritualistic Slayings': Sharon Tate, Four Others Murdered." News of the sensational crimes travelled quickly from California to Cape Cod and every city and small town in between.

The national press turned its attention to what was being dubbed the Tate-LaBianca murders in Los Angeles. Leno LaBianca, a forty-four-year-old grocery store owner, and his thirty-eight-year-old wife, Rosemary, were slaughtered by Manson, Watson, and another family member, Leslie Van

Houten, while the bodies of Sharon Tate and others were still being processed at the LA County Morgue. After the couple was separated, Leno was stabbed twenty-six times, and the word *WAR* was carved into his stomach with a metal fork. Rosemary LaBianca suffered forty-one knife wounds. The killers wrote *Healter* [sic] *Skelter*, *Rise*, and *Death to Pigs* in blood on the walls and the refrigerator inside the home.

"The Sixties ended abruptly on August 9, 1969," writer Joan Didion later wrote. "The tension broke that day. The paranoia was fulfilled."

Suddenly, media calls to Ed Dinis's office about the Tony Costa case ceased. It was almost as if the murders and dismemberment of four young women in the North Truro woods had never happened. The DA's big case, the one that just might save his career after Chappaquiddick, was becoming a footnote to history right before his very eyes. Now, a deputy district attorney from Los Angeles named Vincent Bugliosi was stealing all the headlines.

"Fuck, fuck, fuck!" he shouted again. This time, Dinis's secretary did not unravel from the sound of the outburst. She had become accustomed to the office explosions that were brought on by her boss's fragile ego.

Tony Costa shared the feelings of his prosecutor, as did his alter ego, Cory Devereaux.

We should have murdered somebody famous, Costa's inner voice told him. *Whoever murdered Sharon Tate and those other pigs in LA is now the wolf. The killer is now the wolf of the steppes, and we're stuck here in this cage on a pile of sand.*

Newspaper columnist Evelyn Lawson believed that Costa and his disciples were somehow responsible for the bloodshed in Los Angeles.

"Our evil has spread west," Evelyn Lawson told Norman Mailer. "Witches are involved. I can feel it. I lived out there among them. The killing moon has waned on Cape Cod, so the coven has traveled to California to kill again."

Linda Kasabian, a.k.a. "Yana the Witch," surrendered to police in

Concord, New Hampshire, for her role in the murders on December 1, 1969. Tex Watson and Patricia Krenwinkel were also arrested based on information given by Susan Atkins. In the days and weeks that followed, the Manson family would be brought more clearly into view along with their messianic leader, who emerged as America's most vile killer.

CHAPTER THIRTY-FOUR

Vonnegut first read about Charles Manson's bloody orchestration of the Tate-LaBianca murders while he was visiting Indianapolis, Indiana, for a book signing. He had grown weary of Cape Cod, especially following the criticism of his *Life* magazine article. Vonnegut retreated to his hometown in the heart of the Midwest, where he expected to be treated as a conquering literary hero. *Slaughterhouse-Five* was in its sixth printing after having spent sixteen weeks on the *New York Times* bestseller list. Behind Steve McQueen and actress Frances Farmer, Kurt Vonnegut was perhaps the most famous person to hail from Indianapolis, and he envisioned fetes with the mayor, being handed the keys to the city, and maybe even a parade in his honor. None of that happened. The views of conservative Cape Cod were amplified in Indianapolis, where folks had grown tired of the writer's thumbing of his nose at the American flag. In fact, much of the hate mail delivered to CBS News after his disastrous appearance during the moon landing had been sent from his hometown.

Vonnegut arrived for his book signing at L. S. Ayres, a high-priced department store, to little or no fanfare. He was escorted by a store employee to the store's small book section. There was no excitement in the employee's voice. The man could not care less about his opportunity to rub elbows with the superstar author. It was as if Vonnegut were there to fix the air-conditioning. He was shown to a table where a stack of books awaited him. Vonnegut settled his long frame into a wooden chair, pulled out a fine ballpoint pen, one he had purchased for the special occasion, and waited for the throngs of fans to arrive. He sat there for three hours and sold less than a dozen books. His only visitors were family members who purchased signed copies as something of a charitable act. Between small talk with his cousins, Vonnegut smoked, sipped coffee, and read the latest edition of the *Indy Star* newspaper.

Scanning an article about Manson, Vonnegut learned that the accused killer had spent time in Indianapolis as a youth, where he had worked as a messenger boy while his mother had sex with strangers for money in their rented hotel room. She was charged with adultery and fled the small city, leaving her troubled son behind. Manson was arrested for petty crimes and served time at the Indiana Boys School, a juvenile detention center in Plainfield, Indiana, before finding his way west.

As he continued reading, Vonnegut learned that Manson had lived in San Francisco at or around the time that Tony Costa stayed there.

"I wonder if they knew each other." Vonnegut pondered. "Two young men in their transformative phase from hippie gurus to cold-blooded killers. So it goes."

As he sat in the department store staring at the large pile of unsold copies of *Slaughterhouse-Five*, Vonnegut let his mind wander, drawing more comparisons between the so-called Murderous Messiah and the Cape Cod Vampire. Both men had recruited, in his mind, dim-witted girls, homeless girls, or girls who felt homeless at any rate. They were all simple and young, and family meant so much to them that they would do anything for it. Manson had his accomplices, and Costa had his victims. Each man had the charm and willingness to be *father*, to take charge and collect followers. In both cases, the father figure was pure evil, but the girls, those buried on Cape

Cod and those locked up in California, may have sensed the danger but took their chances anyway.

When Vonnegut returned home to Barnstable, his wife, Jane, and the kids gave him a wide berth. Fame and fortune were supposed to satisfy him and quash his demons. Instead, Vonnegut had become more volatile than ever. He agonized over book sales of *Slaughterhouse-Five*. The novel had made him rich, allowed him to close the Saab dealership, but it also came at a cost to his soul.

"I'm the only one to have profited from the firebombing of Dresden," he told a reporter from the BBC. "One way or another, I got two to three dollars for every person killed. Some business I'm in."

His mood swings turned his Cape Cod home into a war zone of its own.

A simple chess match with his twenty-two-year-old son, Mark, would end up with the board getting flipped in anger if Vonnegut lost. He was drinking again and jousting with Jane. She had grown sick of her role as a verbal punching bag and a "picker-upper of all the crap" in his life. Cape Cod could hold Vonnegut's restless spirit no more, and he was looking for a way out of his marriage and off the sandy peninsula.

———

Meanwhile, Mailer was back in Provincetown, enjoying time with his new live-in girlfriend, a dark-haired jazz singer named Carol Stevens. Mailer collected women like a young boy collected baseball cards. While married to Beverly Bentley, he had engaged in a torrid affair with Carol. The writer was drawn to her dark features and her raspy singing voice, fueled by chain-smoking Duke cigarettes. Carol now slept in Mailer's bed, the one he had shared with Beverly. He wrote his Apollo 11 book by day, the one he would call *Of a Fire on the Moon*. At night, he crawled into bed with Carol to make love and collapse in her warm arms.

But restful sleep evaded Mailer as his subconscious mind brought him to a place in the North Truro woods. In his dream, he was followed there by three vacant-eyed girls on bicycles. They covered their narrow mouths with their delicate hands as they giggled, while Mailer stumbled in the brush at the base of a massive pine tree. He reached his hands into the dirt up to his forearms and pulled out a plastic bag. There was a woman's head inside, and this time, it had the catlike eyes and pouting lips of Carol Stevens.

The next morning, Mailer crisscrossed Commercial Street looking for the young witches who had plagued his dreams, but they were nowhere to be found. He met Evelyn Lawson for coffee at Adams Pharmacy, where she updated him on her book about the Costa case.

"I'm calling it *The Charmer*," she said excitedly. "You like it?"

"It has a certain sex appeal to it," Mailer told her.

"I plan on incorporating the Manson case into the book."

"Is that a bit of a stretch?" Mailer asked.

"Not at all. Linda Kasabian is from here. Well, she's from New Hampshire. I bet she worshipped with the witches of Provincetown at some point. Once initiated into a coven, they become magnets."

Mailer shrugged his shoulders. "First Costa and now fucking Manson. This young generation is making us all pay for our sins."

"Did you read what Gore Vidal is saying about you?" Lawson asked.

"Yes, the bastard claims that I'm in alliance with Manson in some sort of sick way. He's also lumped me in with Henry Miller, calls us the three Ms, and he claims that we all view women as at best, breeders of sons, and at worst, objects to be poked, humiliated, and killed. You can throw Tony Costa into that mix as well."

"Does Vidal have a point?"

Mailer slammed down his coffee mug on the counter.

"I do not exploit women," he argued. "It is impossible to exploit her, because she has magical powers. I am against the emancipation of women just because I respect them. I have had four marriages, and I have four daughters, and Gore has none. He's neither wed nor has he bothered to sire, because he's put womankind in such high regard that he does not wish to injure their tender flesh with his sharp tongue. You know what I am going to do the next time I see him?"

"Who?"

"Gore Vidal. I am going to headbutt that cocksucker!" Mailer promised.

"And what are your true thoughts about women?"

"This question has dogged me since the incident with Adele. Feminists have been killing my wallet, my ego, and my reputation for the past decade. For that, I believe women are sloppy beasts and should be kept in cages."

Lawson raised a pitcher of water from the table. "And I should pour this ice water over your curly little head."

He held his hands up in mock surrender.

"That was a joke," Mailer explained. "I said it for fun and idiocy."

Lawson did not see the humor.

"You are an infant. Like all men, you emerge from the vagina and attach yourself to our breasts," she said, seething. "From then on, those become the only two female body parts that you are most interested in. You refuse to believe that a woman has a brain and a purpose. You are most afraid of the dune witches, but it's feminism as a whole that has you running scared. There's a storm brewing, and the strong women of this land will leave you buried in the sand."

Lawson pulled herself off the stool and marched out of the pharmacy.

––––––––––

Nearby on Bradford Street, Maurice Goldman was seated in his law office, perusing the latest copy of *Newsweek*, which featured a detailed investigation of the Chappaquiddick incident. The attorney studied the article with unbridled glee.

"They're kicking the shit out of Dinis over his treatment of Ted Kennedy,"

Goldman told his colleague Justin Cavanaugh. "The story also mentions how he's botching the Costa case. This is exactly what we need right now. If the jury has no confidence in the district attorney, this trial could blow up in his face."

Goldman wondered if the chance of another public embarrassment for Dinis would be enough leverage for him to float the idea of a plea deal. Before approaching the district attorney, Goldman would have to get the approval of his client, Tony Costa.

"Dinis is on the ropes," Goldman told Costa during a meeting at the Barnstable House of Correction. "He's become a national embarrassment thanks to Chappaquiddick. It might be time to approach both the judge and the DA with a compromise."

"Yes, I have contemplated such a deal before," Costa informed him. "What concerns me is the amount of time I would serve for four murders."

Goldman explained the judge's decision to deny severance in the case— which meant separating the murders into four trials.

"I've got to be able to prove your use of drugs during this time," the attorney said. "This strategy could take a first-degree murder charge off the table. After we agree to a sentence, I can then appeal it. With any luck, you just may be back on the street in three to four years."

Costa contemplated the offer for a moment.

"What do you have for a straight defense?" he asked.

Goldman was floored by the question.

"A straight defense? Are you still on drugs? You tell me what the straight defense is? You have not been telling us the truth since day one of this thing. The prosecution will pick us apart, and you'll be headed for the hangman's noose."

Costa shook his head no. Such an offer was unacceptable to him.

"My idea is to attempt to persuade Mr. Dinis to listen to reason. We could offer him a package deal," he suggested. "I could cop out on a larceny charge, turn over the real murderer to him, and ultimately offer my services to his office in cleaning up Cape Cod. This would benefit him, his position, and would appease his power-mad, glory-seeking desires. Aren't I a sly fly?"

You are a madman, Goldman thought to himself.

"Tony, I don't think that Dinis will accept your offer. First, we don't have the real killer. Cory Devereaux passed the polygraph test like a champ. And I know that the DA won't go for the idea of deputizing his so-called Cape Cod Vampire."

"I suggest we prepare for trial then, Mr. Goldman."

"Yes, Tony. We will plan to go to trial."

CHAPTER THIRTY-FIVE

Cecilia Bonaviri entered King's department store, just across from the airport in Hyannis, and she could feel the eyes of store clerks and fellow customers upon her. It was just before Christmas, and the store was brightly lit and decorated with colorful fake trees and large cardboard cutouts of Santa Claus and his tiny reindeer. Costa's mother grabbed a shopping cart and navigated her heavy figure through the aisles, overstuffed with toys and other holiday gift ideas.

The front wheel of her cart made a screeching noise as it rolled, causing shoppers to turn their heads toward the direction of the irritating racket. The mature woman pushing the cart looked familiar to them. In fact, they had seen her photograph on the front page of the *Cape Cod Standard-Times*, accompanied by a picture of her now infamous son.

"That's her," one shopper whispered to her companion. "That's Tony Costa's mother."

Cecilia heard her son's name being muttered in the distance, so she quickly moved to another aisle of the department store, where she was once again recognized by a customer. There was no place for her to hide.

"Is your son the Cape Cod Vampire?" the customer asked her while Bing Crosby's "White Christmas" played over the loudspeaker.

Cecilia's dark eyes narrowed, and her swollen hands began to shake. She pretended not to hear the question as she examined a pink angora cardigan that was two sizes too small for her. Suddenly, Cecilia could feel herself falling as she pulled down the sweater from its rack. Her body hit the floor, and she saw nothing but darkness. Cecilia heard muffled sounds around her as customers called for help.

"Tony," she whispered. "My Tony."

Soon after, an ambulance arrived at the scene and rushed her to Cape Cod Hospital, but by that time, there was nothing the doctors could do to save her. Tony Costa's mother had suffered a massive cerebral hemorrhage, and she died on a gurney in the emergency room.

Her eldest son was notified of her death by Goldman's colleague Justin Cavanaugh.

Costa showed no emotion while the attorney delivered the news. Instead, he returned to his cell and put pencil to paper.

"Through your eyes, you saw nothing," he wrote. "Yet, you sensed freedom had approached you and you succumbed to its power gracefully; allowed it to draw you closer to its womb, magnetically. Then you envisioned me. 'Come,' I called, 'I'll show you the way.' You came. A child you thought. A baby. Freedom! Independence. A mother, wife, lover. A free woman. And me... I was your teacher."

Costa stared down at the paper. Was he writing a poetic tribute to his dead mother? Was she worth his adoration? He continued to express his thoughts on the page.

"You considered only you. With each new lesson, your world unraveled. Soon my world would shrink to black oblivion—lost! You considered only you. You alone reigned supreme, casting knowledge aside to grow damp and dusty in the dungeons of your mind. The only book you had cherished, its pages plank, now lies filled cluttered with decomposed memories of your wickedness. You have never read it. It speaks to you aloud, shouting the tales of all those you have destroyed. And me... I loved you."

On Christmas Eve 1969, a light snow fell on Cape Cod. Tony Costa could see the white frozen crystals dance their way past the small window of his jail cell. He could only wonder what his ex-wife, Avis, had purchased for their children under Santa's name. The kids had been kept away from St. Paul's, the Catholic cemetery in Provincetown, where the caretaker was digging a hole into the frozen ground a few feet away from a large pine tree. The task took two hours to perform, and the caretaker's gloved hands ached each time he drove the spade deeper into the earth. Tony Costa understood how tough that ground was in the dead of winter.

A wooden casket carrying the body of his mother, Cecilia, was lowered into a burial plot and prayed over by a small group of family members and friends. They brushed the snow off the shoulders of their winter coats, hugged one another, and said goodbye before returning home for their Christmas Eve dinners. After day turned to night, three young women entered the cemetery holding hands. Sadie, Thumper, and Strawberry Blonde stood over the mound of fresh dirt by the tall pine tree and placed three black roses on the top of Cecilia's grave.

Costa's lawyer Maurice Goldman had lost his petition to have the murder trial moved to Greenfield, Massachusetts, in the western part of the state, but in early January 1970, he celebrated a well-earned victory for his client as a state judge ordered a motion to halt publicity in the weeks and months leading up to the trial. The judge cited a story that appeared in *Time* magazine that was filled with erroneous information given by Ed Dinis. "All were nude at the time of their deaths and there were teeth marks on their bodies," the reporter claimed. "In none of the random graves could they find any of the four girls' hearts."

The judge's gag order sent Evelyn Lawson into a tailspin. She was harvesting information from both sides of the case for her book, and the spigot had been abruptly turned off. Lawson used her column in the *Barnstable Register* as a platform to rail against the judge while defending the First Amendment. "This is a first for Massachusetts," she wrote. "The first blow against one of our basic freedoms... Since (the judge's decision), no reliable information from law enforcement agencies investigating the case has been made public. Consequently, fantastic rumors and pernicious gossip have taken the place of responsible reporting."

Lawson argued that the decision, which was made to protect Costa from being tried in the press before trial, could backfire on the defense. The columnist compared it to the strategy employed by Ted Kennedy to win his privacy in the wake of Chappaquiddick.

"In a series of obvious mistakes by Senator Kennedy, who drove that car that became a death trap for the young woman, and his many powerful friends, this blaming of the media could backlash to become one of the biggest public relations mistakes of all-time... The publishers who belonged to the school of journalism in which I was trained consider themselves the watchdogs of the people. They would have barked long and loud, bared their teeth and even bitten, if necessary, the thieves who attempted to rob the people of their right to know." Lawson closed her piece with a quote from Patrick Henry. "The Price of Freedom is Vigilance," she wrote.

Lawson was greeted with a round of applause from her fellow reporters when she showed up at Barnstable Superior Court for the first day of jury selection in the Costa trial on May 11, 1970.

The Boston Bruins had celebrated a Stanley Cup victory the night before with a dramatic, high-flying overtime goal from superstar Bobby Orr. Cape Codders partied into the early morning hours, and most people were still groggy and hungover. Gallons of coffee and cartons of cigarettes helped the throngs gathered outside the courthouse get themselves into the right mindset to greet the fateful day.

Kurt Vonnegut slipped into the courthouse unhurried and unseen. He sat on a long wooden bench in the back of the courtroom, wearing his customary tweed coat, rumpled shirt, and khakis with white tennis shoes. He was happy to be back on Cape Cod, but he did not know for how long. He had recently appeared on *The Dick Cavett Show* to discuss a journey he had taken to Biafra in January 1970 to write about war and famine in a country filled with living skeletons that walked like men. The trip had changed him, the impact almost as profound as the conflagration in Dresden more than two decades before. Vonnegut wept for the living and for the dead of Biafra, where systematic murder was commonplace, an amendment built into the constitution of the toppled West African state. He had returned to the Cape, where killing was not used as a political and socioeconomic tool but as a method to satisfy the demonic urges of a sickly, disturbed young man.

That individual, Tony Costa, was driven from the jailhouse down the hill to the courthouse in a police car accompanied by two deputy sheriffs. He was almost unrecognizable to reporters, courthouse gawkers, and the carloads of hippies who had traveled from Provincetown to wish the accused killer well.

The mustache and scruffy beard that he had grown while incarcerated were gone. Maurice Goldman cleaned his client up with a smooth shave, a Dutch-boy haircut, and a black suit, starched white collared shirt, and black tie. If it weren't for the handcuffs on his wrists, one might have mistaken him for a potential juror.

As the suspect was being led into the rear entrance of the courthouse, Sadie emerged from the gathered crowd to kiss his manacled hands.

"Tony, we love you!" she cheered.

News photographers and television news crews elbowed their way closer for a better view of the Cape Cod Vampire.

See, we're just as big, if not bigger than Manson, Cory told Costa.

Costa did not respond to his alter ego. Instead, he grinned for the cameras before disappearing inside the building. The 204-seat courtroom where the trial would take place had to be modified to support up to 300 spectators, although no member of the public would be allowed to witness the first day of jury selection. Temporary press quarters were set up in the basement of the old granite courthouse. The Manson trial in California was scheduled for July 1970, which meant that a full accounting of Tony Costa's crimes would dominate the national news cycle for the month of May. This idea tickled Ed Dinis, who bought himself a new suit and got his hair coiffed at the Beauty Nook hair salon in Hyannis, the same place where the Kennedys were known to get their hair styled.

Ninety-eight potential jurors shuffled into the courthouse for questioning. Thirty-nine were later excused, citing "personal reasons." One prospective juror was dismissed because of his name—Antone Costa—although he was of no relation to the accused killer. Costa himself played an active role in the selection of those who would decide his fate. He objected harshly to one candidate, an unemployed chef from Yarmouth, for no other reason than the fact that he wanted everyone in the courtroom to believe that he was ultimately in charge of the proceedings.

"The type of juror we're looking for here is someone who's been around a bit, whose world view wasn't formed here on this sandbar," Maurice Goldman told Costa. "When we have to confront the marijuana issue, along with other drugs, we want them to see them as no big deal. I'd much rather have a jury made up of six lawyers and six psychiatrists because they won't be able to agree on anything. But we're stuck with this jury pool, and we need to make the best of it."

Evelyn Lawson was one of the reporters allowed into the courtroom to monitor jury selection. She was gathering information for both her column and her book project, but she also served as Norman Mailer's eyes and ears. Unlike Vonnegut, Mailer had decided not to attend Costa's trial in person. He had uprooted his girlfriend Carol Stevens and a few of his children and moved them from spooky Provincetown to idyllic Stockbridge, Massachusetts, in the heart of the Berkshires and once home to Norman Rockwell. He purchased the rambling fifteen-room mansion known as Wyndcote for $75,000 and vowed to make it his permanent residence.

"I need to get my family as far away from those fucking witches as I can," he told Lawson before the move. "This case is plaguing my mind, and I cannot sleep. I have much writing to do, and Tony Costa and his disciples make those efforts all but impossible."

Mailer hoped the leafy seventy-five-acre estate would stop his nightmares. But as he worked to finish his book about the moon landing while also preparing for the release of his film *Maidstone*, he remained haunted by visions of a severed head in a plastic bag.

Lawson could not help but laugh at Mailer's predicament.

"Here's a man that reeks of toxic masculinity, and he's petrified by three skinny hippie girls on bicycles," she told Vonnegut, who also enjoyed the idea that his literary rival was not *man enough* to stand his ground against the young women who were camped outside the courthouse, singing and handing out flowers to anyone entering or leaving the building.

"And so *he* goes," Vonnegut said of Mailer's retreat from Helltown.

By the second day of jury selection, six panelists were chosen, including James Blackmore, a heating engineer from North Harwich, and Charles Horton, an airline pilot from East Orleans. When asked his views on capital punishment, Horton looked over at Costa and said, "In all fairness, I question whether the death penalty serves a deterrent."

Ten more names would be added to the jury list. Goldman made sure that none of them had daughters the same ages as Pat Walsh and Mary Anne Wysocki. Among them was a young woman from Orleans named Irene McCoubrey. The attractive woman quickly became a favorite among news photographers, who snapped pictures of her alluring profile each day she arrived at the courthouse. McCoubrey was chosen for the panel because, like the others, she pledged to keep an open mind regarding the gruesome crimes that Costa was charged with.

Presiding over the Costa trial was Judge Robert Beaudreau, a former FBI agent and U.S. marshal. The son of a prominent superior court judge, Beaudreau operated by the book, despite his genial personality. He knew that the trial would be a media circus and therefore had sequestered the jury to a local motel.

After Irene McCoubrey's selection to the jury panel, when her photo appeared on the front page of the *Cape Cod Standard-Times*, the judge received an anonymous letter, delivered by Goldman, questioning whether the woman had been honest with the court.

"She's a personal friend of Sydney Monzon's mother," Goldman summarized to Beaudreau. "They both work together at the A&P grocery store in Orleans. I'm disturbed by this because a portion of the remnants of Sydney Monzon will appear in one or two of the graves exhibited, and there will no doubt be testimony."

The judge summoned the female juror to his chambers.

"Did you ever work with Mrs. Monzon?" Beaudreau asked her.

"Yes," she said meekly.

"And of course you know that her daughter was allegedly murdered by the defendant, Costa?"

"Yes," she replied. "I just worked with her in the summertime. I was on produce. She was on meat."

"How long had you worked with her?"

"Well, it was just a summer thing," McCoubrey explained. "There was no particular friendship. I mean, it wasn't social."

The juror was wringing her hands and appeared outwardly nervous. Judge Beaudreau attempted to put her at ease.

"Mrs. Monzon was just another employee?"

McCoubrey nodded.

"Now, of course, I didn't give you an opportunity to answer such a question because the Monzon case is not before us," the judge told her. "I only asked about Patricia Walsh and Mary Anne Wysocki, and you answered truthfully about that."

"Yes."

Both sides in this trial would have to walk a fine line regarding Sydney Monzon and Susan Perry, as District Attorney Edmund Dinis had decided against putting Costa on trial for all four murders. It was a calculated move by the lawman.

"Walsh and Wysocki are slam dunks," he told his assistant DA Armand Fernandes. "Costa shot them both, and we have the murder weapon. But we can't say the same about Monzon and Perry. Sure, it looks like he cut their bodies up, but we have to prove beyond a reasonable doubt that Costa murdered them. I can't do that, and I can't afford to lose."

Dinis told the parents of Sydney Monzon and Susan Perry that justice would be served for their daughters and that he would order another trial so that Costa would answer for those crimes. Of course, Dinis had no intention of doing this. Instead, he would get a conviction on the Walsh and Wysocki murders and put the killer in the electric chair or send him away for life. Either way, he would serve the greater good, and by that, the lawman meant protecting his own political and legal legacy. The families of Sydney Monzon and Susan Perry would have to find closure and justice by proxy, through the two young women from Providence, Rhode Island.

Standing before the judge now was another piece of collateral damage from Dinis's selfish decision.

"Mrs. McCoubrey, in view of the fact that you did know Mrs. Monzon, I am going to ask Mr. Goldman if he would feel better if you were excused."

The defense attorney stood up from his chair. "I would, Your Honor. I think this woman is a very honest woman, but I think in the interest of my defendant, I would appreciate it if Your Honor would consider my request that she be excused, so that I could feel safe with my client."

"I know nobody connected with this case, honestly," McCoubrey stated, feeling the need to defend herself. "Mrs. Monzon was not a social friend. It's just that I know a lot of people in that area. You can't help it."

"But you'd feel better also, in light of this, to be dismissed from the jury?" the judge asked.

"Oh, of course. Yes!"

"I don't want you to feel the least bit embarrassed about this, because you were never given an opportunity to answer that question," Beaudreau said in a comforting tone. "I want to caution you though that you'll be asked by the newspapers why you were excused."

"Will they do that?" she asked nervously.

"They already have done that," Goldman told her. "You happen to be a very attractive woman. You made the front page."

"Oh, dear," McCoubrey sighed.

The juror could feel the defense attorney's eyes on her. She wanted to run from the room. Irene McCoubrey had promised to do her civic duty, to weigh the evidence against a man accused of the most grotesque sexual violence imaginable. But now, she felt like a victim herself.

"You're in several papers," Goldman continued. "You are the prettiest juror."

"Now I'm scared," McCoubrey told the judge, hoping he would call off Goldman. "This is frightening."

Goldman would not stop badgering her. "You're the prettiest juror and therefore, you photograph well."

Judge Beaudreau told the woman that she did not have to speak to the press if she did not want to.

"I just want to remain anonymous," she pleaded.

The judge ordered a bailiff to drive over to a nearby motel and retrieve McCoubrey's belongings.

"What room are you in?" he asked her.

"I'm in 261. I'm scared to death."

Ed Dinis offered his own advice, which, unfortunately for the juror, was similar to Goldman's. "You just smile pretty and you will be all right," Dinis said.

"You'll be photographed again. You see, you made all the newspapers," Goldman stressed once more, in a state of near arousal. "Just smile!"

Irene McCoubrey left the courthouse feeling completely violated.

Although there was no way around the Monzon issue, both Maurice Goldman and his client Tony Costa were sad to see her go.

CHAPTER THIRTY-SIX

The yellow school bus rumbled along the Mid-Cape Highway with sixteen jurors—twelve panelists and four alternates—inside. Most had not ridden in a vehicle like this since they were kids. Taking Irene McCoubrey's place on the jury was Mrs. Frances Leonardi, a retired school teacher who promised the judge that she would vote for the death penalty if warranted, despite her personal opposition to capital punishment.

Ed Dinis sat in the front seat of the school bus next to the driver.

"Today, we are going to take a view of areas that have a particular relevance to this trial," he told the group. "We will be stopping at several points in Provincetown and North Truro where these crimes occurred. You are allowed to take notes as they will aid you when you examine certain exhibits in the trial. I am going to point out to you a room in a boarding-house. I am going to point out to you an area in the forest where the bodies of the two young women were discovered. I will point out also a speakeasy or bar called the Fo'csle in Provincetown that, you will observe, is frequented by younger people in the Provincetown area."

Frances Leonardi sat in the back seat of the yellow school bus. Occasionally, she looked back at the vehicle traveling close behind them. It was a fortified army surplus Jeep driven by a court officer. Sheriff's deputy

Elwood Mills, armed with a shotgun, sat in the passenger seat. Maurice Goldman squeezed his flabby frame into the back seat next to his client Tony Costa, who was wearing a dark-blue suit and striped tie that he Goldman had loaned him. The suit was short in the arms and legs and loose in the middle. Costa kept his arms slightly bent so that the sleeves did not ride up his long arms near the elbows. There was another yellow school bus following behind the Jeep, and it was filled with journalists, including Kurt Vonnegut and Evelyn Lawson. Vonnegut placed both of his thumbs on the latches of a window, lowering it so that he could blow smoke out, while Lawson was seated next to him with her nose stuck in a book of magic spells.

"Reading for pleasure?" he asked her.

"No, I'm just making sure that we stay out of harm's way today," Lawson said. "The devil himself is riding in the car in front of us, and he can make anything happen. Bad things."

Vonnegut laughed. "Looks like you're not taking a true journalistic approach to this whole thing."

"I'm writing about the deeper truth," she whispered. "Tony Costa is a necromantic. He and his witches can conjure up the spirits of his victims to do us all harm."

Lawson opened her purse and asked Vonnegut to look inside.

"I've got betony, hawthorn, and garlic in my pocketbook," she pointed out. "These will protect both of us from evil spirits."

Vonnegut rolled his eyes, took one last deep drag from his Pall Mall, and flicked it out the bus window.

The convoy continued up the long arm of Cape Cod toward the village of Wellfleet before pulling into the parking lot of a doctor's office and pharmacy. The buses were unloaded, and Costa was assisted out of the Jeep and flanked by his lawyer and the sheriff's deputy.

"This is the medical office of Dr. Sidney Callis," Ed Dinis announced in his booming voice. "You will learn during the trial that the defendant, Mr. Costa, broke into the office to obtain large amounts of hallucinogenic drugs."

Goldman then approached the jurors. "You will also learn much about Dr. Callis himself," he told them. "You will understand that this so-called man of medicine got my client hooked on dangerous drugs that impaired his decision making."

The jurors took some notes before the foreman, a retired machinist named Russell Dodge, urged them back to the bus.

The caravan continued into Provincetown, where the white dunes, topped by sea grass, goldenrod, and wormwood, rose up just beyond placid East Harbor.

"We're home," Costa muttered to his alter ego. "We never thought we would see this place again."

Our names will be remembered long after this day, Cory told him. *Nobody will speak about Helltown without mentioning us and what we achieved here.*

Costa let out a loud, sinister laugh.

The driver and the sheriff's deputy wondered who the accused murderer was speaking to, but Maurice Goldman said nothing. He had become accustomed to his client's one-sided conversations.

The vehicles all turned left onto Conwell Street, opposite Race Point Road. The street was narrow, and the convoy travelled slowly. Sadie, Thumper, and Strawberry Blonde were straddling their bicycles and waiting at the corner of Old Ann Page Way as the Jeep carrying Costa motored passed. The trio pedaled hard to catch up with the vehicle, and they rode alongside, acting as escorts for the murder suspect's homecoming.

"Should we be concerned?" Elwood Mills asked as he tightened his grip on the rifle.

"Nah, they're just girls," the driver said. "They don't pose a threat to us."

Costa smiled out the back seat window and made a V for victory sign with the fingers of his manacled hands.

"We believe in you, Sire!" Strawberry Blonde shouted as she blew a kiss his way.

The vehicles turned right onto Bradford Street and arrived at Mrs. Morton's rooming house a few moments later. The girls pulled alongside the Jeep and pressed their faces against the back windows.

"I can feel your love," Costa said through the glass. "We will all be back together very soon. I promise you that."

Mills climbed out of the passenger seat with his rifle and shooed the girls away.

"Come now, ladies. That's enough," he told them. "We have serious work to do here."

Sadie, Thumper, and Strawberry Blonde rode their bikes to the opposite side of the street facing the door of the jury bus. As the panelists stepped out at the corner of Bradford and Standish Streets, the three young women stared them all down.

Sadie then began reciting a banishing spell for the jurors to hear.

"Let this visit be ended. Be gone, and follow me no longer," she chanted. "Let my spirit be mended. So mote it be."

Thumper continued with the invocation of the god of death. "I call you, the comforter. From the underworld, come. I name you the keeper of men's souls. The walker of dark spirals. Come embrace us in your dark sleep."

The jurors tried to pay no attention, but with the Manson murders still fresh in their minds, they were all a bit spooked, although none would admit to it. The bailiff again tried to drive the girls away.

"Play your little fucking games somewhere else," Mills said angrily. But the girls did not move. They straddled their bicycles and held their ground.

"This is a public sidewalk, pig!" Sadie shouted. "We're here to show our love and support for an innocent man."

"Well, if you interfere with this business, I'll haul your skinny asses in for obstruction of justice!"

The sheriff's deputy motioned the jurors to keep moving toward the rooming house. The busload of reporters filed passed the witches next, and Sadie's demeanor quickly changed.

"Hello, Mr. Vonnegut!" she said happily as the author stepped off the school bus.

"Hello, girls!" He waved back, smiling.

"Keep writing the truth about our Tony," Sadie added. "He's being framed, just as you said."

Vonnegut had only alluded to that possibility in his *Life* piece, but he did not correct the young woman. He fished another cigarette from his pack and let it dangle under his mustachioed lips as he took his place with the others. Meanwhile, Evelyn Lawson pulled out a sprig of betony from her purse and clutched it in her thick palm as she walked swiftly past the trio without making eye contact. The girls could sense the columnist's trepidation.

"Now begin my evil spell, a thunderbolt to mix it well," Strawberry Blonde muttered in Lawson's direction.

Lawson stepped onto the sidewalk and fell in behind Vonnegut.

"Don't tell me you're worried about those little girls," he said to her. "Collectively, they look like they weigh only a hundred pounds."

"I can see their auras," she told Vonnegut nervously. "A murky redness surrounds them all. They are each filled with anger and violence."

He looked over at them and shrugged his bony shoulders. "I don't see anything. So it goes."

Ed Dinis announced that the group would enter the boardinghouse single file. They all climbed the front steps and crossed the threshold into the home, with the district attorney leading the way.

"We are now going to see where Pat Walsh and Mary Anne Wysocki were last seen alive, along with the bedroom that was once occupied by the defendant."

Dinis led the groups up a narrow staircase near the back of Patricia Morton's basement office.

"Will the jury please observe that this room is in the westerly part of the house, on what is referred to as the first floor."

The jurors and reporters all took turns examining Costa's former bedroom. Ed Dinis showed them the closet where Mary Anne Wysocki's hairdryer was found and where the rope, stained by human blood, was discovered by Tom Gunnery.

"The rope was used to tie up the girls and dismember them after they were shot," Dinis informed the group. "You'll be hearing more about this during trial."

Maurice Goldman chimed in. "And you'll also hear that the rope was placed in the closet after my client had moved out. We ask you all to be open-minded and impartial."

The groups climbed another flight of stairs to the bedroom once occupied by the victims.

"Here is where the defendant left a note asking Ms. Walsh and Ms. Wysocki for a ride to Truro," Dinis said, pointing to the bedroom door.

"And as we will state during trial, Mr. Costa readily admits that he met both ladies," Goldman added. "But he didn't kill them."

The verbal volleys continued between the DA and defense attorney throughout the tour, which also included a trip to the Foc'sle, where the regulars, all hardened day drinkers, cast suspicious bloodshot eyes at the strangers who were invading their boozy oasis.

"I feel like I'm visiting the zoo," Vonnegut whispered to Lawson. In fact, it reminded him of the human zoo on Tralfamadore in *Slaughterhouse-Five*.

"It's safer here than out there," she replied, pointing out the door to Commercial Street. "The witches are the real danger in this town."

Jurors and reporters were then led back to the buses for the final stop on their field trip—the woods of North Truro.

*Costa and his lawyer Maurice Goldman look on as
District Attorney Ed Dinis describes the murder scene in the Truro, Massachusetts, woods in
1970. © IMGN.*

Sitting shackled in the Jeep, Tony Costa could feel his hands sweating as they neared the old cemetery and Hatch Road.

Our masterpiece, Cory said, beaming with pride. *Now, they will see us for who we really are. We are the wolf of the steppes.*

Costa stepped out of the Jeep, smiling as if attending an exhibition where he was the featured artist. Elwood Mills handcuffed himself to the murder suspect so that Costa would not try to make an escape in the dense woods.

"This is area one. The parking space," Ed Dinis announced. "I would like to draw your attention to a small hole by the side of the road where Mary Anne Wysocki's pocketbook had been buried. And a short distance away from that is where a state trooper uncovered both the gun and the knife, tools used to murder and cut up the two victims."

Should we take our bow now? Cory asked.

"No, not yet. The big reveal is coming," Costa muttered.

"Shh!" Goldman whispered. "Not here in front of the jurors."

This time, the groups were led not single file but in pairs down the winding, leafy path until they got to a clearing.

"Mr. Foreman," Dinis said, nodding to Russell Dodge. "Members of the jury. Please notice the tree to my left. There are broken branches that protrude from the tree." He walked closer to the towering pine. "Now please observe the depression behind this tree. It is simply a hole in the ground. I want you to remember this location as hole number one, in area nine."

Jurors took out their pencils and pads and jotted notes, while reporters did the same. The groups looked down into the ditch, all wondering what butchery had happened there. Ed Dinis walked another thirty yards and waved for the jury panel's attention.

"This hole, this area where I am now standing is to be considered and remembered as hole number two."

Vonnegut gazed over at the second depression and then looked back at Costa, who was standing nearby with his attorney and the armed bailiff.

Look at him, Vonnegut thought to himself. *He's absolutely giddy. He's reliving the experience. Who did you cut up and stuff into this hole, Tony? Why don't you just tell us right now? You're the perfect tour guide for this, not Dinis. You know what happened here, and I'm sure we'll all find out soon enough.*

Costa caught Vonnegut's stare. *Don't you see, Mr. Vonnegut? We are both artists,* the killer wanted to say. *You express yourself with trippy stories about aliens and faraway places, while I create sculptures of flesh and bone out here in the forest. We are very much alike, you and me. We both yearn to be eternal in our work.*

Costa's attorney then alerted jurors and reporters to the side of a small hill that was covered by moss.

"Ladies and gentlemen of the jury. I would like to direct your attention to this spot," Goldman said. "This is what is known as the defendant's so-called marijuana patch. You cannot see it now, but large cannabis plants were grown and nurtured here, and they will be discussed at length by both sides in this case."

We haven't had a good high in days, Cory reminded Costa. *But I think it's wise to stay clean through the trial. If Goldman does his job, we'll be celebrating again soon enough.*

Dark clouds rolled in off Cape Cod Bay, indicating that a spring storm was fast approaching. The tops of trees began to rustle and sway as the groups were led, two by two, back to the buses and vehicles in the parking lot. It had been an exhausting six-hour tour, but Tony Costa was fully invigorated.

I could stay out here for hours, he told himself. *The forest is my studio.*

Costa could feel a few raindrops falling lightly on the shoulders of his borrowed coat. He then watched Vonnegut step up into the yellow school bus like an overgrown child.

"I hope you enjoyed the show," he said softly while staring at the famous author.

Elwood Mills then grabbed Costa's elbow and lifted him into the Jeep. Goldman got in on the other side next to his client.

"That was most pleasant," Costa gushed. "It was just like that show, *This Is Your Life.*"

"I'm glad you enjoyed yourself," Goldman replied with a trace of annoyance in his gravelly voice. "Just remember, I'm trying to save your life here. Those are the stakes we are facing. This is not some game show."

Costa nodded. "I understand fully well, Mr. Goldman. I have faith in you, the jury, and in God. We will win this thing, and I will be set free."

The defense attorney could not understand where Costa's confidence was rooted. Maurice Goldman knew that they were both in a hole as deep as the ones the jury had just seen in the North Truro woods.

CHAPTER THIRTY-SEVEN

"Describe to me exactly what it was like," Mailer said to Evelyn Lawson by telephone. "You were in the woods with Costa himself?"

Lawson told him that she was and then described the two burial pits where the bodies of the young female victims were pulled out.

"Did you see the grave site where the Perry girl was found?"

"We did, but the dopey district attorney didn't even mention it," Lawson replied. "It's like Susan Perry and Sydney Monzon never existed. Are you still having those dreams?"

Outside Carol Stevens, Lawson was the only person that he had confided in about his constant nightmares.

"I am," he grumbled. "I took the family away from the Berkshires to a home on the coast of Maine on Mount Desert Island. It's nearly four hundred miles away from Provincetown. My family should be safe up here, and I'm confident that the nightmares will go away."

"In those dreams, are you still seeing the severed head?" Lawson asked.

"Yes, and I can't seem to shake it. My mind vomits that despicable image nightly."

"You must write about it, after my book is published, of course."

"The unconscious has an enormous teleological sense," Mailer explained. "It moves toward a goal. One day, that goal will be to write about the Costa case in my own way."

Lawson then told Mailer about her encounter with the three witches during the jury tour.

"They were casting spells on me. But I made a gris-gris, a charm bag that kept me safe."

"Was Vonnegut there?"

"Yes, and he thinks it's all very funny. The witches I mean."

"I figured he would."

"He's also wondering why you left Provincetown," Lawson said. "He thinks that despite all your machismo, you are afraid of little girls."

"I'm twice the man he will ever be," Mailer contended before hanging up the phone.

Mailer curled his fist in anger. He wanted to punch something, someone. But Carol was pregnant with their child, and his rage might startle her and she could lose the baby.

Mailer squeezed a tennis ball in his hands until his fury subsided.

He began thinking about his new movie, *Maidstone*, which he planned to screen in Provincetown before its world premiere overseas.

But what if the witches lock the doors of the theater and burn us alive inside? he thought to himself. *What if they invade my home and butcher my pregnant wife like Manson's girls did to Sharon Tate?*

He stepped out of his kitchen and walked across the well-manicured lawn to the rocky beach, where the men of the Abenaki Indian tribe shucked clams in the flats and battled one another amid the nearby spruce trees thousands of years before. Locals claimed that the ancient warriors still haunted the beach and cursed the land, but Mailer did not feel their angry spirits. He was at peace here, the same peace and solitude he had found in Provincetown decades before. But his true home had been taken away from him, at least for now, by a generation that had seen their friends and brothers sent off to war and had slain their heroes.

"What is happening now in California and on Cape Cod is retribution," Mailer said to himself. "We are doomed for the life we created for them. We enslaved them in commercialism, and now the only spiritualism left for them is that of a demonic manifestation."

He quickly decided that he would postpone the Ptown film screening and preview the film at the Whitney Museum of American Art in New York City, selling out its entire two-week run before taking it to the Venice Film Festival. As director, Mailer had chosen to include the real-life fight scene with Rip Torn, who reminded him of the newly infamous Tex Watson from the murderous Manson gang, in the final cut. Despite praise for Torn's smoldering performance, critics were lukewarm, even cruel to Mailer's cinematic effort, one he described as a "guerrilla raid on the nature of reality."

While Mailer worked tirelessly to promote his new film, far outside his amplitude, the very nature of reality was facing one of its greatest challenges inside a Cape Cod courtroom.

The judge took his seat on the bench on Friday morning May 15, 1970, and thanked the jurors for participating in what he called "a nature walk" through the North Truro woods the day before.

"Had I known the trip would have been as exciting as it was yesterday, I would have asked you if you had any prior Boy Scout or Girl Scout experience. I think that would have been a qualifying question that would have been appropriate."

The jurors laughed politely. Judge Beaudreau then reintroduced Ed Dinis and Maurice Goldman, who would each provide opening statements to the jury. For Dinis, it was his time to shine and repair some of the luster that had been stripped away from him for his handling of Chappaquiddick.

He would leave much of the trial's grunt work to his assistant, a young prosecutor from New Bedford named Armand Fernandes Jr. Since both men were also of Portuguese descent, they hoped to eliminate any claims of cultural bias surrounding the defendant.

The district attorney stood up from the prosecutor's table and strode past Goldman on his way to the jury box. Physically, the two lawyers could not have been more different. Dinis was dark, tall, and lean, while Goldman was pale, squat, and pudgy.

"It looks like a Great Dane squaring off against a bulldog," Vonnegut said to Evelyn Lawson as both were seated in the back of the courtroom.

Dinis placed both hands on the wooden gate of the jury box and addressed the panel, making sure that he made eye contact with each juror.

"May it please the Court, Mr. Foreman, and ladies and gentlemen of the jury, we are about to try Antone C. Costa. Our system is known as an adversary system. The Commonwealth offers the evidence to support the indictments, and the defense in its rebuttal will offer their reply to these accusations."

Dinis turned his head away from the jury box and pointed his finger at Tony Costa, who sat expressionless at the defense table next to Goldman and his team.

"The Commonwealth says that Antone Costa, on or about the twenty-fifth day of January, 1969, did murder Patricia H. Walsh and Mary Anne Wysocki of Providence, Rhode Island. And the Commonwealth further says that after murdering these girls, he stole the automobile owned by Patricia Walsh."

Dinis began pacing the floor. It looked like a natural action, but each step had been choreographed and exhaustively rehearsed in the days prior. Armand Fernandes marveled at Dinis's performance. In Fernandes's opinion, the district attorney lacked the tenacity and commitment to detail needed to make for a good trial attorney, but the man was a natural performer. Dinis had even taken a Hollywood screen test years before and could have had a career in movies had he not decided to pursue a life in politics instead.

"The tragedy began when these two women, approximately the age of twenty-three, one teaching school and the other going to college, decided to take a weekend trip to the town of Provincetown. They drove in an automobile belonging to Patricia Walsh, a blue Volkswagen with a registration KV-978. When they arrived in Provincetown, they went to that rooming house that we visited yesterday, and they checked in with Mrs. Pat Morton. They were given that room on the second floor, that room that I asked you to observe."

Ed Dinis went on to describe the note left by Costa on the girls' bedroom door and, later, the discovery of Pat Walsh's car in Truro.

"Now when the police, the detectives of the state police attached to my office, and the Provincetown police became involved, they approached Mr. Costa, and he was duly advised of his constitutional rights repeatedly. But then Mr. Costa indicated a willingness to cooperate. In order to explain the whereabouts of the girls and the position of the automobile, Mr. Costa began to tell conflicting and contradictory stories as to his activities involving the missing girls and the automobile. He told one story that he had purchased the car because the girls had owed him money in a marijuana transaction. He told another story that one of these girls, and pathologically this is proven untrue, was in need of an abortion and was trying to raise money to go to Los Angeles to take care of that particular problem. And he told another story that he drove these girls to Burlington, Vermont, from which they flew to Canada to go and make more marijuana deals."

The district attorney paused to allow the jurors to catch up with their note taking.

"Now, the pathology will show that the defendant did murder these girls with deliberate premeditated malice aforethought and that he further murdered them with extreme atrocity and cruelty," Dinis stated. "The pathology will report to you that these girls had been shot, that one of the girls had been shot twice in the head and that the other had been shot once. The pathology will further reveal to you that these girls were cut up in seven parts."

Those words triggered a gasp from some trial watchers seated in the courtroom. Although the details had been printed time and time again in newspapers, hearing it in open court made it feel more real to them.

"The testimony will also show and will reveal that the examination by the ballistics expert in removing the slugs from the bodies of these two girls will testify that the weapon that fired these slugs came from a revolver owned and possessed by Antone Costa."

Dinis walked over to the prosecution table and lifted a thick manila folder in the air for everyone in the courtroom to see.

"Now further, in the examination of these bodies, the medical men, the pathologists made an examination, and they found in the bodies, in the cavities of the vagina and rectum of these dead girls, they found spermatozoa, male sperm, and that will be testified by the pathologist who made the examination of these bodies, or these parts of butchered bodies."

For one courtroom observer, a housewife and neighbor of Vonnegut's, the details of the gruesome killings were too much to bear. She got up and ran out of the courtroom weeping, never to return. The accused killer felt differently about the whole affair. Ed Dinis's opening statements stimulated him and made him feel aroused. Once again, Costa's palms began to sweat as his mind drifted back to his masterpiece.

Following the district attorney's hour-long oration, Maurice Goldman approached the jury box with only a few words to say on his client's behalf.

"We are going to offer some evidence to try and prove in substance that the defendant was a victim of drug dependency and that each and every stage of the proceedings, he was under the domination, intoxication, and the use of mind-altering drugs," the defense attorney told jurors. "We are going to show you, and we hope to prove, as the government intends to prove its case, just what effect of the use of these chemicals and drugs will do to a mind."

Maurice Goldman wanted to convince the jury that America's drug culture, not Tony Costa, was being put on trial inside the Cape Cod courtroom.

"The defendant at this moment stands absolutely innocent," Goldman continued. "Wait until you have heard all the evidence. There is much that is going to be revealed in this case. It is on evidence alone that you will make your determination of guilt or innocence in this case."

Costa's lawyer had also practiced the delivery of his opening remarks to the jury. Unlike the smooth district attorney, Maurice Goldman moved about the courtroom in a lumbering, folksy way. He pulled on his starched collar as the temperature rose in the courtroom. The actions were calculated. The defense lawyer was presenting himself to the jury as an everyman. *I'm just like you*, he wanted them to believe. Finally, after trying to explain the difference between what constituted evidence and what did not, Goldman put the question in its simplest terms for the jury to understand.

"A question will be first presented to the witness, and then the witness will answer," he told the panel. "It is the answer that is evidence, not the question. Now let me give you an exaggerated example of this. If I should say to you, Mr. Foreman, 'Did you beat your wife last night?' and you say, 'No,' well, the evidence is no, unless somebody else gets on the stand and testifies as to evidence of having seen you or some evidence which would show that you did."

Many of the jurors nodded. Satisfied with their response, Goldman returned to the defense table and waited for the first witness to be called.

CHAPTER THIRTY-EIGHT

The judge ordered a five-minute recess at 10:35 a.m. It was just enough time for Vonnegut to go outside for a quick smoke. He wondered why he had decided to attend the trial. After all, his special report in *Life* magazine had already been published months before.

"It's time to move on, isn't it?" he asked himself between puffs off his Pall Mall.

At least the murder trial allowed him some time away from his house and his family. His wife, Jane, breathed a sigh of relief each time he walked out their front door and headed up to the courthouse.

Vonnegut was gearing up for a rewrite of a play that he had written called *Penelope*. He had performed the show a few times on Cape Cod at the Orleans Arena Theater, and Evelyn Lawson had told him that it had potential. But that was during the time before *Slaughterhouse-Five*, when Vonnegut had chucked his scripts in an old beer carton and left them, forgotten, in the back of his writing studio. Now, publishers and even Hollywood producers were clamoring for his work. Paramount wanted to option *Penelope* for a feature film, but Vonnegut knew that the script needed work. He came up with a new title, *Happy Birthday, Wanda June*, and was eager to begin writing that summer. Having a Hollywood movie adapted from his play would be another feather in Vonnegut's cap and would help him continue to shift the balance of power in his ongoing rivalry with Mailer. The story's plot involved a girl who was run over by an ice cream truck and ascended to heaven where Jesus, Judas, Einstein, and Hitler were happily playing shuffleboard together. As for Wanda June, she too was overjoyed to have gone to heaven and was very thankful to the truck driver who had sent her there.

I wonder if those poor girls feel the same way about Tony Costa, he thought.

Vonnegut dropped his cigarette onto the granite steps of the courthouse and stamped it out with his tennis shoes. He then returned to the courtroom, where the father of Patricia Walsh was about to take the stand.

Wearing a dark suit, thickly framed eyeglasses, and close-cropped white hair, Leonard Walsh was sworn in as the first witness in the murder trial. Assistant prosecutor Armand Fernandes approached the witness stand and began his direct examination of the father and retired postal clerk.

"Could you tell the court and jury when was the last time you saw your daughter, as you best remember?"

"It was Wednesday or Thursday, on the twenty-second or twenty-third of January," Walsh answered. "I cashed a check for her."

"Now do you recall filing a missing person's report?" Fernandes asked.

"I called the Rehoboth barracks of the Massachusetts State Police and asked them if they would try to determine for me whether or not my daughter had met with an accident on the Massachusetts highway and had been hospitalized. She should have been in school at that time. I received a phone call from her principal that she didn't show up for school that morning."

Fernandes then returned to the prosecution table to consult his index cards. The tiny cards referenced what was inside twenty boxes that were being used for exhibits during the trial. He reached into one box and pulled out a photograph, which he then handed to the father. It was the smiling image of Patricia Walsh taken for her high school yearbook. The man gripped the picture tightly, and his hands began to shake.

"Could you tell whether or not it is a fair representation of your daughter?"

"It is," Walsh said softly. "It is definitely, yes."

Fernandes then asked the girl's father to describe her car.

"She had a Volkswagen with a sunroof," the witness stated. "It was light blue with the registration KV-978."

Fernandes handed Leonard Walsh a photograph of his daughter's automobile, and the father positively identified it. The prosecutor then offered more exhibits: Patricia Walsh's dental records and her final college term paper on psychological research methods.

"Is this your daughter's handwriting?"

"Yes, with corrections that I presume were made by her college professor."

Fernandes returned to the prosecution table, pulled a piece of clothing from a cardboard box, and brought it over to the witness. Leonard Walsh instinctively looked away as a tear rolled down his cheek.

"I'll show you this item. Whether or not you can identify that?"

"Well, it is a sweater very similar to the type that my daughter had," the father answered. "It appears to be her sweater."

Unlike his daughter's photograph, Leonard Walsh was reluctant to touch Pat's white cable-knit sweater. While her graduation picture symbolized her life, her sweater only reminded the distraught father of her tragic death. He was excused from the witness stand and avoided eye contact with his daughter's accused killer as he returned to his seat in the courtroom next to his two sons and their girlfriends.

Catherine Walsh, Pat's mother, was called to testify next. Unlike her husband, Mrs. Walsh locked eyes with Tony Costa as she made her way to the witness stand.

"Please state your full name for the court, Mrs. Walsh."

"Catherine Madeline McCarthy Walsh," the mother answered.

"And your occupation?"

"I am a second-grade teacher in the only inner-city school in Providence, Rhode Island," she replied proudly.

"And you are the mother of Patricia Walsh?"

"Yes I am."

Armand Fernandes brought the white sweater back to the witness stand for identification.

"I recognize it as a sweater that Patricia came in to me one day and said, 'Mommy, I'm getting like you. I got a bargain on this sweater.' And I said, 'I think the sleeves might be a little short for you. You have long arms.' She tried it on. It was all right."

The mother went on to identify a long-sleeved blouse and a pocketbook that had belonged to her daughter. She examined the items in evidence and then looked over at Costa, shooting daggers with her eyes. Catherine Walsh reached swiftly into her own handbag. It was a sudden move that startled both the judge and the jury. Everyone in the courtroom believed she was grabbing for a gun. Tony Costa ducked below the defense table as sheriff's deputy Elwood Mills reached for the woman's hand.

"How dare you?" she shouted as she pulled out a handkerchief from the bag. "I needed to blow my nose. I'm no killer. He is!" Catherine Walsh added, pointing at Tony Costa.

"Objection!" Goldman yelled.

"Sustained." The judge complied.

Catherine Walsh was escorted off the witness stand with no further questions from either side.

Once excused, Walsh's parents left the courthouse in a hurry. It was impossible for either of them to breathe the same air as the monster who murdered and chopped up their daughter like firewood. As they descended the granite steps, they bumped into Steve "Speed" Grund, who was scheduled to testify for the prosecution that afternoon. Dressed in striped bell-bottom slacks, a purple shirt, and a leather jacket, the long-haired, oafish hippie appeared unsteady on his feet. While Sadie, Thumper, and Strawberry Blonde kept their distance from the Walsh family outside the courthouse, seeing Grund, they rushed over immediately and began hurling obscenities in his direction.

"You're a fucking snitch, Steve," Sadie hissed. "How could you speak out against Sire?"

"I was ordered here by the court," he replied. "You think I wanna be here talking about Tony?"

Thumper then blew sprinkles of pepper from the palm of her hand in Grund's direction.

"The wicked shall decay," she chanted. "You foul Tony, and you shall be fouled in return."

"You chicks are fucking crazy," Grund shouted as he ran up the granite steps away from the three witches.

He had ingested a tab of acid in the parking lot of the courthouse, and its effects were just starting to take hold. He pushed open the large wooden doors and stumbled into the ornate lobby. Grund steadied himself against a marble column, and he felt safe, at least for the moment. As he waited for his turn to testify, he placed his ear to the door of the courtroom but heard nothing.

"I wonder what the hell is happening in there?" he said aloud.

Inside the courtroom, Armand Fernandes and Maurice Goldman were sparring over a pair of witnesses about Pat Walsh's stolen Volkswagen Beetle. One witness, William Watts, ran a garage and gas station at the junction of Routes 6 and 6A in North Truro. Watts told the court that he had known Tony Costa for five years and recalled a telephone conversation he had with the defendant in late January 1969.

"What did he say to you?" Fernandes asked.

"He wanted to know how much it would cost to paint a Volkswagen," Watts replied. "I found out from my brother that it would cost one hundred dollars if it didn't have any dents and if he didn't want the inside painted. Tony told me that the car was in pretty good shape and that he'd like to have it painted some exotic color."

"Did he tell you the color of the car at all at this time?"

"No, he just said he'd stop by, but he never did. We never painted it."

During cross-examination, Maurice Goldman fixated on Watts's use of the word *exotic*.

"Was it a gay color? Like a brilliant yellow or an offbeat color?"

"A color that was not ordinary is what I understood it to mean," Watts replied.

The line of questioning was going nowhere for Goldman, so he excused the witness.

Carl Benson came next, and he recounted the morning that he discovered Pat Walsh's blue Volkswagen Beetle parked in an odd spot off Old Proprietor's Road near the old cemetery.

"Where was the car in reference to the road you were traveling on?" Fernandes asked.

"Oh, I should say it was off the road about thirty feet," Benson answered. "In a little clearing."

The witness told the court that he met up with Truro police chief Harold Berrio and returned to the scene a short time later.

"And what, if any observation, did you make of the automobile at this time?"

"There was an object in the right-hand side of the windshield which wasn't there before," Benson replied. "It was a piece of brown paper with some markings on it."

"No further questions."

Attorney Goldman waved off the witness also. "No further questions. Thank you."

If it was a football game, both sides were still in the first quarter, but

Ed Dinis liked his chances so far. Armand Fernandes had given jurors an emotional gut punch by putting Pat Walsh's grief-stricken parents on the witness stand. Now, he had established the fact that Costa was in possession of Walsh's Volkswagen and had tried to get it painted in an attempt to camouflage the evidence. The prosecution was on a roll. Landlady Patricia Morton was called to testify next.

"Did you know Tony Costa?" Fernandes asked her.

"Yes, he stayed at my house for three weeks."

"Was his appearance different than it is now?"

"I'm near-sighted, but I do see him," Morton replied. "He looks fatter and his hair is done differently, and he's dressed in business clothes."

Did that bitch just call us fat? Cory asked Costa. *We should have sliced her up and dumped her with the rest of them. She may be old and ugly, but we could have made an exception for her.*

Costa did not engage with his alter ego; that would come later when he was back in his jail cell. For now, he was enjoying his time in court, playing his own macabre version of the Rolling Stones Rock and Roll Circus. Only he, not Mick Jagger, was the star of this show.

Fernandes showed Morton a page from her guesthouse register, and she identified Costa's signature and the date of Saturday, January 18, 1969. Morton was then shown photos of Pat Walsh and Mary Anne Wysocki.

"They came to the door of my guesthouse, at my office, looking for a room on January 24. I took them through the house first, and then they registered."

"At this time, was Mr. Costa in the establishment?"

"Yes he was," she answered. "I merely introduced them and said that he was one of our guests, and they nodded faintly and we proceeded on our way."

"Did you see the girls after they registered?"

"Yes, just before I was going to bed very early," Morton replied. "I went upstairs in my bathrobe, and they were sitting up fully dressed, on top of their beds, with the spare bed blanket wrapped around each girls' shoulders, and they were talking animatedly and seemed quite happy. I was afraid it would be cold because of the bitter, bitter night, about five degrees."

When asked if she visited their room another time, Morton testified that she had gone up to the room the next morning.

"I check on all the rooms each day, wastebaskets and general disorder. Our house is neat, clean, and organized."

"And what observation did you make?"

"In the tongue and groove wood construction of the door, there was a note torn from a piece of brown paper bag, and it was stuck there just carelessly with a pin in the groove, so I read it."

"What did the note say?"

"Something like, 'Could you possibly please give me a ride to Truro early in the morning,' or something. And it was signed by Tony."

"And on January 26, Sunday, did you go to that room again?" Fernandes continued.

"I did. I thought, well goodness, all their things are gone. The room was cleared out, and then I noticed the note. It was written on a brown paper bag again, and it said, 'We are checking out. Thank you for your many kindnesses.' It was signed by Mary Anne and Pat."

"What about Mr. Costa's room?"

"Things were gradually being taken out of the room without a note saying, 'I'm leaving.'"

Patricia Morton finished her testimony without any cross-examination from Maurice Goldman. She strode out of the courtroom, confident that she had delivered her most important message to the court and to reporters that although she once had a killer for a tenant, she kept a clean house.

Robert Turbidy and Gerry Magnan followed Mrs. Morton on the stand. Pat Walsh's boyfriend wept as he examined the leather bag he had made for her, while Magnan identified the hair dryer found in Costa's room as one that had belonged to his girlfriend, Mary Anne Wysocki.

Ed Dinis's next witness would surely be the highlight to an already eventful first day of trial, because he had been an unwitting accomplice to Costa's plot to cover up the murders of Pat Walsh and Mary Anne Wysocki.

Steve Grund was called into the courtroom, and he was tripping out.

CHAPTER THIRTY-NINE

Fuck, fuck, fuck, Ed Dinis thought. The district attorney recognized immediately that Steve Grund was on drugs. But he nodded to Fernandes to proceed with the witness and hope for the best. Maurice Goldman saw that the witness was barely awake and licked his lips. The drugged-out hippie would make his case for him.

"Please give the court your full name," Armand Fernandes told him.

"Stephen Wayne Grund, G-R-U-N-D."

"How long have you known Mr. Costa?"

The witness began counting on his hand. "Since approximately November, December, around that period of time." Grund could not remember if they had met in 1968 or 1969. "I'm not positive on dates at all," he said.

"Let me direct your attention to February 2, 1969. It was a Sunday. You recall going to Boston with Mr. Costa?"

"I was walking up Commercial Street, and I saw him in a phone booth. I approached the phone booth and he said, 'Hey Steve, Weed, hello. What are you doing?'"

"How do you spell 'weed'?" Fernandes asked.

The question drew some snickers from courtroom observers.

"That's Tim Atkins's nickname. That is *w-e-e-d*."

Over the next several minutes, Fernandes asked the witness to take the jury back to the night that he, Atkins, and Tony Costa took the stolen Volkswagen on a trip to Vinnie Bonaviri's apartment in Boston. Grund's eyes were dilated, and his mouth was dry. He asked for a glass of water and finished it with one long gulp.

"Did Mr. Costa say that the car was a gift, or did he purchase it?"

"He said he fronted the girls a pound of hashish."

"Do you know what hashish is?" Fernandes asked.

Grund laughed. "Hashish is a type of smoking material derived from a marijuana plant, a hemp plant. Tony said the girls had ripped him off. In other words, they had not paid for the hashish. He said that the girls then owed him seven hundred dollars for the pound of hashish, so they made what you might call a trade. They gave him the car, and he gave them a couple hundred dollars because they were going to split. They were going to just completely leave town and go up to Canada."

"Now, you had another conversation with Mr. Costa later in Provincetown?"

"Yeah, he said he was gonna split because the cops were hassling him too much."

Grund was getting jumpy. He bit down on his lower lip and began bouncing his knees on the witness stand.

"Do you need a rest?" Fernandes asked him.

"I think I'd better," Grund slurred. He staggered off the witness stand, and Judge Beaudreau ordered the jurors out of the courtroom.

During this time, Dinis and Fernandes debated whether to continue their questioning. The prosecutors still needed to associate Costa with the murder weapon, and the only way to do that was to keep Grund on the stand. After twenty minutes, the witness was asked back to the courtroom along with the jury. The hippie took his seat on the witness stand and was in worse shape than before. Grund closed his eyes and nodded off. Bernie Flynn was seated at the prosecution table and rushed over with another glass of water. This time, Grund could not hold the glass, as his hands were shaking badly. Grund stood up to get his bearings. He gripped the wood railings tightly.

Armand Fernandes had to wrap up his questioning quickly.

"Okay, you'll stand. Before we suspended, you were describing your last conversation with Mr. Costa. What else did Mr. Costa discuss with you?"

"He asked me if I wanted to buy a gun. It was supposed to be a twenty-two-caliber pistol," Grund slurred. "It was hidden in the Truro woods, and it was hot. I didn't buy it. I wanted no part of it."

Bingo, Fernandes thought. "No further questions."

Now, it was Goldman's turn.

"You are known as Speed or Speedy. That's right, isn't it?" he asked Grund.

"Yes, in the past, yes."

"And Speed had some reference to LSD, didn't it?"

Fernandes shot up from his chair. "Objection!"

Judge Beaudreau called both lawyers to the bench.

"What are we going into now?" the judge asked Goldman.

"I'm going to show the use of drugs between Tony and him on occasions."

"Mr. Grund's use of drugs is totally immaterial to this case," Fernandes argued. "And if he did use drugs, he runs the risk of criminal responsibility."

"I think I'll allow this," Judge Beaudreau decided. "We are going to hear a lot of this talk from now on. There is no crime unless you are caught with possession."

Goldman agreed. "No crime at all. And then again, there is no crime for the use of LSD if he gets it by prescription from a doctor. That is the point I am getting at."

"Costa used, because he's the man on trial, not Grund," Fernandes contended. "I object to any questions which ask him, Grund, if he used LSD."

"I'm going to show the effects of the drugs," Goldman insisted, turning his head to Grund, who was swaying back and forth while standing in the witness box. "Look at him. This fellow is in bad shape right now. He's under LSD. He's having a freak-out moment right now."

"It's evident from his conduct that he has some problem. I don't know what it is," the judge said.

Grund sat down and finished his glass of water. His hands were steady now. The judge saw this as a sign to proceed with testimony.

Attorney Goldman approached Grund and began questioning him about Costa's drug use.

"You told me that Tony had used heroin, didn't you?" he asked the witness.

"Not that I recall."

"What about the night that you drove the Volkswagen to Boston?"

"Before we left to go to Boston, we picked up some vitamin B-12 and a joint that I had left in my house."

"Tony was high that day too, in the parlance of the street."

Grund shrugged his shoulders. "I don't recall."

"Is it that you can't recall exactly now because you are experiencing a trip now?"

"Objection," shouted Fernandes.

"It is Costa who is on trial!" the judge reminded Goldman.

Beaudreau called an end to the day's proceedings, and Grund went to a nearby motel to get his head straight as Goldman planned to call him back to the stand on the following Monday.

The jurors were sent to a different motel, where they were sequestered for the duration of the proceedings. The reporters, including Kurt Vonnegut and Evelyn Lawson, went home to either file their stories or compile their notes and relax for the weekend, while Ed Dinis went out and enjoyed an elegant dinner with a companion. But the day was not over for Armand Fernandes or Tony Costa. The young prosecutor spent the next several hours in the law library of the Barnstable Superior Courthouse, studying legal briefs about psychosis. Fernandes wanted to read a particular edition of the *Harvard Law Review* that focused on the subject, but it was not on the library shelf. Instead, the book was in the hands of Tony Costa, who was seated at a nearby table under armed guard, conducting research for his own defense.

"Nice work today, Mr. Fernandes," the killer said, smiling. "We certainly have our work cut out for us."

"Mr. Goldman is a fine attorney," Fernandes replied. "He'll do just swell."

"From your last name, I gather that you are Portuguese," Costa said. "Where are your people from? Mine came over here from the Azores."

"My mother's family came from the island of Madeira," Fernandes told him. "My mother, Rosaria, is from New Bedford. Her parents immigrated here in 1933."

Fernandes did not know why he felt comfortable offering such personal information to the accused murderer, but Costa had a gentle and disarming way about him. He then thought about his younger brother James, who had been born with spina bifida, which left him paralyzed from the waist down. Their mother had to quit her job as a factory worker to take care of him. An act of God had taken the legs of his brother, but it was an act of the devil that had ripped apart the legs of the young women that had been buried in North Truro. Fernandes had seen all the dismembered body parts that were put back together like broken dolls on the examination tables at the funeral home on Cape Cod.

I need to get justice for those girls, he thought to himself.

Costa spoke up, getting the prosecutor's attention. "I've read about Madeira. It sounds lovely. I can't wait to go there when this trial is over."

You cocky son of a bitch, Fernandes wanted to say. *You think you're gonna just walk away from this thing? You're either going to the electric chair or to jail for the rest of your life. But you sure as hell ain't going to Madeira. I'll see to that.*

Instead, the prosecutor kept his cool and just smiled.

"Sure, Tony, sure," he said.

Costa was escorted back to the jailhouse, where other inmates had learned to keep their distance. Most were incarcerated for petty offenses, and their girlfriends, wives, and mothers fed them all the grisly details that were printed in the newspapers or described on the evening news.

"Stay away from that sicko!" they were warned. "He butchers women."

Prisoners began referring to Costa by the nickname Cold Cuts behind his back.

He felt more isolated. Cory, his alter ego, had become less of a presence in his warped mind.

He continued writing, adding new verses to a poem he had titled "You. In Memory of All Broken Men."

> *I wait—listening to the echo of your pain. Haunting you as you stumble through the stolid crypts...crawling, searching for me amidst the gunk and stench of dead man's bones. From the tombs of your mind from the ebony past. I hear you scream, "I will help you, you need it, please allow me." Yes—you are irony itself! And me... I lay silent.*
>
> *Now you search the fortress, the citadel you once destroyed, but only the cobwebs remain. Even the spiders know you. They hide, rushing from their webs to seek the secure dark crevasses beneath the rubble you peruse. Yet, even some of them, cannot escape your crushing foot.*
>
> *And me... I lay broken.*

It was late in the evening, and Norman Mailer was also writing at his rented home, Fortune's Rock in Mount Desert, Maine. He gazed out the sliding doors to the timbered balcony, which appeared virtually suspended twenty feet high over Somes Sound. He scoffed at the idea that he was hiding out at the secluded retreat in Acadia National Park, far away from the dark elements of Provincetown, but in his mind, he knew it to be true. Mailer feared that he had lost his courage, so he challenged himself by scaling outside the living room of Fortune's Rock over the jagged, boulder-strewn basin and punishing tides below. This landscape was more rugged than the soft, dune-covered terrain of Cape Cod, but to Mailer, it was far less dangerous.

Helltown was weighing heavily on his mind. He pulled out a yellow notepad and a pencil and wrote a description of its past as it related to its present. He called it "a vanished place…something of a perished Klondike of whores and smugglers, and whalers with wages hot in their pockets… What a Biblical scene Hell-Town must have offered of catamites and sodomites and whores passing the infections of the ages on to each pirate with blood in his beard… I had lived most mornings with the unseen presence of much of the population of Hell-Town."

He paused and stared at the page, and a story began to form in his mind. It was a story about a severed head and a marijuana patch. "The Truro woods are haunted," he wrote. "A young Portugee in Provincetown killed four girls, dismembered their bodies and buried them in several graves in these low woods. I was always immensely aware of the dead girls and their numb, mutilated, accusing presence."

"Okay, that's it for now," Mailer said to himself. "It's a start to a novel, maybe not a good start, but a start nonetheless."

CHAPTER FORTY

Patricia Walsh's parents returned to the courthouse when testimony resumed on Monday, May 18, 1970. Catherine Walsh wanted to look into the eyes of her daughter's killer when he was sentenced to death. The idea of life in prison was not enough for the traumatized mother, especially after Bernie Flynn described to her how Costa had killed her only daughter.

Her resilience would be put to the ultimate test on this day. Steve Grund resumed his testimony that morning. Ed Dinis and Armand Fernandes were both happy to see that the witness was clear headed and focused during Maurice Goldman's cross-examination. Grund's sidekick, Tim "Weed" Atkins, followed him on the witness stand. The young hippie's mother had tried to get him excused from the trial, claiming that he had been constantly harassed by police in Ptown because of his friendship with the so-called Cape Cod Vampire. Her plea fell on deaf ears at the district attorney's office, and Atkins was ordered to testify about the night he drove Pat Walsh's stolen Volkswagen with Tony Costa. Weed Atkins filled in some of the details that were missing from Steve Grund's drug-addled testimony, but he could not supply any specific dates to the court. "I don't remember," was Atkins's standard response to questions about the timeline of events on February 2, 1969, the night they drove to Boston. When questioning was turned over to the defense, Atkins said he recalled seeing Tony Costa at a "pot party" in Provincetown sometime around Christmas in December 1968. He was asked to point out Costa in the courtroom, which he did. Atkins averted his eyes, though, when Costa shot him a steely glare from the defense table.

When his testimony concluded, Atkins left the courthouse with Steven Grund by his side. Both were cornered by Costa's disciples, Sadie, Thumper, and Strawberry Blonde, in the parking lot.

"You'll burn in hell for what you did," Sadie told them. "You turned your back on Tony, and you'll pay for it in the everlasting fire."

Thumper then pulled a piece of writing paper from the pocket of her tight jeans and unfolded it.

It was the poem Costa had written a couple of nights before and was able to smuggle out of jail through his cellmate.

"Now you search the fortress, the citadel you once destroyed, but only the cobwebs remain," Thumper recited from the note. "Even the spiders know you!"

Feeling spooked, Atkins grabbed Grund's shoulder, and together they ran to a waiting car parked down the hill and drove away.

With both witnesses now out of the way, Armand Fernandes set the prosecution's focus on the exhaustive police work involved in the murder case. The false statements made by Ed Dinis aside, the district attorney's office as a whole had performed exemplarily in their duties. Fernandes called Trooper Tom Gunnery to the witness stand. Fernandes wanted to follow the trail of the murder weapon, Costa's pistol, from the time he tried to sell it to Steve Grund to the moment it was discovered in the North Truro woods. The prosecutor pointed Gunnery's attention to a large photograph fastened to a blackboard in front of the jury box. The black-and-white image was labeled Area 3, the parking area.

"I show you this photograph," Fernandes told Gunnery. "Is that photograph a fair representation of the area?"

"Yes," Gunnery confirmed.

"At that time, did you have occasion to find anything?"

"At the base of a pine tree, I uncovered the turf, and I found a plastic bag," Gunnery replied. "I observed in this bag a small gun which had white grips on the handle."

Fernandes consulted his index cards once again before reaching into another box of evidence. This time, he pulled out an envelope containing a large plastic bag. He brought it to the witness stand.

"Trooper, I ask you to examine the contents of the envelope."

Gunnery opened the envelope and found a large plastic bag, and inside was an unloaded firearm.

"With reference to the item you now hold in your hand, can you identify it?"

"Yes, sir. It's a twenty-two-caliber revolver, make EIG."

"Was that the same caliber weapon, make, and model used to shoot and kill Patricia Walsh and Mary Anne Wysocki?"

"Yes, it is," Gunnery replied definitively.

Fernandes went back and pulled another envelope out of the box and handed it to the witness.

"What do you identify that as?"

Gunnery pulled out another plastic bag and examined it closely. "It's a knife."

"Is that the same knife that you found in that area?"

"Yes, sir, it is."

With both murder weapons established for the jury, Fernandes then called Bernie Flynn to the stand. The state police investigator touched Catherine Walsh's shoulder as he made his way through the courtroom.

This time, Fernandes showed the court photographs of the two holes where the victims' bodies were recovered.

"Lieutenant Flynn, can you state what you found inside the holes depicted in these photos?"

"I reached into the first hole, by that time it was approximately a foot,

foot and a half deep," Flynn stated. "And I pulled out a severed head of a white female."

"And what did you do at this time?"

"I held the head in my arms, and I brushed the dirt, sand, and gravel from the eyes and her face, and I opened her mouth and took the dirt and sand from her mouth. As a result of doing that, I recognized the face of Mary Anne Wysocki."

Wysocki's parents did not attend the trial. But Catherine Walsh let out a loud sob on their behalf.

Fernandes let Flynn's words linger in the air.

Sitting in the media rows, Vonnegut raised his bushy eyebrows, while Evelyn Lawson shook her head in disgust. This was the first time that Vonnegut had heard the gruesome details directly from one of the investigators who found the bodies and not the sensational version of the events recounted for him by Ed Dinis, who was nowhere near the murder scene at the time of the discovery.

"Now, what did you do next?"

"Along with Trooper Gunnery, we dug further into the hole to remove the portion of the body that was exposed; and by reaching our hands under the armpits; we pulled up the upper half of a female body, severed at the mid-abdomen. We placed that next to the head on top of the pile of sand."

It was the same white sand that vacationers from around the world yearned for and had flocked to each summer season. And now inside this courtroom, it symbolized excruciating pain and death. This cruel irony was not lost on Vonnegut.

If you're fond of sand dunes and salty air, you're sure to fall in love with old Cape Cod, the writer hummed to himself.

"And what did you discover in the second hole?" Fernandes asked Flynn.

"Lieutenant George Killen reached into the hole and he came up with an arm, and an arm protruded above the surface from the wrist and the hand was exposed. As a result of that, we started taking the dirt out by hand, and we dug down approximately a foot, and I saw what appeared to be hair. I reached into the hole, pulled the hair, and as I did, it removed itself from the scalp. As a result, we dug further into the hole. I reached into the hole and lifted what appeared to be the head of a female. I lifted it out and it was the head of a white female girl. We had discovered Patricia Walsh."

Fernandes then showed jurors photographs of the detached remains of both young women taken during their autopsies. Pat Walsh and Mary Anne Wysocki did not appear to be human anymore. They looked like slabs of meat on display in a butcher-shop window.

Patricia's mother let out a heartrending wail and collapsed against her husband. Leonard Walsh hugged his wife and wept. On the stand, Bernie Flynn chewed the inside of his cheek and tried not to cry.

With emotions running high in the courtroom, Judge Beaudreau called for a much-needed recess.

CHAPTER FORTY-ONE

The discussion about headless corpses unnerved everyone in the courtroom, most notably Pat Walsh's parents, who kept their eyes focused on Tony Costa during Bernie Flynn's grisly testimony. Catherine Walsh wished that she had slipped a pistol in her purse so that she could bring Biblical justice to the man who had shot her beautiful daughter and desecrated her precious body. Kurt Vonnegut also spent time studying Costa in the courtroom. The defendant was not a casual observer at his own trial; instead, he was taking notes and whispering in the ear of his attorney at various times during witness testimony.

Costa's outward appearance gave no indication as to the depravity that had been associated with him. Sure, his lawyer had cleaned him up for the trial. He had his sideburns trimmed down, his hair cut shorter, and he was freshly shaven.

He looks like the accountant that handles my taxes, Vonnegut thought.

Costa was a sharp contrast to Charlie Manson, who showed up to court with wild hair, a mangy beard, and a swastika carved into his forehead. Yet as gruesome as the Manson family murders were, they did not equal the gore that prosecutors and witnesses were describing in the Tony Costa trial.

"This is a whole new level of evil," Vonnegut told Evelyn Lawson.

"It's beyond ghoulish," Lawson agreed. "But how could he have managed this on his own? You saw the autopsy photos. It took some time to *saw* those women apart. I think he had help with the killings. Those hippie-dippie girls standing vigil outside the courthouse were involved. I'm sure of it. They look sweet and innocent, but they're really witches. They should be on trial or in jail just like the Manson girls."

Once again, Vonnegut chuckled and rolled his eyes.

"Mr. Vonnegut, you are not a native of Cape Cod, so you don't know. Witches have always been part of the fabric of this land, for both good and bad," Lawson stressed. "When able young men first took to the sea to fish George's Bank, their wives, girlfriends, sisters, and daughters formed a union to design spells to bring them home safely. As for those fishermen who treated their wives like horses, riding them and beating them whenever they wanted, the witches cast different spells, ones that would send their men to the bottom of the ocean."

Lawson stopped talking as the prosecutor called Dr. George Katsas to the witness stand.

The pathologist provided his credentials to the court and then testified that he was able to determine the identification of Pat Walsh and Mary Anne Wysocki through their dental charts.

Fernandes held several photographs from the autopsies in his hand and gave them to Dr. Katsas for review.

"If you would please, with reference to these two bodies, would you please tell us what gross observations you made during your examination?"

"Well, the body of Patricia Walsh was cut into two pieces," Dr. Katsas said in a thick Greek accent as he studied the first photograph. "Essentially it was cut at about the midline of the abdomen, so that the upper part of the body contained the chest, part of the abdomen and the upper extremities, the hands and arms."

The pathologist held the second black-and-white picture in one hand while he adjusted his eyeglasses with another.

"The body of Mary Anne Wysocki was cut in five pieces," he told the court. "One included the head and part of the neck. The second included the chest, with the skin going all the way to the pubic area. The third part was the pelvis, the hip bones, and the genitalia. The fourth part was the right lower extremity, from the hip below. And the fifth part was the lower left extremity, again, from the hip below."

The prosecution wanted the autopsy photos shared with jurors, but the defense quickly objected.

Both sides approached the judge for a bench conference. Lawrence Shubow, a respected Boston lawyer and Goldman's co-counsel, argued against showing the horrific images to the jury.

"If Your Honor please, in view of the fact that the defendant does not contest the identity of the person or the remains shown in this group of photographs, and in view of the fact the defendant does not contest any testimony given by the present witness as to the wounds, the place of the wounds, and the details of dismemberment, we object to the introduction of these photographs on the ground that they add no probative evidence on any issue in the case and are so extreme and so horrible and so unusual as to pose a hazard of overwhelming judgment of the jury," Shubow pleaded to Judge Beaudreau.

"These were cruel and atrocious murders," Fernandes fired back.

The judge pondered the argument for a moment before announcing his decision on the matter. "You already have photographs of the bodies taken from the graves; you do not need the autopsy photos as well."

Armand Fernandes lost the argument but recovered quickly as his direct examination of Dr. Katsas resumed.

"May we start with the victim Walsh?" the prosecutor asked.

"Externally, the skin was peeled off of the chest in a fashion like a sweater. On the back of the neck, there was an entrance gunshot wound. There were several hemorrhages including the sub tissues of the neck leading to the left cheek where the bullet was found. Incised wounds, or stab wounds were present on the back of the chest." Dr. Katsas noted that the victim's genitals were "present and unremarkable."

"And what did you find next?"

"I took smears from the rectum and the vagina of Patricia Walsh, and when I examined this material under a microscope, I found spermatozoa in both the rectum and the vagina."

Hearing this, Catherine Walsh placed her face in her hands and wept once again for her daughter.

"Now with reference to the victim Wysocki?"

"The skin was cut sharply at the areas where the skin was separated," Dr. Katsas explained. "In other words, there was no break of the bone in that area. The cuts were precise and clean."

Tony Costa listened intently to Katsas's testimony. The killer was proud of his work.

We didn't spend years in medical school to earn some fancy degree, Cory told him. *We don't have the initials MD after our name. We learned our trade from an old book about taxidermy. And yet he just called our dissection precise and clean!*

"In the back of the neck, just to the right of the midline, there was an entrance gunshot wound, and against the bone of the back of the head, the occipital bone, there were fragments of a bullet," the pathologist continued. "The low extremities were completely cut off the body, and also the buttocks showed many incised wounds or stab wounds, big slashes, which involved both the skin and the underlying muscles and soft tissues."

Dr. Katsas also said that he had found no evidence of any injuries that were consistent with abortion in either victim, which further disputed Costa's claims that the women had left town to take care of an unwanted pregnancy. But like his autopsy of Pat Walsh, the pathologist had discovered sperm in the vagina and rectum of Mary Anne Wysocki.

His testimony was beyond disturbing, and some jurors even shed tears for the two young victims. But Dr. Katsas's graphic descriptions of the murders also bolstered the defense, because no one in their right mind could be capable of such barbarous acts.

Lawrence Shubow hoped to drill this point home during his cross-examination of the witness. The left-leaning Shubow had once been labeled a communist sympathizer for working to block local investigations of suspected communists launched by Senator Joe McCarthy during the Red Scare in the 1950s. He was also an ardent opponent of the death penalty, which ultimately led him to join Maurice Goldman's defense team. As despicable as Costa's alleged acts were, the attorney would fight valiantly to save the man's life. According to Shubow, Tony Costa was a sick and deranged individual who should be committed to a mental hospital instead of being put on death row.

"The peeling of the skin with what you called a sweater-like effect, that is not connected to the division of the body into two portions, is it?"

"No, this involved the upper part of the body," Dr. Katsas answered.

"There'd be no need to do that peeling in order to accomplish the separation of the body into two parts?"

"No, sir. It's a separate process."

"And is the peeling consistent with having been done after death?"

"Yes, sir, it is."

"That's a rather bizarre finding, isn't it?"

Fernandes voiced his objection, but it was overruled.

"Would I be fair to say that it was a very bizarre finding, having in mind your experience as a pathologist?"

"It was very bizarre and very unusual, sir."

The mild-mannered Shubow then uttered a word that had never been spoken before inside the old granite courthouse.

"Doctor, as a forensic pathologist, have you ever run into the term necrophilia? For the record, I am going to spell it out: *n-e-c-r-o-p-h-i-l-i-a.*"

"Yes, sir. I have."

"What does the term necrophilia mean to you?"

"It's the psychiatric term indicating the perversions of certain persons to have sexual attraction to dead bodies."

"Are the pathological findings consistent with a person that has this certain type of psychiatric condition?" Shubow asked.

"If one assumes that the sperm was inserted after death, one may be talking about necrophilia," Dr. Katsas explained.

"In the case of the stab wounds, described as slashing-type wounds, there is no surrounding hemorrhage, is there?"

"That is correct, sir. I found none."

"Doesn't that support the inference that these were inflicted after death?"

"Yes, sir."

"All right, I think that's it," Shubow said to the pathologist. "I think that's it."

The prosecution's final stake in the so-called Provincetown Vampire's coffin came from a state blood expert who described "dark brown human head hair consistent in length with female hair" on a piece of rope discovered in Costa's room by Tom Gunnery. He also detected blood in the trunk of Pat Walsh's Volkswagen and on a pair of work boots belonging to Costa.

Serological blood testing and DNA testing were still years away, so the experts could not state with authority whether the blood and sperm belonged to Costa, but with any luck, the jurors presumed they did.

Cory Devereaux had just turned eighteen years old, and he now found himself on the witness stand in the Costa murder trial.

He pulled at the whiskers of his beard while Armand Fernandes asked him about his friendship with the defendant.

"How long have you known him [Costa]?"

"I've known him for about two years."

Fernandes showed Devereaux the .22-caliber revolver used to kill Pat Walsh and Mary Anne Wysocki.

"Can you identify it?"

"That gun used to belong to my grandfather," Devereaux replied. "I brought it back to Provincetown when I left my grandparents' place in West Virginia. I sold it."

"To whom did you sell it?" Fernandes asked.

"Antone Costa. I think Tony heard that I had a gun. He asked me if I wanted to sell it, and I did for twenty dollars."

That was all the prosecution needed to know.

It was now Goldman's turn to question the witness.

This is the moment that I've been waiting for, Costa thought to himself. *We're finally going to expose the real killer.*

"Cory, you and Tony were close friends, weren't you?"

Devereaux considered the question for a moment. "I would say fairly close. We were good friends, yes."

"You socialized together? You went to his place, and he went to your house?"

"Occasionally," he answered. "My father didn't like him. He didn't believe someone that old should be hanging around with me, because I was much younger than him. I was sixteen at the time, and my father didn't approve of it."

I became your father, Costa wanted to say. *And now you're betrayed me.*

"Did you ever go to Truro to visit his marijuana patch?"

"No."

Costa stared at the witness from across the room. He was seething. *That's a fucking lie, and we both know it.*

"Did you ever go to Truro at all with Tony?" Goldman asked.

"Yes, twice. Tony had a stash of pills in the woods."

Okay, now we're getting somewhere, the killer thought.

"Where was the stash of pills located?"

"Behind a big funny-looking tree. There was some kind of metallic container that was directly behind the trunk of the tree. We walked a while and we saw this big, funny-looking tree and he said, 'that's it.' And there was a hole there, and it was covered with leaves."

"Can you tell us what was contained in the can, the type of drugs?"

"There were different kinds of amphetamines and barbiturates. Some were Nembutal, Seconal, phenobarbital, and sodium amytal."

"Did you ever see Tony use drugs?"

"I saw Tony smoke marijuana, smoke hashish, use amphetamines, and use barbiturates."

"How many times?" Goldman asked.

"Very many," Devereaux replied.

"Did you ever see Tony stoned?"

"Yes, too many times to count. I would say well over a hundred."

"Was he ever violent when he was on any drug?"

"I've never seen Tony violent in my life."

Good boy, Costa thought. *Now, ask him if he murdered those girls.*

But Goldman stayed clear of that line of questioning.

"No more questions," the defense attorney told the judge.

Cory Devereaux was dismissed.

Costa's big moment never came.

During a recess, he exploded at Goldman.

"Why didn't you ask him about the girls?" Costa shouted. "Why didn't you place him at the scene of the crime? He's the one that should be sitting here, not me!"

"Look, Tony. No matter what you believe, this kid is clean. He passed his polygraph test," Goldman reminded him. "But Cory did us a favor by testifying to your drug use."

"That's not fucking good enough. I want you to call him back to testify when you open your defense, *my defense*. I will question him myself if I have to."

CHAPTER FORTY-TWO

———————

Try as he might, Vonnegut could not shake the day's graphic testimony. He sat hunched over his old Smith and Corona typewriter, and for once, the words did not magically appear on the page in front of him. How could he attempt to explain the sexual mutilation of the two young women from Providence, Rhode Island? How could he get inside the mind of the twisted killer? He had witnessed murder with his own eyes before in the prisoner of war camp in Dresden, Germany, but that was war after all, when madness could be justified and even rewarded if you were lucky enough to find yourself on the winning side.

Vonnegut checked his watch. It was 5:30 p.m. and the sun was slowly dipping along the backside of Cape Cod Bay. He poured himself a small glass of scotch and water. It would be the first of many on this spring evening. He had convinced Ed Dinis to let him review the autopsy photos that were shielded from the jury, but now he wished he hadn't.

One of the photos, stamped March 6, 1969, showed the severed head of Mary Anne Wysocki, with her brown hair pulled back from the scalp. Her eyes were closed, but the mouth was slightly open, with the top row of her teeth showing. Another shocking image showed Pat Walsh's legs and buttocks, positioned knees down on a blood-soaked examination table.

There were long, deep slashes and giant gashes to the backs of her calves, thighs, and buttocks, just as the pathologist had described in court.

"That could have been my daughter," Vonnegut said to himself.

Working as a true crime reporter had lost its appeal and excitement. Vonnegut wondered what, if anything, he would do with the materials and notes that he was gathering in the trial. He also hoped, for Edie's sake, that the maniac behind the murders was no longer on the loose and that he was now locked up at the jailhouse on the hill, just two miles from his home. As he sipped his scotch, his mind returned to his conversation with Evelyn Lawson earlier in the day. Vonnegut thought she was entertaining, but he had dismissed her as a crackpot columnist who had lost her grasp on reality with all that witch talk. She had just published a new column claiming that Tony Costa was a high priest of the black arts and that he had followers on the outer Cape. The jury was sequestered and could not read a word of it. Still, the column frustrated prosecutors, who adamantly believed, at least publicly, that Costa had committed these murders on his own. Evelyn Lawson had a dedicated following of readers on Cape Cod, although most journalists did not take the theater critic turned crime reporter seriously.

"But is she on to something that I just can't see?" Vonnegut muttered.

After leaving the courthouse that day, Lawson drove back to Hyannis for a screening of the new film *Easy Rider*, which had opened the week before. She planned to review the film for her newspaper. Sitting in the balcony at the Hyannis Theater on Main Street, Lawson nibbled on popcorn as the plumes of marijuana smoke wafted in the air. The movie house was packed with long-haired hippies who hooted and hollered each time Peter Fonda and Dennis Hopper rode across the screen straddling their motorcycles. Lawson could not hear the actors or follow the plot due to the thunderous noise of empty beer bottles rolling down the aisles. Frustrated, she got up and left the theater after only twenty minutes. She then drove to her cottage at the edge of Estey Avenue, overlooking Nantucket Sound. Lawson parked in the driveway and turned off the headlights of her Ford Skyliner. The car was thirteen years old and had a bum engine and bald tires, but the two-door sedan had a retractable hardtop, and it looked dramatic, just like its eclectic driver. She approached the back gate and was surprised to see that the door had been left open.

"Stella, Stella, where are you, frisky cat?" she called.

Normally, the shaggy-coated Maine coon cat greeted Lawson at the back gate, making figure eights around her ankles to welcome her home. She reached for the porch light and flipped the switch, but nothing happened. The light was out. Lawson inspected it closely and saw that the light bulb was gone. Nervous now, she fumbled for her house key with shaking hands. The key slipped out of her grip and landed on the patio. Lawson bent down to pick it up and noticed drops of dark liquid spread out in a line across the stone floor. She followed its trail to the back of the patio, where she found Stella the coon cat lying in a pool of blood. One of Stella's ears had been sliced off.

"Oh dear! Oh dear!" Lawson screamed.

Next to the dead cat sat a ceramic bowl that had been filled with blood from the pet's still-beating heart. Lawson recognized the ritual. She had read about the Satanic practice of spilling blood into mixing bowls under a full moon in places like Catemaco, Mexico.

"The witches performed a black mass with my beloved Stella," she muttered before running to a neighbor's house to call the police.

The cat's remains were taken to the local veterinarian for inspection. A detective from the Barnstable police department handed the pet, which was wrapped in a blanket, over to the vet, who laid it on a metal table. The veterinarian placed the animal on its back and could see that it had been cut with a sharp utensil from its stomach to the bottom of its sternum. He lifted the greater omentum, the honeycombed layer of fat covering the stomach, and saw that the intestines were missing. The vet also noted that Stella's uterine tubes and ovaries had been cut out.

"This cat was dissected," he told the detective.

"Its owner believes the pet was used in some satanic sacrifice," the cop said. "Have you seen anything similar happen around here?"

"Not that I'm aware of," the vet replied. "They teach dissection over at the high school in biology class. I believe they use cats too. My guess, it's just some kids playing a sick prank."

The detective nodded. "I bet you're right."

"But their work is quite good," the veterinarian added. "I will give them that."

Tony Costa was allowed one outside phone call per week, and he used his five-minute allotment that same night to telephone his ex-wife, Avis, whose testimony would be critical to his defense, which was set to begin the following Monday. Costa placed a quarter in the payphone outside the prison mess hall and dialed the mother of his three young children.

"Baby, it's me."

Avis did not like the warm affections that he still tried to use on her. "Hello, Tony."

"Mr. Goldman told me that you are willing to testify on my behalf, and I want to say that I appreciate your assistance here," he told her. "I know how difficult it must be for you."

"I'm wishing you luck and steady nerves in the weeks to come," she said.

"I don't need luck. It's now my time to tell the truth about this case. Many so-called friends are gonna get busted, including one for murder," he promised her. "They should have kept their mouths shut. I predict that some will run in fear, but Cory Devereaux will have no excuse when he shows his face again. We are ready to blow the lid off this whole thing!"

At this time, Costa was paying closer attention to the Manson case in Los Angeles. He had read that prosecutors had offered immunity to New

Hampshire native Linda Kasabian in exchange for her cooperation and testimony against other members of "the family." Costa was now demanding the same treatment, despite being on trial for murder.

"Justice is important, and I don't want to pay for a crime while the murderer roams free," Costa told his ex-wife.

When testimony resumed on Tuesday, May 19, 1970, Vonnegut was surprised to see that Evelyn Lawson was not there. He did not know that she was digging a hole in the side of a small dune across the street from her cottage to bury her pet cat Stella. Lawson lifted three feet of soft sand with a shovel that she normally used for gardening and placed a small wooden box in the hole. The distraught columnist wept for her Maine coon cat and then cursed the witches of Helltown.

Six miles away on the other north side of Cape Cod, Tony Costa's attorney opened his defense and addressed the jury. "For over a week now, we've heard some devastating and shocking evidence. Perhaps you've never heard such testimony before in your life, concerning the atrocities of two young ladies who were killed on a weekend visit to Provincetown. A certain young man is charged with these atrocities. His name is Mr. Costa. We propose to show you that Mr. Costa, as a result of an unconscious mind, has been made fully sick as the result of mind-altering drugs. We will show you the impact of these drugs and its abuse. Tony Costa is on trial here, and so are drugs."

Costa clenched his fists under the defense table. He could see how his attorney was setting up the defense argument, and he was strongly against it. On the previous day, Costa had written and delivered a long note to Goldman, expressing his ideas for what he believed to be a winning courtroom strategy.

Mr. Goldman,

My whereabouts during that fateful weekend can be corroborated by a number of witnesses including a friend who will testify that

I was at the Foc's'le on Saturday night, January 25th, and Mrs. Morton who will say that I was in bed Saturday night and on Sunday morning when she collected the rent. When well presented in court, how could I have possibly committed the murders and buried the girls. Also, how could I have destroyed my own bloody stained clothing—as they certainly would be if I dismembered anyone? At least 30 other persons had access to that can of drugs and weapons. This must be brought out in court! As for Avis, I will not allow any previous sexual activities testimony under any circumstances. Our private lives must remain private in court. Devereaux must be implicated and broken down on the stand with witnesses against him, or I shall be forced to do so myself. We must place the blame in his hands and thereby influence the jury into possibly believing that I am a victim of circumstances.

Goldman discussed the note with his team members Lawrence Shubow and Justin Cavanaugh, and both agreed that Costa was delusional. The amount of evidence against him in the murders of Pat Walsh and Mary Anne Wysocki was staggering. There was no way that they could convince the jury that Costa was an innocent man. They decided that they would not recall Cory Devereaux to the witness stand.

Armand Fernandes was also concerned over Goldman's remarks and asked for a bench conference.

"Your Honor, he used the defendant's capacity to know what he was doing," the prosecutor pointed out. "Are you now maintaining that this is an insanity defense?" Fernandes asked Goldman.

"You can figure it out," Goldman shot back. "It's a diminished capacity under the McHoul case."

The defense lawyer was referring to a case before the Massachusetts Supreme Judicial Court two years prior where a judge ordered a new trial for a violent rapist named James McHoul, who had escaped a mental hospital and assaulted a woman in her apartment, choking her until she passed out. His lawyers argued that McHoul could not have been responsible for the crime because he was already sick and being treated as a sexually dangerous person at Boston State Hospital.

"If the issue is going to be a plea for insanity, then maybe we can shorten this trial tremendously," Fernandes countered.

Finally, Judge Beaudreau broke in. "The defense team is leaving the door open for, let's say, a legal gimmick for want of better words. Or am I being too sloven in my talk when I say that?"

This time, Lawrence Shubow spoke up. "We are introducing evidence of diminished capacity, which is relevant to the issue of clemency if the evidence warrants a conviction of first-degree murder or to a conviction of second-degree murder if the jury decides this man does not have the requisite mental capacity for criminal responsibility."

"Then we have no problem here," the judge stated before allowing Goldman to continue his remarks to the jury.

While Armand Fernandes returned to the prosecution table, Costa's lawyer made his way back to the jury box.

"What happens to a personality such as this as a result of a total, long-lasting drug dependency?" Goldman asked rhetorically. "We are going to show you step by step how it increases until it ultimately controls you, that you now have no mental capacity to know what you are doing; you have no control over yourself. We propose to show you that an unconscious force controls a man's deeds. He didn't possess premeditation to commit a crime. He wasn't capable of committing it because he didn't know what he was doing by virtue of being under the influence of drugs—drugs that are mind altering, drugs that will absolutely so control you, you don't know what you're doing."

Attorney Goldman then pointed his stubby finger at his client. "We propose to you that Tony was incapable of committing a crime if he were not under the domination, the control of drugs!"

The defense called a Wellfleet doctor named Sidney Callis as its first witness. Costa's lawyers aimed to convince the jury that if Tony Costa was indeed a monster, it was Callis serving in the role of Dr. Frankenstein, who had created him.

CHAPTER FORTY-THREE

Tony Costa had first visited Dr. Sidney Callis's office in 1965, when he sought help for a nervous condition brought on by the deterioration of his marriage to Avis, his child bride.

"It's a gnawing pain," Costa said at the time, pointing to his stomach.

"I'll give you something to alleviate the soreness," the physician replied. "I think you're getting an ulcer, so I'm going to give you some capsules for it. They will stop the pain and make you less nervous. It's a new tranquilizer called Solacen."

Dr. Callis had his assistant put together two envelopes filled with the large orange capsules, about a hundred in all, and handed them to Costa. Tony took two pills later that day and nearly passed out while having dinner with Avis and their kids. But the feeling they gave him was unlike anything he had ever experienced before.

"It's like the aftermath of an unholy orgasm," he later told Avis. "It was such a beautiful experience, such peace. The sensation only grew stronger, and I thoroughly enjoyed every minute of it."

Costa was immediately hooked, and his drug use got worse from there.

Now, he was on trial for two vicious murders, and his defense lawyers were desperately trying to shift the blame to his former physician, Cape Cod's very own Dr. Feelgood.

Costa recited the lyrics to an Aretha Franklin song in his head. *And after one visit to Dr. Feelgood, you'll understand why Feelgood is his name. And the man sure makes me feel real good.*

Sidney Callis was sworn in by the bailiff and took his seat on the witness stand.

"I practice general medicine, but I also practice psychosomatic medicine," he told the court. "The patient, Mr. Costa, had complained of nervous tension, a gnawing pain in his stomach. After a careful examination and review, I concluded that he was a strong, healthy fellow and that there was some question of an emotional problem."

"What was it about his physical condition that called for Solacen?" attorney Shubow asked Callis.

"His physical condition was manifested by his nervousness," Dr. Callis replied. "He stated that he was having marital problems with his wife and that she was unhappy with him."

"Do you remember any discussions of a problem of sexual compatibility?"

"That was not mentioned by him, sir."

Costa's demand that his private life be kept private had been completely discarded by his defense team.

"At some time, did Costa become an employee of yours?" Shubow asked.

"In the spring of 1967, he was asked by me, and he agreed to help paint the outside trim of my office building," Dr. Callis answered. "He was usually behind on his payments. He owed, as I recollect, about one hundred forty dollars. That was the reason for asking him to work off some of his bill."

"Was there a theft upon your premises some time in 1968?"

"Yes, there was."

"And was Tony Costa, at the time, a suspect?"

"He was."

"And you so indicated to the police?"

"I reported it immediately to the Wellfleet police," the witness stated. "I told them I felt that he could be a suspect."

"You reported stolen, one thousand four hundred and eighty amphetamine sulfate, ten milligrams, white tablets—known as speed?"

"That's right."

Shubow also pointed out that nine hundred Solacen capsules were stolen in the robbery.

"Did you describe Tony Costa as a 'pothead' to police at the time?" the defense attorney asked.

"I have no recollection of that," Dr. Callis replied. "From my observations and examination of the patient, if he were addiction prone, I wouldn't have been prescribing him any drugs."

Later, Costa's lawyers called a Wellfleet police officer named Patrick Padden to the witness stand to further discuss the May 1968 break-in at Sidney Callis's medical office. Lawrence Shubow asked the officer to read aloud from his original police report.

"Callis stated that he had been treating the subject, Costa, for about three years, during which time he had prescribed the drug Solacen, issuing fifty capsules at a time and allowing two refills," Officer Padden told the court. "Callis stated that he was aware that Costa was a 'pothead' and 'pill user.' Callis stated that Costa had painted his offices to pay some debts; therefore, Costa would have some knowledge of the building's layout."

Padden's appearance before the court was followed by testimony from a friend of Costa named Mark McCray, who said under oath that Costa had once told him that he was "copping" barbiturates from Dr. Callis.

"Did Tony ever appear violent to you?" Goldman asked McCray.

"No, sir," the witness replied, shaking his head. "He always appeared to be a nice, peaceful, and ordinary guy."

Sitting toward the back of the courtroom, Kurt Vonnegut scribbled the words *nice, peaceful, and ordinary guy* into his notebook. He looked over at the defense table where Costa was seated in his borrowed suit and tie.

How does one go from being nice, peaceful, and ordinary to the wolf of the steppes? Vonnegut asked himself.

He would have posed the question to Evelyn Lawson, but she had not turned up at all during this critical day of the trial, where Costa's lawyers had successfully established the suspect's long history of drug use for the jury. Across the street from her home on Estey Avenue, Lawson had covered the hole in the side of the dune where Stella's remains were now buried and returned the shovel to her gardening shed. Lawson was sad, angry, and scared. She wanted to drive up to the courthouse and bash the witches' heads in with the steel blade of her shovel.

"I should get them before they get me," Lawson muttered.

But she quickly thought better of it. She did not want to go to jail, but she also did not want to give up the case. The cruel act had served as a warning, and she needed to go back to reporting the story straight, without editorializing about witchcraft. Lawson reached for her phone and called Mailer to seek his advice. The columnist was told by Mailer's pregnant girlfriend, Carol Stevens, that he was in jail for the weekend. Mailer flew to Washington, DC, to serve the last three days of his jail sentence in Alexandria, Virginia, after his conviction for disorderly behavior during the march on the Pentagon in October 1967. The U.S. Supreme Court had refused to hear his appeal, so Mailer surrendered to local authorities.

"I'm a believer in the rules of the game," he told reporters. "If you cross that line, you get arrested."

Mailer used the occasion to speak out against the recent massacre at Kent State University in northeast Ohio, where on May 4, 1970, national guardsmen opened fire on a group of students who were gathering to protest the war in Vietnam. Four students were killed that day.

As Mailer walked into the Alexandria city jail to serve his weekend sentence, he said to a group of newsmen gathered outside, "The winning hand this weekend is to have no violence. The point to be made is it's the administration shedding blood, not the New Left. When President Nixon called the protesters 'bums,' it gave the soldiers an out to pull the trigger."

After his short stint in jail, which Mailer found "near agreeable," he was driven back to the airport by Rip Torn. The two men were on friendly terms now that the actor's *Maidstone* performance was being hailed by critics. When Mailer returned to Maine, he decided that it was time to face his greater fear. Climbing across the narrow railing of his deck at Fortune's Rock was a test of his courage but not the ultimate test. He told Carol to pack him a bag. Mailer was headed back to Helltown, and this time, he would rent a shack in the dunes and lie in wait to see if the coven of witches was only playing childish games or whether Costa's disciples were hell-bent on his destruction.

Mailer climbed into his Jeep and drove seven hours from Mount Desert, Maine, to the Peaked Hill district of Provincetown, where nineteen shacks dotted the hilly landscape that stretched across 1,960 acres of shoreline. He parked his Jeep at the foot of Snail Road, just off Route 6A, grabbed his duffel bag and a shotgun out of the back seat, and began hiking through the scrub thickets that would eventually give way to sand dunes that rose to about a hundred feet in some places.

"There are few places on the Eastern Seaboard where one could bury a man as easily and leave one's chances so to nature," he said to himself as he trudged through the heavy sand while beads of sweat gathered on his thick brow. After thirty minutes of walking, he arrived at a small one-room cabin, which was nothing more than a wooden shed repurposed from the old lifesaving station there. Mailer pushed open the door and placed his duffel bag on the floor. He looked around the sparse room, which had just a wooden chair, a single bed, and an oil lamp. There was no electricity or running water here.

"This must have been how Thoreau felt when he was here," he muttered.

Mailer placed the twelve-gauge shotgun on the bed and grabbed a handful of shells from his bag. He had used the gun for skeet shooting and to hunt birds, but he never imagined that he would fire the weapon at another human being. He hoped that he would not have to, but he was also ready to shoot a big hole in anyone who might come calling in the dead of night.

There was a mirror hanging on a peg on the wall. It was cracked and covered with dust. Mailer walked over and brushed the sediment away with his hand and looked at his reflection.

How did he compare to other men? What he saw staring back at him was someone who was less strong than others, more fidgety, more determined, more inept, yet more successful. Mailer was a walking contradiction. He didn't like himself enough to follow his instincts, and he had not had the courage to be truly authentic. The writer was determined to change that. And if it meant killing a group of young hippies out here in this hostile, barren environment, so be it.

Mailer loaded the shotgun, sat himself on the wooden chair, and waited.

Sadie, Thumper, and Strawberry Blonde spotted Mailer's vehicle parked on the side of Snail Road. They had seen him driving the Jeep around town and knew it to be his.

"We should kill the chauvinist pig," Strawberry Blonde said. "Cut his throat and let his body bake in the sun."

"Nobody likes him in this town anyway," Thumper added. "They'd probably throw a parade in our honor."

"Killing a man is a lot different that murdering someone's cat," Sadie argued. "Plus, it wouldn't help Tony."

"It would show the world that no one is out of Sire's reach," Strawberry Blonde replied.

"Tony has nothing against Norman Mailer. He's our beef," Sadie said. "We can curse him, but we can't kill him."

As they rode their bicycles back into town, Strawberry Blonde was overcome by a vision; it was an image of the world-famous author on his knees begging for his life.

She kept the image to herself for the time being.

Mailer took with him some K rations, dried sausages, and chocolate bars to get him through the night. He wondered what his old army sergeant, Donald Mann, would think if he knew Mailer was offering himself up as bait to three skinny witch bitches in the vast wilderness of the Provincetown dunes. He felt like the junior man in his platoon once again, hugging his carbine and waiting to spot a Japanese patrol on the island of Luzon during WWII. A stiff wind rolled off the ocean, and by nightfall, Mailer had wrapped himself in an old blanket for warmth.

He smoked cigarettes to keep alert, but so far, nothing had happened, and his blue eyes were growing heavy.

"What did you think, Norman? That you'd lead the witches here with bread crumbs?" he asked himself. "It's all nothing but a folly. You believed all the hocus-pocus that that crank Evelyn Lawson planted in your brain."

Mailer nodded off with the shotgun resting on his lap as Strawberry Blonde was making her stealthy approach from fifty yards away.

"You can do this," she whispered to herself as she crept slowly between the peaks of two giant dunes. The night was almost pitch-black, but the young witch had grown up on this spit of sand and knew the terrain well. She was holding a small oyster knife in her right hand, one she had swiped from her job at the Lobster Pot restaurant on Commercial Street.

"In goes the knife, a quick turn of the wrist, and off pops the shell," a Portuguese fisherman had once taught her as a kid. She had been shucking for years in restaurants downtown and was skilled with the sharp blade.

If she could just get close enough to her prey, it would be easy. Strawberry Blonde believed that she held the element of surprise on her side because the writer could have no idea she was coming.

"If Charlie's girls can do it, so can I," she promised herself. "Tony will applaud me for this."

There were two cabins up ahead, but there was light coming from only one of them. There were no blinds on the windows, and as she tiptoed closer, she could see inside thanks to the flickering light of a kerosene lamp hanging from one of the walls. The screen door of the camp was left wide open, as if the slumped figure sitting on a chair by the bed was inviting her in to do mayhem.

The Devil's business, Tex Watson had called it.

Strawberry Blonde was alone. The other girls did not share her vision for his night. In her mind, they did not love Tony Costa enough to kill in his name.

"He's a pig, and he needs to die," she convinced herself.

Strawberry Blonde was now only ten feet away from the door of the cabin. She placed the oyster knife in her left hand, her shucking hand. The knife, called the Large Frenchman, came with a blade two and a half inches long with a razor-sharp edge that ran to a point at the tip. She could slip inside the cabin and slice his throat from ear to ear before he could open his eyes.

Mailer was still asleep, but just barely. He had what experts would call light sleep spindles, meaning that his brain waves could not block out even the slightest noise. The disorder had kept him alive in the Philippines during the war. The wind had picked up again, and the rustling of sea grass jostled him awake. He saw a dark silhouette standing at the threshold of the cabin. Mailer lifted the shotgun and placed his finger on the trigger. The silhouette took a step closer, and Mailer could make out a woman's lithe figure and long hair, which was the color of wheat. He saw her eyes. She did not look crazed now; instead, she looked frightened. He noticed the outline of the knife in her hands. He gave pressure to the trigger and was about to fire. Strawberry Blonde stood, frozen at the threshold of the cabin. Mailer could not shoot.

"Get away from here, little girl," he shouted. "I will blow a hole in that tiny stomach of yours."

Strawberry Blonde stepped back from the door and turned away.

"That's right, run, witch!" Mailer urged her. "Never come back to this place or to me. I will show you mercy at this moment, but only at this moment. If you turn back to me, I will shoot you dead where you stand."

Strawberry Blonde kept her back to Mailer. She dropped the shucking knife in the sand and started to run, disappearing moments later in the darkness of the dunes.

Mailer jumped from his chair and stepped out of the cabin. He could almost hear her heavy breathing and her pounding heartbeat amid the howling wind. He lifted the barrel of the shotgun to the sky and fired. The loud blast sounded like a wave crashing to the shore. Mailer picked up the shucking knife, slung the shotgun over his shoulder, and went back inside.

The witch was gone, and he had confronted and defeated his darkest fear, at least for now.

CHAPTER FORTY-FOUR

———

The following day in court, Maurice Goldman paraded several medical experts before the jury, one of them testifying that Tony Costa suffered from borderline schizophrenia disorder and was legally insane at the time of the murders.

"These people in distress actually become mentally ill. If anybody, including myself, kills somebody, he must be angry, but if we mutilate the body, we must be a little nuts," Dr. Jack Ewalt, a Harvard professor, told the court when asked about the possibility that Costa had had sex with his victims after he murdered them.

Dr. Ewalt had interviewed Costa on eight occasions and testified that drugs had jolted his underlying personality, the one he called "Cory Devereaux," into violence. The psychiatrist described one therapy session with Costa where he experienced a vivid flashback of the murders and told Ewalt that he had killed one of the young victims after finding her lying on the ground making gurgling sounds.

"Mr. Costa told me that he could not get help for the girl because he was too far from civilization, and he sort of killed her to put her out of her misery," Dr. Ewalt testified.

Lawrence Shubow then referred to Dr. Ewalt's report on Costa.

"He began accumulating a group of teenage drug users during the winter of 1967, and he was called by them Sire and Lord Antone," Shubow said, reading from the report. "He calls these kids his disciples, and letters from several of these people to him address him as 'Sire of all that is true.'"

It was the first time that any reference to the witches' coven had been brought up in trial.

Evelyn Lawson, sitting on a court bench next to Vonnegut, stirred uneasily. Vonnegut saw that her hands were shaking, and he touched her shoulder.

"Are you okay?" he asked.

"I'll be better when Costa is sent to prison for good," she told him. "Hopefully by then, his disciples will abandon him and move on with their miserable little lives."

Shubow then read from another psychological report, this one explaining Costa's bizarre, love-lust-hate relationship with his late mother, Cecilia Bonaviri.

"He is preoccupied by death. Costa over-idolized his war hero father," Shubow read aloud. "Costa believed that females, like his mother, betrayed his father by remarrying and having another son. When asked about his mother, he is blinded by fury. There is also an underlying sexual attraction there. Mr. Costa is a very sick and angry man."

With their client's psychiatric condition now firmly established for the jury, it was time for the defense team to call the one person who had known both sides of the suspected killer's dual personality better than anyone: his ex-wife, Avis Costa.

At first, Avis was reluctant to testify, but Goldman convinced her that she might be the only one who could get Costa's life spared. The young mother thought of their three children and decided that she would take the witness stand for their sake.

The twenty-one-year-old ex-wife showed up for court on May 21, 1970, holding a bouquet of lilacs in her hand.

Avis Costa wore a maroon knit vest and a brown tartan skirt with a thick belt that hung low over her hips. She looked better suited to attend Woodstock than her ex-husband's murder trial. Avis giggled nervously, switching the flowers from her right hand to her left so she could be sworn in.

"Do you swear to tell the truth, the whole truth, and nothing but the truth?" the bailiff asked.

"Yeah, sure," Avis replied, giggling once again.

Maurice Goldman then approached the witness stand.

"Why are you holding flowers?" he asked her.

"For security."

Avis swept a strand of her long, brunette hair away from her face and waved to Costa, who was seated twenty feet away at the defense table.

"You keep looking at Tony," Goldman noted. "Do you still like him?"

"Sure," she replied.

Avis spoke softly and kept her hand over her mouth.

"Can you speak up and hold the flowers with both hands so that they're away from your mouth?" the judge asked.

"Now, don't be nervous," Goldman told her. "How old are you now?"

"Twenty-one."

"And how old were you when you married Tony?"

"Fourteen," she replied.

"You had known him for how long?"

"I had known him when I was about five," Avis told the court. "Then I didn't see him for a while. I had known him for over a year before we got married."

"So you were childhood sweethearts then?"

"Yeah."

Avis Costa then provided the names and ages of their children: six-year-old Peter, five-year-old Michael, and three-year-old Nicole, or Nico as she was called.

"Did some family disagreements take place in your household between you and Tony?" Goldman asked her.

"Yeah, mostly because I'm a lazy housewife," she said and laughed.

"Was that what Tony said?"

"Yeah."

"Why did he call you a lazy housewife?"

"I don't know, because his mother was clean. I guess."

Goldman asked her to speak up.

"Because his mother was a very fastidious person and I'm not."

"Do you know whether Tony went to see some doctor as the result of some problem?"

"He was having trouble with his stomach because of his nerves," Avis replied. "It's because we were arguing all the time and hassling each other so much."

"Now, what happened after Tony started going to see Dr. Callis?"

"The more Tony saw him, the more he took the tranquilizers. He got very uptight when he wasn't taking them. He was hard to live with."

"Did he visit you and your three children often after your divorce?"

"Most of the time I saw him, he was stoned," Avis pointed out. "I mean, I never saw him not stoned. He was smoking hash at the time, dealing hash."

"How are the children being supported now?"

"ADC Welfare."

"And you also?"

"Mm-hmm." She nodded.

Listening to his ex-wife on the witness stand, Costa began to cry.

Keep it together, Cory told him. *We cry for no one. Remember who we are. We are the wolf of the steppes, and we hunt without remorse.*

"Did you ever see Tony in December 1968 or January 1969 take any amphetamines or any barbiturates in your presence?"

"Yeah, I can't tell you how many times, but a lot. You know, almost every day. He could take handfuls of them. He'd try to give them to every-body, you know. He was playing Santa Claus."

"Did he use any other type of drugs during that period?"

"Yeah, LSD, marijuana, everything. He'd had a lot, and nobody could take a lot. He'd take a lot."

"Did Tony come see you while he was living on Standish Street?"

"I guess he came by almost every day. He was talking about going to Boston, and then buying a car, buying a Volkswagen."

It was now time for the prosecution to cross-examine Avis Costa. District attorney Ed Dinis led the questioning of the witness. Thus far, the flamboyant lawman had kept a low profile during the trial, allowing Armand Fernandes to handle much of the questioning. But after seeing how nervous Avis Costa had been answering Goldman's questions, Dinis could taste blood. He felt confident that he could get the ex-wife to unravel on the witness stand and reveal Costa's darker side to the jury.

"Do you recall an incident where Dr. Hiebert was either called or you were taken to him?" Dinis asked.

Avis's shoulders sank on the witness stand, and she looked over to Maurice Goldman for guidance and support. The defense lawyer avoided eye contact and stared down at his notes.

"Yeah," she replied softly.

"Would you tell us about that?"

"I'd rather not."

"Did it involve a situation where you needed medical attention as a result of something you ingested?"

Avis, the former child bride, clutched the flowers in her hand. "Uh-huh."

"Did you take a chemical of some kind?"

"Chloral hydrate," she replied.

"Who gave you that drug?"

"Nobody gave it to me. I took it on my own volition."

"You got it from Tony Costa, didn't you?" Dinis pressed. "What prompted you to take the drug?"

"That's really personal. I really would not like to go into that."

"Wasn't it the practice of your husband at the time, Tony Costa, to give you the drug to make you unconscious?"

"That's not true," Avis shouted back. "You have your stories messed up."

"You were interrogated after Tony's arrest by Lieutenant Flynn of the state police, were you not?"

"I was interrogated several times," Avis stated. "I don't remember by who."

"Do you remember saying that early in your marriage, your husband, Tony Costa, liked to put a plastic bag over your head?"

"That's not the way I would put it."

"Well then, how would you put it?"

Avis Costa looked over at the judge. "Look, I really would not like to talk about this in front of all these people. I'm sorry, but that's just the way it is."

Judge Beaudreau ordered her to keep answering questions.

"Is it true or not that Tony Costa would put a plastic bag over your head, endeavoring to knock you out, before he had sexual relations with you?"

Costa wished he had had his "pig stabber" at that very moment. He would have leapt from the defense table and gutted the arrogant district attorney and would have done the same thing to his own lawyer for exposing his ex-wife to such harassment.

Avis fought back against Dinis's sordid question. "I'm not going to agree to that. You have that completely wrong. I'm not gonna say 'yes' to that because it's completely untrue!"

Ed Dinis did not relent. "As a result of using the plastic bag, were you not afraid of Tony Costa at the time?"

"No, I wasn't afraid of him. I was never forced into anything!"

"Did you tell investigators that Tony Costa tried to smother you with pillows?" he added.

"I don't remember saying it in those words, no," she replied. "I don't want to talk about that. I'm telling you that you are wrong. You're trying to make it sound like these are acts of violence that he insisted upon, or forced onto me, but that's not the way it was."

"There was the use of a pillow to cut short your breath, was there not?"

"Maybe once, yes," Avis said with a sigh.

"And the same thing with the plastic bag?" Dinis asked. "Your cooperation was required with the plastic bag?"

"At one time, yes."

"Did he knock you out?"

"No!" she shot back.

"At one time, did your husband ask you to hang by your heels?"

"Yeah," Avis replied. She fought her own sudden urge to get up and run out of the courtroom. Maurice Goldman had promised her that she would be protected on the witness stand. Now, Avis was up there alone, answering for her ex-husband's twisted fetishes.

"Did the hanging upside down involve a sexual experience?" Dinis asked with a trace of excitement in his voice.

Avis shot another glance over at attorney Goldman. "Do I really have to answer this?" she asked. "This period of things you are talking about lasted about a week. It was never anything inflicted on me. It was never a horror scene. It was an experiment that I wouldn't have anything to do with. And once we established that, Tony and I got along just fine."

"Was there an incident involving a belt? Did you and Tony beat each other with belts?"

"No!"

"You never told investigators that?"

"I don't remember that, no."

Serial killer Tony Costa greeted by his ex-wife, Avis Costa, outside the courthouse in Barnstable, Massachusetts, during his 1970 trial. © Stanley Forman.

"Did Tony Costa burn the soles of your feet with cigarettes?"

"That's absolutely absurd!"

"Did you tell investigators that Tony beat the heads of your children against the crib when he was angry?"

"He did not beat them. I never said that!"

Ed Dinis had one more question for the badgered witness.

"Mrs. Costa, are you writing a book about this case?"

"No!" she responded defiantly.

"No more questions," Dinis said with a grin.

Goldman stood up. He would call no more witnesses.

"The defense rests," he told the judge.

Avis clutched her lilacs as the bailiff helped her down off the witness stand. She blew a kiss at Costa and flashed a peace sign. As she left the courthouse, she gave a deputy her bouquet of flowers. Each lilac stem was wrapped in a small piece of paper with mementos belonging to their three children. "They represent life," she told the bailiff.

Avis waited at the back of the courthouse for her ex-husband to be escorted back to the jail. Sadie, Thumper, and Strawberry Blonde, knew better than to approach her. Instead, they kept their distance. Avis was still Costa's dark queen, after all. There had been tension among the witches all day. Strawberry Blonde evaded questions from Sadie as to her whereabouts the night before. As the youngest and newest member of the coven, Strawberry Blonde had never disobeyed Sadie, their de facto leader. She kept quiet about her activities in the Provincetown dunes for that reason. Plus, Mailer's would-be killer was embarrassed that she did not finish the job and leave his bloody body in the sand for the crows to feast on.

Minutes later, the suspected killer emerged from the courthouse, his hands once again in shackles. Avis stepped forward to touch her ex-husband's arm, but a sheriff's deputy knocked it away.

CHAPTER FORTY-FIVE

"You sent Avis to the slaughter," Costa shouted at Maurice Goldman during a meeting at the Barnstable House of Correction while the court was in recess. "And because that bastard Dinis had her flipped around so much, Avis may have just sent me to the electric chair with her testimony."

"We figured that she'd make a good witness because someone needed to humanize you," Goldman replied. "So far, everybody thinks that you are a monster."

"And now after Avis's testimony and the questions about plastic bags over her head and hanging her by her feet?"

The defense attorney shook his head. "We didn't think the prosecution would go after her as hard as it did. Fernandes wouldn't have battered her around like that. Ed Dinis is a piece of shit, and he has no conscience."

"That's why I have decided to testify myself," Costa told Goldman. "I will not fall for any of his tricks."

Putting the so-called Cape Cod Vampire on the witness stand was the last thing that Goldman and the rest of the defense team wanted to do.

"Tony, if you take the witness stand, the jury will be out just long enough to take a piss. Ed Dinis will eat you alive in there."

"Well, I want my voice to be heard," Costa stressed. "I am in charge of my own defense, and I demand it."

Goldman had to figure out a solution quickly. He thought for a moment and then convinced his client to write a statement that he could present to the jury.

"By reading a statement, you will not be subject to cross-examination. Tony, you always wanted to be a writer," Goldman said. "This is your chance. Convince the jury that you don't deserve the death penalty for this."

Costa liked the idea. "Hell, once I'm done writing, they will finally know the truth, and I'll be set free."

After Costa was sent back to his cell, he grabbed a pencil and notepad. He flipped it open to an empty page and wrote "Part of my Jury Speech:" at the top. He then listed all the reasons why he believed he should be found not guilty of the murders of Pat Walsh and Mary Anne Wysocki. Once again, he would place the blame with Cory Devereaux.

1. The prosecution has failed to place me at the scene of the crime— where ever that is!
2. Bullet heads which match those found in the girls' bodies were not lodged in the walls of my room, but I can tell you whose room they might be found in.
3. The gun that killed those girls was not stolen by me from West Virginia.
4. The gun that killed those girls was not used by me, but I can tell you who used it to kill them.
5. My room was not redecorated many months ago to conceal and cover up the bullet holes in the walls and the bloodstains.
6. I can also tell you that these girls also met this same person [Devereaux] by pre-arrangement, at his mother's cosmetic shop, just two short blocks away from where the girls were staying... After their subsequent meeting at the area directly surrounding the shop, the girls were never seen alive again!

An hour later, Costa delivered his statement to Goldman, who called a meeting with his co-counsel Justin Cavanaugh and investigator Lester Allen.

"Somebody's got to rewrite this nonsense," Goldman told them. "Please take turns drafting a new statement for Tony to read to the jurors. Otherwise, we're sunk."

It appeared that Judge Beaudreau did not believe that Tony Costa stood any chance at an acquittal.

He had offered several potential verdicts that the jury would be allowed to check off on a piece of paper. Appearing nowhere on the document was a box that read simply "not guilty."

Larry Shubow brought the blatant oversight to the judge's attention during a brief bench conference.

"The jury might disbelieve everything they've heard," Shubow argued. "And they might say that a circumstantial case was not proved beyond a reasonable doubt."

Prosecutor Armand Fernandes agreed and suggested that the judge add "not guilty" in pen or a magic marker before handing the document over to the jury for deliberation.

The judge agreed and motioned for Maurice Goldman to begin his closing argument.

"There is a serious problem in the search for truth in this case," Goldman told the jury. "What have you heard during the last eleven days of this trial? You heard that he graduated from Provincetown High School, and while there he met and married a young girl, he himself at a young age. There is no evidence of any kind introduced at this trial to indicate that Tony was anything other than a good boy."

Vonnegut shared a confused look with Lawson. They had both heard Costa described many ways over the course of the trial, necrophiliac being the worst. But never did anyone say or even indicate that Tony was a *good boy*.

"Tony Costa was sick; he had some stomach disorder, and he was nervous," Goldman continued. "He needed some medical help and attention, so he went to see a doctor. He went to what was purported to be a medical center in Wellfleet, and there he found one doctor, and I think his name was Dr. Callis. He went there seeking help, and what did he get? Pills, pills, pills!"

The defense attorney pointed over at his client.

"Up until that time, Tony Costa never took a single pill, even so much as aspirin. When he went to that doctor, the doctor started him on pills. I am not passing judgment upon Dr. Callis; he is not here on trial today. But I want you to consider how Tony got started on his downfall in life. Drugs took possession of a sick man."

Goldman returned to the jury box and placed both hands on the railing. "The crime was best described by Dr. Katsas," he recalled. "He said it was the most bizarre killing he had ever seen! Let's see what that amounts to. Mary Anne Wysocki, mutilation of the body in five distinct portions, gunshot wounds, stab wounds of the chest, abdomen, and legs, with the peeling off of the skin. And at present as you recall, spermatozoa in the vagina and rectum."

The defense attorney sighed and shook his head. "Is that a sane man? Do I have to tell a Barnstable County jury that any man that does that can possibly be sane?"

Goldman then described the murder of Pat Walsh. "The same mutilation of the body into two distinct portions, the gunshot wound, the stab wounds of the chest, abdomen, and legs, and again, the peeling of the skin and the presence of spermatozoa in the vagina and rectum. Is this the action of a mentally well-balanced person? Or is it the action of a truly sick person? You heard the leading psychiatrists in America on the stand say that Tony is nuts, Tony is crazy. There's no question about that in my mind."

Goldman then looked into the eyes of each juror. The defense attorney was tired, and his voice was hoarse. The lines on his face were engraved deep over his brow, and he had heavy bags under his eyes. Goldman looked like he had aged ten years during the trial, and perhaps he had. He often thought what his life would be like had he not met Tony Costa at a construction site on that fateful day one year ago. Since then, he had spent thousands of hours working on the case and had nothing to show for it except seeing his name attached to lurid headlines in the newspaper. Costa had not paid him but promised that he would make good on his debt when he sold his story to the publishing houses in New York and to Hollywood. The attorney was skeptical that he would ever see a dime from his infamous client. But if anything, Goldman was a man of his word and would see this case to the end, whatever that may be.

"The defense in this case does not and will not ask you to set Tony Costa free. But I want you to consider that you are dealing with a mentally sick person, and all of it was triggered by the use of drugs. His mind was completely gone by the time of the killing of those girls, that terrible tragedy in January of 1969. Drugs are now on trial in the Costa case. May God bless you in your verdict, in the consideration of a mentally sick and drug-dependent defendant."

Maurice Goldman took his seat next to Tony Costa at the defense table. His closing summary was not what his client wanted to hear, but it was what he needed to hear. The ridiculous notion that Costa had not committed the murders would not be uttered by Goldman or anyone else on his team. Costa was a killer, a sick and mentally disturbed killer. The defense attorney prayed that jurors would take that last crucial element into their consideration as they debated whether Costa should live or die.

Ed Dinis stood once again from the prosecution table. This was the moment he had been waiting for. He had been practicing his speech in front of the mirror in his office during the morning recess. Every move he would make was choreographed ahead of time, each dramatic pause scripted. Dinis had brought in his personal hairstylist for a trim and had a new suit made for him by the tailors at Puritan Clothing in downtown Hyannis. This was the ultimate screen test, and Ed Dinis was ready. Despite being prone to gross exaggeration, he was a realist who understood that he would be voted out of office by his constituents in the next election cycle. Ed Dinis had been chewed up and spit out by the Kennedy political machine over his actions during the Chappaquiddick investigation. F. Scott Fitzgerald was right as far as Ed Dinis was concerned; there are no second acts in American lives, especially if one challenged a Kennedy on his home turf. If this was to be his swan song, the district attorney would give a masterful performance. While Maurice Goldman looked like a beaten prizefighter answering the final bell of a fifteen-round bout, the district attorney had fresh legs and looked relaxed as he strolled confidently over to the jury box.

"The defendant stands before you today charged with the double slaying of Mary Anne Wysocki and Patricia Walsh," he said. "I submit that even though Tony Costa has a mental illness, the defendant was never deprived of the capacity to understand the wrong that he was doing when he did it. He knew what he had in mind when he asked those girls for a ride to Truro that morning, when he rode out of Provincetown with these girls to their unfortunate and most tragic death in those woods. There is no evidence that Costa was on drugs in that rooming house. Did you feel for a single moment that these two girls, one a school teacher, one a junior in college, would drive off with a man that they did not know if he was under the spell of drugs?"

Dinis turned toward Costa. "I submit to you that he was his charming self; that when these girls walked into that rooming house and were introduced to him by the landlady, that he began making plans for them; and he subsequently lured them to their deaths. Tony Costa wasn't addicted. He was on kicks, self-gratification, playing with himself. He was always conscious of what he was doing. In every phase of this man's life, he was trying to manipulate other people for his own gratification, to the extent that he would lure them into the woods and butcher them. He has a *problem*, because he was detected, apprehended, and tried."

The district attorney walked around the room, letting his words hang in the air, before approaching the jury box once again.

"The final adjudication of this matter lies with you," he told the panel. "It is your duty to impose a finding as to guilty or not guilty under our system of law. And I submit to you that Antone Charles Costa is guilty of murder in the first degree, that he is guilty of murder, premeditation, and forethought."

Dinis took a moment to clear his throat. He had a surprise in store for the jury that neither the judge, the defense, the media, or the public could see coming.

"Although I ask you to find him guilty of murder in the first degree in both of these butcherings of Mary Anne Wysocki and Patricia Walsh, I ask you to temper that finding with clemency. Let Costa *live*, so that he can think and meditate, because he is a man of high intelligence. Let him think about the unwarranted butcherings of these two helpless souls on that day in January in the woods of North Truro. Let him *live* with it, because that is what he deserves, to *live* with that. But he deserves no other consideration."

Dinis was focused solely on securing a guilty verdict in this case. The idea that jurors might waver under consideration of the death penalty was the last thing he wanted. The district attorney needed to ensure a win at any cost. His startling decision to advocate against the death penalty for Tony Costa created a huge uproar in the courtroom. Some onlookers clapped and cheered, openly applauding his decision. Others loudly booed the lawman. Catherine Walsh cried, while reporters and courtroom artists scribbled and sketched, capturing the drama as it unfolded.

Judge Beaudreau pounded his gavel.

"Order in the court!" he shouted.

CHAPTER FORTY-SIX

It was noon on Friday, May 22, 1970, and Judge Beaudreau was preparing to charge the jury. The panel, made up of eleven men and one woman, retired school teacher Frances Leonardi, had been sequestered for nearly two weeks, and all were ready to go home and put this nightmare behind them. Typically, juries on Cape Cod were called to weigh the evidence of minor crimes, such as theft of lobster traps or a neighborly dispute over farmland. This group had been taken into the depths of hell. These jurors had heard and seen things that would no doubt haunt them forever. But now they had their own chance to play God. Tony Costa's fate rested in their hands, and it was a responsibility that none of them took lightly.

"You may reserve your opinion as to whether you enjoyed the case or not until you have arrived at the threshold of your homes," Judge Beaudreau told the jury. "The woman juror, I am sure, will be greeted with remarks such as: There hasn't been a hot meal in this house in eleven days. And the men will be greeted by their ever-loving spouses with regards to things: that the car isn't running right, the grass needs mowing, and other things you will have to catch up on. You can't volunteer for another tour of duty, though. We know the sacrifices that you people went through here in taking this time out of your lives and out of your work; but we need conscientious, devoted citizens such as yourselves, particularly in these trying times, to make our judicial system work."

The judge then asked Tony Costa if he would like to speak. The defendant rose from his chair, adjusted his tie, and leaned against the railing that separated spectators from litigants. Maurice Goldman had done everything in his power to convince the jury that his client was crazy and that he should be sent away to a mental hospital. He had pleaded with Costa not to address jurors. "Let them think you're a drooling loony," Goldman advised him. "They'll be less likely to send you away to prison."

But Costa would not listen to his lawyer. Instead, he would perform a sober soliloquy of his own.

"Your Honor, at this time, I would like to thank you for your kindness and consideration in this matter," Costa said. "I have always had a high respect for the legal system in this country, and your consideration has reinforced that, one-hundred fold. I would also like to thank my chief counsel, Mr. Goldman, and his assistant, Mr. Cavanaugh, who I consider dedicated pursuers of justice. And I want to apologize to the jury for any inconvenience in having you sequestered and keeping you from your loved ones. I now realize that I was involved in some nightmarish events, and I can't explain how or why. I do know that it is one heck of a thing to have to live with and to realize at this point. Before this event took place, my wife and I led a very good, very decent life. And marital problems developed; and I realized I needed help. At that time, I sought that help. I did not receive help, I received drugs instead. And in receiving these drugs, I became dependent on them instead. I could no longer carry on as I had done in the past. I was no longer the person I used to be. It became a constant downhill fall. I lost everything that I had worked for. I had a business, a good life, I had a home and I had children. And in using these chemicals, I lost all this. And I started to lose contact with reality. And I held great contempt for myself for getting involved in this situation; but at this point, there was nothing I could do. My mind was shackled by chemicals."

Costa was doing his best to convince the jury that he was not the demon butcher of Pat Walsh and Mary Anne Wysocki but a victim himself of the sixties drug scene.

"Gaining authority and confidence, I tried to decrease my capacity and tolerance for drugs. In these attempts, I got into what I believed to be much milder drugs. And this only led to a complete state of further confusion. And I met a girl who I was very much in love with; and I made the determination to stop using drugs at that time. Then, one unfortunate evening I was in Provincetown, I received word that she had taken an overdose of drugs and had passed away. And with this knowledge, I just fell to pieces. I went right back to drugs. I felt that everything had collapsed around me. I felt I had nothing anymore."

Costa was referring to Christine Gallant, the woman he had murdered and left dead in a bathtub in New York City. The killer's words angered Bernie Flynn, who was standing in the back of the courthouse next to his partner Tom Gunnery.

"Can you believe the balls on this guy?" Flynn said with astonishment. "He should be tried for that murder as well as the deaths of Sydney Monzon and Susan Perry."

"Their ghosts are here in this courtroom today," Gunnery told him. "I can feel them."

Tony Costa continued his story. "In February 1969, I had access to great quantities of LSD. I had heard that it was an enlightening drug, that it could possibly open one's mind and help one's self. And in taking LSD, I simply found that it did nothing but cause nightmarish hallucinations. It caused me to become so far from reality that I could not exist as a man anymore. All I wanted to do was just go somewhere and die. I had flashbacks, or bad trips from LSD, without even using any drugs. And I realized that I was mentally ill…and I gradually diminished my capacity for drugs. I was not using any drugs, but I had lost contact with reality. And then I came to my final realization in March that I was going to return to society and be the man that I once was. I cleaned myself up and went out and got a job. I was to start work the next day, but unfortunately, I was arrested. And that is about where I had stopped along the line of rehabilitation. I am hoping now that I can seek the help that I desperately sought then. I am hoping that you will give me this chance to accomplish my achievement in life with the help that I need...so that someday, perhaps in the far-off, foreseeable future, I may be able to return to society as the man that I once was."

Bernie Flynn bit down hard on his lower lip. "This fucking guy thinks he's gonna walk free someday," he muttered.

The killer then offered advice to his followers and hippies across the country.

"And I have a message at this time that I would like to give young people, I want these people to know from what I have experienced that drugs are destruction. You cannot find happiness in a capsule; you cannot find happiness shooting it into your veins. You can only destroy yourself. And I hope that all these young Americans realize the power and potency of destructive drugs and exactly what they can do to the mind. At our birth, we are given the most precious, God-given gift that we could have, and that is our brain. And I pray that these young Americans will start using their brain and stop using drugs. I now realize that I must suffer for my drug domination, and I leave my fate in your hands."

Tony Costa returned to the defense table and leaned toward his lawyer.

"I think I did it. I think I may have just won the case," he told Goldman. The attorney said nothing.

The jury entered deliberations at 12:30 p.m. Costa beamed with confidence as he was taken back to the Barnstable House of Correction. Sadie, Thumper, and Strawberry Blonde had covered the walkway from the back of the courthouse to the hill leading up to the jail with mandrake leaves, which they hoped would protect Costa and increase his strength and courage.

Two hours later, Costa returned to the courthouse, where one of the jurors had a question—they wanted clarification of Goldman's statement that he did not want Costa allowed back on the streets. Judge Beaudreau read aloud from the stenographer's transcript of Goldman's closing argument, in which he stated that the defense did not wish Costa to go free. The twelve jurors returned to the jury room, where they deliberated for five more hours.

Evelyn Lawson hung around the courthouse while Vonnegut went home for an early dinner. At 7:00 p.m., Lawson called him from a pay phone to let him know that the jury had reached its verdict. Vonnegut grabbed a pack of cigarettes and his notepad and jogged up the street toward Barnstable Superior Court. A large crowd had gathered outside, and spectators spilled into the lobby, hoping they would get the opportunity to witness the verdict. Vonnegut showed his press pass and squeezed through the crowd before entering the courtroom. The jury was called in thirty minutes later.

"Mr. Foreman, have you agreed upon your verdict?" the superior court clerk asked Russell Dodge.

"We have."

"In case number 27664, Commonwealth versus Antone Costa, what do you say, Mr. Foreman: Is the defendant guilty or not guilty?"

"We find the defendant guilty of murder in the first degree," Dodge announced. "But we recommend that the sentence of death not be imposed."

There was an audible gasp in the courtroom as spectators learned that Costa's life would be spared.

Russell Dodge delivered the same verdict for the murder of Patricia Walsh.

Ed Dinis stood up proudly. It was the result that he had passionately advocated for. "The commonwealth moves for sentencing at this time," he requested.

The court clerk motioned to the defendant. "Antone Charles Costa, please rise. Under the indictment number 27664, the court, having considered the offense whereof you stand convicted, orders you to be punished by imprisonment in the Massachusetts Correctional Institution at Walpole for and during the term of your natural life."

The killer's false hope was dashed in an instant. He truly believed that he would be allowed to return to Helltown one day after being fully cured of what he called his "drug domination." Judge Beaudreau vowed that he would not let this happen and that Tony Costa would spend the rest of his days caged for the cruel acts he had committed against the two young women from Providence, Rhode Island, as well as the victims that were not represented in the murder trial.

Tony Costa was visibly shaken, and his confidence was gone. "Thank you," he said softly.

Outside the courthouse, Ed Dinis addressed reporters. "Justice was served," he told them. "This is a terrible tragedy and the most unfortunate incident in the lives of all concerned."

Catherine Walsh shook her head with disgust as she and her family passed the district attorney on their way out of the building.

"I'm glad it's all over," Joe Walsh, Patricia Walsh's older brother, told a reporter in the parking lot. "We can now close the book. We've lived with this for a long time."

Defense counsel Larry Shubow was still arguing the case on the courthouse steps, and he called for the law to be changed in the wake of the trial.

"The jury should be allowed to return a verdict of guilty but insane," he told the press. "Everyone agrees that Antone Costa is sick. But it is an insurmountable task to convince a jury to convert that finding into the words *not guilty.*"

Tony Costa spent the night at the Barnstable jailhouse, from where he would be transported by armed guard to Walpole State Prison the next morning. As he sat in his cell, he penned a letter to Maurice Goldman, announcing that he wished to appeal his sentence.

"I would rather be free than a martyr," Costa wrote.

Sadie, Thumper, and Strawberry Blonde held a vigil outside the prison that night. Thumper cranked the volume of her portable radio and danced under the moon to the song "Daughter of Darkness" by Tom Jones. "Heaven, we had our own kind of heaven, sharing together, the magic of love… Oh daughter of darkness, daughter of darkness."

CHAPTER FORTY-SEVEN

Kurt Vonnegut emptied his ashtray and set his typewriter on a narrow desk next to a window overlooking East Forty-Eighth Street in New York City, where he now lived. It was 1974, and Cape Cod was a distant memory for him. He had walked out on his long-suffering wife, Jane, four years before, just after Tony Costa was handed two concurrent life sentences for the murders of Mary Anne Wysocki and Patricia Walsh. Vonnegut was still not divorced, but he was living the life of a pseudo bachelor and super-star author in Manhattan, his own version of the Emerald City, where he was fully participating in the literary life, which included dinner parties at Elaine's and hobnobbing with fellow scribes like George Plimpton. It was a far cry and a world away from the years he had spent in Barnstable, running a failing car dealership, writing on the side, and struggling to care for his family. He had a new girlfriend, Jill Krementz, an acclaimed photojournalist who had covered the war in Vietnam and the march on the Pentagon but who now specialized in photographing writers. In 1974, there was perhaps no more famous writer in America than Kurt Vonnegut Jr.

Breakfast of Champions, his follow-up to *Slaughterhouse-Five*, was a smashing commercial success, spending fifty-six weeks on the *New York Times* bestseller list. Universal Pictures had produced a big-screen adaptation of *Slaughterhouse-Five*, which premiered at the Cannes Film Festival and won the coveted Jury Prize. Vonnegut screened the movie more than twenty times and called director George Roy Hill's take on his material flawless. Vonnegut's play *Happy Birthday, Wanda June* also made its way to the cinema in a film starring Rod Steiger. Both movies performed well at the box office, better than any of Norman Mailer's films did. The rivalry between the two writers had never been more equal.

Vonnegut had watched with glee while *60 Minutes* correspondent Mike Wallace eviscerated Mailer on the television program over his latest book, *Marilyn: A Biography*, about the life and death of Hollywood icon Marilyn Monroe. In the book's final chapter, Mailer alleged that Monroe may have been murdered by rogue agents of the FBI and CIA to cover up her alleged affair with Bobby Kennedy. Wallace seized on the theory, which at that point had been given little credence by journalists.

"It's a bizarre theory," Wallace told Mailer during their interview for a segment titled "Monroe, Mailer, and the Fast Buck." "If *Marilyn* does become the book of the year, its last chapter will be the reason, for it deals in sensational fashion with Monroe's relationship with the Kennedys, both the president and his brother Bobby."

"I could not ignore the possibility of a murder," Mailer countered. "All Hollywood was gossiping about Marilyn having an affair with Bobby Kennedy, which I believe in fact she was not having, although they were dear and close friends. So of course she could be murdered in such a way that it would look like a suicide, for unrequited love of Bobby Kennedy. It would be a huge embarrassment for the Kennedys."

"You can tell, no one's talking. No one is going to talk about that night," he added.

Wallace then asked Mailer why he did not interview Monroe's housekeeper, who was with the actress when she died. "She is the one person who could invalidate all of Mailer's tortured theorizing about the Monroe murder plot."

Mailer shrugged his shoulders and said that he hated doing telephone interviews. "I hate that way of getting facts… I was doing something that you don't normally do with a book, which is I was getting into the end of the book with a half-finished exploration, and I decided it was important enough to get out there half-finished rather than not get into it at all."

At the close of the segment, Mike Wallace editorialized for his *60 Minutes* audience. "The best criticism of the book we've heard so far is Norman Mailer's own: 'It got out there half-finished.' But no matter, the book will sell."

Wallace was right. Mailer's book sold over six hundred thousand copies and was translated into fifteen languages. But it continued to be plagued by controversy. Mailer was accused of plagiarism by the British publisher of two previous biographies on Marilyn Monroe. He fought back against the claims. "No one is going to call me a plagiarist and get away with it," he fumed. "I do not need other writers' words or thoughts to make myself a book."

Playwright Arthur Miller, Monroe's former husband, would later summarize the murder plot theory this way: "[Mailer] was himself in drag, acting out his own Hollywood fantasies of fame and sex unlimited and power."

As much as Vonnegut enjoyed seeing Mailer sweat, he was fighting a battle within himself about his writing future. He was disappointed, even embarrassed by his work on *Breakfast of Champions*, which was partially cobbled together from pages he had intended for *Slaughterhouse-Five*. "I feel like an animal in a wicker cage," he told Jill Krementz. "For so long, money motivated me, and now there is nothing to move me off center. I don't know what to do."

He enjoyed living in the four-story town house on Forty-Eighth Street between Second and Third Avenues, which was a short walk from the United Nations. His home office was roughly the size of his writing studio on Cape Cod, but it did not help foster the same creativity that had fueled him in years past. Without the idea for a new novel floating around in his brain, Vonnegut decided to publish a patchwork of his old essays, which he titled *Wampeters, Foma & Granfalloons*.

One of the stories that he had decided to resurrect was the piece he wrote about Tony Costa for *Life* magazine in 1969. Vonnegut had never quite shed the skin of the grisly murders that took place in North Truro, and he thought about Tony Costa often. The serial killer turned prison lifer had corresponded with Vonnegut several times since his conviction. In the preface for *Wampeters*, the author wrote, "There is a piece in this book about Tony Costa, a Cape Codder who was a friend of my daughter Edith. He was accused of several murders. It was decided that he was insane, and thus beyond ordinary punishment. I have heard from him. He cannot believe that a decent, sensible person like himself could possibly have done the killing police thought he had done."

Vonnegut's version of Costa's crimes was at odds with the facts, as he failed to mention that Costa was indeed convicted of first-degree murder and was serving two concurrent life sentences. But he was also able to tap into a greater truth.

"As his trial approached, incidentally he was the most famous American then accused of mass murder," Vonnegut added. "And then, on the other shore of the continent, Charles Manson and some members of his artificial extended family were arrested for murdering celebrities. Costa himself ceased to be a celebrity—became overnight what he had been in the beginning, a nobody, a mere wisp of an implication."

Kurt Vonnegut's assessment was dead-on. Manson was by that time a cult figure. His menacing profile on the covers of magazines such as *Life* and *Rolling Stone* terrified readers. The so-called rock 'n' roll bible had anointed Manson as the most dangerous man alive.

Like Tony Costa, Charles Manson was serving life without parole after the death penalty had been ruled unconstitutional in the state of California.

Linda Kasabian was spared a prison sentence after agreeing to serve as the star witness for the prosecution. She was now back in New Hampshire, living with her young children and her mother, Joyce Byrd, who told a *Boston Globe* reporter that she blamed herself for Linda's newfound notoriety. "I tried to protect her by regulating her life. I told her what to eat, what to wear, and what friends she could have… Linda felt thoroughly rejected as she had so often before, and she turned again to life in the hippie communes. She was a set-up for Charles Manson and his cultist movement."

Unlike Manson's growing legion of followers, Tony Costa's cultist movement had diminished over time. Of the three witches, only Strawberry Blonde remained in touch with him behind bars. Shortly after Costa's conviction, Sadie was found dead on a friend's couch with a needle stuck in her arm. Thumper got knocked up by a local fisherman. They got married and enjoyed domestic life in a small cottage on the edge of Ptown. Strawberry Blonde still shucked oysters on Commercial Street but had abandoned the Wiccan lifestyle for something more sinister. After a trip to London and a visit to a basement coffee bar known as Satan's Cave, she had adopted the teachings of the Process Church of the Final Judgment. Strawberry Blonde attended secret meetings and read the church's twisted scripture under candlelight. She was especially drawn to the Process Church's exploration of the duality between Christ and Lucifer, which reminded her of Sire.

"The humans are trapped in God's game, and God will have its way," one member told her. "So be it."

So it goes, thought Strawberry Blonde. In Provincetown, she was a church of one, waiting for the perfect disciple to appear before her, like an apparition in the nighttime fog of Helltown. She kept up with her routine of writing Tony Costa two letters each week. He had responded eagerly during his first three years of incarceration, but the mail had slowed, because he told her that he needed to focus all his energy on his book, a book that would rewrite the history of his case and present him as the hero he had longed to be.

He was working on a borrowed typewriter and asked his lawyer Maurice Goldman to loan him $100 so he could buy a new machine. He stacked the typewritten pages on a small shelf next to several books in his collection, including *Ceremonial Magic*, *A Treasury of Witchcraft*, and *The Satanic Bible*. Costa separated the final chapters of his book and read them aloud.

Suddenly, a thunderous, explosive sound pierced and shattered the air around me! At first, I didn't recognize the sound, but unexpectedly, it penetrated the forest again a second time…and then three times consecutively. Each sounded like a resonant, vibrating explosion, and in a sense they were. Then all at once, I realized what those ugly, frightening sounds were; or must have been… Gunshots! Five gunshots in the night.

I beamed the flashlight around the area at ground level, stopping its beam upon a strange, unnatural clump on the ground. It was what appeared to be, a body… Dizziness and nausea prevailed, overwhelming me… It was indeed a body, Pat's body, barely conscious, laying on her right side, her right arm extended over her head. I prodded at her shoulder gently, "Pat?" I called feebly, fearfully…

"Tony…ple…please hold me…" came her soft, raspy deathlike whisper. "I'm so…cold. I…love you."

No breathing.

No sound.

No movement.

No Nothing!

Acid games again or reality?

Behind me, I heard someone or something furiously thrashing through the bushes… I finally realized it was Carl… Carl had forcefully wrapped his hands around my throat while he kneeled on my chest… His cold stare, burning with vengeance, seared my brain but I dared not move a muscle… Carl had the power of life or death over me.

The manuscript, "Resurrection," was the truth as Tony Costa believed it to be. He had decided to change Cory's name to Carl in the manuscript. His alter ego did not want his name revealed in Costa's *real* story. Costa dedicated the book to his children, whom he had not seen since before his arrest in 1969. His ex-wife, Avis, was remarried and out of his life altogether.

They'll read about us one day, Cory told him in their prison cell. *The world will know what we created together, a masterpiece for the ages. Our work here is done. It's time to go.*

Tony Costa was an old man at age twenty-nine. *Van Gogh shot himself at thirty-seven,* Cory reminded him. *Fitzgerald drank himself to death at forty-four. You've created your greatest work of art. Now go!*

"To hell with Vonnegut and all the other pretenders," Costa muttered. "I want to live forever."

The killer pushed his bunk over to the bars of his prison cell. He removed his leather belt and wrapped it around his neck. He then looped the opposite end around the upper bars, making sure it was tightly secured. He stood on his bunk and took a deep breath. Tony Costa stepped off and let the leather belt do the rest of the work.

At approximately 8:15 p.m. on May 12, 1974, a prison guard made his rounds in the first-floor, minimum-security wing of Walpole State Prison. When he approached Costa's cell, he found him collapsed on the floor with the belt choking his neck. Blood dripped from the sides of the killer's mouth. To the prison guard, Costa resembled a vampire. The blood was his own, however. Costa had bitten down so hard on his tongue that it was barely attached. The killer had pissed himself, and his dark eyes remained wide open. But they were lifeless. He had no pulse. The wolf of the steppes was dead.

CHAPTER FORTY-EIGHT

Strawberry Blonde stood in mud up to her ankles next to an open plot at St. Paul's Cemetery in Provincetown. She looked down into a fresh hole, dug six feet deep, which had been the custom for all burials since the Lord Mayor of London's decree in the seventeenth century that all bodies must be laid to rest at least six feet in the ground in an attempt to curb the spread of the plague.

Four caretakers lowered the simple oak coffin that held Tony Costa's body into a burial plot next to his mother, Cecilia Bonaviri. Heavy rain pounded the newly laid sod as Father Leo Duarte recited the Catholic prayer for the dead.

"Deliver him now from every evil, and bid him eternal rest," the priest told the small group gathered at the grave site.

Strawberry Blonde held a book to her chest as she wept for her dark prince, the only man she had ever loved. After the brief ceremony, she returned to her basement apartment on Creek Road and placed the book on a table, allowing the pages to dry.

Strawberry Blonde poured herself a cup of tea mixed with dried rue, opened the book, and read, "The art of taxidermy is very ancient, and doubtless had its origin among the very early races of man."

Strawberry Blonde guided the young woman along a sandy path about a mile east of the Race Point Coast Guard Station. They could see the white, three-and-a-half-story building standing in the distance. It was after eight o'clock, and the sky over Cape Cod had turned purple.

"Do we need a flashlight?" the young woman asked.

"Just follow me," Strawberry Blonde replied. "I've been coming here since I was a kid. We won't get lost. I promise."

"We just need to get away from these flies," the companion said as she swatted a tiny swarm of greenheads away from her face.

She stopped and fished a rubber band from the front pocket of her blue jeans. She then pulled her hair back into a tight ponytail and wrapped the elastic around her long, reddish-blond strands. Her hair was similar to Strawberry Blonde's, which was their first point of attraction to each other. They had met the night before at the Foc'sle and spent the rest of the evening and most of the following day exploring each other's bodies in bed at Strawberry Blonde's apartment. The young woman wanted to see the sunset at land's end, so Strawberry Blonde brought her here to Race Point. She carried a heavy backpack, filled with a cotton beach blanket and a bottle of red wine, over her narrow shoulders. Strawberry Blonde dropped the pack on the side of a dune that would give them a perfect view of the bright constellations as they appeared in the gloaming. She placed her hand carefully in the bag and pulled out the blanket.

"Need my help?" the young woman asked.

"No, my darling. You just sit there looking beautiful."

Strawberry Blonde spread the blanket across the incline of the dune and invited her companion to join her. They huddled closely, kissing and caressing as they undressed each other. The young woman folded her blue jeans and placed them at the edge of the blanket. Strawberry Blonde bundled her blouse and shorts and stuffed them inside the backpack. She opened the bottle of wine, took a long pull, and offered a taste to her new friend.

"I don't drink," the young woman told her. "I don't need wine. I just need you."

Strawberry Blonde pressed her naked body against her companion's and devoured her with her lips and tongue. Afterward, the young woman wanted to be held.

"I could stay here with you forever," she whispered lovingly.

Strawberry Blonde moved the friend's hands from her bare breasts and inched herself off the blanket.

"Where are you going?"

"I have to pee."

Strawberry Blonde grabbed the handle of the backpack and disappeared around the other side of the dune.

"Don't take so long. I miss you already," the young woman shouted in the darkness.

Strawberry Blonde put her clothes back on and dug deeper in the backpack and pulled out a sturdy hammer and then a sheathed knife. Silently, she crept back to the blanket from the opposite side of the tall dune. Her companion was still naked, leaning back on her elbows, watching the sky. The young woman did not hear the approach. Suddenly, she felt a powerful blow to the back of her head. She fell forward on the blanket as Strawberry Blonde swung the hammer down once more, crushing the left side of her skull. A river of blood flowed from the gaping wound onto the blanket. She appeared to be dead, but Strawberry Blonde needed to be sure.

"Watch for any rise and fall of the chest cavity," she told herself.

The killer thought she saw the body moving slightly in the darkness. Taking no risk, she unsheathed the knife, grabbed her prey by the ponytail, and cut into her neck just below the jaw line. Strawberry Blonde plunged the blade deeper, sawing through the digastric muscle until the victim's head was almost completely separated from the body.

"Now it's time to cut the feathers," she said.

Once that bloody task was completed, Strawberry Blonde stood over her specimen and admired her work.

"A naked girl, fair haired and in the prime of youth, lies like a human sacrifice upon your altar," she chanted. "Nothing stirs, no sound but the sighing wind. Here is a gift for you, Sire, to satisfy your restless spirit."

Strawberry Blonde returned her murderous tools to her backpack and marched to the ocean, where a moonlight swim in the cold water would absolve her of her sins.

Ten days later, on July 26, 1974, twelve-year-old Leslie Metcalfe chased after her dog in the remote dunes near the Coast Guard station at Race Point. She was hiking with her parents back to the Province Lands Visitors Center at the end of Race Point Road after visiting with family friends at one of the dune shacks.

The retriever caught a smell of something and jerked away from its leash. The dog ran about twenty yards before stopping, sniffing, and barking at the edge of what appeared to be a blanket surrounded by scrub pines. Metcalfe jogged in the sand ahead of her parents, turned the corner of the dune, and saw a figure lying on its side on the blanket. At first, she thought it was a deer because of the discoloration of the skin. The girl then recognized that it was a young woman.

As the dog inched its nose closer to her, she did not move.

"Are you okay?" Metcalfe shouted.

She did not answer.

The girl approached the blanket and pushed the retriever away for a closer look.

The young woman was naked, and her head rested on a pair of folded blue jeans. Her skull was cracked wide open, and blood had congealed in a scarlet halo around the deep wound. There were other blood stains on the blanket just below the victim's elbows. The teenager ran her eyes down the woman's body to her hands. Both had been cut off and were missing from the blanket.

Leslie Metcalfe screamed for help.

Provincetown police were called to the scene. James Meads was now the chief of police, having taken over for Cheney Marshall. He inspected the young woman's body, her nearly severed head and dismembered hands. Meads had seen this type of killing once before in North Truro during the winter of 1969. He immediately thought of Tony Costa, his former police informant turned butcher of women.

"It can't be Costa," Meads said to himself. "Tony's dead now. He can't hurt anybody anymore."

He searched the pair of blue jeans located at the scene but found no wallet. The young woman's body was taken to the local funeral home, but no one came forward to claim her. The victim was as mysterious as her killer. News of the murder was slow to trickle out. The *Cape Cod Standard-Times* ran a headline four days later that read "Homicide Victim Still Unidentified."

Evelyn Lawson read the article while sipping her tea on the patio at her cottage in Hyannis. Her new pet, a male coon cat named Stanley, sat at her feet. The cat jumped when it noticed its owner's hands begin to quake. Lawson gripped the sides of the newspaper as the words *severed head* and *missing hands* leapt off the page.

"Costa's disciples are still out there," she muttered breathlessly.

Lawson ran into her writing office and pulled a bound manuscript from her desk. It was the final, edited version of her book on the Costa murder case, a project she had spent the past five years toiling over. She had planned to send it to her publisher the following day. Instead, Lawson carried her book outside and dropped it into a steel garbage bin. She soaked the pages with lighter fluid, struck a match, and watched them burn.

CHAPTER FORTY-NINE

Norman Mailer squeezed his stocky frame into the narrow stairway that led up to his writing office on the third floor of his home. The wooden planks groaned with each step as he lumbered forward, his hand holding tightly to the metal railing. The writer was sixty-one years old now, but he looked a decade older. He wore heavy bags under his blue eyes and was round in the middle. His once barrel chest now appeared sunken. His curly hair was nearly all white. The near-constant turmoil of the last ten years had aged him badly.

Mailer had recovered from the sting of media sniping regarding his half-baked biography of Marilyn Monroe. In 1979, he published his seminal work, *The Executioner's Song*, a true crime novel about the execution of convicted double murderer Gary Gilmore, who faced the firing squad at Utah State Prison two years before. The idea for the book came from a *Newsweek* article about Gilmore's sheer determination to be put to death for his crimes. Mailer was intrigued by the story and by Gilmore's face. He was handsome, like Tony Costa, but in a different way. Whereas Costa used his silky dark features to seduce and kill, Gilmore's profile was long and full of character. Mailer saw Gary Gilmore, like Costa, as both a saint in his ability to connect with people and a psychopath who placed no value on human life.

Working with Larry Schiller, his collaborator on the Marilyn Monroe book, Mailer dove into the project with great energy, absorbing hours of audiotaped interviews that Schiller had conducted with Gilmore on death row before his execution and traveling to Utah and Oregon, where Gilmore had also done time, on his own research quest.

"Gilmore embodies many of the themes that I've been living with all my life," Mailer said while writing the book. "He's the perfect character for me."

The Executioner's Song spent twenty-five weeks on the *New York Times* bestseller list and was hailed as a work of genius. It also earned Mailer the coveted Pulitzer Prize. But the achievement came at a painful cost. During his research for the book, Mailer met and began a relationship with an inmate named Jack Abbott, who had written to him with an offer to describe what it was like to be incarcerated in a maximum-security prison. Mailer was struck by Abbott's evocative writing style, and the two men began sending letters back and forth.

"He has a mind like no other I have encountered," Mailer later wrote about the prisoner. "It speaks from the nineteenth century as clearly as it speaks from the twentieth... Freedom and justice are oxygen to Abbott."

Jack Abbott asked his famous friend to champion his parole. Mailer met him behind bars in Marion, Illinois, and believed that he deserved a second chance, that he could be rehabilitated.

Mailer wrote letters to the parole board and even got Abbott his own book deal worth $12,500. Abbott was soon set free.

On July 18, 1981, just six weeks after his parole, Jack Abbott found himself in a Manhattan restaurant called Binibon, at the corner of Second Avenue and Fifth Street. Abbott asked an employee, twenty-two-year-old Richard Adan, if he could use the bathroom. Adan, the owner's son-in-law, told Abbott that the restroom was reserved for employees only. He led Abbott to a back alley, where Abbott took out a knife and plunged its four-inch blade into his heart, killing him.

Abbott called Mailer in Provincetown shortly after the murder. The killer then fled New York City and was later arrested in Louisiana. Seven months after the crime, Mailer testified at Abbott's manslaughter trial. The author acknowledged that he shared in the responsibility for the deadly crime.

"Richard Adan's death is an absolute tragedy," Mailer told the court. "Who's pretending it isn't? It's a hideous waste, it's a horror. The fact that Richard Adan is killed is something that the people who are closest to Abbott are going to live with for the rest of their lives. I mean, you can't have my blood unless you go for it, but you can have my psychic blood, because naturally, I, like many other people, are upset about the death of Richard Adan."

Jack Abbott was sentenced to fifteen years to life in prison for the killing of Adnan.

Later, when confronted by reporters, Mailer said, "This is another episode in my life in which I can find nothing to cheer about and nothing to take pride in."

It was the darkness explored in the writing of Gilmore's story and the relationship with a killer like Jack Abbott that had prepared Mailer to finally confront the murders that had taken place in the shadow of Helltown back in 1969.

The haunting image of a woman's severed head encased in a plastic bag had never faded. But her facial features had changed over time, depending on whom Mailer was sleeping with at the moment. His relationship with jazz singer Carol Stevens produced a daughter named Maggie but fizzled soon after. He was now married to a model turned artist named Norris Church. And like everything in his life, their courtship was not easy. They had met in 1975, while Mailer was in Arkansas promoting his Monroe biography. Her name was Barbara Jean Norris then, and she was a high school art teacher. They struck up a conversation at a cocktail party and discovered they shared the same birthday and were born just one minute apart, minus the twenty-six-year age difference. Barbara was tall, with dark eyes and long legs. Mailer urged her to move to New York to pursue a modeling career. He also recommended that she change her name to Norris Church. Norris was the last name of Barbara's ex-husband, and the name Church was a nod to her father, a Baptist deacon. She quickly replaced Carol Stevens in Mailer's bedroom and his life. When they decided to get married, Mailer had to complete two tasks first. He had to ask Barbara Bentley for a divorce after years of separation, and he had to marry and then divorce Carol Stevens in an effort to legitimize their daughter, Maggie, who was then nine years old. Bentley battled him in court before settling, while Stevens allowed herself to get married and then divorced all in one crazy month. Amazingly, Mailer had pulled it all off, and he and Norris were now happy and settled in Provincetown.

Although Mailer's wife had aspirations of her own, Norris was more committed to him and his work than any of his former wives and lovers had ever been. But now it was her face that he saw being dug from a hole in the woods of North Truro. It was finally time for him to explore and then exorcize that demon, and the only way that he could accomplish this was through his writing.

After reaching the top of the stairway leading to his office, Mailer ducked his head to avoid skinning his brow on the low, pitched ceiling. He passed three shelves that extended into the middle of the room, bulging with books and papers dedicated to his past works and future projects. The space was dark. The only light came from the large window next to his desk, which offered a panoramic view of Provincetown with its monument illuminated in the distance. In his prose, Mailer was about to bring murder and grisly dismemberment back to the community, one that was still healing from the killings of local residents Susan Perry and Sydney Monzon as well as Mary

Anne Wysocki and Patricia Walsh, the two women from Providence, Rhode Island.

Evelyn Lawson had recently died at age seventy-six after a long bout with cancer, so Mailer felt the story was his to write. He never did learn why she had abandoned the project, only to go back to reviewing local theater productions for the *Barnstable Patriot*. Another book had been published about the case. It was a solid journalistic effort written by a Cape Cod crime reporter named Leo Damore, who later committed suicide by shooting himself in the head. But nobody could get inside the head of a killer such as Tony Costa quite like Norman Mailer, or at least that was what he thought. He flicked the switch of an old brass floor lamp, sat at his desk, and went to work.

Since Mailer felt he had little in common with the actual killer, he decided to morph Costa into a fictional character that was more Norman than Tony. Mailer's protagonist, Tim Madden, was struggling to make it as a writer while spending the off-season in Provincetown, a place that Mailer described as "funky." "We sell room-space to tourists," he wrote in the novel. "One hundred rented rooms can end up having one hundred outside stairways. Provincetown, to anyone looking for gracious living, is no more unclutttered than twenty telephone poles at a crossroads." Mailer was convinced that the original inhabitants of Helltown still had a hauntingly sexual influence on all those who lived in the village. "A bawdy force came down on us from one-night stands of whores and seamen more than one-hundred years dead," he wrote.

He developed a fantastical story that examined the idea of "ego splitting," the psychological disorder that turned Tony Costa into a sadistic killer. In Mailer's fictional version of the story, his protagonist, Tim Madden, wakes up one morning in a fog and finds the passenger seat of his car covered with blood. Later, he treks out to the Truro woods to check on his marijuana patch, located at the base of a dwarf pine, only to make a terrifying discovery:

"I felt something—it could be flesh or hair or some moist sponge—I didn't know what, but my hands, fiercer than myself, cleared the debris to pull forward a plastic garbage bag through which I poked and saw enough at once to give one frightful moan, pure as the vertigo of a long fall itself. I was looking back at a head. The color of its hair, despite all the stains of earth, was blonde. Then I tried to see the face, but when to my horror the head rolled in the bag without resistance—severed!"

Later in the novel, another severed head would be unearthed from the dirt in North Truro. Was Madden the killer? Mailer's main character did not know for sure, as he had been under the influence of highly potent marijuana, a strain that the writer called Hurricane Head.

Mailer wrote his novel, which he called *Tough Guys Don't Dance*, in sixty-one days. He worked from eleven in the morning until nine at night. He delivered the manuscript to his publisher, Little, Brown, in September, but the editor refused to publish it without major revisions.

Mailer refused and asked the publisher to release the book. He was shocked and angry that the editor had seen little value in his hard-boiled whodunit. But like the real-life murders that had inspired the story, *Tough Guys* was seen as too graphic—too disturbing to attract a wide audience.

Mailer resold the novel to Random House, where he had recently signed a long-term book contract worth $4 million. *Tough Guys* became a massive bestseller, with two million copies sold. Two years later, Mailer secured a film deal for the novel with Cannon Films. At that time, Cannon was known for violent revenge movies like Charles Bronson's *Death Wish II* and martial arts flicks such as *Enter the Ninja*. The production company was in search of elevated material that would attract the art-house crowd, and Cannon executives saw Mailer as someone who could create a new, more sophisticated audience for their films. Mailer offered to write the screenplay for *Tough Guys Don't Dance* and direct the movie, his first effort behind the camera since *Maidstone*. Adapting his novel into a script, Mailer kept in place the heart of the story and its characters, which he described in a Costa-esque way. "Monsters with charm have always appealed to me," he told a friend. "And something that I hope is still in the screenplay."

He insisted on shooting the movie in Provincetown, even using his own waterfront home for a party scene. Mailer employed extras from town, many of them disturbed by the fact that he was further sensationalizing the Costa murder case but, in the same vein, excited for the chance to rub elbows with the film's two stars, Ryan O'Neal and Isabella Rossellini. Film critic Roger Ebert joined Mailer on location in Ptown. Ebert found the sixty-three-year-old writer-director wearing an ill-fitting goose-down parka, blocking out a scene involving a rented Rolls Royce in the middle of Commercial Street. During a coffee break, Ebert asked Mailer about the difference between novel writing and directing a film.

"When you write a novel, it's all yours, but you can use one part of yourself," he replied. "When you direct, you use every last part of yourself—especially a practical side that's been frustrated all my life. In novel writing,

Norman Mailer on the Provincetown set of his film Tough Guys Don't Dance, adapted from his novel and loosely based on the Costa murders. © PictureLux/The Hollywood Archive/ Alamy Stock Photo.

you can get by with a lot of fire and smoke. In the movies, there is less margin for error."

At the end of each day of filming, Mailer would host the cast and crew for cocktails at the Red Inn, at the far end of Commercial Street, where the director had set several scenes. There, he would regale the crowd, which included O'Neal and his wife, Farrah Fawcett, with stories and legends about Helltown and the macabre murders that had inspired his book and their film.

"The decapitations in *Tough Guys* came out of that case with Tony Costa here in Provincetown where he dismembered four women's bodies," Mailer told them as he sipped a tall glass of Bacardi and tonic, his new favorite drink. "That thing haunted me for years. In the sixties, while I was working on my novel *Why Are We in Vietnam*, I was going to write about a group of people hiding out in the sand dunes of Provincetown who were making raids and killing people, and then along came Costa, and Manson after that. It really freaked me out."

Mailer did not mention his near-deadly encounter with the knife-wielding hippie girl at the dune shack a decade before. He had not seen her since and did not feel the need to rustle up any old spirits. He called the project his "Valentine to Cape Cod." However, many villagers called it a bloody valentine and a dark moment they did not wish to relive. The author's son Michael, then a student at Harvard, worked closely with his father on the film set.

"Tony Costa, or Tony 'Chop-Chop' as we called him, was like the boogeyman for us kids growing up in Provincetown," Michael Mailer later recalled. "In *Tough Guys*, my father wanted to explore the mythology and lore of the Costa case and also tell a story about the underbelly of Ptown that still exists today."

The day after sharing Costa's story at the Red Inn, the film's production shifted to the woods of Truro for the pivotal severed-head scene. The area was

The ghosts and memories of Helltown are still vivid in Provincetown today.
© *Casey Sherman.*

teaming with crew members, cameras, and bright lights. A crowd of spectators, mostly townspeople, stood at the edge of the movie set, hoping for a glimpse of Ryan O'Neal, who had charmed movie audiences in Massachusetts with his heartfelt performance in *Love Story* nearly two decades before. But there was one onlooker who had no interest in the Hollywood star. She had come to see Norman Mailer.

Strawberry Blonde had finally come home. She had not set foot on Cape Cod since killing her lover and cutting off her hands in 1974. Strawberry Blonde found refuge from her crime in another eclectic community, Salem, Massachusetts, where she worked in an occult book store. She was still fascinated and committed to the dark arts, but she had never killed again. Once an eager apprentice, Strawberry Blonde never found the right mentor for murder after Tony Costa's death.

She still did not know why she was standing out in the cold on a starless night in Truro, but she felt a gravitational pull to be there. She held an oyster knife in the front pocket of her hooded jacket. A voice told her that she had to kill Norman Mailer and complete the work that she was too scared to finish so many years before. Strawberry Blonde waited for two hours while the director ordered several takes. During this time, she thought back to the letters she had received from Costa while in prison. He was so desperate to have his story told. Strawberry Blonde felt conflicted about her mission.

If I kill Mailer, the world may not get to see the masterpiece that my prince had once created here, she told herself.

The director and his cinematographer huddled together to discuss an adjustment of camera positions. As that work began, Mailer took a moment to thank the locals for supporting his film project. He chatted with a few townsfolk before setting his eyes on Strawberry Blonde. Her hair was trimmed short, she had added thirty pounds to her once lean body, and wrinkles crowded the edges of her eyes. But Mailer had recognized those determined yet terrified eyes immediately. He paused for a moment and took a step back. Strawberry Blonde leaned forward and extended her hand. For some odd reason, Mailer felt compelled to take it. Their skin touched for a brief moment, and she smiled at him. He grinned back and then returned to the director's chair. She left the knife in her pocket and walked away in the darkness.

In 2000, the body of the young woman found butchered near the Race Point Coast Guard station in 1974 was exhumed by police investigators in an attempt to confirm her identity. DNA samples were taken, and a new composite profile of the victim was created by forensic experts from the National Center for Missing and Exploited Children and the Smithsonian Institute using cutting-edge computer technology. The murder victim, now known as the Lady in the Dunes, was approximately five feet six inches in height, and she had a striking resemblance to both Patricia Walsh and Mary Anne Wysocki. After the exhumation, she was reburied under a flat grave marker that read *Unidentified Female Body* at St. Paul's Cemetery in Provincetown, a short distance from Tony Costa's final resting place.

AUTHOR'S NOTE

Helltown is a work of fact told with elements of fiction storytelling. While the chronology of some events had to be shifted to satisfy this book, the majority of what you read here really happened, sadly. The murders depicted in this book are all too real. Details of the shocking trial were pulled directly from court transcripts. Norman Mailer and Kurt Vonnegut Jr. were both obsessed with this case, although I recreated their dialogue and reimagined some scenarios with Costa's so-called disciples. I had never married journalism with narrative storytelling before, but I felt that *Helltown* warranted a deeper exploration of Tony Costa's crimes and the minds and attitudes of Norman Mailer and Kurt Vonnegut Jr. In fact, I was inspired by their classic works, especially *Slaughterhouse-Five* and *The Executioner's Song*, in my attempt to use elements of fiction to reach a greater truth.

As *Newsday* reporter Mike McGrady once wrote of Mailer, "he took his considerable skills as a novelist and used them unstintingly in reporting... There was background, mood, sound and smell, secondary levels of meaning, ethical considerations, personal insights." I have attempted to do the same but in reverse. I have used my skills and decades of experience as a journalist and true crime writer to enter an area that Mailer had once mastered— new journalism. I was also inspired to break free from the shackles of strict reportage by the great thriller novelist James Patterson, with whom I had the honor of cowriting my last book, *The Last Days of John Lennon*. There's also a subtle influence from Quentin Tarantino in my latest writing. Seeing how he reimagined the Manson murders offered me a new perspective on storytelling as well as a new challenge.

If it worked, that's great. If it didn't, so it goes...

Despite growing up on Cape Cod, it took me years to confront the horror and depravity of the Tony Costa murders. I had been too consumed by my reinvestigation of the Boston Strangler case at the time, which I chronicled in my first book, *A Rose for Mary*. My aunt, Mary Sullivan, was the youngest and final victim of the notorious 1960s murder case, and I did not wish to explore that darkness again in my writing. After discussing the decades-old Costa case with my brother Todd during a drive through Provincetown at the height of the pandemic, when the village was completely shut down, I decided that the crimes were worth a second look. I chased after all the court documents and police files in the case and was not prepared for what I found. As an investigative journalist with thirty years' experience covering hundreds of homicides, I was shaken to my core when I first viewed the autopsy photos of Mary Anne Wysocki, Patricia Walsh, Susan Perry, and Sydney Monzon. What happened to these women was pure evil and so unnatural that their murders almost appeared to be the work of fiction.

Everything you read about Costa's crimes in this novel is true. The information that I used in my story was pulled from thousands of pages of documents, including court transcripts, autopsy reports, psychological examinations, Massachusetts State Police interviews, eyewitness accounts, and hours of audiotaped interviews with Tony Costa. I also gained access to Costa's unpublished manuscript, "Resurrection," in which he described the murders as they happened while blaming them on his alter ego. I interviewed retired state police trooper Tom Gunnery, former prosecutor Armand Fernandes, Bernie Flynn's widow, Jacqueline Flynn, and Vonnegut family friend James

Leonard. I also had correspondence with Avis Costa Johnson, Edie Vonnegut, and Michael Mailer. Details surrounding the death of Mary Jo Kopechne came directly from grand jury testimony from the Chappaquiddick incident. I consulted dozens of articles that had appeared in the *Boston Globe* and the *Barnstable Patriot* about the Costa case as well as numerous published stories about the lives and work of both Norman Mailer and Kurt Vonnegut. Much of their dialogue was pulled from interviews they did.

With regard to the enduring mystery surrounding the Lady in the Dunes, the theory explored in this book is as plausible as any. Years ago, reporters floated the idea that Boston crime boss James "Whitey" Bulger was responsible for the young woman's murder. Having previously written a nonfiction book about Bulger called *Hunting Whitey*, I feel confident in my belief that Bulger had nothing to do with it. It wasn't his style. He was a killer of two women, strangling them because they knew too much about his criminal enterprise, but he left the more gruesome work to others. The fact that the victim's body was discovered shortly after Costa's prison suicide and the dismemberment of her hands should not be ignored. Like Charles Manson, Tony Costa had disciples who may have been willing to kill in his name.

Growing up in Hyannis, I had an ill-conceived notion about who Kurt Vonnegut was as a person. My perspective was shaped by a letter Vonnegut wrote to my father, Donny Sherman, in 1973. It was in response to a query letter that my dad, a talented artist, had sent to the author in the hope that he might one day have the opportunity to design the cover art for a Vonnegut novel. It was a long shot for sure. My father was surprised to receive a response from Vonnegut but was also disheartened by what he wrote:

Dear Mr. Sherman,

    I thank you for letting me see your artwork. It is vivid and well drawn. You have chosen a very tough field in which to compete. It is my publishers who pick my jacket artists. They are here in New York, and so are hundreds of first rate commercial artists. It is highly unlikely that a beginner can ever get an assignment by mail.

My daughter Edith, incidentally, is one of New York's best commercial artists, a real pro. She has gone to a lot of art schools and served a lot of apprenticeships in order to become that. She has also hustled jobs in the city, where the action is.

You must do the same.

As for your artwork's reflecting the madness of my writing: that could be so. You should understand though, that the purpose of jackets is to sell books, not to reflect the contents of the books they cover. They are eye-catching packages, just like the packages for breakfast foods. A commercial artist may be a fine artist, but he must also be a shrewd salesman. Understand?

I have a book coming out in May, and the jacket is bright and simple. It is an eye-catcher. To a person browsing in a bookstore, psychedelic artwork like yours would not only seem dated, but, from a few feet away, would be an incomprehensible blur.

I wish you luck. At the same time, I pity you or any beginning commercial artist, since so much frustration and hard work and mad scrambling lie ahead. Again: you can't work from a mailbox.

Yours truly,
Kurt Vonnegut, Jr.

During the process of researching and writing this book, I have had the opportunity to reread the letter several times with a fresh set of eyes. In my view, Vonnegut was not attempting to cut out the creative heart of a young artist; instead, he was writing this letter to a younger version of himself. Had Vonnegut known early that novel writing on Cape Cod would lead to years of commercial frustration and financial disappointment, he would have opted for life in New York City decades earlier. In this letter, which was written just before the release of *Breakfast of Champions*, Vonnegut was sharing his wisdom with a young artist, hoping that my father would learn from the writer's mistakes. It's a beautiful letter, really, and it taught me a great deal more about Vonnegut. I have come to have a greater appreciation for Vonnegut, who was grappling with the effects from the firebombing of Dresden throughout his lifetime without getting the proper help to treat his PTSD, and also for Mailer, who explored darkness within himself while also confronting many of the great injustices of his time. Regarding their literary rivalry, it's worth noting that Vonnegut's novels have staying power and continue to outsell Mailer's work today. But I strongly recommend reading both of these incredible artists.

For this book, I also relied on several wonderful books about both authors, including *And So It Goes: Kurt Vonnegut: A Life* by Charles J. Shields, *Norman Mailer: A Double Life*, by J. Michael Lennon, *Mailer* by Peter Manso, and *Conversations with Norman Mailer*, edited by J. Michael Lennon. For more details on the Tony Costa murder case, I found Leo Damore's *In His Garden* incredibly compelling. Another good read is *The Babysitter*, written by Liza Rodman and Jennifer Jordan. The Manson murders were brought into greater focus for me during this project by reading *Manson: The Unholy Trail of Charlie and the Family*, coauthored by John Gilmore and Ron Kenney, and *Chaos: Charles Manson, the CIA, and the History of the Sixties* by Tom O'Neill with Dan Piepenbring. Charles Johnson Maynard's *Manual of Taxidermy* offered me, as it had Tony Costa, a greater understanding of the practice, although hunting of any kind doesn't appeal to me. I also incorporated what I learned about Cape Cod lore and witchcraft by reading Elizabeth Raynard's *The Narrow Land: Folk Chronicles of Old Cape Cod* and *Practical Magic: A Beginner's Guide to Crystals, Horoscopes, Psychics & Spells* by Nikki Van De Car.

I would also like to thank my wife, Kristin Sherman, for keeping me sane and dealing with the night terrors brought on by repeated studies of the crime scene and autopsy reports in the Costa case. I love you. I would like to thank my daughters, Mia and Bella, who joined me on tours of the crime scenes. You both make me so proud. I would like to thank my brother, Todd Sherman, who planted the seed for this book after a visit to Provincetown. I would like to thank my mother, Diane Dodd, who for years has shared information with me about what it's like to have a loved one taken so early and to be involved in a sensational crime. Thanks to my uncle Jimmy Sherman for sharing his memories of meeting Kurt Vonnegut during his brief courtship of his daughter Edie. Thanks also to the helpful staff at the Kurt Vonnegut Museum and Library.

A special thanks to literary agent Peter Steinberg and to my editor Anna Michels and the team at Sourcebooks for your tremendous enthusiasm for this project. A big thank you to Susan Downey and Amanda Burell, my partners at Team Downey, who are working to adapt this novel for a limited series for television. Thanks to Gotham Group for securing another Hollywood deal. Thanks to my Fort Point Media partner, Dave Wedge, for being a sounding board for ideas. Thanks also to the Goldsmith-York family for your love and support.

Norman Mailer was once asked how he felt when he wasn't working. "Edgy, I get into trouble," he replied. "I would say I'm wasting my substance completely when I'm not working."

I feel the same way. I look forward to sharing my next book with you all sooner rather than later. I hope you will look forward to that as well.

Casey Sherman, 2021

READING GROUP GUIDE

REFERENCES

AUTHOR INTERVIEWS

Armand Fernandes, former assistant district attorney

Jacqueline Flynn, wife of former Massachusetts State Police detective Bernie Flynn

Tom Gunnery, former Massachusetts State Police trooper

James Leonard

Michael Mailer, son of Norman Mailer

Jim Sherman

CORRESPONDENCE

Avis Costa Johnson, former wife of Tony Costa

Edie Vonnegut, daughter of Kurt Vonnegut

DOCUMENTS AND TRANSCRIPTS

Commonwealth v. Antone C. Costa, trial transcripts and exhibits, May 15–22, 1970.

Autopsy Report and Photos for Patricia Walsh, Case A 69–50.

Autopsy Report and Photos for Mary Anne Wysocki, Case A 69–51.

Postmortem Examination of the Body of Susan E. Perry, Case A 69–32, 1969.

Pathological Diagnosis of the Body of Sydney Lee Monzon, 1969.

Somerville, Massachusetts, Police Report, Commonwealth v. Anthony C. Costa, November 18, 1961.

Burlington, Vermont, Police Department Detective Bureau Report, Complaint # 6005, Lieutenant Richard Beaulieu, 1969.

Grand Jury Testimony, Death of Mary Jo Kopechne, Edgartown, Massachusetts, August 27, 1969.

Lester Allen interview of Tony Costa, 1969.

Maurice Goldman and Justin Cavanaugh interview of Tony Costa, 1969.

Massachusetts State Police interview of Larry Andresen, 1969.

Massachusetts State Police interview of Timothy Atkins, 1969.

Massachusetts State Police interview of Carl Benson.

Massachusetts State Police interview of Wayne Blanchard, 1969.

Massachusetts State Police interview of Vincent Bonaviri, 1969.

Massachusetts State Police interview of Dr. Sydney Callis, 1969.

Massachusetts State Police interview of Antone C. Costa, 1969.

Massachusetts State Police interview of Avis Costa, 1969.

Massachusetts State Police interview of Cory Bond Devereaux.

Massachusetts State Police interview of Steve Grund, 1969.

Massachusetts State Police interview of Irene Hare, 1969.

Massachusetts State Police interview of Brenda Dreyer, 1969.

Massachusetts State Police interview of Paula Hoernig, 1969.

Massachusetts State Police interview of Ronald Karnes, February 14, 1969.

Massachusetts State Police interview of Gerry Magnan, February 14, 1969.

Massachusetts State Police interview of Linda Monzon, 1969.

Massachusetts State Police interview of Patricia Morton, 1969.

Massachusetts State Police interview of Martha Mowery, 1969.

Massachusetts State Police interview of Russell Norton, February 14, 1969.

Massachusetts State Police interview of Stella Smith, 1969.

Massachusetts State Police interview of James Steele, 1969.

Massachusetts State Police interview of Robert Turbidy, February 14, 1969.

Massachusetts State Police interview of Catherine Walsh, 1969.

Massachusetts State Police interview of Leonard Walsh, 1969.

Massachusetts State Police interview of William Watts Jr., 1969.

Massachusetts State Police interview of Martha Wysocki, February 14, 1969.

Massachusetts State Police interview of James Zacharias, 1969.

NEWSPAPER AND MAGAZINE ARTICLES

"Drugs Blamed on Death of Ex-Baystate Girl." *Boston Globe*, November 26, 1968.

Adams, Laura. "Existential Aesthetics: An Interview with Norman Mailer." *Partisan Review* 42, no. 2 (Summer 1975): 197–214.

Bloom, Arthur, dir. *60 Minutes*. "Monroe, Mailer, and the Fast Buck." Aired July 13, 1973, on CBS.

Bragg, Mary Ann. "New Look at Old 'Lady of the Dunes' Mystery." *Cape Cod Times*, April 14, 2019.

Connolly, Kate. "'We Thought Dresden was Invincible': 70 Years after the Destruction of a City." *Guardian*, February 13, 2015. https://www.theguardian.com/world/2015/feb/13/we-thought-dresden-invincible-70-years-after-destruction-second-world-war.

Davis, William A. "Dismembered Body Found in Lonely Truro Grave." *Boston Globe*, February 9, 1969.

Denby, David. "A Great Writer at the 1968 Democratic Disaster." *New Yorker*, August 26, 2018. https://www.newyorker.com/culture/cultural-comment/a-great-writer-at-the-1968-democratic-disaster.

Ebert, Roger. "Norman Mailer: Tough Guy Directs." *Chicago Sun-Times*, October 25, 1986.

Lawson, Evelyn. "Murders of Girls Recall to Writer Weird Killings by Black Arts Cults." *Barnstable Register*, March 13, 1969.

———. "Threat to Press Seen in Court Curbs on Hearings, Probes." *Barnstable Patriot*, November 9, 1969.

Macdonald, Dwight. "Massachusetts vs. Mailer." *New Yorker*, October 1, 1960. https://www.newyorker.com/magazine/1960/10/08/massachusetts-vs-mailer.

Miller, Tim. "Hanging out with Jack at the Hole." *Cape Cod Times*, October 26, 2019.

Morse, Donald. "Bringing Chaos to Order: Kurt Vonnegut's Literary Remains." *Los Angeles Review of Books*, February 24, 2013. https://lareviewofbooks.org/article/bringing-chaos-to-order-on-kurt-vonneguts-literary-remains/.

Muñoz-Alonso, Lorena. "Adele Mailer, Visual Artist Once Stabbed by Husband Norman Mailer, Dies at 90." Artnet News, November 26, 2015. https://news.artnet.com/art-world/artist-adele-mailer-dies-at-90-372473.

Nash, Tom. "Kurt Vonnegut: The Story Behind the Legendary Author's Cape Cod Dealership." *Massachusetts Auto Dealer* 24, no. 8 (August 2011): 16–18. https://www.vonnegutlibrary.org/wp-content/uploads/2009/12/MSADA-AUGUST-Vonnegut-single-pages.pdf.

Powers, Richard. "Cape Pushes Probe in Murder of 4 Girls. Two Victims Unidentified and There May Be Others." *Boston Globe*, March 6, 1969.

———. "Cape Search Yields 4 Bodies." *Boston Globe*, March 6, 1969.

———. "Dist. Atty. Dinis Terms Mystery 'Most Bizarre.'" *Boston Globe*, March 6, 1969.

Roth, Jack. "Norman Mailer Sent to Bellevue Over His Protest in Wife Knifing." *New York Times*, November 23, 1960.

Sales, Robert J. "Costa Found Guilty." *Boston Globe*, May 23, 1970.

Saltzberg, Rich. "The Crash That Launched Chappaquiddick." *MV Times*, July 17, 2019. https://www.mvtimes.com/2019/07/17/crash-launched-chappaquiddick/.

Stack, James. "Mother Accepts Blame for Linda." *Boston Globe*, August 23, 1970.

Torgerson, Deal. "'Ritualistic Slayings': Sharon Tate, Four Others Murdered." *Los Angeles Times*, August 10, 1969. https://www.latimes.com/about/archives/story/2019-07-27/manson-family-murder-sharon-tate-1969-archives.

Vonnegut, Kurt, Jr. "Excelsior! We're Going to the Moon!" *New York Times*, July 13, 1969. https://www.nytimes.com/1969/07/13/archives/excelsior-were-going-to-the-moon-excelsior.html.

———. "Have I Got a Car for You!" *In These Times*, November 24, 2004. https://inthese-times.com/article/have-i-got-a-car-for-you.

———. "'There's a Maniac Loose Out There." *Life*, July 25, 1969.

Walker, Charles. "He Butchered the Beauties Before Burying Them!" *True Detective*, 1969.

Walsh, Kenneth T. "50 Years Ago, Walter Cronkite Changed a Nation." *U.S. News & World Report*, February 27, 2018. https://www.usnews.com/news/ken-walshs-washington/articles/2018-02-27/50-years-ago-walter-cronkite-changed-a-nation.

BOOKS AND MANUSCRIPTS

Costa, Tony. "Resurrection." Unpublished manuscript.

Damore, Leo. *In His Garden: The Anatomy of a Murderer*. Westminster, MA: Arbor House, 1981.

Hesse, Hermann. *Narcissus and Goldmund*. New York: Penguin Books Ltd, 1990.

———. *Steppenwolf*. Translated by Basil Creighton. New York: Picador, 1961.

Lennon, J. Michael. *Norman Mailer: A Double Life*. New York: Simon & Schuster, 2013.

Mailer, Norman. *Miami and the Siege of Chicago: An Informal History of the Republican and Democratic Conventions of 1968*. New York: World Publishing, 1969.

———. *Of a Fire on the Moon*. Boston: Little, Brown, 1969.

———. *Tough Guys Don't Dance*. New York: Random House, 1984.

Maynard, Charles J. *Manual of Taxidermy: A Complete Guide*. Boston: S. E. Cassino, 1883.

O'Neill, Tom, with Dan Piepenbring. *Chaos: Charles Manson, the CIA, and the Secret History of the Sixties*. Boston: Little, Brown, 2019.

Shields, Charles J. *And So It Goes: Kurt Vonnegut: A Life*. New York: Henry Holt, 2011.

Vonnegut, Kurt, Jr. *Slaughterhouse-Five*. New York: Delacorte, 1968.

———. *Wampeters, Foma & Granfalloons*. New York: Delacorte, 1974.

NOTES

PROLOGUE

"Truth demands courage": Tony Costa, "Resurrection" (unpublished manuscript, n.d.).

CHAPTER 1

Edie Vonnegut was nervous: Jim Sherman, in discussion with the author, July 17, 2020.

she wanted a new life: Linda Monzon, interview by Lieutenant Bernie Flynn, Massachusetts State Police, 1969.

she wrote that she was leaving: Nauset Tides yearbook (Eastham, MA: Nauset Regional High School, 1967).

Linda Monzon left: Monzon, interview.

"And then I'll take you": Costa, "Resurrection."

CHAPTER 2

Linda Monzon walked up: Monzon, interview.

"Do you know where Sydney": Monzon, interview.

Bertram Monzon immediately: Tom Gunnery, in discussion with the author, February 27, 2021.

Marshall's officers had made nearly: *Annual Report of the Town of Provincetown, Massachusetts, for the Year Ending December 31, 1968* (Provincetown, MA: Advocate Press, 1968), http://www.provincetownhistoryproject.com/PDF/mun_200_101-annual -town-report-1968.pdf.

Linda was born: James Stack, "Mother Accepts Blame for Linda," *Boston Globe*, August 24, 1970, https://www.cielodrive.com/archive/mother-accepts-blame-over-linda/.

Vonnegut called himself: Tom Nash, "Kurt Vonnegut: The Story Behind the Legendary Author's Cape Cod Dealership," *Massachusetts Auto Dealer* 24, no. 8 (August 2011): 16–18, https://www.vonnegutlibrary.org/wp-content/uploads/2009/12/MSADA-AUGUST -Vonnegut-single-pages.pdf.

"The Saab then as now": Kurt Vonnegut, "Have I Got a Car for You!," *In These Times*, November 24, 2004, https://inthesetimes.com/article/have-i-got-a-car-for-you.

They had first met: Charles J. Shields, *And So It Goes: Kurt Vonnegut: A Life* (New York: Henry Holt, 2011), 132.

"He wasn't shy": Peter Manso, *Mailer: His Life and Times* (New York: Simon & Schuster, 1985), 178.

NBC dubbed it: *NBC News Special Report*, aired January 31, 1968, on NBC.

"For it seems": Kenneth T. Walsh, "50 Years Ago, Walter Cronkite Changed a Nation," *U.S. News & World Report*, February 27, 2018, https://www.usnews.com/news/ken-walshs -washington/articles/2018-02-27/50-years-ago-walter-cronkite-changed-a-nation.

CHAPTER 3

"tough, keen eyed ladies": Norman Mailer, *Miami and the Siege of Chicago: An Informal History of the Republican and Democratic Conventions of 1968* (New York: World Publishing, 1969), 88.

"an orgy of gorging": Mailer, *Miami and the Siege*, 90.

"hecklers, fixers": Mailer, *Miami and the Siege*, 119.

"dowager's humps": David Denby, "A Great Writer at the 1968 Democratic Disaster," *New Yorker*, August 26, 2018, https://www.newyorker.com/culture /cultural-comment/a-great-writer-at-the-1968-democratic-disaster.

"the vegetable memories": Mailer, *Miami and the Siege*, 32.

"looking like an undertaker's": Mailer, *Miami and the Siege*, 42.

"Of course the reporter": Mailer, *Miami and the Siege*, 95.

"as the kid with a rocky, sharp glint": Denby, "Great Writer."

"the best journalist": J. Michael Lennon, *Norman Mailer: A Double Life*, (New York: Simon & Schuster, 2013), 390.

"superficial, flat": Rejection Letters Collection, Kurt Vonnegut Museum and Library, Indianapolis, Indiana.

"Doing that job": Jim Romensko, "Surviving City News Job was like getting a Purple Heart," *New York Times*, December 13, 2005.

The republic is hovering: Mailer, *Miami and the Siege*, 10.

This is a generation: Mailer, *Miami and the Siege*, 152.

"washed with battle": Mailer, *Miami and the Siege*, 154.

Do my loyalties: Mailer, *Miami and the Siege*, 203.

"You're beautiful": Mailer, *Miami and the Siege*, 205.

CHAPTER 4

"Our fathers preach peace": Costa, "Resurrection."

A friend spotted: Paula Hoernig, interview by Lieutenant Bernie Flynn, Massachusetts State Police, May 7, 1969.

"One way, Do Not Enter": Costa, "Resurrection."

"Skinning Birds": Charles J. Maynard, *Manual of Taxidermy: A Complete Guide in Collecting and Preserving Birds and Mammals* (Boston: S. E. Cassino, 1883), 38.

"This is ghastly": Costa, "Resurrection."

This got the attention: Gunnery, discussion.

CHAPTER 5

"as colorful as St. Tropez": Norman Mailer, *Tough Guys Don't Dance* (New York: Random House, 1984), 5.

"Your attachment to this place": Manso, *Mailer: His Life and Times*, 101.

"I'll move when": Dwight Macdonald, "Massachusetts vs. Mailer," *New Yorker*, October 1, 1960, https://www.newyorker.com/magazine/1960/10/08/massachusetts-vs-mailer.

"Do you know what Cobra means?": Macdonald, "Massachusetts vs. Mailer."

"Don't give up your job": Shields, *And So It Goes*, 128.

"Not a striking plot": Shields, *And So It Goes*, 116.

"a nice guy": Shields, *And So It Goes*, 132.

You're about my age: Shields, *And So It Goes*, 132.

"gone broke, was out": Kurt Vonnegut, Jr., "Despite Tough Guys, Life is Not the Only School for Real Novelists," *New York Times*, May 24, 1999.

CHAPTER 6

"I'm a beast astray": Hermann Hesse, *Steppenwolf*, trans. Basil Creighton (New York: Picador, 1961), 32.

"For me to needlessly": Costa, "Resurrection."

"People who use": "Drugs Blamed on Death of Ex-Baystate Girl," *Boston Globe*, November 26, 1968.

CHAPTER 7

"My name is Yon": Kurt Vonnegut Jr., *Slaughterhouse-Five* (New York: Delacorte, 1968), 13.

"There must be": Shields, *And So It Goes*, 136.

"I love him": Shields, *And So It Goes*, 149.

"I've come through this God awful": Shields, *And So It Goes*, 77.

"Giants stalked the earth": Charles J. Shields, "Kurt Vonnegut and the Dresden Bombings," History Reader, February 13, 2012, https://www.thehistoryreader.com/military-history/kurt-vonnegut-dresden-bombings/.

"Well, it's those criminals": Kate Connolly, "'We Thought Dresden Was Invincible':

70 Years after the Destruction of a City," *Guardian*, February 13, 2015, https://www.theguardian.com/world/2015/feb/13/we-thought-dresden-invincible-70-years-after-destruction-second-world-war.

"looked like a streetcar": Volker Jannsen, "Why Was Dresden So Heavily Bombed?," History.com, February 12, 2020, https://www.history.com/news/dresden-bombing-wwii-allies.

"terribly elaborate Easter egg hunt": Shields, *And So It Goes*, 89.

"Listen, I'm writing": Vonnegut, *Slaughterhouse-Five*, 14.

"I don't think": Vonnegut, *Slaughterhouse-Five*, 28.

"I have been a sore-headed": Shields, *And So It Goes*, 203.

"The place is awful": Shields, *And So It Goes*, 206.

"Shut the fuck up!": Shields, *And So It Goes*, 238.

"It was as though": Alexander McKee, *Dresden 1945: The Devil's Tinderbox* (New York: Dutton, 1984), 35.

"A fourth-generation": Vonnegut, *Slaughterhouse-Five*, author's note.

CHAPTER 8

The killer spent: Costa, "Resurrection."

"I haven't seen her in such": Tony Costa, interview by Maurice Goldman, audiotape, 1969.

"You're handsome enough": J. Michael Lennon, *Norman Mailer: A Double Life* (New York: Simon & Schuster, 2013), 423.

"The disease of the 20th century": Lennon, *Norman Mailer: A Double Life*, 423.

"the poorest part": Lennon, *Norman Mailer: A Double Life*, 424.

"I cannot say Mailer": Harry Medved and Michael Medved, *Hollywood Hall of Shame: The Most Expensive Flops in Hollywood History*, (New York: Perigee Trade, 1984), 71.

"I wanted to get below": Manso, *Mailer: His Life and Times*, 445.

"We're making a movie"; Manso, *Mailer: His Life and Times*, 445.

"So good, and tough": Vincent Canby, "Norman Mailer offers Beyond the Law," *New York Times*, September 30, 1968.

"I'm interested in sexuality": "D. A. Pennebaker on the Films of Norman Mailer," Criterion Collection, October 17, 2012, video, 6:04, https://www.criterion.com/current/posts/2518-pennebaker-on-mailer-maidstone.

"Daddy, Daddy": *Maidstone*, directed by Norman Mailer (New York: Supreme Mix Productions, 1970).

"You're supposed to die": *Maidstone*.

CHAPTER 9

"I'm being threatened": Costa, "Resurrection."

"My mind is bent!": Costa, "Resurrection."

"I would like to inquire": Patricia Morton, interview by Massachusetts State Police, 1969.

"Although…many valuable": Maynard, *Manual of Taxidermy*, 16.

Norton was waiting: Russell Norton, interview by Massachusetts State Police, February 14, 1969.

Pat and Mary Anne knocked: Morton, interview.

"Make yourselves at home": Costa, "Resurrection."

"I'm so sorry": Morton, interview.

"I've been through there": Costa, "Resurrection."

Pat wore bell-bottom: Autopsy report for Patricia Walsh, Case A 69–50, Massachusetts State Police Bureau of Photography, 1969; autopsy report for Mary Anne Wysocki, Case A 69–51, Massachusetts State Police Bureau of Photography, 1969.

They soon were joined: Irene Hare and Brenda Dreyer, interviews by Massachusetts State Police, 1969.

They pedaled their bicycles: Costa, "Resurrection."

"A wolf of the Steppes": Hesse, *Steppenwolf*, 20.

CHAPTER 10

Zacharias was holding: James Zacharias, interview by Massachusetts State Police, June 3, 1969.

"I suffered": Costa, "Resurrection."

The bullet struck Pat Walsh: Autopsy report for Patricia Walsh, March 7, 1969.

The first bullet penetrated Mary Anne's skull: Autopsy report for Mary Anne Wysocki, March 7, 1969.

The killer unzipped his pants: Autopsy report for Mary Anne Wysocki; autopsy report for Patricia Walsh.

He attended to the body of Pat Walsh: Autopsy report for Patricia Walsh.

Costa carved her body: Autopsy report for Mary Anne Wysocki.

CHAPTER 11

"You bastard, you're the cause": Costa, "Resurrection."

he buried the weapons: Gunnery, discussion.

Costa had worn a fresh pair: Costa, "Resurrection."

Russell Norton was both frustrated: Norton, interview.

She visited each of her tenants: Morton, interview.

She entered their room: Morton, interview.

Dear Mrs. Morton: Note to Patricia Morton, Exhibit 9, Commonwealth v. Antone C. Costa, May 14, 1970, 79.

Leonard Walsh hung up: Testimony of Carl Benson, Commonwealth v. Antone C. Costa,

May 14, 1970, 147; Carl Benson, interview by Massachusetts State Police, February 18, 1969.

The worried father then rushed out: Walsh, interview.

The registration number is: Testimony of Leonard Walsh, Commonwealth v. Antone C. Costa, May 14, 1970, 56; Leonard Walsh, interview by Massachusetts State Police, February 3, 1969.

"Put this information": Provincetown Police Department internal report, January 1969.

I have bought bread: Leo Damore, *In His Garden: The Anatomy of a Murderer* (Westminster, MA: Arbor House, 1981), 4.

Turbidy arrived in Provincetown: Robert Turbidy, interview by Massachusetts State Police, February 14, 1969.

"There's no way those girls are": Damore, *In His Garden*, 12.

Carl Benson left his home: Carl Benson, interview by Massachusetts State Police, 1969; trial transcripts, Commonwealth v. Antone C. Costa, May 15, 1970, 147.

CHAPTER 12

"Hey, Speed and Weed": Costa, "Resurrection."

He asked the driver: Steven Grund, interviews by Massachusetts State Police, 1969; trial transcripts, Commonwealth v. Antone C. Costa, May 15, 1970, 155.

Since Costa did not have a valid driver's license: Grund, interview.

"They took a plane to Vermont": Steven Grund, interview by Massachusetts State Police, March 13, 1969.

Russell Norton twisted his entire: Norton, interview.

Meads recognized the address: Provincetown Police Department internal memo, 1969.

The landlady also mentioned: Provincetown Police Department internal memo, 1969.

"Only through his [Costa's] efforts": Trial transcripts, Commonwealth v. Antone C. Costa, 1970.

The next day, Mary Anne's mother: Opening Statement of Edward Dinis, Commonwealth v. Antone C. Costa, May 14, 1970, 27.

"Where is he now?": Testimony of Patricia Morton, Commonwealth v. Antone C. Costa, May 14, 1970, 64; Patricia Morton, interview by Massachusetts State Police, February 26, 1969.

"I gave her a flat, no!": Testimony of Patricia Morton, Commonwealth v. Antone C. Costa, May 15, 1970, 64; Patricia Morton, interview by Massachusetts State Police February 26, 1969.

Magnan then opened the closet door: Gerald G. Magnan Testimony, Commonwealth v. Antone C. Costa, May 15, 1970, 105.

"When I dumped out": Patricia Morton Testimony, Commonwealth v. Antone C. Costa, May 15, 1970, 65.

CHAPTER 13

"The girls had become friendly": Patricia Morton Testimony, Commonwealth v. Antone C. Costa, May 15, 1970, 67.

Berrio telephoned: Patricia Morton Testimony, Commonwealth v. Antone C. Costa, May 15, 1970, 67; George Killen Testimony, Commonwealth v. Antone C. Costa, May 18, 1970, 302.

The slip was from: George Killen Testimony, Commonwealth v. Antone C. Costa, May 18, 1970, 310.

Costa saw his buddy: James Steele, interview by Massachusetts State Police, April 17, 1969; James Steele Testimony, Commonwealth v. Antone C. Costa, May 18, 1970, 336.

Patrolman James Cook: Trial transcripts, Commonwealth v. Antone C. Costa, 1970.

He found a Volkswagen owner's manual: Interview with Tom Gunnery, February 6, 2021; Edward "Tom" Gunnery Testimony, Commonwealth V. Antone C. Costa, May 18, 1970, 351.

He stopped at a gas station: Wayne Blanchard interview by Massachusetts State Police, March 12, 1969, George Killen testimony Commonwealth v. Antone C. Costa, May 18, 1970, 325.

He paid the landlord: Stella Smith interview by Massachusetts State Police, March 11, 1969, George Killen testimony Commonwealth v. Antone C. Costa, May 18, 1970, 325.

He then found a bookstore: Stella Smith interview by Massachusetts State Police, March 11, 1969, George Killen testimony Commonwealth v. Antone C. Costa, May 18, 1970, 325.

CHAPTER 14

Gunnery woke up with a strange feeling: Gunnery, discussion.

He then joined: Interview with Tom Gunnery, February 6, 2021, Edward "Tom" Gunnery Testimony, Commonwealth V. Antone C. Costa, May 18, 1970, 353.

The pathologist then made: Postmortem Examination of the Body of Susan E. Perry, Case A-69–32, 1969.

IDENTIFICATION WANTED: Massachusetts State Police report, March 13, 1969.

The headline at the top: William A. Davis, "Dismembered Body Found in Lonely Truro Grave," *Boston Globe*, February 9, 1969.

"One of them [critics]": Vonnegut, *Slaughterhouse-Five*, 270.

"The scene and the film reflect": "D. A. Pennebaker on the Films."

CHAPTER 15

"Good day, Sergeant": Costa, "Resurrection."

"Good morning, Tony": Costa, "Resurrection."

I pulled you over back in September: Gunnery, discussion.

"First of all, I want you": Tony Costa, interview by Massachusetts State Police, February 10, 1969.

CHAPTER 16

Beaulieu raced over: Lt. Richard Beaulieu, Burlington Police Department, Detective Bureau Report, Complaint # 6005, February 10, 1969.

Dear Mrs. Smith: Beaulieu, report.

Gunnery also found: Interview with Tom Gunnery, February 6, 2021, Edward "Tom" Gunnery Testimony, Commonwealth V. Antone C. Costa, May 18, 1970, 347.

WILL RETURN FROM BURLINGTON: Note to George Killen, Exhibit 12, John Dunn Testimony, Commonwealth v. Antone C. Costa, May 18, 1970, 337.

"Look, Tony, as far as I'm concerned": George Killen testimony, Commonwealth v. Antone C. Costa, May 18, 1970, 326.

"There, you goddamned hypocrite": Costa, "Resurrection."

"I met Donna Welch on Thursday": Somerville Police Report, Commonwealth v. Anthony C. Costa, November 18, 1961.

"I trust the present": Charles Johnson Maynard, *Manual of Taxidermy: A Complete Guide in Collecting and Preserving Birds and Mammals* (Boston: S. E. Cassino, 1883), xviii.

CHAPTER 17

Avis was just thirteen years old: Avis Costa, interview by Massachusetts State Police, 1969.

"What kind of sick individual": Gunnery, discussion.

"I blame myself": Norton, interview.

"I want to point out": Magnan, interview.

"We all miss her": Ronald Karnes, interview by Massachusetts State Police, February 14, 1969.

"Pat loved music": Turbidy, interview.

"She brought the bag to Cape Cod": Martha Wysocki, interview by Massachusetts State Police, February 14, 1969.

"My daughter would never sleep with": Catherine Walsh, interview by Massachusetts State Police, February 14, 1969.

The chemist found miniscule: Melvin Topjian, Massachusetts Department of Public Safety Report, Lab. No. 29620, March 14, 1969.

"She mentioned it once or twice": Monzon, interview.

"An examination of the bill of sale": FBI Boston Office to Massachusetts State Police, memo, February 21, 1969.

Dear Jim: Note to James Meads, Exhibit 21, James Meads Testimony, Commonwealth v. Antone C. Costa, May 19, 1970, 421.

CHAPTER 18

It appeared to be a torn piece: Bernard Flynn Testimony, Commonwealth v. Antone C. Costa, May 18, 1970, 362.

They caught up with Tony Costa: Gunnery, discussion; Jacqueline Flynn, in discussion with the author, May 17, 2021; Bernard Flynn testimony, Commonwealth v. Antone C. Costa, May 18, 1970, 362.

"Tony, if you hear from the girls": Gunnery, discussion.

He visited Toronto: Costa, "Resurrection."

CHAPTER 19

"What happened? We waited as planned": Note from Costa, Exhibit 31, Bernard Flynn Testimony, Commonwealth v. Antone C. Costa, May 18, 1970, 365.

"Tony's been really nice to me": Larry Andresen, interview by Massachusetts State Police, February 25, 1969.

"I've known him for three years": Marsha Mowery, interview by Massachusetts State Police, February 25, 1969.

"I know Tony's ex-wife": Marsha Mowery, interview by Massachusetts State Police, February 26, 1969.

"Two men to be arraigned": Note to Massachusetts State Police Yarmouth Barracks from Massachusetts State Police Rehoboth Barracks March 2, 1969.

Kimpel came across: Ray Kimpel, interview by Massachusetts State Police, March 9, 1969; testimony of Ray Kimpel, Commonwealth v. Antone C. Costa, May 18, 1970, 455.

He pulled out Pat Walsh's Rhode Island: Ray Kimpel, interview by Massachusetts State Police, March 9, 1969; Testimony of Ray Kimpel, Commonwealth v. Antone C. Costa, May 18, 1970, 456.

Kimpel dug further: Ray Kimpel, interview by Massachusetts State Police, March 9, 1969; Testimony of Ray Kimpel, Commonwealth v. Antone C. Costa, May 18, 1970, 456.

CHAPTER 20

"In parting, all of life's": Hermann Hesse, *Narcissus and Goldmund* (New York: Penguin Books Ltd, 1990), 238.

Gunnery took a closer look: Interview with Tom Gunnery, February 6, 2021, Edward "Tom" Gunnery Testimony, Commonwealth V. Antone C. Costa, May 18, 1970, 353.

CHAPTER 21

A tenant informed the investigators: William White and James DeFuria, Massachusetts State Police memo, March 7, 1969.

Costa had showered: Costa, "Resurrection."

The marijuana had already: Costa, "Resurrection."

Killen handed the warrants to Gunnery: Interview with Tom Gunnery, February 6, 2021, Edward "Tom" Gunnery Testimony, Commonwealth V. Antone C. Costa, May 18, 1970, 356; Bernard Flynn Testimony, Commonwealth v. Antone C. Costa, May 18, 1970, 367.

"We have four warrants here": Interview with Tom Gunnery, February 6, 2021, Edward "Tom" Gunnery Testimony, Commonwealth V. Antone C. Costa, May 18, 1970, 357; Bernard Flynn Testimony, Commonwealth v. Antone C. Costa, May 18, 1970, 368.

"I don't have to answer to either of you": Costa, "Resurrection."

In Costa's wallet: Interview with Tom Gunnery, February 6, 2021, Edward "Tom" Gunnery Testimony, Commonwealth V. Antone C. Costa, May 18, 1970, 357; Bernard Flynn Testimony, Commonwealth v. Antone C. Costa, May 18, 1970, 368.

"Don't hug me": Flynn, interview.

Dr. George Katsas carefully placed: Autopsy report for Mary Anne Wysocki.

"The victim's pelvis": Autopsy report for Mary Anne Wysocki.

Mutilation of the body in two distinct: Autopsy report for Patricia Walsh.

"Spermatozoa are found": Autopsy report for Patricia Walsh.

Sydney's body was cut into four: "Pathological Diagnosis of the Body of Sydney Lee Monzon," March 6, 1969.

"The lungs are markedly decomposed": "Pathological Diagnosis."

CHAPTER 22

Both Flynn and Gunnery had sifted: Interview with Tom Gunnery, February 6, 2021, Edward "Tom" Gunnery Testimony, Commonwealth V. Antone C. Costa, May 18, 1970, 357; Bernard Flynn Testimony, Commonwealth v. Antone C. Costa, May 18, 1970, 368.

"What do I think?": John Dunn Testimony, Commonwealth v. Antone C. Costa, May 18, 1970, 338.

"I'm here to announce": Edmund Dinis press conference, Associated Press, March 6, 1969.

Boston Globe **reporter Richard Powers:** Richard Powers, "Cape Search Yields 4 Bodies," *Boston Globe*, March 6, 1969.

"We have a signed complaint": Arraignment transcript, Commonwealth v. Antone C. Costa, March 7, 1969.

"I expect more bodies": Richard Powers, "Dist. Atty. Dinis Terms Mystery 'Most Bizarre,'" *Boston Globe*, March 6, 1969.

CHAPTER 23

"You want a fucking bookcase?": James Leonard, in discussion with the author, January 25, 2021.

"Suspect—Antone Costa": Richard Powers, "Cape Pushes Probe in Murder of 4 Girls. Two Victims Unidentified and There May Be Others," *Boston Globe*, March 6, 1969.

"I'm ready to take all my fame": Lennon, *Norman Mailer: A Double Life*, 422.

"You know something?": Lennon, *Norman Mailer: A Double Life*, 425.

The day's lead story: "The Truro Murder Case," aired March 8, 1969, on WNAC-7 Boston.

"Aja toro, aja": Lennon, *Norman Mailer: A Double Life*, 294.

"Let the bitch die!": Lorena Muñoz-Alonso, "Adele Mailer, Visual Artist Once Stabbed by Husband Norman Mailer, Dies at 90," Artnet News, November 26, 2015, https://news.artnet.com/art-world/artist-adele-mailer-dies-at-90–372473.

"I don't think he's fully": Lennon, *Norman Mailer: A Double Life*, 295.

"Do you know that": Lennon, *Norman Mailer: A Double Life*, 296.

"I need to get outta": Lennon, *Norman Mailer: A Double Life*, 297.

"In Cuba, hatred runs": Lennon, *Norman Mailer: A Double Life*, 297.

"In my opinion": Jack Roth, "Norman Mailer Sent to Bellevue in Protest over Wife Stabbing," *New York Times*, November, 23, 1960.

"Naturally, I have been a little upset": Jack Roth, "Norman Mailer Sent to Bellevue Over His Protest in Wife Knifing," *New York Times*, November 23, 1960.

"his good intellectual energies": Dr. Lawrence Barrows Testimony, Commonwealth v. Antone C. Costa, May 19, 1970, 410.

Fleece-lined lavender clouds: Note to Maurice Goldman, Exhibit 47, Dr. Lawrence Barrows Testimony, Commonwealth v. Antone C. Costa, May 19, 1970, 410.

CHAPTER 24

"Mr. Vonnegut pronounces": Review of *Slaughterhouse-Five, or The Children's Crusade*, by Kurt Vonnegut Jr., *New York Times*, March 31, 1969, https://www.nytimes.com/1969/03/31/books/vonnegut-slaughterhouse.html.

"beautifully done": Michael Crichton, review of *Slaughterhouse-Five, or The Children's Crusade*, by Kurt Vonnegut Jr., *New Republic*, 1969.

"The short, flat sentences": Susan Lardner, "So It Goes," *New Yorker*, May 17, 1969.

"devastating and supremely human": Christopher Wordsworth, "Slaughterhouse Five Review," *Guardian*, March 19, 1970.

"Let others bring order": Donald Morse, "Bringing Chaos to Order: Kurt Vonnegut's Literary Remains," *Los Angeles Review of Books*, February 24, 2013, https://lareviewofbooks.org/article/bringing-chaos-to-order-on-kurt-vonneguts-literary-remains/.

"My experience with Tony Costa": Edie Vonnegut, correspondence with the author, July 17, 2020.

"If Tony's really the murderer": Kurt Vonnegut Jr., "There's a Maniac Loose Out There," *Life*, July 25, 1969.

"It's sort of hard": Charles Walker, "He Butchered the Beauties Before Burying Them!," *True Detective*, June, 1969.

"He's talking about the possibility": Damore, *In His Garden*, 163.

"this encounter with a strangeness": Damore, *In His Garden*, 164.

"With Tony Costa's life at stake": Pretrial hearing transcript, Commonwealth v. Antone C. Costa, 1969.

"Barnstable County and the Town of Truro": Editorial, WEEI Radio 590, March 13, 1969.

At the top of the staircase: Gunnery, discussion.

"He also told us that Tony tried to sell": Steele, interview.

CHAPTER 25

"I have done much thinking": Costa Note to Massachusetts State Police, March 17, 1969, Exhibit 38, Bernie Flynn Testimony, Commonwealth V. Antone C. Costa, May 19, 1970, 617.

"I simply requested": Tony Costa, interview by Maurice Goldman and Justin Cavanaugh, June 7, 1969.

CHAPTER 26

"I'd piss on it!": Lennon, *Norman Mailer: A Double Life*, 428.

"He called it his suicide kit": Steven Grund, interview by Massachusetts State Police, March 13, 1969.

"The first time I met him": William Watts Jr., interview by Massachusetts State Police, March 14, 1969.

Trooper Gunnery returned: Interview with Tom Gunnery, February 6, 2021, Edward "Tom" Gunnery Testimony, Commonwealth V. Antone C. Costa, May 18, 1970, 358.

the knife showed a presence of blood: Melvin Topjian Testimony, Commonwealth V. Antone C. Costa, May 18, 1970, 371.

"We have a strong suspicion": Tony Costa, interview by Maurice Goldman and Justin Cavanaugh, April 16, 1969.

CHAPTER 27

"I'm an existentialist who": Laura Adams, "Existential Aesthetics: An Interview with Norman Mailer," *Partisan Review* 42, no. 2 (Summer 1975): 197–214.

"Cannibalism is a feature": Evelyn Lawson, "Murders of Girls Recall to Writer Weird Killings by Black Arts Cults," *Barnstable Register*, March 13, 1969.

Costa would sneak out of the apartment: Costa, "Resurrection."

CHAPTER 28

"Cory Devereaux shot her": Tony Costa, interview by Maurice Goldman and Justin Cavanaugh, April 16, 1969.

"I got the gun while visiting my grandmother": Devereaux, interview with Massachusetts State Police, March 11, 1969; testimony of Cory Devereaux, Commonwealth v. Antone C. Costa, May 18, 1970, 672.

"Did you tell the police": Charles Zimmerman testimony, Commonwealth v. Antone C. Costa, May 19, 1970, 710.

"Do you know who killed these girls, Tony?": Charles Zimmerman testimony, Commonwealth v. Antone C. Costa, May 19, 1970, 710.

CHAPTER 29

"I can't answer that totally": Tony Costa, interview by Lester Allen, June 26, 1969.

Costa received good marks: Dr. Lawrence Barrows Testimony, Commonwealth v. Antone C. Costa, May 19, 1970, 412.

"I suffered as a result": Costa, "Resurrection."

"The good Tony": Dr. Harold Williams Testimony, Commonwealth v. Antone C. Costa, May 19, 1970, 815.

It is now my pleasure to inform you: Note to Maurice Goldman, Exhibit 62, Commonwealth V. Antone C. Costa, May 1970.

CHAPTER 30

"You stand in the vast expanse": Poem to Maurice Goldman, Exhibit 68, Commonwealth V. Antone C. Costa, May 1970.

CHAPTER 31

"You wouldn't let a commercial pilot": Lennon, *Norman Mailer: A Double Life*, 434.

"Thirty seconds and counting": "Sounds from Apollo 11," NASA, updated November 22, 2007, https://www.nasa.gov/mission_pages/apollo/apollo11_audio.html.

they looked like two enormous wings: Norman Mailer, *Of a Fire on the Moon* (Boston: Little, Brown, 1969), 103.

"If it's the devil": Mailer, *Fire on the Moon*, 83.

"Excelsior! We're going to the Moon!": Kurt Vonnegut Jr., "Excelsior! We're Going to the Moon!," *New York Times*, July 13, 1969, https://www.nytimes.com/1969/07/13/archives/excelsior-were-going-to-the-moon-excelsior.html.

"Tranquility base here": "Sounds of Apollo 11."

"Putting space exploration": Shields, *And So It Goes*, 279.

"He was really sour": James Jeffrey, "Dark Side of the Moon Mission," *Progressive Magazine*, July 18, 2019.

"a man who has": Shields, *And So It Goes*, 279.

CHAPTER 32

"Did you hear anything this morning?": Grand jury testimony regarding the death of Mary Jo Kopechne, Edgartown, MA, August 27, 1969.

Dr. Mills instructed: Grand jury testimony, death of Mary Jo Kopechne.

"The body is almost": Grand jury testimony, death of Mary Jo Kopechne.

"I'd like you to come over here": Grand jury testimony, death of Mary Jo Kopechne.

"On July 18, 1969": Grand jury testimony, death of Mary Jo Kopechne.

"Look, Chief": Grand jury testimony, death of Mary Jo Kopechne.

"The driver of the car was": Grand jury testimony, death of Mary Jo Kopechne.

"The official cause of death": Grand jury testimony, death of Mary Jo Kopechne.

"Next morning came the news": Mailer, *Fire on the Moon*, 112.

A woman from Stockton: Rich Saltzberg, "The Crash That Launched Chappaquiddick," *MV Times*, July 17, 2019, https://www.mvtimes.com/2019/07/17/crash-launched-chappaquiddick/.

CHAPTER 33

"Now, Cape Cod has a mutilator": Kurt Vonnegut Jr., "'There's a Maniac Loose Out There,'" *Life*, July 25, 1969.

If you spend an evening: Patti Page, vocalist, "Old Cape Cod," by Claire Rothrock, Milton Yakus, Allan Jeffrey, recorded 1957.

"you'll be known as Yana": Tom O'Neill and Dan Piepenbring, *Chaos: Charles Manson, the CIA, and the Secret History of the Sixties* (Boston: Little, Brown, 2019), 266.

"'Ritualistic Slayings'": Deal Torgerson, "'Ritualistic Slayings': Sharon Tate, Four Others Murdered," *Los Angeles Times*, August 10, 1969, https://www.latimes.com/about/archives/story/2019-07-27/manson-family-murder-sharon-tate-1969-archives.

"The Sixties ended abruptly": Joan Didion, *The White Album* (New York: Simon & Schuster, 1979), 47.

CHAPTER 34

"I'm the only one": Kurt Vonnegut's Unpublished WWII Scrapbook, Meilan Solly, Smithsonian Magazine, December 14, 2018.

"My idea is to attempt": Costa Note to Maurice Goldman via Lester Allen, Commonwealth V. Antone C. Costa, September 11, 1969.

CHAPTER 35

"Through your eyes": Poem to Maurice Goldman, Exhibit 69, Commonwealth V. Antone C. Costa, May 1970.

"All were nude": "Crime in the Dunes," *Time Magazine*, March 14, 1969.

"The first blow against our": Evelyn Lawson, "Threat to Press Seen in Court Curbs on Hearings, Probes," *Barnstable Patriot*, November 9, 1969.

"The type of juror": Maurice Goldman Note to Antone C. Costa, Justin Cavanaugh, Commonwealth V. Antone C. Costa, May 1970.

"In all fairness": Jury Selection Transcripts, Commonwealth V. Antone C. Costa, May 12, 1970, 13.

"She's a personal friend": Jury Selection Transcripts, Commonwealth V. Antone C. Costa, May 13, 1970, 17.

"Walsh and Wysocki are slam dunks": Armand Fernandes, in discussion with the author, May 6, 2021.

"Mrs. McCoubrey, in view": Jury Selection Transcripts, Commonwealth V. Antone C. Costa, May 13, 1970, 17.

CHAPTER 36

"Today, we are going to take": Jury View Transcripts, Commonwealth V. Antone C. Costa, May 13, 1970, 19.

"This is the medical office": Jury View Transcripts, Commonwealth V. Antone C. Costa, May 13, 1970, 20.

"We are now going to see": Jury view, Commonwealth v. Antone C. Costa, 1970.

"Now please observe the depression": Jury View Transcripts, Commonwealth V. Antone C. Costa, May 13, 1970, 22.

"This is what is known as": Jury View Transcripts, Commonwealth V. Antone C. Costa, May 13, 1970, 24.

CHAPTER 37

"Had I known the trip": Jury View Transcripts, Commonwealth v. Antone C. Costa, May 15, 1970, 25.

"May it please the court": Opening statement by Edmund Dinis, Commonwealth v. Antone C. Costa, May 15, 1970, 11.

"We are going to offer some evidence": Opening statement by Maurice Goldman, Commonwealth v. Antone C. Costa, May 15, 1970.

CHAPTER 38

"Could you tell the court": Testimony of Leonard Walsh, Commonwealth v. Antone C. Costa, May 15, 1970, 58.

"Catherine Madeline McCarthy Walsh": Testimony of Catherine Walsh, Commonwealth v. Antone C. Costa, May 15, 1970, 61.

"He wanted to know how much": Testimony of William Watts, Commonwealth v. Antone C. Costa, May 15, 1970, 74.

"Oh, I should say": Testimony of Carl Benson, Commonwealth v. Antone C. Costa, May 15, 1970, 65.

"Yes, he stayed at my house": Testimony of Patricia Morton, Commonwealth v. Antone C. Costa, May 15, 1970, 77.

CHAPTER 39

"Stephen Wayne Grund": Testimony of Steve Grund, Commonwealth v. Antone C. Costa, May 15, 1970, 104.

"From your last name": Fernandes, interview.

Now you search: Costa, "Resurrection."

"a vanished place": Mailer, *Tough Guys Don't Dance* (New York: Random House, 1984), 54.

CHAPTER 40

"Yes," Gunnery confirmed: Testimony of Tom Gunnery, Commonwealth v. Antone C. Costa, May 18, 1970, 353.

"I reached into the first hole": Testimony of Bernie Flynn, Commonwealth v. Antone C. Costa, May 18, 1970, 353.

CHAPTER 41

"The body of Patricia Walsh was cut into": Testimony of Dr. George Katsas, Commonwealth v. Antone C. Costa, 1970.

"I've known him for about two years": Testimony of Cory Devereaux, Commonwealth v. Antone C. Costa, May 18, 1970, 519.

CHAPTER 42

"I'm wishing you luck and steady nerves": Transcript of Avis Costa Phone Call Antone Costa, Commonwealth V. Antone C. Costa, May 1970.

My whereabouts: Antone C. Costa Note to Maurice Goldman, Commonwealth V. Antone C. Costa, 1970.

"You can figure it out": Maurice Goldman Bench Sidebar, Commonwealth V. Antone C. Costa, May 19, 1970, 768.

"What happens to a personality": Opening Statement of Maurice Goldman, Commonwealth v. Antone C. Costa, May 19, 1970, 777.

CHAPTER 43

"It's a gnawing pain": Dr. Sidney Callis, interview by Massachusetts State Police, March 22, 1969; Costa, "Resurrection."

"I practice general medicine": Testimony of Dr. Sidney Callis, Commonwealth v. Antone C. Costa, May 19, 1970, 928.

"Callis stated that": Testimony of Officer Patrick Padden, Commonwealth V. Antone C. Costa, May 19, 1970, 945.

"Did Tony ever appear violent": Testimony of Mark McCray, Commonwealth v. Antone C. Costa, 1970.

"I'm a believer in the rules": Lennon, *Norman Mailer: A Double Life*, 440.

"A winning hand": Lennon, *Norman Mailer: A Double Life*, 440.

"There are few places on the Eastern": J. Michael Lennon, "Norman Mailer's Provincetown," Norman Mailer Society, April 27, 2015, https://normanmailer.us /norman-mailer-s-provincetown-66943d75e164.

CHAPTER 44

"These people in distress": Testimony of Dr. Jack Ewalt, Commonwealth v. Antone C. Costa, May 19, 1970, 1002.

"He is preoccupied by death": Testimony of Lawrence Shubow, Commonwealth v. Antone C. Costa, May 19, 1970, 1025.

"For security": Testimony of Avis Costa, Commonwealth v. Antone C. Costa, May 21, 1970, 1113.

CHAPTER 45

The prosecution has failed: Note from Costa to Maurice Goldman, "Part of my Jury Speech", Commonwealth V. Antone C. Costa, May 21, 1970.

"The jury might disbelieve": Lawrence Shubow Bench Conference, Commonwealth v. Antone C. Costa, May 22, 1970, 1151.

"There is a serious problem": Closing statement by Maurice Goldman, Commonwealth v. Antone C. Costa, May 22, 1970, 1216.

"The defendant stands": Closing statement by Edmund Dinis, Commonwealth v. Antone C. Costa, May 22, 1970, 1271.

CHAPTER 46

"You may reserve your opinion": Judge Beaudreau Jury Instructions, Commonwealth V. Antone C. Costa, May 22, 1970, 1301.

"Your Honor, at this time": Statement by Tony Costa, Commonwealth v. Antone C. Costa, May 22, 1970, 1332.

"We find the defendant guilty": Russell Dodge Verdict Announcement, Commonwealth V. Antone C. Costa, May 22, 1970, 1356.

"I'm glad it's all over": Robert J. Sales, "Costa Found Guilty," *Boston Globe*, May 23, 1970.

"Everyone agrees that Antone Costa is sick": Sales, "Costa Found Guilty."

CHAPTER 47

"It's a bizarre theory": Norman Mailer, "Monroe, Mailer, and the Fast Buck," interview by Mike Wallace, *60 Minutes*, CBS, July 13, 1973.

"[Mailer] was himself": Arthur Miller, *Timebends: A Life*, (New York: Grove Press, 1987), 527.

"There is a piece in this book about Tony Costa": Kurt Vonnegut Jr., *Wampeters, Foma & Granfalloons* (New York: Delacorte, 1974), preface.

"I tried to protect her": Stack, "Mother Accepts Blame for Linda."

Suddenly, a thunderous: Costa, "Resurrection."

CHAPTER 48

twelve-year-old Leslie Metcalfe: Mary Ann Bragg, "New Look at Old 'Lady of the Dunes' Mystery," *Cape Cod Times*, April 14, 2019.

"The Cape Cod Standard Times": "Homicide Victim Still Unidentified," *Cape Cod Standard Times*, July 30, 1974.

CHAPTER 49

"Gilmore embodies many of the themes": Norman Mailer, interview by William F. Buckley Jr., *Firing Line*, PBS, October 11, 1979.

"He has a mind like no other": Lennon, *Norman Mailer: A Double Life*, 530.

"Richard Adan's death": Lennon, *Norman Mailer: A Double Life*, 574.

"This is another episode": "OBITUARY—Mailer—towering figure of U.S. literature," *Reuters*, November 10, 2007.

"We sell room-space": Mailer, *Tough Guys Don't Dance*, 25.

"A bawdy force": Mailer, *Tough Guys Don't Dance*, 55.

"I felt something": Mailer, *Tough Guys Don't Dance*, 60.

"When you write a novel": Roger Ebert, "Norman Mailer: Tough Guy Directs," *Chicago Sun-Times*, October 25, 1986.

There, he would regale: Michael Mailer, in discussion with the author, 2021.

"Tony Costa, or Tony 'Chop-Chop'": Michael Mailer, interview.

In 2000, the body: Bragg, "New Look."

AUTHOR'S NOTE

"he took his considerable": *Conversations with Norman Mailer*, edited by J. Michael Lennon, (Jackson: University Press of Mississippi, 1988), 110.

"Edgy, I get into": *Conversations with Norman Mailer*, Edited by J. Michael Lennon, (Jackson: University Press of Mississippi, 1988), 130.

ABOUT THE AUTHOR

Casey Sherman is the *New York Times*, *USA Today*, and *Wall Street Journal* bestselling author of fifteen books, including *The Finest Hours* (now a major motion picture starring Casey Affleck and Chris Pine), *Boston Strong* (the basis for the film *Patriots Day* starring Mark Wahlberg), *Animal*, *Hunting Whitey*, and *The Last Days of John Lennon*. He is a contributing writer for *TIME*, *Esquire*, *Washington Post*, *Boston Herald*, and *Boston Magazine* and has appeared as a guest analyst on more than 100 television news programs. Sherman is a graduate of Barnstable High School (Cape Cod), Fryeburg Academy (Fryeburg, Maine), and Boston University.